Citizen Review Resource Manual

by
Samuel Walker
with the assistance of
Betsy Wright

Department of Criminal Justice
University of Nebraska at Omaha

Police Executive Research Forum

The opinions expressed herein are those of the author and do not necessarily reflect those of PERF's members.

Police Executive Research Forum, Washington, D.C. 20036

Printed in the United States of America

Library of Congress Catalog Number 95-71263

ISBN 1-878734-37-7

Cover by Marnie Deacon

Contents

Preface	v
Acknowledgments	vii
Guide to the Citizen Review Resource Manual	1
Document	**Number**
Albuquerque, N.M.	1
Baltimore	2
Cambridge, Mass.	3
Cincinnati	4
Dayton, Ohio	5
Denver	6
Detroit	7
Dubuque, Iowa	8
Evanston, Ill.	9
Flint, Mich.	10
Houston	11
Iowa	12
Kansas City, Mo.	13
Minneapolis	14
New Orleans	15

Contents

Document	Number
New York City	16
Omaha, Neb.	17
Phoenix	18
Pittsburgh (employees' and citizens' guides)	19
Pittsburgh (functions and procedures)	20
Portland, Ore.	21
Rochester, N.Y.	22
San Diego	23
San Diego County (citizen complaint form)	24
San Diego County (rules and regulations)	25
San Francisco (annual report)	26
San Francisco (citizen complaint form)	27
San Jose, Calif.	28
Seattle	29
St. Petersburg, Fla.	30
Tucson, Ariz.	31
Winston-Salem, N.C.	32
Yonkers, N.Y.	33

Preface

As more and more police agencies adopt the philosophy of community policing, a philosophy that stresses better relations between the police and the citizens they serve, it is imperative that police and community members cooperate on a variety of issues. One such issue is police accountability. Citizen review of complaints against the police is on the rise nationwide, not only in large cities but also in medium-sized and small ones. More and more jurisdictions are establishing committees of community members to determine the validity of complaints against the police and, if necessary, to recommend appropriate disciplinary measures.

Citizen review has sometimes proved to be a source of controversy, but regardless of whether one agrees that it is an effective means for holding the police accountable for their actions, current trends indicate that it is here to stay. Thus, it is crucial that policymakers from a variety of fields be familiar with the range of citizen review policies and procedures in place at police departments across the country.

The *Citizen Review Resource Manual* provides readers with a broad assortment of ordinances and statutes, executive orders, departmental orders, and other documents pertaining to citizen review. These documents were collected from over 30 police departments nationwide. This manual is of interest not only to police practitioners, but also to civil libertarians, attorneys, city managers, and others who are concerned about police accountability and professionalism.

As the trend toward adopting citizen review continues both here and abroad, policymakers will need a range of alternatives from which to choose when implementing or changing citizen review procedures in their jurisdictions. This manual will provide policymakers with the information they need to make their decisions informed ones.

Ellen Hanson
Chief, Lenexa, Kan., Police Department
At-Large Member, PERF Board of Directors

Acknowledgments

Several people helped to bring this project to fruition. My graduate assistant, Betsy Wright, was primarily responsible for collecting the documents included here. She was always prompt, efficient and cheerful in carrying out this rather mundane assignment. Dennis Kenney, PERF's research director and my former colleague at the University of Nebraska at Omaha, was immediately enthusiastic when I first suggested this project to him. Martha Plotkin, PERF's communications director, provided insightful substantive comments and suggestions that will greatly enhance the manuscript's overall value to those in the field. Finally, Suzanne Fregly, PERF's senior editor, did an extremely efficient job editing the manuscript. The final version is much improved because of her efforts.

Samuel Walker
University of Nebraska at Omaha
October 1995

Guide to the Citizen Review Resource Manual

Introduction

Citizen Complaints and the Community

The review of citizen complaints is an important and rapidly changing aspect of police oversight. Police officer misconduct results in public dissatisfaction with police services, particularly when citizens who file formal complaints believe that their charges are not investigated thoroughly. Problems associated with the complaint process have inhibited positive relations between law enforcement agencies and the communities they serve. This issue is even more important today, as American law enforcement moves into the era of community policing, with its emphasis on closer interaction between police departments and community residents.

Traditionally, police departments have reviewed citizen complaints internally. Sworn officers assigned to the internal affairs or office of professional standards unit investigate individual complaints and recommend a final disposition to the chief executive. But nationally, municipal law enforcement agencies sustain an average of only 10.1 percent of all citizen complaints reviewed internally (Pate and Fridell 1993:113–120).

Because many citizens have been dissatisfied with the police's internal complaint review, community groups have long demanded some form of external or citizen review. After many years of controversy and conflict, external review has gained acceptance. By late 1994, there were an estimated 66 external complaint review bodies (Walker and Wright 1995a).[1] This represents a 400 percent increase over the 13 that existed in 1980 (figure 1).

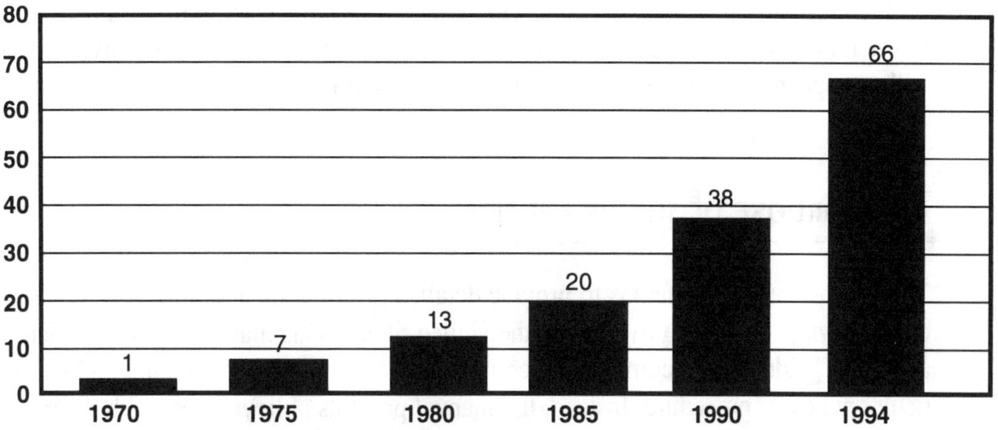

Fig. 1. The growth of citizen review, 1969 to 1994

1. Additional citizen review bodies have been established since the Walker and Wright (1995a) survey was completed in late 1994, and at least one has been abolished. Additional bodies were under consideration as this manual went to press.

One index of the growth of external review was the creation in 1985 of a professional association for civilian review staff and board members, the International Association for Civilian Oversight of Law Enforcement (IACOLE). IACOLE publishes a newsletter, holds an annual meeting and has published compendia describing external complaint review procedures (IACOLE 1989). Many IACOLE members are from other countries. External review of police complaints is now found in almost all English-speaking countries (Goldsmith 1991).

A Definition of Citizen Review

As a result of the rapid growth of external review, there is a wide variety of approaches used, differing with respect to organizational structure, role and mission, staffing, and operating procedures. No one term for external review has gained universal acceptance. Citizen review, civilian review and civilian oversight are used interchangeably. This manual uses the term *citizen* review, as *civilian* review suggests a "civilian-military" dichotomy that is inappropriate for American policing.

For the purposes of this manual, citizen review is defined as a procedure for handling citizen complaints about police officer misconduct that, at some point in the process, involves people who are not sworn officers.

Several aspects of this definition merit explanation. First, the involvement of people who are not sworn officers is the crucial factor that gives a complaint review system its "external" or "citizen" character. Second, there are many different ways in which nonsworn people may participate in complaint review. These variations are explained below. Third, this definition does not use the term review *board*. Many existing bodies involve an agency with a single director rather than a multimember board.

The Purpose of this Manual

The purpose of this manual is to provide detailed information about the different forms of citizen review that currently exist in the United States. This manual is not intended to offer a "model," "ideal" or recommended complaint review system. It does not endorse any particular policy or procedure. Instead, the manual presents policymakers with the range of currently available alternatives. Policymakers who are considering changing their existing systems are free to choose those elements that appear best suited to their needs or to reject all the examples presented here. This manual is designed to help make that choice an informed one.

The manual provides documents related to policies and procedures currently in place in at least one jurisdiction in the United States. Thus, the options offered are not hypothetical ones. Additional variations of external review models exist in other countries, but they have not been included here.

How to Use This Manual

The manual includes a variety of ordinances and statutes, executive orders, departmental orders, rules and procedures, annual reports, and other documents. They have been carefully selected to highlight the most important issues related to citizen review. The documents have been arranged alphabetically by jurisdiction, and each document has been assigned a document number. In this guide, important points are illustrated by reference to specific document numbers (e.g., San Diego County, #24).

Characteristics of Citizen Review

The Prevalence of Citizen Review

Citizen review is both a national and an international phenomenon. The majority of the big U.S. cities have adopted it, and medium-sized and small cities are increasingly adopting it, as well (Walker and Wright 1995a). As already mentioned, citizen review is almost universal in the other English-speaking countries (Goldsmith 1991).

No analyst has offered a conclusive explanation for the recent spread of citizen review. The concept was first proposed in 1935, and it was implemented in a few cities in the 1940s and 1950s. The procedures New York City and Philadelphia adopted were abolished in the 1960s, however. One factor contributing to the recent growth of citizen review has been the increase in African-American political activity, resulting in the election of mayors and city council members who consider police misconduct a major issue. It should be noted, however, that many cities with very small minority populations have also adopted citizen review. Opposition from police chiefs has declined significantly, as they increasingly recognize the importance of responding effectively to citizen complaints.

Geographic Distribution

Citizen review procedures are found in all regions of the country—neither more prevalent in nor significantly absent from any particular region. They are found in the Northeast (New York City, #16); the Southeast (St. Petersburg, #30); the Midwest (Kansas City, #13); the Southwest (Tucson, #31); and the West Coast (Seattle, #29; San Diego County, #24).

Type of Law Enforcement Agency

Most of the existing citizen review procedures apply to municipal police departments. By 1994, seven applied to county sheriffs' departments (San Diego County, #25). The Public Safety Review Commission in Denver (#6) handles complaints against both the municipal police department and the county sheriff's department. The Iowa Citizens' Aide/-Ombudsman (#12), meanwhile, is a state agency that handles complaints against any government agency in Iowa, including all city and county law enforcement agencies.

City or County Size

Citizen review procedures are most common in the largest cities (e.g., New York City, #16), but they are also increasingly common in medium-sized cities (e.g., Dayton, #5) and many small cities (e.g., Evanston, #9; Dubuque, #8). By 1994, 72 percent of the 50 largest cities had some form of citizen review, compared with only 26 percent of the second 50 largest cities. Ten citizen review procedures were found in small cities. Seven additional procedures applied to county sheriffs' departments (Walker and Wright 1995a).

Citizen review procedures are most common in big cities because of the political dynamics affecting police misconduct. Since the 1950s, police misconduct has been primarily a civil rights issue. The African-American community has been the leading advocate of citizen review, and in most cities, an incident involving an African American has precipitated the creation of some form of external review. Consequently, citizen review is most prevalent in those cities with large minority communities and/or effective local civil rights organizations.

Source of Legal Authority

Citizen review bodies have been established in six different ways: by municipal ordinance, state statute, voter referendum, mayoral executive order, police chief administrative order, and memorandum of understanding. Municipal ordinances have established the vast majority. State statute created the Iowa Citizens' Aide/Ombudsman Office (#12). A voter referendum authorized the San Diego Citizens' Review Board (#23). A mayoral executive order established the Omaha Citizen Review Board (#17). Police chiefs' administrative orders have authorized other citizen review bodies (Yonkers, #33). Finally, the Community Advisory Panel in Dubuque, Iowa (#8), was established by a memorandum of understanding between the city and the local NAACP, as part of a settlement the U.S. Justice Department's Community Relations Service negotiated.

The various sources of legal authority reflect underlying differences in the nature of support for citizen review. The enactment of an ordinance indicates support by the majority of the elected representatives in that jurisdiction. From a historical perspective, it is worth noting that the two most important citizen review procedures in the 1950s and 1960s (in New York and Philadelphia) were created by mayoral executive order in the face of opposition from the cities' respective city councils. The lack of broad political support left both of them vulnerable to attack, and both were eventually abolished. The fact that ordinances have created most of the current procedures demonstrates the growing public support for citizen review.

The growing number of review procedures that police chiefs' administrative orders have created suggests increased support for citizen review within the law enforcement profession. This represents a significant change in attitude—in 1965, the International Association of Chiefs of Police (IACP 1965) adopted an official policy statement opposing citizen review. However, in recent years, the Police Executive Research Forum (PERF) and the Commission on Accreditation for Law Enforcement Agencies (CALEA) have recognized the need for effective (although not necessarily external) procedures for reviewing citizen complaints.

Organizational Structure

Board vs. Agency

Citizen review takes many different organizational forms. Although the term civilian review *board* is still commonly used, it is inappropriate because many systems do not involve a multimember board. Of the 66 citizen review bodies that existed in 1995, 54 (82%) involved a multimember board, and 11 (17%) were agencies with a single director (Walker and Wright 1995b).

Boards are found in Minneapolis (#14), San Francisco (#26), Baltimore (#2), and many other cities. Examples of agencies with a single administrator include the Office of Municipal Investigation in Cincinnati (#4), the Office of Citizen Complaints in Kansas City (#13), and the Flint, Mich., Ombudsman (#10).

The majority of citizen review bodies are separate municipal or county agencies, such as the Cincinnati Office of Municipal Investigation (#4) and the Kansas City Office of Citizen Complaints (#13). Some, however, are essentially committees within the police department that include citizen members. Examples include Phoenix (#18) and Yonkers (#33). Another variation exists in Evanston, Ill. (#9), where one of the city council's standing committees is responsible for hearing complaints about the police.

There appears to be no clear explanation for why different forms of citizen review are found in various cities. Some are apparently borrowed from other cities, while other arrangements are unique. In the absence of any detailed comparative evaluations, it is impossible to say that any particular approach to citizen review is more appropriate for certain kinds of jurisdictions than others.

Employees Covered

Citizen review has traditionally applied only to complaints against police officers. Understandably, police officers have objected to being singled out for special scrutiny. In several cities, however, the citizen review agency is authorized to review complaints against other municipal employees as well. Nationally, 17 percent of the citizen review bodies in 1995 handled complaints against police officers and employees in other agencies (Walker and Wright 1995b). In Cincinnati (#4), New Orleans (#15) and Flint (#10), the citizen review body handles complaints against any municipal employee. The Flint Ombudsman, for example, investigates complaints about the purchasing procedures of the city and the management of the cable television franchise.

The San Diego County Citizens Law Enforcement Review Board (#25) not only hears complaints against sheriff's deputies, custodial officers and probation officers, but is also responsible for conducting an annual inspection of the county adult detention facilities. The Denver Public Safety Review Commission (#6) has jurisdiction over complaints involving both the Denver Police Department and the Denver County Sheriff's Department.

Role and Mission

The concept of citizen review originated as an alternative mechanism for reviewing individual citizen complaints. Case-by-case review of complaints is still the primary function of citizen review bodies.

Policy Review

In addition to reviewing individual complaints, many citizen review bodies are authorized to review police department policies and procedures and to recommend changes where necessary. Almost two-thirds of all citizen review bodies (42 of 66) are authorized to review police policy (Walker and Wright 1995b). Examples of policy review models include those in Dayton (#5), Rochester (#22), San Diego County (#25), San Francisco (#26), and Denver (#6).

Seattle (#29) and San Jose (#28) have created auditor systems wherein the primary function is the review of police department policy. The auditors do not review individual complaints, in the sense of conducting the initial fact-finding. The San Diego County Citizens Law Enforcement Review Board (#25) is also responsible for conducting an annual inspection of the county adult detention facilities.

Policy review is meant to be a preventive measure: to identify and correct problems that have either generated complaints or may cause complaints in the future. It is important to note that the policy review function is advisory only. Citizen review bodies may recommend changes in law enforcement policy but have no power to impose them.

Citizen review agencies have reviewed a variety of police department policies. The San Francisco Office of Citizen Complaints (#26), for example, recommended that the police department develop written policies regarding the arrest of disabled people and specialized training for handling "[people] whose gender may not be immediately apparent." The Denver Public Safety Review Commission (#6) recommended changes in how the Denver Police Department compiled its gang list. The San Jose Independent Police Auditor (#28) recommended and secured changes in how internal affairs handled complaints, including changes in the system for classifying complaints and in how investigators maintained their notes.

The Nature of Citizen Input

The most important distinction among various citizen review procedures involves the nature of citizen input. Several different classification systems have been developed to categorize citizen review bodies in this regard (Walker and Bumphus 1991; Kerstetter 1985; Perez 1994; Goldsmith 1988). Despite some differences in terminology, the various classification systems are roughly similar. This manual uses the classification system Walker and Bumphus developed (1991).

Class I

The most independent citizen review bodies are those where people who are not sworn police officers handle complaints. A full-time professional investigator who is not a sworn officer conducts the initial fact-finding investigation of each complaint. Nonsworn personnel also review investigative reports and make recommendations to the law enforcement chief executive. Complaint procedures of this type have been labeled Class I systems and are found, for example, in New Orleans (#15) and Cincinnati (#4).

Class II

In some jurisdictions, sworn officers in the police department investigate citizen complaints. A nonsworn individual or a board that contains at least some nonsworn people reviews the officers' reports. The individual or board then recommends action to the chief law enforcement executive. Procedures of this type have been labeled Class II systems. Examples are found in Kansas City (#13), Portland (#21) and Albuquerque (#1). Because sworn officers conduct the initial fact-finding investigation, Class II systems are considered less independent of the police than Class I systems.

Class III

Citizens participate even less in Class III systems. In these systems, the police department investigates and reviews citizen complaints. Internal affairs then recommends action to the chief executive. If the complainant is not satisfied with the final disposition, however, he or she may appeal the decision to a board containing at least some nonsworn individuals. This board reviews the complaint and may recommend a different disposition to the chief executive. Omaha (#17) is an example of a Class III system.

Class IV

Two cities (Seattle, #29; San Jose, #28) have established auditors for citizen complaints; these cities have Class IV systems. In both Seattle and San Jose, the auditor does not investigate individual citizen complaints. Instead, the auditor reviews the police department's complaint procedure and recommends changes where necessary. The San Jose Independent Police Auditor, for example, reviews all unnecessary-force complaints and at least 20 percent of all complaints involving other allegations. It employs a call-back system, interviewing complainants to assess their satisfaction with the complaint process.

As table 1 indicates, Class II systems are currently the most common form of citizen review; 31 of the 66 citizen review bodies (47%) that existed in early 1995 were Class II systems. Class I systems represent 33 percent (22 of 66) of the current citizen review procedures. Class III systems represent 17 percent of the existing procedures.

Table 1

Distribution of Citizen Review Procedures

	50 Largest Cities	Second 50 Largest Cities	Small Cities	County Sheriff's/ Police Departments	Total
Class					
I	17	0	3	2	**22**
II	13	10	4	4	**31**
III	4	3	3	1	**11**
IV	2	0	0	0	**2**
Total	**36**	**13**	**10**	**7**	**66**

Board Composition

Eighty-three percent of the citizen review bodies in the United States involve multi-member boards. These boards range in size from a high of 24 members to a low of three members (Walker and Wright 1995b). Among the boards cited in this manual, the Rochester Civilian Review Board (#22) has three members, while the Baltimore Complaint Evaluation Board (#2) has 12 members. There does not appear to be any connection between the size of boards and the size of the jurisdictions they represent; large and small boards are found in cities of all sizes.

Police Officer Participation

Sworn police officers' participation as members of citizen review boards is a particularly controversial issue. Many citizen review advocates believe that police participation eliminates the independent or "citizen" character of external review.

Nationally, 26 percent of citizen review boards have sworn officers as members (Walker and Wright 1995b). The number and percentage of these officers vary considerably. For example, the Baltimore Complaint Evaluation Board (#2) has 12 members, one of whom is a sworn police officer. The Yonkers Police Professional Standards Review Committee (#33) is evenly balanced with four sworn officers and four citizens. On the other hand, five of the seven members of the Phoenix Disciplinary Review Board (#18) are police officers. In Tucson (#31), the police union has explicit authority to nominate two of the 13 members of the complaint review board. In Omaha (#17), the police union selects three of the Citizen Review Board's nine members.

There are different patterns with respect to public officials' participation on review boards. The citizen (i.e., non-police officer) members of most boards are presumed to be people who do not hold public office. The Baltimore Complaint Evaluation Board (#2), however, is dominated by high-ranking public officials (e.g., the state's attorney of the city of Baltimore, the attorney general of Maryland, the city solicitor of Baltimore, the police commissioner, the executive director of the Maryland Human Relations Commission, etc.).

Disciplinary Authority

Virtually all citizen review bodies in the United States have the authority only to recommend disciplinary action to the police chief executive. Local or state civil service law generally specifies the chief executive's responsibility regarding officer discipline.

A few exceptions to the general rule exist. In Detroit (#7), the Board of Police Commissioners has ultimate authority to "[a]ct as final authority in imposing or reviewing discipline of employees in the department." The Milwaukee Fire and Police Commission (not included here) is also the final arbiter of police disciplinary cases.

Rules and Procedures

Some citizen review bodies have elaborate sets of rules and procedures, while others have only short statements of general goals. Where a review board exists, the rules and procedures tend to be longer because they specify the rules for the board itself (e.g., selection of officers, quorum, etc.). Such is the case with Minneapolis (#14) and San Diego County (#25).

Models of Citizen Review

With respect to the content of rules and procedures, some of the most important questions involve such issues as subpoena power and public hearings. A useful way to make sense of the variations that exist regarding these issues is to identify different models of the complaint process.

Some review bodies adopt a criminal trial model in which the investigation of citizen complaints resembles the traditional criminal trial. These bodies tend to have subpoena power, public hearings and strict rules of evidence, and they permit legal representation for police officers accused of misconduct. Other bodies, however, adopt an administrative review model, which resembles a traditional personnel disciplinary procedure. In this approach, the investigation of complaints is confidential, closed to the public, and without many of the other procedures associated with a criminal trial. Minneapolis (#14) follows the criminal trial model, while Cincinnati (#4) and New Orleans (#15) follow the administrative review model.

Subpoena Power

There has been much controversy over whether citizen review agencies should have the power to subpoena witnesses, including police officers. Citizen review advocates argue that subpoena power is necessary for the thorough investigation of complaints. Police officers, on the other hand, generally oppose granting citizen review bodies subpoena power. Nationally, almost 40 percent of review bodies (25 of 66) have subpoena power (Walker and Wright 1995b). Examples of such bodies include those in San Diego County (#25) and New Orleans (#15).

Public Hearings

Some complaint review bodies conduct public hearings on individual complaints, while others keep hearings closed to the public. Nationally, almost half (46.2%) conduct public hearings (Walker and Wright 1995b). Even where public hearings are permitted, however, they are not necessarily mandatory. Most complaints are disposed of without a public hearing. Review bodies with public hearings include those in Minneapolis (#14) and San Diego County (#25). Bodies that do not permit public hearings include those in Cincinnati (#4) and New Orleans (#15).

Legal Representation

About one-third (21 of 66) of citizen review procedures specifically allow legal representation for the police officer, the citizen or both (Walker and Wright 1995b).

Mediation/Conciliation

Some citizen review bodies have adopted mediation or conciliation procedures to resolve citizen complaints. This approach is designed to be less costly and time-consuming than the full criminal trial model approach, in addition to being satisfactory to both sides in the complaint. The Minneapolis Civilian Police Review Authority (#14) has a mediation procedure.

Subject Officer's Disciplinary Record

One of the most significant new developments regarding police officer misconduct has been the recognition that a small percentage of the officers in any department tend to generate a disproportionate share of citizen complaints (Christopher Commission 1991). Some departments have instituted special training sessions for such officers.

Existing citizen review bodies have different rules about the handling of an officer's disciplinary history. In San Diego County, the Citizens Law Enforcement Review Board (#25) may consider an officer's prior disciplinary record only after it has "sustained" a complaint against that officer.

In Denver, the Public Safety Review Commission (#6) compiled a list of officers with three or more citizen complaints in the previous 21 months and reported that approximately 5 percent of all sworn officers were responsible for 43 percent of the complaints filed during that period. The Public Safety Review Commission discussed issues related to training, assignment and policy development, based on these data.

San Jose (#28) has a formal procedure for monitoring the number of complaints and requiring special training for officers with frequent complaints. Any San Jose police officer who is the subject of three or more formal complaints within a 12-month period is required to receive intervention counseling.

In Minneapolis (#14), any officer who has participated in mediation for a serious misconduct allegation in the previous 12 months is not permitted to mediate a current complaint.

Information Dissemination

As public agencies, virtually all citizen review bodies publish information about their activities. There is considerable variety, however, in the nature of the information published and the manner of its release.

Annual Reports

Most civilian review bodies publish annual reports. The San Jose Independent Police Auditor (#28) also publishes quarterly reports. The Seattle Investigations Auditor (#29) is directed to publish reports twice a year.

Annual reports generally provide a statistical summary of complaints and their disposition. Some reports, however, provide far more detailed data. The annual report of the New York City Civilian Complaint Investigative Bureau (#16) includes, for example, data on where complaints were filed, how complainants learned about the complaint process, what injuries were associated with use-of-force allegations, and how complaints were handled, in addition to summary information on officers who were the subjects of complaints. Such officer information includes length of service on the police force, place of residence, race, ethnicity, and gender. Data on the race of the officers are cross-tabulated with data on the race of the complainants.

Generally, annual reports provide only summary data on complaints. Some of the reports of the Flint Ombudsman (#10) are unique in that they provide detailed descriptions of individual cases, including the name of the investigator who handled each case. The annual reports of some of the citizen review bodies in Canada and other countries contain the names of the complaining citizens.

Whether some or all of the data available to a citizen review body should be confidential is a matter of controversy, involving a conflict between the public's right to information about a public agency and the complainants' and officers' rights to privacy. In particular jurisdictions, the confidentiality of data is governed by state statutes regarding public records and/or privacy, as well as police union contract provisions.

The rules and procedures of complaint review bodies often include guidelines regarding confidentiality. For example, the administrative rules of the Minneapolis Civilian Police Review Authority (#14) and the New Orleans Office of Municipal Investigation (#15) specify which data are public and which are confidential in those jurisdictions.

Publicity

Several cities have taken extra steps to publicize or otherwise facilitate the complaint process. Some cities have published information brochures or complaint forms in several languages. The San Francisco Office of Citizen Complaints, for example, has published a complaint form (#27) in four languages. Pittsburgh has published an employee's guide (#19) to the complaint process, including a statement of employee rights.

Conclusion

Citizen review of complaints against police officers is an important and rapidly changing aspect of American policing. Citizen review procedures have spread quickly in the last 10 to 15 years. All indicators suggest that they will continue to spread in the near future.

Because of this rapid growth, there is a wide variety of citizen review models. This manual attempts to highlight the most important features of citizen review. The documents included here are offered for information purposes only. The author does not recommend any one "model" or "ideal" form of citizen review. It is hoped that policy-makers will use the manual to make informed choices when considering changes in their agencies' existing complaint review procedures.

The "References" section that follows cites additional literature on citizen review for those readers interested in obtaining further information.

References

Abbott, David W., Louis H. Gold, and Edward T. Rogowsky (1969). *Police, Politics and Race: The New York City Referendum on Civilian Review*. New York: American Jewish Committee.

Adams, Kenneth (1995). "Measuring the Prevalence of Police Abuse of Force," *And Justice For All: Understanding and Controlling Police Abuse of Force*, eds. William A. Geller and Hans Toch. Washington, D.C.: Police Executive Research Forum.

"Administration of Complaints by Civilians Against the Police," *Harvard Law Review* 77 (1964):499–519 (no author given).

American Civil Liberties Union (1964). Policy no. 204, "Civilian Review Boards," *Policy Guide*. New York: ACLU.

——— (1966). *Police Power and Citizens' Rights: The Case for an Independent Police Review Board.* New York: ACLU.

——— (1992). *Fighting Police Abuse: A Community Action Manual.* New York: ACLU.

American Civil Liberties Union of Northern California (1992). *A Campaign of Deception: San Jose's Case Against Civilian Review.* San Francisco: ACLU of Northern California.

American Civil Liberties Union of Southern California (1992). *The Call for Change Goes Unanswered.* Los Angeles: ACLU of Southern California.

Americans for Effective Law Enforcement (1976). Brief no. 73-5 (1973), *AELE Defense Manual.* Rev. ed. San Francisco: AELE.

——— (1982). Brief no. 82-3, "Police Civilian Review Boards," *AELE Defense Manual.* San Francisco: AELE.

Barton, P.G. (1970). "Civilian Review Boards and the Handling of Complaints Against the Police," *University of Toronto Law Journal* 20:448–469.

Bayley, David (1992). "Police Brutality and Civilian Oversight," *Another Viewpoint*, no. 2. Evanston, Ill.: IACOLE.

Bellush, Jewell (ed.) (1971). *Race and Politics in New York City.* New York: Praeger.

Bray, Robert J. (1962). "Philadelphia's P.A.B.: A New Concept in Community Relations," *Villanova Law Review* 7 (Summer):656–673.

Brown, D. (1983). *Civilian Review of Complaints Against the Police: A Survey of the United States Literature*. Home office research paper no. 19. London: HMSO.

——— (1987). *The Police Complaints Procedure: A Survey of Complainants' Views*. Home office research study no. 93. London: HMSO.

Brown, Lee P. (1991). "President's Message: The Civilian Review Board: Setting a Goal for Future Obsolescence," *The Police Chief* 58 (July):6–7. Also in *IACOLE Newsletter* 16 (September 1991).

Caiden, Gerald, and Harlan Hahn (1979). "Public Complaints Against the Police," *Evaluating Alternative Law-Enforcement Policies*, eds. Ralph Baker and Fred A. Meyer Jr. Lexington, Mass.: Lexington Books. Pp. 169–176.

Carter, David L. (1991). "Police Disciplinary Procedures: A Review of Selected Police Departments," *Police Deviance*, eds. Thomas Barker and David L. Carter. 2nd ed. Cincinnati: Anderson. Pp. 351–371.

Chevigny, Paul (1969). *Police Complaints: A Handbook*. New York: ACLU.

——— (1969). *Police Power: Police Abuses in New York City*. New York: Vintage Books. Pp. 258–266.

Christopher Commission (1991). *Report of the Independent Commission on the Los Angeles Police Department*. Los Angeles: City of Los Angeles.

Cohen, Bernard (1970). *Police Internal Administration of Justice in New York City*. New York: Rand Institute.

——— (1972). "The Police Internal System of Justice in New York City," *Journal of Criminal Law, Criminology and Police Science* 63 (March):54–67.

Corbett, Claire L. (1991). "Complaints Against the Police: The New Procedure of Informal Resolution," *Policing and Society* 2(1):47–60.

Coxe, Spencer (1961). "Police Advisory Board," *Connecticut Bar Journal* 35:138–155.

——— (1965). "The Philadelphia Police Advisory Board," *Law in Transition* 2:179–193.

Culver, John H. (1975). "Policing the Police: Problems and Perspectives," *Journal of Police Science and Administration* 3(2):125–135.

Decker, Scott H., and Allen E. Wagner (1982). "Race and Citizen Complaints Against the Police: An Analysis of Their Interaction," *The Police and the Public*, ed. Jack Greene. Beverly Hills, Calif.: Sage.

Dugan, John R., and Daniel R. Breda (1991). "Complaints About Police Officers: A Comparison Among Types and Agencies," *Journal of Criminal Justice* 19:165–171.

Epstein, David G. (1992). "The Complaint: Advisory Reflections to the Law Enforcement Agency Head," *The Police Chief* (May):58–61.

Fogel, David (1987). "The Investigation and Disciplining of Police Misconduct: A Comparative View—London, Paris, Chicago," *Police Studies* 10:1–15.

Fyfe, James J. (1985). "Reviewing Citizens' Complaints Against Police," *Police Management Today*, ed. James J. Fyfe. Washington, D.C.: ICMA.

Geller, William A., and Hans Toch (eds.) (1995). *And Justice For All: Understanding and Controlling Police Abuse of Force.* Washington, D.C.: Police Executive Research Forum.

——— (1995). "Improving Our Understanding and Control of Police Abuse of Force: Recommendations for Research and Action," *And Justice For All: Understanding and Controlling Police Abuse of Force*, eds. William A. Geller and Hans Toch. Washington, D.C.: Police Executive Research Forum. Pp. 277–337.

Gellhorn, Walter (1969). *The Ombudsman and Others*. Cambridge, Mass.: Harvard University Press.

Goldsmith, Andrew (1988). "New Directions in Police Complaints Procedures: Some Conceptual and Comparative Departures," *Police Studies* 11:60–71.

——— (ed.) (1991). *Complaints Against the Police: The Trend to External Review*. Oxford: Clarendon Press.

——— (1991). "External Review and Self-Regulation: Police Accountability and the Dialectic of Complaints Procedures," *Complaints Against the Police: The Trend to External Review*, ed. Andrew Goldsmith. Oxford: Clarendon Press. Pp. 13–61.

——— (1993). "Necessary But Not Sufficient: The Role of Police Complaints Procedures in Police Accountability," *Accountability in Criminal Justice*, ed. P. Stenning. Toronto: University of Toronto Press.

——— (1994). "Recognizing Difference in Civilian Review: The Limits of Mono-Logical Thinking in a Polyphonic World." Paper. IACOLE annual meeting.

Goldstein, Herman (1967). "Administrative Problems in Controlling the Exercise of Police Authority," *Journal of Criminal Law, Criminology and Police Science* (June):160–172.

Grant, Alan (1976). "Complaints Against the Police—The North American Experience," *Criminology Law Review* (June):339–343.

Griswold, David B. (1994). "Complaints Against the Police: Predicting Dispositions," *Journal of Criminal Justice* 22(3):215–221.

Hudson, James R. (1968). "The Civilian Review Board Issues as Illuminated by the Philadelphia Experience," *Criminologica* 6:16–29.

——— (1970). "Police-Citizen Encounters That Lead to Citizen Complaints," *Social Problems* 18 (Fall):179–193.

——— (1971). "Police Review Boards and Police Accountability," *Law and Contemporary Problems* 36 (Autumn):515–538.

——— (1972). "Organizational Aspects of Internal and External Review of the Police," *Journal of Criminal Law, Criminology and Police Science* 63:427–432.

IACOLE (1985). *Compendium of Civilian Oversight Agencies*. Chicago: IACOLE.

——— (1989). *International Compendium of Civilian Oversight Agencies*. Chicago: IACOLE.

International Association of Chiefs of Police (1960). Resolution (Oct. 6).

——— (1964). "Police Review Boards" (critique of the Harvard study), *The Police Chief* (February):12–34.

——— (1965). "Position Statement of Police Review Boards," *The Police Chief* 9 (June):6.

International City Management Association (1992). "Police Review Systems," *MIS Report* 24(8) (August).

Jolin, Annette I., and Don C. Gibbons (1984). "Policing the Police: The Portland Experience," *Journal of Police Science and Administration* 12 (September):315–322.

Kahn, Ronald (1975). "Urban Reform and Police Accountability in New York City: 1950–1974," *Urban Problems and Public Policy*, eds. R. Lineberry and L. Masotti. Lexington, Mass.: Lexington Books. Pp. 107–127.

Kappler, Victor E., David Carter, and Allen Sapp (1992). "Police Officer Higher Education, Citizen Complaints and Departmental Rule Violation," *American Journal of Police* 11(2):37–54.

Kerstetter, Wayne A. (1985). "Who Disciplines the Police? Who Should?" *Police Leadership in America: Crisis and Opportunity*, ed. William A. Geller. Chicago: American Bar Foundation.

——— (1995). "A 'Procedural Justice' Perspective on Police and Citizen Satisfaction With Investigations of Police Use of Force: Finding a Common Ground of Fairness," *And Justice For All: Understanding and Controlling Police Abuse of Force*, eds. William A. Geller and Hans Toch. Washington, D.C.: Police Executive Research Forum. Pp. 223–232.

Kerstetter, Wayne A., and Kenneth A. Rasinski (1994). "Opening a Window Into Police Internal Affairs: Impact of Procedural Justice Reform on Third-Party Attitudes," *Social Justice Research* 7(2):107–127.

Lenzi, M.A. (1974). "Reviewing Civilian Complaints of Police Misconduct," *Temple Law Quarterly* 48:89–125.

Letman, Sloan T. (1980). "Chicago's Answer to Police Brutality: The Office of Professional Standards," *The Police Chief* (January):16–17.

——— (1981). "The Office of Professional Standards: Six Years Later," *The Police Chief* (March):44–46.

Lewis, Clare E. (1991). "Police Complaints in Metropolitan Toronto: Perspectives of the Public Complaints Commissioner," *Complaints Against the Police: The Trend to External Review*, ed. Andrew Goldsmith. Oxford: Clarendon Press. Pp. 153–175.

Littlejohn, Edward (1981). "Civil Liability and the Police Officer: The Need For New Deterrents to Police Misconduct," *University of Detroit Journal of Urban Law* 58:365–431.

——— (1981). "The Civilian Police Commission: A Deterrent of Police Misconduct," *University of Detroit Journal of Urban Law* 59 (Fall):5–62.

——— (1981). "The Cries of the Wounded: A History of Police Misconduct in Detroit," *University of Detroit Journal of Urban Law* 58:173–219.

Loveday, B. (1988). "Police Complaints in the USA," *Policing* 4 (Autumn):172–193.

Luna, Eileen (1994). "Accountability to the Community on the Use of Deadly Force," *Policing By Consent* I (December):4–6.

Lustgarten, Laurence (1986). "Controlling Police Misconduct," *The Governance of Police*. London: Sweet and Maxwell. Pp. 126–159.

Maguire, Mike (1991). "Complaints Against the Police: The British Experience," *Complaints Against the Police: The Trend to External Review*, ed. Andrew Goldsmith. Oxford: Clarendon Press. Pp. 177–209.

Maguire, Mike, and C. Corbett (1991). *A Study of the Police Complaints System*. London: HMSO.

McMahon, M. (1988). "Police Accountability: The Situation of Complaints in Toronto," *Contemporary Crises* 12:301–327.

Muir, William Ker, and Douglas W. Perez (1995). "Administrative Review of Alleged Police Brutality," *And Justice For All: Understanding and Controlling Police Abuse of Force*, eds. William A. Geller and Hans Toch. Washington, D.C.: Police Executive Research Forum.

NAACP (1995). *Beyond the Rodney King Story: An Investigation of Police Misconduct in Minority Communities*. Boston: Northeastern University Press. Pp. 52–71, 130–131.

Naegele, Timothy D. (1967). "Civilian Complaints Against the Police in Los Angeles," *Criminology* 3(1):7–35.

National Advisory Commission on Civil Disorders (Kerner Commission) (1968). *Report*. New York: Bantam Books. Pp. 291–292.

Neier, Aryeh (1966). "Civilian Review Boards—Another View," *Criminal Law Bulletin* 2(8):10–18.

Nelson, Penelope (1986). "Beyond the Blue Curtain: The Ombudsman's Role in Investigating Complaints Against the Police in New South Wales," *Australian Journal of Public Administration* XLV (September):230–238.

New York City Civilian Complaint Investigative Bureau (1992). *Survey of Civilian Complaint Systems*. New York: CCIB.

New York Civil Liberties Union (1990). *Police Abuse: The Need For Civilian Investigation and Oversight*. New York: NYCLU.

——— (1993). *Civilian Review Agencies: A Comparative Study*. New York: NYCLU.

Pate, Anthony M., and Lorie A. Fridell (1993). *Police Use of Force: Official Reports, Citizen Complaints and Legal Consequences*. Washington, D.C.: Police Foundation.

Paulsen, Monrad G., et al. (1970). "Securing Compliance With Constitutional Limitations: The Exclusionary Rule and Other Devices," *Law and Order Reconsidered*, eds. James S. Campbell et al. New York: Bantam Books. Pp. 390–436.

Perez, Douglas W. (1994). *Common Sense About Police Review*. Philadelphia: Temple University Press.

Walker, Samuel, and Vic W. Bumphus (1991). *Civilian Review of the Police: A National Survey of the 50 Largest Cities*. Omaha, Neb.: University of Nebraska at Omaha.

Walker, Samuel, and Betsy Wright (1995a). "Citizen Review of the Police, 1994: A National Survey," *Fresh Perspectives*. Washington, D.C.: Police Executive Research Forum.

——— (1995b). "Citizen Review of the Police, 1995: An Analysis of Roles, Structures and Procedures." Presentation at the annual meeting of the Academy of Criminal Justice Sciences, Boston, March 1995.

About the Police Executive Research Forum (PERF)

The Police Executive Research Forum (PERF) is a national professional association of chief executives of large city, county and state law enforcement agencies. PERF's objective is to improve the delivery of police services and the effectiveness of crime control through several means:

1. the exercise of strong national leadership,
2. the public debate of police and criminal issues,
3. the development of research and policy, and
4. the provision of vital management leadership services to police agencies.

PERF members are selected on the basis of their commitment to PERF's objectives and principles. PERF operates under the following tenets:

1. Research, experimentation and exchange of ideas through public discussion and debate are paths for the development of a comprehensive body of knowledge about policing.
2. Substantial and purposeful academic study is a prerequisite for acquiring, understanding and adding to that body of knowledge.
3. Maintenance of the highest standards of ethics and integrity is imperative in the improvement of policing.
4. The police must, within the limits of the law, be responsible and accountable to citizens as the ultimate source of police authority.
5. The principles embodied in the Constitution are the foundation of policing.

About the Police Executive Research Forum (PERF)

Document No. 1
Albuquerque, N.M.

CITY OF ALBUQUERQUE

SEVENTH COUNCIL

COUNCIL BILL NO. 0-103 ENACTMENT NO. 4-1987

SPONSORED BY: Pete Dinelli

ORDINANCE

CREATING THE OFFICE OF INDEPENDENT COUNSEL; SPECIFYING DUTIES AND RESPONSIBILITIES; PROVIDING FOR MORE EFFECTIVE REVIEW AND DIRECTION OF ALBUQUERQUE POLICE DEPARTMENT INTERNAL AFFAIRS INVESTIGATIONS; PROVIDING FOR SUPPLEMENTARY INVESTIGATIONS.

BE IT ORDAINED BY THE COUNCIL, THE GOVERNING BODY OF THE CITY OF ALBUQUERQUE:

Section 1. SHORT TITLE.--This ordinance may be cited as the "Independent Counsel Ordinance".

Section 2. PURPOSE.--The Council finds the public confidence could be enhanced in handling of internal affairs investigations concerning the conduct of members of the Albuquerque Police Department. The Council finds that employment of an outside, independent counsel with authority necessary to insure a fair, objective and impartial investigation would enhance the credibility of this process. The purpose of the Independent Counsel Ordinance is to establish the mechanism for implementing the process in a manner that will have the confidence of the public, the police officers and the complainants.

Section 3. OFFICE ESTABLISHED.--The office of Independent Counsel for the City of Albuquerque is hereby created. The Independent Counsel shall direct the overall manner in which the internal affairs investigations of the Albuquerque Police Department are conducted and shall assure confidentiality in the process. The Independent Counsel shall be an attorney with the necessary background and experience to direct and oversee the internal affairs

Underscored Material - New
[Bracketed Material] - Deletion

EXHIBIT
A

investigations. The City Attorney shall contract, with the advice and consent of the City Council, with the Independent Counsel for a term of no more that one year at a time, and the Independent Counsel shall not be considered an employee of the City for any purpose. The contract may be terminated in accordance with its provisions, but any such termination by the City shall be subject to the approval of the City Council.

Section 4. DUTIES OF INDEPENDENT COUNSEL.--The Independent Counsel shall establish by written directive to the Chief of Police the manner and procedure for such investigations.

Section 5. INVESTIGATIONS.--The Independent Counsel shall review all Albuquerque Police Department Internal Affairs Unit investigations for the purpose of making recommendations to the Chief of Police as to whether disciplinary action should be taken; he shall send copies of all such recommendations to the City Attorney. The Independent Counsel shall also make recommendations to the Chief Administrative Officer, the City Attorney, the Chief of Police and, where appropriate, the City Council, on procedures to be changed or any other matter the Independent Counsel deems appropriate. The Independent Counsel may, upon his own motion or upon request, initiate investigations of police misconduct by his staff or the Internal Affairs Unit or may supplement investigations already conducted through investigations conducted by his staff. All investigations subject to the control of the Independent Counsel shall be conducted in a manner to assure their objectivity, fairness and impartiality. The Independent Counsel shall be provided with resources, and any and all information requested, sufficient for investigative services necessary to assure an adequate investigation and shall be authorized to employ such investigators as are necessary to provide an objective, fair and impartial review.

Section 6. REPORTS.--In order to assure that elected officials are properly informed of the activities of the Office of Independent Counsel, the Independent Counsel shall report quarterly, or upon request, on his investigations to the Mayor and the members of the City Council.

Section 7. ATTEMPTS TO INFLUENCE.--It shall be the duty of the Independent Counsel to assure that all investigations are objective, fair, impartial and free of political influence. He shall conduct all investigations in a manner which assures objectivity, fairness, impartiality and freedom from such influence.

Section 8. COMPILATION.--This ordinance shall be compiled as part of the Revised Ordinances of the City of Albuquerque, 1974.

Section 9. EFFECTIVE DATE.--This ordinance shall become effective five days after publication in full.

PASSED AND ADOPTED THIS 2nd DAY OF February, 1987.

BY A VOTE OF 8 FOR AND 0 AGAINST.

Yes: 8
Excused: Hoover

Patrick J. Baca, President
City Council

APPROVED THIS 23rd DAY OF February, 1987.

Ken Schultz, Mayor
City of Albuquerque

ATTEST:

City Clerk

Underscored Material - New
[Bracketed Material] - Deletion

Document No. 2

Baltimore

same manner as other members of the Baltimore City Police Department. Any person who is a member of the Baltimore City Police Department shall be given credit for all the purposes aforesaid for all time spent as a member of the said Park Police Division. (P.L.L., 1969, sec. 16-40. 1961, ch. 290.)

COMPLAINT EVALUATION BOARD

16-41. Created; members and powers.

(a) The Complaint Evaluation Board (C.E.B.) of Baltimore City is created to provide a permanent, statutory agency in Baltimore City through which complaints lodged by members of the general public regarding alleged acts of discourtesy and excessive force by personnel of the Police Department of Baltimore City are to be processed and evaluated.

(b) The Board is composed of the following members or their delegates:

(1) The State's Attorney of Baltimore City

(2) The Attorney General of Maryland

(3) The City Solicitor of Baltimore City

(4) The Police Commissioner of Baltimore City

(5) The Executive Director of the Legal Aid Bureau, Inc., of Baltimore City

(6) The Executive Director of the Maryland Human Relations Commission

(7) The Executive Director of the Baltimore City Community Relations Commission.

(c) The City Solicitor of Baltimore City shall be the permanent chairman. The representative of the Legal Aid Bureau shall serve as secretary.

(d) The Board shall meet in executive session as often as necessary to perform its functions and duties, but it shall meet not less than once a month.

(e) In all matters where a quorum is present, a majority vote of the Board shall prevail. A quorum consists of 5 members. (1975, ch. 889.)

16-42. Complaint procedures.

(a) Any person who claims to have been subjected to, or any person who claims to have personal knowledge of an act or acts of discourtesy, use of excessive force, or injury allegedly resulting from excessive force caused by Police personnel, may make a complaint of such conduct at the Office of the Internal Investigation Division of the Police Department of Baltimore City, the Legal Aid Bureau, the Maryland Human Relations Commission, the Baltimore Community Relations Commission, or at any of the Police District Stations.

(b) The complaint shall be reduced to writing on a special C.E.B. Form serially numbered, signed by the complainant, and notarized before a duly authorized Notary Public.

(c) One copy of the completed form shall be retained by the recipient of the complaint and a copy given to the complainant. A copy hall be mailed within 48 hours to the Internal Investigation Division and to the Secretary of the Board.

(d) The Secretary of the Board shall assign a consecutive number to each complaint and, within 48 hours, shall mail a copy to each member of the Board. The Secretary shall also maintain on file a record of each complaint.

(e) The Internal Investigation Division shall make a comprehensive investigation of each complaint and submit its report thereof to the Board within 90 days from the date of the complaint.

(f) The Board shall review the Internal Investigation Division's report and submit in writing to the Police Commissioner within 30 days from receipt thereof, a statement of its findings and recommendations as provided under Section 16-43(b). The Police Commissioner shall, within 30 days of his receipt of the findings and recommendations of the C.E.B. forward to the Board a statement of his disposition in each case. Concurrent with this, the Police Commissioner will also forward a copy of the Board's recommendation and the Police Commissioner's statement of disposition to the complainant and respondent police personnel. (1975, ch. 889.)

16-43. Jurisdiction and disposition of complaint.

(a) Jurisdiction of the Board shall extend only to complaints against police personnel with respect to discourtesy and use of excessive force as defined by Police Department rules and regulations.

(b) Upon review of the investigative report of each case, the Board shall make forthwith any one of the following four recommendations to the Police Commissioner:

(1) Sustain the complaint and approve, disapprove or modify the proposed Internal Investigation Division's action against the police personnel.

(2) Dismiss the complaint because of lack or insufficiency of evidence.

(3) Exonerate the police personnel because of the complainant's failure to prove his case by clear and convincing evidence.

(4) Remand the case for further investigation to the Internal Investigation Division or to the Maryland State Police.

(c) The Board may request the complainant, witnesses, and the police department personnel involved in a particular complaint to submit voluntarily to a polygraph test or to appear voluntarily before the Board. (1975, ch. 889.)

16-44. Final action.

The Police Commissioner has final decision-making responsibility for the appropriate disciplinary action in each case, but no final action may be taken until the recommendation of the Board has been reviewed. (1975, ch. 889.)

16-45. Rights not abrogated.

Nothing contained in this article may abrogate any constitutional, statutory or common law right of police personnel against whom a complaint is filed, nor of the complainants, investigators or witnesses who participate in the complaint procedure. (1975, ch. 889.).

16-46. Suspension and dismissal procedures not changed.

This procedure may not be construed to affect or change the methods and procedures for suspension or dismissal of members of the Baltimore City Police Department. (1975, ch. 889.)

16-47. Procedural Requirements.

Police personnel may not be penalized or affected adversely in any way as a result of the procedure set forth in this Article without having been first afforded proper written notice of charges lodged against him and the right to a hearing before the Police Trial Board in accordance with due process of law. (1975, ch. 889.)

16-48. Records; public disclosure.

Records containing the names or identification of police personnel, complainants, investigators and witnesses may not be disclosed or released to the general public. (1975, ch. 889)

16-49. Rules of procedure.

Subject to the provisions of this Article, the Board may adopt reasonable and proper rules to govern its procedure. (1975, ch. 889.)

16-50. Semi-annual report.

The Board shall prepare and publish a semi-annual statistical and analytical report regarding the complaints processed under this Article. (1975, ch. 889.)

Document No. 3
Cambridge, Mass.

RULES AND REGULATIONS

The following rules and regulations are the operating procedures and guidelines for the City of Cambridge Police Review and Advisory Board, as approved by the board on 5/5/88.

I. REMOVAL OF BOARD MEMBERS

a) If any board member misses three unexcused regularly scheduled monthly meetings of the board during a calendar year, that position of said board member shall be automatically vacated upon certification to the City Manager by the board.

b) If a board member changes his/her legal residence to one outside of the City of Cambridge, that position of said board member shall be automatically vacated upon certification to the City Manager by the board.

RULES AND REGULATIONS

The following rules and regulations are the operating procedures and guidelines for the City of Cambridge Police Review and Advisory Board, as approved by the board on 5/5/88.

BOARD VACANCIES

a) If a vacancy occurs prior to the expiration of the member's terms, an appointment shall be made for the remainder of the term.

b) The board shall continue to meet, subject to the appearance of a quorum of its total membership, whenever a vacancy exists. However, if a vacancy exists without an appointment being made for a period of three (3) months or longer, the board may discontinue further meetings until such appointment has been made to fill the vacancy.

RULES AND REGULATIONS

The following rules and regulations are the operating procedures and guidelines for the City of Cambridge Police Review and Advisory Board, as approved by the board on 9/1/88, and revised as of 1/5/89.

III. COMPLAINTS

a) Types of complaints

1. Formal complaints - these are written complaints utilizing the board's complaint form and signed by the complainant. The filing of such a complaint will trigger a preliminary investigation.

2. Requests for information, assistance - informal complaints which request that the board obtain information for the complainant and resolve issues through an informal process or the gathering and/or dissemination of information.

b) Filing a complaint; limitations
1. A complaint may be filed up to 30 days from the date of the occurrence of the incident complained of.
2. The board may, at its discretion, and in response to written petition, investigate and hear complaints brought to its attention after the 30 day period has expired.

c) Duties of Cambridge Police Department employees - not withstanding any other provision of law, every officer or employee of the police department shall cooperate fully with any investigation or inquiry of the board, its staff, or its investigator.

d) Copies of formal complaints - copies of formal complaints shall be made available to the chief of Police, the Internal Affairs Division, and to the complained of individuals within five (5) days business days from the filling of the complaint with the board. Delivery to the Police department shall constitute delivery to the specific individuals mentioned herein.

e) The filing of the complaint, the failure to file a complaint, or the dismissal of the complaint by the board shall not bar the complainant from seeking relief in any other administrative or judicial forum.

f) "No contest" response - the complained of individual may enter a written response of "no contest" at any time before a hearing.

1. A response of "no contest" indicates that the complained of individual accepts the allegations of the complainant as substantially true in fact and interpretation. The complained of individual shall be bound by the terms of the "no contest" response in any consideration of the complaint by the City Manager.
2. Upon receipt of a "no contest" response, the Board investigator or staff member conducting the investigation shall refer the file of the case and the finding of "no contest" to the board, which shall then make recommendations to the City Manager for appropriate action. Recommendations to the City Manager shall be made within thirty(30) days of the filing of the "no contest" response with the board.

III. COMPLAINTS, CONTINUED

g) Resolution of complaints

1. Complaints concerning the Police Department and filed with the Police Review Board shall be investigated immediately by the Board. The Board will not delay the investigation of a complaint because of the existence of unresolved criminal charges or civil suits relating to the incident complained of.
2. A preliminary investigation shall be completed within ten(10) days, unless at least one Board member has agreed to extend such time. No preliminary investigation shall be extended for longer than thirty(30) days.
3. After conducting a preliminary investigation, the Board shall either order a full investigation or dismiss the complaint.
4. After conducting a full investigation, the board shall either schedule a hearing or dismiss the complaint.
5. If a complaint is not resolved as a result of #1-4 above, to the satisfaction of the complainant, the respondent employee, or a member of the Board, either the complainant, the respondent employee, or the Board member may request that the full Board hear or review the matter.
6. If a hearing or review is requested, the staff of the Police Review Board shall query the members of the Board, to determine if they wish to hear or review the matter. A majority of the members voting in the affirmative shall constitute an order to hold such hearing or review.

IIIg. RESOLUTION OF COMPLAINTS, CONTINUED

7. The Board may, at its discretion, order a hearing <u>or</u> a review.
8. The purpose of a review shall be to <u>reconsider</u> a decision to dismiss a complaint. If a review is held to reconsider a decision to dismiss made prior to a full investigation, the board shall either order a full investigation or affirm the previous decision to dismiss. If a review is held to reconsider a decision to dismiss made after conducting a full investigation, the board shall either order a hearing or affirm the previous decision to dismiss. No appeal may be made of an affirmation of a decision to dismiss.

9. The purpose of a hearing shall be to reach a final disposition of a complaint. The board shall either dismiss the complaint or recommend to the City Manager any discipline to be imposed. A hearing before the Board shall be conducted according to Section V of these rules and regulations.

RULES AND REGULATIONS

The following rules and regulations are the operating procedures and guidelines for the City of Cambridge Police Review and Advisory Board, as approved by the board on 5/5/88.

IV. PUBLIC INFORMATION

a) The following documents shall be available for inspection by all parties and the public during normal business hours upon request. Duplication of materials available for inspection shall be subject to whatever charges, if any, that the board may require for copying:

1. Complaint
2. Response to the complaint by the complained of individual.
3. Any letters of pre-hearing reconciliation
4. Any letters of pre-hearing dismissal of the complaint.
5. Orders by the board, requesting that a full investigation commence.
6. Written responses to all complaints
7. Notice(s) of board hearings
8. Any pleadings, briefs, subpoenas, motions and responses, orders filed or issued after certification of a case to public hearing.
9. Transcript, exhibits, and other evidence of record in connection with a public hearing.
10. Decisions issued by the board after the public hearing.

IV. PUBLIC INFORMATION, CONTINUED

b) Information not public.

The following materials shall not constitute public information:

1. Interrogatories and answers of the Respondent
2. All file materials dealing with efforts at conciliation.
3. Investigatory materials, including but not limited to investigatory memoranda, memoranda of law, interview forms, affidavits, notes, and worksheets.

c) The docket of the board is public information and shall contain the following information:

1. Case number
2. Date of the complaint
3. Name(s) of the complainant(s)
4. Nature of the complaint
5. Final disposition of the complaint

RULES AND REGULATIONS

The following rules and regulations are the operating procedures and guidelines for the City of Cambridge Police Review and Advisory Board, as approved by the board on 5/5/88.

V. HEARINGS

a) Function - the board shall review the investigative report and the evidence gathered in connection therewith, hear testimony, prepare findings, and shall advise the City Manager of its conclusions and recommendations.

b) All parties to the hearing shall receive notice of the hearing at least five(5) business days prior to the date of the hearing.

c) Subpoena power - the board's subpoena power shall be used to the extent necessary to insure fairness to all parties.

d) Procedure - the hearing will not be conducted according to the strict rules of evidence that apply in a court of law. However, irrelevant material may be excluded and other objections will be heard. The chairperson of the board will rule on objections to the evidence, and can initiate objections. All rulings of the chair will be subject to being overruled by a majority of the board members. This is not a public hearing in the sense that audience participation is invited. The public, however, is invited to witness the hearing, and may ask questions concerning procedures prior to the commencement of testimony; after that, no audience participation will be permitted.

V. HEARINGS, E, CONTINUED

e) Order of testimony:

1. The board will first obtain testimony and other evidence from a complainant about his/her case. After the complainant is questioned by the board, the complainant can be asked questions by the subject of the

complaint, his/her attorney, and by the staff member who conducted the investigation for the board. Then other witnesses in support of the complaint will be questioned by the board, subject to the same order of questioning. The staff member who conducted the investigation may be asked by the board to provide relevant information or clarification as is appropriate.

2. After the complainant's case has been presented, the subject of the complaint will be asked by the board to present testimony and other evidence.The same rules of questioning will apply as those stated in e-1 of this section, including the right of the complainant to question the subject of the complaint and witnesses in support of the subject of the complaint.

3. After the board obtains all the evidence, each party will be given an opportunity to present any further statement that he/she may wish.

4. Upon the conclusion of the case, the board will deliberate, either in public or private, at its discretion; such deliberations will be limited to discussion of the evidence that is presented at the hearing, and will not go outside such matters. Immediately following the deliberations, the board will publicly announce its findings and then adjourn the hearing.

5. The Cambridge Police Review and Advisory Board is an advisory body only, and as such have the power to advise the City Manager and recommend action to be taken. All parties to a complaint will receive copies of findings and conclusions from the hearing conducted by the board.

VI. CONTINUANCE POLICY, CONTINUED

In view of the problems of scheduling and potential for case backlog involved in the grating of continuances for board hearing, the Police Review directs staff to follow procedures as set here in regard to requests for hearing continuances.

a) Only the board may grant continuance. The board shall grant continuance requests by majority vote. If the request for continuance occurs prior to 72 hours before the time of the scheduled hearing, staff shall contact the board members, inform them of the reasons for the continuance request and determine whether a majority wishes to grant the request. If the request occurs within 72 hours of the scheduled hearing , the hearing will continue as scheduled and the party requesting the continuance (or his/her representative) can address the board at that time to explain the circumstances and the board will decide by majority vote whether to grant the continuance request. In case of inability of the requesting party or that party's counsel to attend the hearing due to illness or other involuntary incapacity staff shall cancel the hearing, inform board members and all parties to the hearing, and rescheduled the hearing.

b) Normally, requests for continuance received within 72 hours of the hearing will not be granted. The board can make exceptions only when there is compelling evidence of involuntary incapacity to take part in the hearing which could not have been foreseen prior to that time.

c) It is the responsibility of the parties involved to make any necessary arrangements for and with counsel if they desire counsel representation. Any scheduling problems which arise due to failure of a party to give timely notice to his/her counsel shall not be the basis for a continuance.

RULES AND REGULATIONS

The following rules and regulations are the operating procedures and guidelines for the City of Cambridge Police Review and Advisory Board, as approved by the board on 5/5/88.

VII. MEETINGS

a) Board members shall receive a written notice of upcoming by the staff at least 48 hours prior to the meeting, with the exception of special meetings, as defined in Ordinance #1018, Section 10. It is the responsibility of the individual board members to keep the staff informed of addresses changes.

b) Quorum - attendance of three (3) board members shall constitute a quorum.

c) Voting - all decisions of the board shall be by majority vote of the board members present and voting.

d) Minutes of the meeting - The executive secretary shall maintain accurate records of board meetings, setting forth the date, time, place, members present or absent and action taken at each meetings, including executive sessions. In the absence of the executive secretary, any board member may maintain the minutes of the meeting.

e) Executive sessions - No executive session shall be held until the board has first convened in an open session for which notice has been given, a majority of the members of the board have voted to go into executive session, and the vote of each member has been recorded on a roll call vote and entered into the minutes.

The purpose of the executive session must be stated and acceptable as defined in the Open Meeting Laws of the Commonwealth, and the board must state before the executive session if the board will reconvene after the executive session.

RULES AND REGULATIONS

The following rules and regulations are the operating procedures and guidelines for the City of Cambridge Police Review and Advisory Board, as approved by the board on 11/16/88.

VIII. CATEGORIES AND DEFINITIONS OF POLICE MISCONDUCT

1) Excessive Force - all allegations concerning the unnecessary use of force that goes beyond reasonable or lawful limits of physical power that may be used upon a person including:

a. improper use or display of a firearm

b. improper use of other objects such as a flashlight, baton, mace, handcuffs, etc.

c. improper use of hands or feet

2) Discourtesy - all allegations concerning a failure to be courteous and civil to the public. Complaints may include improper hand gestures or signs and/or the failure of an employee to give a proper response or explanation to a citizen. All employees are expected to be quiet, orderly, attentive, and respectful and to exercise patience and discretion in the performance of their duties.

3) Improper Stop/Street Detention/Search/Seizure/Arrest - all allegations concerning police actions conducted without sufficient lawful reason, particularly as they relate to improper stops, street detentions, searches, seizures and arrests. This category does not include complaints about improperly issued traffic citations or improper police tows(see 9 below).

4) Improper Detention Procedures - all allegations concerning a failure to follow proper procedures for arrest, booking, incarceration and release of prisoners. May include allegations concerning a failure to advise of the reasons for an arrest; failure to "Mirandize" a suspect; failure to utilize the proper citation release procedure; a failure to follow proper bail procedures; failure to follow proper juvenile processing procedures; failure to allow phone calls and/or access to attorneys, and unnecessary delays in releasing prisoners.

5) Inadequate Investigation or Improper Police Report - all allegations concerning a failure to adequately and impartially investigate and to accurately provide a written account of an

RULES AND REGULATIONS

The following rules and regulations are the operating procedures and guidelines for the City of Cambridge Police Review and Advisory Board, as approved by the board on 11/16/88.

VIII. CATEGORIES AND DEFINITIONS OF POLICE MISCONDUCT, CONTINUED

incident. May include the failure of an employee to take a report or to make a lawful arrest.

6) Discrimination - all allegations concerning a favorable or unfavorable treatment or action by a police employee which exhibits partiality or prejudice based upon a person's race, sex, religion, political persuasion or appearance.

7) Harassment - any allegation asserting a consistent, deliberate annoyance by police employees where the complainant can attest to repetitious contact over a period of time.

8) Improper Police Procedures - any allegation concerning a failure to follow approved Departmental policies, procedures, orders or guidelines.

9) Improper Traffic Citation or Police Tow - all allegations of improperly issued traffic citations or improper towing by a police employee.

10) Other - all other allegations concerning police employee misconduct that do not fit into any of the other listed categories. These allegations may include, but are not limited to complaints concerning criminal misconduct, abuse of discretion, or failure of a police employee to properly identify self.

The following rules and regulations are the operating procedures and guidelines for the City of Cambridge Police Review and Advisory Board, as approved by the board on 11/16/88.

Document No. 4

Cincinnati

City of Cincinnati

J.F.M.

An Ordinance No.__________ - 1984

Repealing and reordaining the provisions of Article II, Section 13 of the Administrative Code deleting the requirements that the Office of Municipal Investigation of Cincinnati consult with the City Solicitor to determine if the investigation should be delayed, authorizing the Office of Municipal Investigation of Cincinnati to immediately commence its investigation at the scene of shots fired, authorizing the Office of Municipal Investigation of Cincinnati to have immediate access to city records, reports and employees at the commencement of its investigation, and requiring city officials to cooperate with the Office of Municipal Investigation of Cincinnati.

WHEREAS, Council has determined that the duties and responsibilities of the Office of Municipal Investigation of Cincinnati should not include consultation with the City Solicitor to determine if its investigation should be delayed until a parallel criminal investigation or criminal action is completed; and

WHEREAS, Council has determined that the duties and responsibilities of the Office of Municipal Investigation of Cincinnati should include commencing its investigation at the scene of a shots fired immediately upon notification without interfering with the criminal investigation, and immediate access to all City records, documents and employees at the commencement of its investigation; and

WHEREAS, Council has determined that existing legislation concerning when the Office of Municipal Investigation of Cincinnati may require the appearance of any City employee, and the obligation of a City official to cooperate with the investigations of the Office of Municipal Investigation of Cincinnati; now, therefore,

BE IT ORDAINED by the Council of the City of Cincinnati, State of Ohio:

Section 1. That existing Section 13 of Article II of the Administrative Code is hereby repealed.

Section 2. That supplementary Section 13 of Article II of the Administrative Code is hereby ordained to read as follows:

ARTICLE II

Sec. 13. Office of Municipal Investigation of Cincinnati.

There is hereby established an office of municipal investigation of Cincinnati (OMIC) to be administered by a chief investigator, appointed by and subject to the control and supervision of the city manager. The OMIC shall have such assistants and staff as may be authorized by the city manager.

(a) Definitions.

For the purpose of this section, the following words and terms shall have the meanings as defined hereunder. Words used in the masculine gender include the feminine, and the feminine the masculine. Where any word or term is not defined, the ordinarily accepted meaning within the proper context shall apply.

New language is underscored. Language which has been deleted is indicated by asterisks as follows:

1 Where an investigation requires an inquiry into the subject of any ongoing criminal investigation, which shall include any investigation into shots fired, the OMIC shall consult with the city solicitor to determine whether the OMIC investigation shall be delayed until the criminal investigation is completed.

2 (3) If a city employee is likely to be arrested for serious misconduct, the chief investigator shall seek the counsel of the city solicitor and the city manager in determining whether the administrative investigative process should be delayed until criminal action is completed.

3 The chief investigator

4 The chief investigator

(1) "Person" means any natural person, proprietorship, corporation, government, partnership, trust, joint venture, group, association, organization or other business or enterprise of any kind or nature and any division, department or other suborganizational unit.

(2) "Serious misconduct" for a city employee means bribery, theft of city property, improper discharge of firearms, coercion, excessive use of physical force in the conduct of official duties, performance of a lawful, official act in an illegal or improper manner and serious violation of a law, rule or regulation which may be considered by the OMIC as reasonable cause for dismissal from public employment or the filing of criminal charges.

(3) "Serious misconduct" for a person who contracts in writing with the city means bribery of a city officer, agent or employee, theft of city property, defrauding the city or any violation of a law involving transactions related to the written contract with the city or compliance with any clause under the written contract.

(4) "Shots fired" means the deliberate and intentional discharge of a firearm by a police officer at or toward another individual or individuals.

(5) "Criminal intelligence information" means information on identifiable individuals compiled in an effort to anticipate, prevent or monitor possible criminal activity.

(b) Department: Chief Investigator.

The chief investigator shall be a bona fide criminal investigator with a proven record of successful investigations, shall be highly trained and experienced in investigative techniques, and shall have been graduated from an accredited university with at least a bachelor's degree. The chief investigator shall be bonded by the city and shall be an unclassified, full-time employee without secondary employment which conflicts with or creates a conflict of interest with the duties and responsibilities as chief investigator. The chief investigator must receive written approval from the city manager before accepting or engaging in any secondary employment. The chief investigator shall have official duties as set forth herein and shall have such duties and powers as delegated by the city manager, pursuant to Article II, Section 3 of the Administrative Code.

(c) Powers and Duties.

(1) The OMIC shall have the responsibility and power to investigate and inquire into any serious misconduct of any city employee or other person who contracts in writing with the city and may review the process and decision of various departmental investigations upon request of the complainant. The OMIC shall immediately commence and conduct an investigation into any shots fired. The OMIC chief investigator, when authorized by the city manager (or the council if the city manager is the object of an investigation) may request assistance from other city departments and/or outside consultants to aid such investigations.

(2) Conduct that is not considered serious by the chief investigator of OMIC or the appropriate department director or commissioner shall be investigated at the department level through the proper administrative channels. Provided, however, that such consideration shall not be construed to prevent OMIC from commencing and conducting an investigation into any shots fired.

(3) All OMIC personnel shall be prepared to participate as witnesses and to present testimony and evidence to those tribunals, administrative or criminal, that retain jurisdiction after an investigation is concluded.

(d) Complaint.

(1) Investigations shall be commenced upon the receipt of a complaint of or knowledge by OMIC of serious misconduct or shots fired. OMIC shall be placed on the priority list for notification when there are any shots fired. **1** Upon notification of shots fired incidents, OMIC shall immediately commence its investigation at the scene of the incident including having access to witnesses, subjects, and evidence, without interfering with the criminal investigation.

(2) All city departments shall report all serious misconduct to and refer all complaints of serious misconduct or other complaints specified herein to the OMIC. Parallel investigations may be necessary and shall be coordinated with OMIC upon consultation with the departments involved, OMIC and the city manager.

2

(e) Employee Protection.

All city supervisors shall refrain from any coercion or reprisal toward any city employee who files a complaint with OMIC. A violation of this section may give good cause for or constitute a ground for reduction in pay, suspension, removal or any other administrative disciplinary action in accordance with Section 124.34, Ohio Revised Code, the rules of the Cincinnati Civil Service Commission and the city's personnel policies and procedures relating to disciplinary action. The city supervisor shall have the right to appeal from any such disciplinary action as provided by law, rules of the Cincinnati Civil Service Commission and such other rights as provided by the city's personnel policies and procedures relating to disciplinary action.

(f) Conduct of Investigation.

(1) **3** At the commencement of its investigation, OMIC shall have immediate access to all city records, documents and employees, including employee personnel records and departmental investigation files and reports. **4** OMIC shall not have access to any record, document, file or report which contains any criminal intelligence information, except by order of the city manager. When, in the opinion of the chief investigator, records, witnesses and documents are needed which cannot otherwise be obtained, the chief investigator may petition council, or any committee thereof authorized by it, to exercise its subpoena power for the purposes of aiding an investigation

under the provisions of this chapter. Said subpoena power shall be exercised in accordance with Section 705.21 of the Ohio Revised Code. Confidentiality of records shall be protected according to law.

(2) Investigations are to be conducted according to law. The use of extraordinary investigative methods shall be in accordance with the law and subject to review by the city solicitor and the city manager prior to implementation.

(g) Appearance.

The chief investigator of OMIC shall have the authority to require the appearance of any city employee during his regular assigned working hours, whenever possible, and to question such employee regarding matters specifically relating to any serious misconduct. Any city employee shall be permitted to have union or legal representation during all questioning by the OMIC. A city employee may not refuse to submit to questioning by the OMIC because of the unavailability within a reasonable time of union or legal representation. An employee's refusal to answer questions propounded to him may give good cause for or constitute a ground for reduction in pay, suspension, removal or any other administrative disciplinary action in accordance with Section 124.34 Ohio Revised Code, the rules of the Cincinnati Civil Service Commission and the city's policies and procedures relating to disciplinary action. No disciplinary action for failure to respond to questions from the OMIC shall be taken unless the employee was warned prior to the questions being propounded to him that the failure to respond may be the basis for administrative disciplinary action, including dismissal. The employee shall have the right to appeal from such disciplinary action as provided by law, the rules of the Cincinnati Civil Service Commission and such other rights as provided by the city's personnel policies and procedures relating to disciplinary action.

(h) Interference With Investigation.

(1) No city employee or any person contracting in writing with the city shall prevent, obstruct or otherwise hinder any investigation conducted by the OMIC. Any violation of this paragraph may give good cause for or constitute a ground for reduction in pay, suspension, removal or any other administrative disciplinary action in accordance with Section 124.34 Ohio Revised Code, the rules of the Cincinnati Civil Service Commission and the city's policies and procedures relating to disciplinary action. The city employee shall have the right to appeal from such disciplinary action as provided by law, the rules of the Cincinnati Civil Service Commission and such other rights as provided by the city's personnel policies and procedures relating to disciplinary action.

(2) Every city official, city employee or office and every person contracting in writing with the city shall cooperate with the OMIC. OMIC shall solicit the voluntary cooperation of all other persons with its investigations.

(i) Report and Confidentiality of Investigation.

(1) At the conclusion of the investigation, OMIC shall submit to the city manager a written report containing final conclusions and pertinent facts. The city manager shall provide such report or a summary thereof to the complainant, to the accused and to the appropriate department director or commissioner. Upon request, the city manager may make available such report or a summary thereof to the public, and with regard to reports on shots fired, the city manager shall make those reports public, unless and except to the extent that the city manager requests and obtains city council approval to withhold all or part of such report. Upon written request, the chief investigator of the OMIC may make available such report to any law enforcement agency or prosecuting attorney.

(2) Except the staff of OMIC, the city manager, the city solicitor and any law enforcement agency conducting a parallel current investigation into the suspected serious misconduct of a city employee, no city employee or any other person shall have access to the investigatory files of the OMIC.

(j) Municipal Integrity Maintenance Task Force.

There shall be a municipal integrity maintenance task force appointed by the city manager. The task force shall be comprised of the OMIC chief investigator; the director of personnel; the director of research, evaluation and budget; the director of finance; the deputy/administration city manager; the city solicitor and the division chief of internal management audit. The duties of the task force shall be to advise the city manager of changes in policy, rules and regulations which will help maintain integrity in municipal government.

Section 3. This ordinance shall take effect and be in force from and after the earliest period allowed by law.

Passed ______________________ A.D., 1984

____
Mayor

Attest: ______________________
Clerk

Document No. 5

Dayton, Ohio

The Dayton Citizens Appeal Board
Policies and Procedures of Operation

Section 1: Definitions

For the purpose of this document the following words shall have the meanings ascribed to them by this section.

a. BOARD means the Dayton Citizens Appeal Board which is established by ordinance of the Dayton City Commission.

b. CHAIRPERSON or CHAIR means the presiding officer of the Board as elected by the members of the Board and shall be the official spokesperson for the Board.

c. MEMBER means a duly appointed member of the Board (Ordinance #28179).

d. EX-OFFICIO MEMBER means a non-voting member of the Board.

Section 2: Purpose of the Board

The Board shall have three (3) basic functions: to hear appeals regarding the investigation and determination in citizen complaints; to hear, on a monthly basis, reports from Internal Affairs regarding cases under investigation; and to review policies and procedures as directed by the City Manager or the Chief of Police. Also central to the Board's functioning is its responsibility for communicating with appellants and the public. The Board shall be careful to notify appellants of progress, hearings and findings in their appeals. The Board shall also communicate its findings with the public. These efforts are focused on the desire of the Board to enhance community confidence in the Dayton Police Department. The Board shall also review recommendations of the Firearms Committee on all shootings, and shall review other misdeeds or misconduct at the request of the City Manager.

Section 3: Jurisdiction of the Board

The jurisdiction of the Board shall be the consideration of appeals of complaints against any member of the Dayton Police Department, which alleges police misconduct, and deficient Police policies and patterns of practice discovered either through the appeals process or reviewed as directed by the City Manager. The Board will report its findings and recommendations to the City Manager regarding these appeals and reviews as well as those recommendations formed as a result of hearing Internal Affairs investigation reports and Firearms Committee shootings. The Board's findings in each appeal will be communicated to the appellant by letter. The Board shall also have jurisdiction to review other misdeeds or misconduct as directed by the City Manager. Should the Board, through its operation, wish to make recommendations on other Police policies and procedures, they may do so to the City Manager in their reports.

Section 4: Powers of the Board

The powers of this Board are limited to those of review and recommendation to the City Manager, without any adjudicatory or disciplinary powers.

Section 5: Effective Date of Jurisdiction

The jurisdiction of this Board will commence 30 days from the effective date establishing the Dayton Citizens Appeal Board. Any incident alleged to have happened prior to the date of adoption of the ordinance shall not be appealable to the jurisdiction of this Board.

Section 6: Membership

The Board will be comprised of five voting members appointed by the City Manager. Members of the Board shall be citizens of Dayton of notable knowledge, experience and upstanding community presence. They shall not have had any criminal convictions, nor shall they be a candidate for public office, and shall serve without compensation. One member shall be a representative of the legal community, thereby lending legal knowledge to the appeal and review process. A second member shall be a former member of the law enforcement community. The remaining three members shall be selected from among members of the community. An Assistant City Manager and the Chief of Police shall serve as ex-officio, non-voting members of the Board. The five voting members of the Board shall represent the racial mix of the city, shall have a representation of both sexes, and resemble a fair representation of the various geographical areas of the city.

Section 7: Term of Service

The Board members shall serve for terms of two years, except that in 1990, one member shall be appointed for three years, two members for two years and two members for one year. All members shall continue to serve until their successors have been appointed. In the initial appointment, or any subsequent membership change, members may be reappointed by the City Manager to serve an additional term. No individual may serve more than three consecutive terms.

Section 8: Removal from Membership

Any member of the Board may be removed for incompetence, neglect of duty, misconduct or malfeasance by the City Manager. Members may be removed for missing two consecutive Board meetings without appropriate excuses delivered to the Chair within a reasonable period of time. It is the purview of the Chair to determine the appropriateness of these excuses. Any vacancy occasioned by resignation, death or removal of a member shall be filled for the balance of the unexpired term by appointment of the City Manager. The replacement member shall be appointed within 30 days of the vacancy date.

Section 9: Conflict of Interest

Should a matter arise in which a Board member feels his or her personal interests may influence his or her ability to hear an issue or case in an impartial manner, that Board member shall indicate to the Chairperson such conflicts of interest, and the Board member shall be excused from the hearing. Should an appellant feel a board member has a conflict of interest in hearing his or her appeal, the appellant may state that concern to the Chair, and the concern will be considered by the Board. The required vote for affirmative action of the Board in such cases where one Board member is excused shall remain at three members.

Section 10: Selection and Duties of the Chairperson

The Board's Chairperson shall be elected by the members of the Board from among themselves. The Chairperson shall be selected on the first meeting date, and a new Chair shall be elected annually in the meeting falling closest to the previous Chair's election date.

The Chair shall preside over all meetings of the Board and shall have the right to vote on all questions. The Chair shall see that the laws of the City pertaining to the activities of the Board are faithfully executed. The Board may meet at such additional times and places deemed necessary by its members, on the call of the Chairperson or the City Manager. The Board may meet outside of its monthly meeting to review evidence in appeals cases before testimony is presented during the formal appeal hearing. The Chair will report the recommendations of the Board regarding each issue and appeal directly to the City Manager through a written report.

Section 11: Quorum

In order for the Board to conduct Board affairs, a quorum of three members will be required, and the affirmative vote of three members present at any meeting will be required for Board action.

Section 12: Location and Placement of the Board within the Organization

The Board will operate at its own location on Monument Avenue. The Internal Affairs Bureau also placed at this location shall be separate from the Board's offices and operation. The Board's operation will be independent of the Police Department organization.

Section 13: Staff

The Board shall be served by one staff member assigned to the Board by the Department of Central Services Director. This staff member shall be responsible for the day to day operations of the Board and preparing all necessary materials for Board meetings, setting meetings, notifying the public of these meetings, taking minutes, and preparing written reports from the Board to the City Manager. The staff member shall also maintain a good working relationship with the Police Department and its Internal Affairs Bureau to ensure the easy flow of information and documents between the two organizations.

The Board shall also be served by a legal advisor for each appeal, to assist the Board in review of each case and to reach a fact-based conclusion. A pool of legal advisors will be retained on contract to the Board through the Department of Central Services.

Legal counsel will be provided to the Board by the City of Dayton Law Department.

Section 19: Hearings

a. Scheduling of Hearings: After reviewing each appeal and the investigation of the initial complaint, appeals will be scheduled by the Board for formal hearing at the next monthly meeting, unless the Board determines that the next monthly meeting is not appropriate . If it is the experience of the Board or the City Manager that bi-monthly meetings would better serve timely disposition of Appeals, then such meetings may be scheduled until the number of appeals heard is once again manageable through monthly meetings.

Should the Board determine that after review of the appeal and the investigation, or after the formal hearing, that additional investigation is warranted, it may request that additional investigation by Internal Affairs for completion in a timely manner. Appeals unresolved pending the outcome of additional investigation will be continued at the next possible regular meeting once the investigation is complete and the Board has reviewed the new information.

b. Notice Requirements

The appellant shall be given ten days notice prior to the date of the formal appeal hearing, the public press, and to the Police officers involved. The notice shall state the date, time and place of the formal hearing.

c. Witnesses and Affirmation

The employees of the Department of Police against whom the complaint is made will be invited to give voluntary testimony to the Board during the Appeal hearing. The Board may, at its sole discretion, and is hereby empowered to issue subpoenas for witnesses to the incident.

All witnesses will be required to make an affirmation.

d. CAB Meetings

CAB meetings shall be conducted as follows unless the Chair orders otherwise:

1. Executive Session

During executive session, the Board shall review the Police Department investigation of each complaint appealed with the legal advisor for the particular appeal and a representative of Internal Affairs. The legal advisor shall seek to illuminate the facts in the investigation and the basis of the citizen's appeal. The legal advisor may also make any other statements of fact regarding the case which the Board should be advised of in order to reach a fact based conclusion. These sessions may be held before or after the appeal hearing.

2. Public Hearing

During the Public hearing, at the discretion of the Board, opening statement(s) may be made by the appellant and officer involved. Witnesses will testify, first for the appellant, then for the officer, and after making their statements to the Board may be asked additional questions only by the Board members. At the discretion of the Board, closing statements may be made by the appellant and the officer, at the conclusion of the presentation of evidence and testimony. Unless otherwise ordered by the Chair, the entire hearing on a given complaint shall be conducted on one occasion. All public hearings shall be recorded by a court reporter, with the official reports maintained in the Board's office.

Section 20: Order of Business

a. The order of business at regular Board meetings shall be as follows:

1. Public Meeting
   - roll call
   - approval of minutes
   - other old business
   - new business
2. Public Hearing
   - statement of Appeal
   - testimony of appellant, witnesses and police officers by appeal
   - discussion and questions
3. Executive Session
   - review of complaint investigation with legal advisor and Internal Affairs representative
   - determination of recommendations related to each issue and appeal

review of ongoing Internal Affairs investigations
review of Firearms Committee recommendations
review of Appeals filed
scheduling of appeals for formal hearing
other old business
new business

4. Adjournment

b. Except as otherwise specified in these policies and procedures, the proceedings of the Board shall be governed by Robert's Rules of Order.

Section 21: Findings of the Board

The Board shall use the preponderance of evidence standard when evaluating the investigation, testimony and other evidence in each appeal. In making its determinations, the Board may or may not concur with the findings of the Chief of Police in the investigation of a complaint. If the Board does not concur, it may do so with a finding that the complaint should have been substantiated, not substantiated, exonerated or unfounded. An appeal is recommended as sustained when the investigation and/or appeal hearing discloses evidence indicating that accused employee has committed all or part of the alleged acts. An appeal is recommended as not sustained when the review and hearing discloses insufficient evidence to clearly prove or disprove allegations made. An appeal is recommended for exoneration when the review and appeal hearing indicate that the act did occur but that it was justified lawful and proper. An appeal is recommended as unfounded when the review and hearing establishes the acts complained of and appealed did not occur.

The findings and recommendations of the Board will be submitted in writing by the Chair directly to the City Manager and the appellant, after they are signed by each of the Board members. The report will contain the votes of each individual Board member, the Board's recommendations and brief statements representing the justification for the decision. Members holding the minority opinion may provide written statements as to their dissension with the report if they wish. The dissenting comments must be prepared in a timely manner and may be assisted by the staff member.

The findings shall be reported to the City Manager, the appellant and the public within 30 calendar days of the Board's decision. The decisions will be made in a timely manner. A summary of the findings of the Board will be reported to Dayton households in the City newspaper, "The Dayton Update."

The City Manager will report back to the Board the disposition of their recommendations.

Section 22: Evaluation and Annual Reporting

The Board shall keep a record of all appeals and disposition thereof. The Board shall file annual reports with the City Manager showing the general activity of the Board. This report is to be made public.

Section 23: Amendment of Rules

These rules may be altered or amended at any regular meeting of the Board by a majority vote of the Board. Copies of revised Policies and Procedures will be made available to appropriate agencies and the public.

Document No. 6

Denver

ANNUAL REPORT

City and County of Denver

PUBLIC SAFETY REVIEW COMMISSION

1994

The Public Safety Review Commission

Chet Whye, Jr.
Chairman

Adrienne H. Benavidez
Vice-Chair

Toni Alcott Tichy
Commissioner

James L. Clement
Commissioner

Kenneth Norman Kripke
Commissioner

Tony Ogden
Commissioner

Joseph G. Sandoval
Commissioner

Victoria H. Calvillo
Secretary of the Commission

The Public Safety Review Commission holds Public Meetings on the third Thursday of every month at 6:30 P.M. in Denver City Council Chambers, Room 450 in the City and County Building. For information on the next meeting, call the Commission office at (303) 640-5825 TDD (303) 640-3132 or FAX 640-4567

First Western Plaza 303 West Colfax Avenue, Suite 150 Denver, Colorado 80204-2621

HISTORICAL PERSPECTIVE

The history of police oversight in Denver includes initiatives by city officials and citizen advocacy groups addressing issues of alleged police abuse and misconduct. Because the police reviewed most allegations of police misconduct and abuse, many individuals suggested that the investigation by the police into these incidents lacked credibility. Efforts to develop civilian oversight of police sought to infuse systematic accountability as a supplement or as an alternative to law enforcement officers investigating themselves.

In 1919, the Italian community in North Denver marched on city hall to demand the removal of Detective George G. Klein for the shooting death of just discharged World War I veteran Jerry Carabetta. Carabetta was shot in the spinal cord by Detective Klein while fleeing. Detective Klein stated he stumbled while chasing Carabetta and that his gun fired by accident.

In 1947 Denver Mayor Quigg Newton, Jr. created a 21-member Charter convention to deliberate over racial hiring practices and the feasibility of establishing a civilian review board to investigate complaints against the police.

In the 1950's Denver's African American community expressed its anger when a young boy, arrested in Five Points for drunkenness, was shot and killed in front of Denver Juvenile Hall (now the Gilliam Youth Services Center). The officer who shot him stated that the boy had bolted when he got to the door of the detention center. The officer then chased the boy with gun drawn. He later claimed that his gun fired accidently when he stumbled on a crack in the sidewalk.

Reports of these types of incidents during the period of the 1950's, 1960's and 1970's outraged not only the African-American community but also the Chicano community. In the late 1960's the police shooting of a young boy, Pineda, as he climbed out of an enclosed car lot in West Denver aroused indignation. Concern about police treatment of citizens in these and other types of situations in which the Denver minority community believed that injury or death resulted under suspicious circumstances gave rise to demand for change.

In April, 1970 the late and humanitarian and community activist Richard Castro objected to the police arrest of Artie Ornelas at Curtis Park. His actions resulted in his arrest accompanied by minor injuries. The subsequent uproar created hearings on police-community relations before Denver City Council and an investigation into the incident by Manager of Safety William Hoch and Director Minoru Yasui of the Commission on Community Relations. Although the report exonerated the police, the issue did not subside.

As a result of this and other incidents, the Denver City Council then created the Community Investigation Committee. The committee authorized reports from a team of psychologists led by Monroe J. Miller from R. J. Hernandez and Associates, and from the Metro Denver Urban Coalition. Then the Community Investigations Committee issued a report addressing problems of police/community relations. However, there was no immediate action taken as a result.

Debate and discussion regarding civilian review of police action gained a new twist with the alleged mistreatment of Councilmember Paul Hentzell in 1974. Apparently, Councilmember Hentzell parking his vehicle in the police parking lot while he attended a Denver Rockets basketball game. When he returned to his vehicle after the game he found flat tires. He went into the police administration building to seek assistance when the incident occurred.

This event triggered proposals by Chief of Police Dill to improve police discipline. Community members and some city officials proposed a citizen review board. However, Mayor Bill McNichols steadfastly refused to consider such a proposal, although police-community relations strained under police killing civilians and civilians killing police in 1975.

The death of Carl Newland in 1976 while in police custody renewed the debate on civilian oversight of police. The Spring/Summer of 1976 witnessed the drafting of a proposal for a Police Commissions based on the Los Angeles, California model. Denver City Council refused to pass the Police Commission bill after Mayor McNichols created a Citizens Police Advisory Review Commission. The following year 1977 a member of that Commission Paul Sandoval resigned calling the police department a "closed club". The Denver Post described it as a "watchdog with rubber teeth".

In July 1977, police shot and killed two men in Curtis Park. This event resulted in protest marches on the police department, a Grand Jury indictment of a police officer and a lawyer hired by Denver City Council to investigate the incident.

The Police Commission idea regenerated and in the 1978 elections voters in Denver defeated it.

However, in part the latter idea was rejected when the incumbent Mayor suggested he would implement a police review process if reelected. That idea did not reach fruition and a year after the election promise the Denver Post questioned the seriousness of the suggestion and expressed a desire for an independent police review process. After 1978-79 attempts to establish a civilian review process to investigate allegations of police misconduct, no formal proposals surfaced beyond the talking stage until 1991.

African-American, Chicanos and a coalition of concerned organizations continued to press the City for civilian review of police. Allegations of police abuse and proposals to have the Colorado legislature investigate police conduct occurred during the early years of the 1980 decade. Indeed, speculation suggested that the Governor might appoint a special prosecutor in the police probe. Nonetheless, the quest for police accountability and public awareness did not evaporate.

In 1988 Denver City Councilmember Hiawatha Davis introduced a resolution before City Council to study the issue of whether civilian review of police should exist. This proposal emerged from community pressure indicating a need for a police review board. The proposal did not pass because of heavy lobbying against it.

The issue continued to simmer until an incident occurred on January 29, 1991, following a police chase. Fifteen year old Jevaun Ivory was apprehended after the chase ended in a crash at East Colfax Avenue and Monaco Parkway. According to Ivory, police kicked and beat him as he was lying down, inflicting cuts, bruises, several loose teeth, and a broken nose. Ivory said he laid down on the ground as ordered, but officers kicked him and called him racial epithets.

The effort that led to the establishment of the Denver Public Safety Review Commission was not sparked by the graphic videotaped beating in Los Angeles of Rodney King. It was prompted by an incident that for many was the last straw: the alleged beating of a 15-year old Denver boy in the streets of Denver by officers of the Denver Police Department.

Within a week the decision was made to hold a hearing where victims and witnesses to alleged police brutality and misconduct could disclose their experiences. A panel of 19 citizens was convened, headed by Denver Councilman Hiawatha Davis, to conduct public hearings. For 15 hours, the panel heard testimony from citizens who had experienced or witnessed everything from rudeness to intimidations, coercion, theft, false arrest, rape, and wrongful death.

For three very emotional nights, citizens vented their pain, their frustration, their anger and their distrust. And many who testified stated very emphatically that they had no confidence in filing a complaint with the very agency they were complaining against. The 19 member panel also held special sessions to hear from experts in the field of oversight, both local and national.

Through those deliberations, it was clearly substantiated that the predominance of individuals who alleged being victimized by police misconduct had not reported these incidents to what is now the Internal Investigations Bureau for four basic reasons:

A. Strong belief that nothing would be done by the police
B. Fear of retaliation
C. Insensitive or unwelcome bureaucracy
D. Pending criminal charges

Of those who actually did file complaints, their experience usually fell into these categories:

A. Police exonerated, complaint unfounded, or action justified
B. No information was provided to complainant
C. Long delay in completing the investigation
D. No appropriate disciplinary action taken

The panel's research culminated in a drive to enact an ordinance that would establish a citizen's review board with the power to subpoena witnesses and documents, and to investigate complaints independently from the onset. However, the initial bills failed passage.

On June 19, 1992, Executive Order No. 106 was issued by Mayor Wellington E. Webb establishing a Public Safety Review Commission consisting of 5 members with the power to review complaints and subpoena only witnesses exclusive of the complainants and officers filed against.

On August 24, 1992, the Denver City Council enacted Ordinance 585, Series of 1992, a compromise sponsored by Councilman Timothy Sandos. The ordinance established the present commission of 7 members that would review cases, but only after internal departmental investigation.

As previously stated, there have been a horde of initiatives to review citizen complaints. But, the most potent of these is Denver's present system of oversight, which encompasses the powers of citizen review, independent investigations and authority to subpoena all pertinent witnesses and documents.

UPDATE: GANG LIST RECOMMENDATIONS

As reported in the Semi-Annual Report, the PSRC had several concerns regarding the Department's use and compilation of the "Gang List". In a memorandum dated April 20, 1994, these concerns were conveyed to Chief Michaud. Additionally, several changes to the Department's use of the "Gang List" were recommended. A response to this memorandum was received from the Chief on December 21, 1994. The following is a summary of the PSRC's concerns and recommendations and the Chief's response.

1. The Department has stated that the "Gang List" is an intelligence gathering and resource management tool. However, it was unable to evaluate the effectiveness of the "Gang List" either as an intelligence gathering tool or as a measure for the allocation of resources. The Commission is concerned that such a list is being maintained despite any objective basis to determine its value to the Department.

   Response: The Department stated that the list is used on a daily basis in the investigation of gang related cases and has proven to be useful as an intelligence gathering and resource management tool. (The Department's response did not provide the PSRC with how the effectiveness is measured).

2. Despite that under Colorado law, a "gang" is defined as a group of three or more individuals with a common interest, bond or activity characterized by criminal or delinquent conduct, the "Gang List" contained the names of 6,567 people in early January 1994. 3,747 names were removed from the list on January 19, 1994, the day before the PSRC held a public hearing on the use of the "Gang List". The PSRC is concerned that tainting someone with the connection of criminal undertaking on the basis of ill-defined and ambiguous criteria can be construed as being in contravention of fundamental safeguards. The PSRC is also concerned that amassing data by such means compromises the integrity of law enforcement and exposes the City to lawsuits. Additionally, the list is supposedly only distributed internally, however, its contents have reportedly been used as additional leverage in court cases and the Denver Public Schools receives a copy of the daily "activity sheet" of gang matters.

   Response: The Department continues to make good faith efforts to maintain the integrity of the list. The Department reports that it does not know to what extent the list is used by the courts and confirms that the Denver Public Schools receives a copy of the "activity sheet" by court order.

3. The seven criteria used to screen individuals placed on the Gang List,"

may constitute a "profile". Such a "profile" may stigmatize those individuals placed on the "Gang List" and infringe upon their associational rights. The use of "profiles" has been sanctioned by several courts throughout the country. The potential that the "Gang List" may be determined to constitute such a "profile", unnecessarily exposes the City and the Department to suit.

Response: The Department stands by the seven criteria and explained that the "Gang List" has not been determined to be a 'profile' by any Colorado court nor have any claims or lawsuits been filed on this issue. (The Department's response did not address whether it has evaluated the 'potential' that a suit may or may not be filed.)

4. The PSRC is also concerned that if an individual whose name is on the list is stopped by an officer, some officers may use that fact to justify sufficient probable cause to search the individual and/or his/her automobile for weapons or other contraband. While this is clearly in violation of the Department's Gang Protocol, the Commission has been told by members of the Department that if a person is stopped and determined to be on the "Gang List", the officer will search the individual because of the probability that gang members may be armed.

Response: The Department stated that "stop and frisk" law requires that the officer have a reasonable concern for his/her safety before conducting the frisk. This is determined by numerous variables within an officer's observations and discretion. An individual's membership in a gang is only one of many factors an officer may consider before making a quick assessment of the situation for his/her individual safety.

5. While answering questions of the PSRC, officers admitted that the commission of certain actions north of Colfax could constitute being put on the "Gang List" while the same activity south of Colfax would only result in a contact card being filed for intelligence purposes.

Response: The Department stated that it did not recall any member of the Urban Street Crime Bureau supplying this information. The Bureau uses the factors as its exclusive criteria in determining gang membership.

6. The PSRC is concerned that the confidentiality of the "Gang List" is compromised because of its use by prosecuting attorneys to justify harsher sentencing recommendations.

Response: The Department responded that the use of the "Gang List"/information during Court sentencing is a decision made by prosecutors that must be approved by the presiding judge. (The Department's response does not explain how the prosecutor is made aware of the confidential "Gang List" information.)

7. The PSRC recommended that the names of those individuals who have not been charged or convicted of gang related criminal activity should be removed from the list.

Response: The Department stated that the "Gang List" contains information on individuals who currently are, were, <u>or are likely to be</u> involved in criminal activity. A conviction or a charge would have to be an addition to the established criteria.

8. The PSRC recommended that the seven criteria specified in the Department's gang protocol, which are used to identify those placed on the list, should be reviewed and changed so that their use results in the identification of only those individuals involved in criminal gang related activity.

   Response: The Department stated that it stands by the criteria and reported that many people on this list are self-proclaimed gang members, coupled with an intimate knowledge of gang practices and protocols.

9. The PSRC recommended that the Department should consider and, if necessary, develop alternate means of maintaining useful intelligence information which are less intrusive.

   Response: The Department responded that the "Gang List" works extremely well and that it will continue their "checks and balance" system to maintain integrity in the process.

10. The PSRC recommended that if a clearance is requested on an individual, dispatch should not release information which identifies the individual as being on the "Gang List."

    Response: The Department stated that this is primarily an officer safety issue. Gang members are very often in possession of dangerous weapons. The information that an individual is 'gang active' provides the officers that extra needed awareness for their own safety.

11. Finally, the PSRC also recommended that the letters sent to parents to inform them that their son or daughter has been placed on the list should specifically state the following:

    - as a result of a police contact, their son or daughter has been placed on the "Gang List;"
    - the period of time their son or daughter's name will remain on the list; and
    - an explanation of their right to discuss with the USCB Captain whether or not their son or daughter's name has been appropriately placed on the "Gang List."

    Further, the letter should be sent in English and Spanish and should be translated so as to contain the same information in both languages.

    Response: The Department stated that their letters are sufficient for their purpose and that the information is specific and an invitation is made to the parents to meet with command/supervisory officers of the Gang Bureau. This correspondence is in English and Spanish. (The Department's response does not address the fact that neither the

"Gang List" nor its procedural aspects is ever mentioned in their correspondence nor that there are material inconsistencies in the Spanish version as compared to the English letter.)

The PSRC is not satisfied with the Chief's response to its concerns and recommendations and will be seeking further information from the Department in the near future.

THE POLICE PROTECTIVE ASSOCIATION

In early 1994, the Police Protective Association filed a lawsuit in Denver District Court against the Commission, its individual members and others. The suit sought to prohibit the Commission from mentioning at public meetings the names of police officers against whom citizen complaints had been filed.

Before the lawsuit was filed, the Commission had established an internal policy to refrain from mentioning the names of officers in public proceedings.

The PPA attempted to obtain a restraining order, but after a hearing, the court refused to enter it. After the City Attorney assigned to the Commission filed an answer on behalf of all of the defendants, the PPA voluntarily dismissed its action.

In an unrelated matter, the PPA made several suggestion to members of the Denver City Council regarding the workings of the Commission. The PPA and the Commission discussed the suggestions at several meetings requested and chaired by City Councilman Timothy Sandos. No further action was taken.

CONCERN OVER OFFICERS WITH FREQUENT COMPLAINTS

At its May 16, 1994 Executive Session, PSRC met with Manager of Safety Fidel Montoya, Jr., Chief of Police David Michaud and IAB Lieutenant David Abrams. One of the topics discussed was officers who have had three or more complaints since the effective date of the Ordinance creating PSRC in August 1992. PSRC had compiled the list with complaint numbers and presented it to the Chief, Manager and the Lieutenant.

Commissioners and public safety officials generally agreed that this compilation of information would assist in managing the Department in terms of training needs, assignments, assessment of personal problems and policy development. A consensus emerged that this material suggested that most police officers performed their duties without any allegations of excessive or unnecessary force, harassment, or abusive treatment. Indeed, comments from Commissioners indicated that most officers performed their thankless tasks in an exemplary manner.

Data from the May 16, 1994 report show that 63 officers were alleged to have engaged in 307 incidents resulting in complaints. Of these 63 officers, one officer had nine complaints; six had seven; eight had six; 20 had five; 23 had four; and five officers had three complaints. During the time August 1992 through May 19, 1994 complainants filed approximately 710 allegations of police misconduct as defined by the Ordinance with either the police department or PSRC.

In May, PSRC compiled a list of officers involved in excessive or unnecessary force complaints. The time frame within which these incidents were alleged to have occurred commenced with the enactment of the Ordinance creating PSRC.

Approximately 216 allegations of excessive or unnecessary force were filed. In at least 109 of these incidents a second officer was present. As many as nine officers were present, as a witness or otherwise, in five of these incidents.

A preliminary analysis of the 216 complaints of alleged excessive or unnecessary force suggested that repeat officers were involved. 154 officers were alleged to have used excessive or unnecessary force resulting in the 216 complaints, 39 officers were alleged to have engaged in 104 of these incidents. Of these 39 officers, one officer had six complaints; one officer had five complaints; five officers had four complaints, nine officers had three complaints and 23 officers had two complaints.

Notwithstanding the fact that police work involves situations of intense human emotion, most of the approximately 1,300 police officers have no complaints filed against them. Of the police officers involved in excessive or unnecessary force situations and identified as primary officers, 25 percent are alleged to have committed 48 percent of the incidents. 63 police officers out of approximately 1,300 are alleged to have committed 43 percent of the 710 complaints made against police officers from August 1992 through May 1994.

As the Commission reviewed complaints against officers, it became apparent that certain behaviors were recurring. On November 30, 1994, the Commission met with the Chief of Police and the Manager of Safety to discuss officers against whom multiple complaints were made. Many incidents involving these officers suggested patterns of activity resulting in complaints.

The Commission presented a summary of the complaints against nine officers to demonstrate the Commission's concern. Of those nine officers, three had 10 complaints, one had nine complaints and five had eight complaints. The Commission requested that the Chief of Police and Manager examine records of these officers to determine what, if any, administrative action would reduce complaints.

The Commission will continue to monitor officers who have frequent complaints made against them. As suggested during the executive session with the Chief and Manager, a change in assignment, additional training or other administrative action may reduce complaints against officers. The Commission continues its desire to improve civilian-police cooperation and views this activity as a means to that end.

COMMITTEE ON RESPONSE DELAYS

The Commission continues to be concerned about the long delays that often occur between the time a complaint reaches the Internal Affairs Bureau of the Police Department and a decision on the complaint is communicated to the complainant.

Such delays, usually without any explanation to complainants, not only creates bad public relations, but also threaten to create a backlog in the Commission's review process.

Chairman Whye, therefore appointed a committee headed by Commissioner Kripke and including Commissioners Sandoval, Benavidez and Whye to study the problem and come up with recommendations.

A number of time lines have been prepared on cases which have reached the Commission for review, and these have revealed that some cases have been processed quickly, while others have taken an inordinate amount of time, during which complainants have not been informed of what is taking place.

It was observed by the committee, in studying the problem, that in many cases the IAB gives the District Commanders as much as thirty days within which to report back their investigation of complaints, and that frequently the report does not come into IAB until the very end of that period. It was the opinion of the committee that ordinarily a fifteen day turn around time was sufficient and on recommendation of the committee to the full Commission, the IAB was requested to reduce that time to no more than fifteen days.

The Commission also requested that IAB keep complainants advised of the progress of investigations in cases which are not completed within thirty days.

The response delay committee will continue to monitor the problems of delay and non-communication and will make further recommendations as needed.

PUBLIC SAFETY REVIEW COMMISSION

1994 Status of Complaints for the Denver Police Department

Number of cases for 1994: 425

Improper Procedure	186
Improper Conduct	132
Law Violations	40
Excessive Force	147

***Disposition of the closed cases in 1994**

Information	16
Unfounded	101
Exonerated	129
Not Sustained	89
Sustained	22

***Disposition definitions from the Denver Police Department, Internal Affairs Bureau brochure.**

Unfounded:	The complaint was not based on facts as shown by the investigation, or the alleged violation or action did not occur.
Exonerated:	The incident did occur but the investigation disclosed that the action was reasonable, lawful and proper.
Not Sustained:	Insufficient evidence is available to either prove or disprove the allegation.
Sustained:	The investigation disclosed sufficient evidence to support the allegation.

For year 1992 (August 28 to December 31, 1992) are	117 cases.
For year 1993	413
For year 1994	425

Total cases open ...85.

Please note that in 1993 the Public Safety Review Commission forwarded approximately 45 citizen complaints to the Internal Affairs Bureau. The 45 complaints are included in the 413 total above.

In 1994 the Public Safety Review Commission forwarded approximately 90 citizen complaints to the Internal Affairs Bureau. The 90 complaints are included in the 425 total.

Cases Review: Commissioners do not select cases for review. According to the ordinance complainants must request a review in writing.

Year 1992- complainants requesting review 22. Twenty-one (21) cases closed. One (1) is still in review. Five (5) had change due to Commission review.

Year 1993- complainants requesting review 86. Seventy-two (72) cases closed. Fourteen (14) are still in review. Seven (7) had change due to Commission review.

Year 1994- complainants requesting review 63. Thirty (30) cases closed. Thirty-three (33) are still in review. Two (2) had change due to Commission review.

Commissioners have reviewed a total of 171 cases; the vast majority were reviewed in 1994.

Following are the cases that had change due to Commission review:

YEAR 1992:

#92-09-33 Ann Green - Improper conduct complaint with findings of exonerated. Commissioners recommended to Chief Michaud and Manager of Safety McCann that the findings be changed from exonerated to sustained. Chief Michaud changed the findings to not sustained. Manager of Safety McCann concurred with the Chief.

#92-10-20 Angel Felton - Improper procedure complaint with a finding of unfounded. Commissioners recommended to Chief Michaud and Manager of Safety McCann that RR-105 "Conduct Prejudicial", RR-114 "Intimidation of Persons" and RR-128 "Impartial Attitude" be changed to sustained against one officer. The Chief and the Manager declined to change the findings. However, Mayor Webb recommended that all 3 charges against one officer be changed to sustained.

#92-10-51 Laird Leyba - Excessive force complaint with findings of unfounded. Commissioners recommended to Chief Michaud that he sustain the case or that the complainant receive an apology from the Department. Chief Michaud chose to apologize for the Police Department for the officers' inappropriate actions. However, no changes were made in the findings. They remain as unfounded.

#92-11-28 R. E. Miller - Improper conduct complaint with findings of information only. The complainant wrote a letter to Mayor Webb posing several questions that he was concerned with and requesting responses. During the review process Commissioners found a letter in the investigation file and concluded that it contained the responses to all the complainants concerns. Complainant was called. He never received the letter. Commissioners recommended to Internal Affairs that they send the letter. They did. The complainant called to say he was satisfied.

#92-12-62 Roger W. Potts - Improper Procedure complaint with a finding of exonerated. Commissioners recommended sustainment for violations of the Denver Police Department's Operations Manual Section 104 (01) (04) Frisking of a Suspect, and RR-128 Impartial Attitude. Chief Michaud and Manager of Safety McCann declined to change the findings. However, Mayor Webb sustained DPD Operations Manual Section 104 (01) (04) and RR-128 Impartial Attitude against both officers.

YEAR 1993:

#93-03-19 Michael L. Alexander - Excessive force and improper conduct complaint with findings of exonerated. Commissioners recommended to Chief Michaud that the charge of excessive force be changed to either unfounded or not sustained. The Chief changed the finding to unfounded.

#93-04-68 Tammera Bravo - Improper Procedure complaint with a finding of unfounded. Commissioners recommended to Chief Michaud that RR-129 "Giving Name and Badge Number" be sustained against two officers further, the Commissioners also recommended that the findings with respect to four officers violated police procedures by attempting to gain access to the complainant's home. Chief Michaud sustained RR-129 against two officers but would not change the second recommendation. That remains the same. The second recommendation in the case is being appealed to Manager of Safety Montoya.

#93-05-48 Simone Smith - Improper procedure complaint with findings of exonerated. Commissioners recommended to Chief Michaud that he change the findings to sustained on RR-127, "Responsibility to Serve Public" on each of two officers and also a recommendation to develop a formal policy on civil stand-by for the operations manual. Chief Michaud changed the findings to sustained on RR-127 on both officers and made a commitment to develop a formal policy on civil stand-bys. The policy was adopted as of May 17, 1994.

#93-06-72 Gerta Bella - Improper conduct complaint with findings of exonerated. Commissioners did not complete the review because they were notified by Chief Michaud that the officer had resigned from the police department rendering the case moot. Case reviewed for procedural violations. There were none.

#93-09-06 Marcus Bolin - Improper conduct complaint with findings of not sustained. Commissioners recommended sustainment of RR-303 Officer shall not make arrest for offenses when a warning or citation would suffice. RR-114 Officer shall not intimidate any person for personal reasons under the color of authority; and RR-128 Members while being vigorous and unrelenting in the enforcement of the law must maintain a strictly impartial attitude toward complainants and violators. Chief Michaud and Manager of Safety Montoya declined to change the findings. However, Mayor Webb sustained RR-128 against the subject officer.

#93-09-101 Rev. Oscar Tillman - Improper conduct complaint with a finding of not sustained. Chief Michaud informed Commissioners that the subject officer resigned from the police department leaving the case moot.

#93-11-27 Daniel G. Jennings - This case had not received a police case number nor a category of complaint. Commissioners recommended to the Internal Affairs Bureau that they investigate this case of information only. A police case number was given and the case was investigated. Commissioners hired an independent investigator because critical information that is needed by them in order to make an informed decision is still lacking. This case is still pending.

YEAR 1994:

#94-02-03 James E. Makris - Improper conduct complaint with a finding of not sustained. Commissioners recommended sustainment of RR-127 "Responsibilities to Serve Public" to Chief Michaud. The chief accepted the recommendation and RR-127 was sustained against the subject officer.

#94-03-13 Rev. Carroll A. Weaver - Excessive force complaint with a finding of information only. Chief Michaud notified Commissioners that the officer on the case retired from the police department rendering the case moot. Commissioners reviewed the case for procedural violations. There were none.

DENVER COUNTY JAIL

Some of our Commissioners spent a day touring what seems to have been every corner of the Denver County Jail. What impressed us was the competence with which the Sheriff's office is operating this dangerously overcrowded, and in many respects, outdated facility.

We reviewed a videotape of a cell block riot which was quelled with quiet efficiency. Additionally, we met with the Inmate Council and discussed complaint procedures, access to PSRC and specific concerns raised by the inmate representatives.

The tour provided us with a needed familiarity of departmental procedures which will be useful in the evaluation of complaints received from inmates and others.

It is commendable that foreword looking City officials are seeking alternatives to an unproductive system which accomplishes little more than jamming the jails with more prisoners. We do believe, however, that the City must make every effort to publicize the realities and shortcomings of our present system so that our citizens can get beyond the poultice approach to seek real, long-term solutions.

INVESTIGATOR SELECTION

Section 2-248 of the Denver Municipal Code that established the Commission authorizes the Commission to employ private investigators to assist the Commission in investigating citizen complaints against Denver Police or Sheriff's officers.

A three member committee was established to develop the "job description" for this position; a sample classified advertisement was developed and specific selection criteria discussed.

Advertisements were placed in, The Weekly Issue, Urban Spectrum, La Voz de Colorado, Denver Post, and the Rocky Mountain News.

As a result of the outreach efforts, more than 250 responses were received.

The committee independently reviewed each application and selected 20 potential candidates. The candidate list was reviewed by the committee chair and a "short list" was developed for interviews.

Following city procedures, the Commission has established a list of on-call investigators. To date, have contracted with one investigator. We expect to contract with other investigators on a case by case rotating basis. This process will give the Commission the greatest amount of input from a variety of investigative resources.

Document No. 7

Detroit

Sec. 7-1102. Board of police commissioners.

The police department is headed by a 5-member board of police commissioners. The members of the board shall be appointed by the mayor, subject to the approval of the city council. However, if the city council does not disapprove an appointment within 30 days, an appointment is confirmed. The term of membership on the board is 5 years and not more than 1 member's term expires each year. The mayor may remove members of the board without cause. All members of the board must be residents of the city. As nearly as possible, the board shall be representative of the total community. The board shall elect a chairman annually. A member of the board may not serve consecutive terms as chairman, nor may a person serve more than 5 years consecutively as a member of the board. The board shall meet at the call of its chairman, but shall meet at least once each week. All meetings shall be public except that the board may, in its discretion, publicly reserve specified subjects for executive session. No member of the board shall have been an employee or elective or appointive officer of the city within 3 years prior to appointment or while serving as a member of the board. Compensation for members of the board may be established by ordinance.

Sec. 7-1103. Duties of the board of police commissioners.

The board shall:

1. In consultation with the chief of police, and with the approval of the mayor, establish policies, rules and regulations;
2. Review and approve the departmental budget before its submission to the mayor;
3. Receive and resolve, as provided in this chapter, any complaint concerning the operation of the police department;
4. Act as final authority in imposing or reviewing discipline of employees of the department;
5. Make an annual report to the mayor, the city council, and the public of the department's activities during the previous year, including the handling of crime and complaints, and of future plans.

The board may subpoena witnesses, administer oaths, take testimony, and require the production of evidence. To enforce a subpoena or order for production of evidence or to impose any penalty prescribed for failure to obey a subpoena or order, the board shall apply to the appropriate court. The board may delegate in writing to a member of its staff the powers to administer oaths and take testimony. A delegation is revocable at the will of the board and does not prevent exercise of any power by the board.

Sec. 7-1104. Staff.

1. *Secretary to the board.* The board shall appoint a board secretary, who serves at its pleasure. The secretary shall not have been an employee or elective or appointive officer of the city within 3 years prior to appointment. The secretary shall attend board meetings.
2. *Investigative staff.* The board shall also appoint a chief investigator and such additional staff of investigators as it deems necessary. The chief investigator shall not have been an employee or elective or appointive officer of the city within 3 years prior to appointment. Investigators serve at the board's pleasure. They must possess skills and experience necessary for investigative work.
3. *Other staff.* The board may hire, in accordance with article 6, chapter 5, such additional staff as is necessary to carry out its duties.

All members of the staff are under the direction of the board, and the chief of police has no authority over any member of the staff.

Document No. 8
Dubuque, Iowa

MEMORANDUM OF UNDERSTANDING

This Memorandum of Understanding, entered into by City of Dubuque, IA (City) and the Dubuque, IA, NAACP (NAACP) has as its purpose the promotion of harmonious relations between the City and the NAACP and the establishment of an equitable and peaceful procedure for the resolution of differences. This agreement is initiated pursuant to numerous meetings that have transpired between the City and its minority community representatives, culminating in a meeting convened by Community Relations Service (CRS) of the U.S. Department of Justice dated 11/19/91. The CRS of the Justice Department has ascertained a commitment from both parties to a serious attempt to resolve the issues on good faith and do agree to the following items:

PROPOSED POLICIES TO SUPPORT EQUAL ADMINISTRATION OF JUSTICE

FOR THE CITY OF DUBUQUE POLICE DEPARTMENT

POLICY GOALS:

General - To support non-discriminatory attitudes and behavior by the City of Dubuque Police personnel.

Specific - (1) To continue non-discriminatory procedures in the hiring, development and supervision of police personnel.

(2) To augment established procedures for the fair and thorough investigation of alleged discriminatory acts by police personnel.

(3) To support procedures in the investigation of bias crimes thereby minimizing harm to victims and the community.

ARTICLE I

Establishment of Community Advisory Panel

The City Manager may establish a Community Advisory Panel in accordance with the following outline:

A. Purpose of Community Advisory Panel:

The purpose of the Community Advisory Panel shall be to provide a reasonable degree of citizen input into the development of Police policies and procedures to assure the continuation of equal administration of justice free from racial or other prejudice and to provide a forum for citizen complaints based on alleged violation of civil rights or discriminatory behavior by police personnel.

B. Scope and Powers:

1. The Community Advisory Panel's activity shall be limited to accepting and reviewing citizen allegations of police misconduct relating to civil rights or discriminatory enforcement of law and or, on its own initiative recommending operational or procedural changes to the City or Police Department designed to ensure equal enforcement of the law.

2. The Community Advisory Panel shall have no powers to force disclosure of investigative files, or reports, or to interfere with or alter internal Police Department discipline, and shall not have access to personnel files, but may request information regarding internal Department investigations or disciplinary policies or make recommendations in regard to such matters. There shall be no obligation to release information which is prohibited from release under existing law or policy, nor shall the failure to release such information on that basis be considered a lack of good faith cooperation with regard to the operation of this agreement.

C. Composition of Community Advisory Panel

It is proposed that the Community Advisory Panel will be composed of nine members to include:

1. City Government Representative designated by the City Manager

2. Police Representative designated by the Chief of Police

3. Three interested adult citizens of Dubuque designated by the City Manager

4. A Human Rights Commissioner appointed by majority vote of the Human Rights Commission of the City of Dubuque

5. Two adult members of the minority community in Dubuque to be chosen by the City Manager from a list of interested applicants provided by the NAACP.

6. A police officer designated by the Police Protective Association.

An alternate may be appointed for each member by the appointing authority for the respective member. The alternate may participate in any meetings or actions by the panel when the primary member is unable to be present. No other person may act as a member of the panel.

D. Terms of Office

Each member will serve a term of two years with no limitation on reappointment.

E. Training of Panel Members

All members of the panel will receive training in police authority, use of force, police procedures, and effects of the job on the person, and will spend some time in discussion with line officers, and individual members will spend several hours riding with an officer on patrol.

F. Procedure

1. The Community Advisory Panel will meet as often as necessary to conduct its business but in no event less than four times per year.

2. No action will be taken by the panel unless a majority of the members are present, and all members have been given notice of the meeting. All actions by the Panel, including determination of its own procedural rules, will be taken by a majority vote of members present.

3. Any citizen who feels discriminated against by police action may file a grievance with the Panel. Citizens will be encouraged, but not required, to first file such complaints with the Police Department for initial investigation under its internal procedures. The Panel may conduct its own investigation of such complaint to whatever level it feels appropriate and to make any recommendations in regard to such complaint as it considers justified after its investigation. Upon receipt of a complaint against an officer or the Department from a citizen, the Panel will advise the Chief of Police of the nature of the complaint. The Panel will also advise the Chief of any officers who are expected to be asked to appear before the Panel, and the officers will not be asked to appear before the Panel before any police investigation of the complaint is completed.

4. The Panel will not have any formal judicial powers such as power of subpoena. However, the Panel may, at its own discretion, take but not compel sworn testimony in pursuance of investigations.

5. Any media release by the Panel requires approval by a majority of its members. The Community Advisory Panel may make public its majority findings, and minority reports and findings (if any), and may submit annual or more frequent reports to the City Manager regarding its activities.

6. The City Manager's Office will provide reasonable support services for the conduct of the Panel's business, including provision of clerical assistance for sending out meeting notices, copying of notes and documents, etc.

ARTICLE II

Policies for Police Recruitment and Supervision

The recruitment of minority officers will ensure integration within the department. We believe, since Dubuque is comprised of various ethnic groups and cultures with each contributing to the overall community, it is desirable to have this diversity of culture and ethnicity represented within the ranks of the Dubuque Police Department.

A. Hiring Policies: The City will by November 1, 1993, issue a written plan of the hiring procedures that will be followed to attempt to identify and prevent the hiring of officer candidates who may have racial or other prejudices. This plan will be maintained and updated as needed. Police selection procedures should include:

1. Psychological testing focused on identifying racial and other cultural bias to the extent reasonably available;

2. Interview questions/techniques designed to expose latent racial and other cultural bias;

3. Some focus or component of the background check designed to uncover racial and other cultural bias;

4. The Police Department will continue to use entrance exams which are products of a professional testing firm and which are validated as being free from gender and cultural bias.

B. Supervision Policies:

1. Written Protocol/Procedures Established

   The Chief of Police will within two months issue orders based on a written protocol (i.e., set of procedures) for investigating potential/suspected bias crimes. Training will be in accordance with state law covering this subject.

2. The Police Chief will be responsible for cooperating with the Community Advisory Panel to be established to assist in the processing/investigation/management of citizen complaints of racial and other discrimination by police personnel within the scope of this memorandum.

ARTICLE III

Training

The Dubuque Police Department will develop a comprehensive and ongoing written curriculum plan of human relations training which will include presentations by qualified minority consultants to include cultural sensitivity and conflict management for all personnel.

Training Policies:

1. Initial training (over and above Law Enforcement Academy)

   a. Each new officer will, as soon as practicable after being hired but not later than two years from hiring, receive racial and cultural sensitivity training.

   b. The City will maintain a written policy specifically addressing racial and other discrimination by police employees against members of the public in the performance of their duties. Each new employee will receive and sign for a copy of the policy and will be warned of possible consequences for violation of the policy in the course of employment.

c. The Police Chief will designate an officer who shall be responsible for all training relating to these policies and for developing ongoing training programs.

2. Continuing Sensitivity/Awareness Training

The Police Department will, by September 1, 1993, develop a comprehensive written plan to provide for ongoing refresher programs or courses relating to sexual and cultural sensitivity. As a parameter, every officer should be exposed to such curriculum for at least two hours every year during their employment. The NAACP will suggest to the department suitable choices such as:

a. Educational films/videos;

b. Speakers/lecturers on the topic;

c. Open forums for local citizens to meet with police and discuss concerns, attitudes, etc.

d. Courses on Civil Rights Laws, etc.

ARTICLE IV

Citizen Complaint Mechanism

A formalized mechanism for citizens to file complaints about police misconduct will be provided. A Citizen Complaint guide will be disseminated to the NAACP and other community organizations.

ARTICLE V NAACP/POLICE COOPERATION

The Dubuque Chapter of the NAACP and the Dubuque Police Department will cooperate to resolve conflicts and to promote racial harmony and peace in the community. The NAACP and the Police Department will support the processes set up by this agreement and will publicly support the Department when an incident which has been questioned is found to have been properly handled. Both parties agree to contact the other regarding any question about the other before making any public statement about the other's policies, procedures or actions.

Memorandum of Understanding

This document establishes an agreement between the City of Dubuque, Iowa, and the NAACP of Dubuque, Iowa. It represents the interests of all citizens of Dubuque, Iowa. The agreement is not regarded as a binding legal contract, but is entered into in good faith efforts to work together to alleviate disputes and misunderstandings. The agreement may be modified by mutual consent.

Michael C. Van Milligen
City Manager, City of Dubuque

3-17-93
Date

Ernestine Moss, President
Dubuque Branch, NAACP

3-29-93
Date

Document No. 9

Evanston, Ill.

86-R-92

A RESOLUTION

Repealing Resolution 68-R-75
(Police Services Committee)

WHEREAS, on April 2, 1991, citizens of Evanston passed a referendum to reduce the size of the City Council from eighteen to nine members; and

WHEREAS, the reduction in the size of the City Council will occur effective upon the election of April, 1993; and

WHEREAS, the reduction in the size of the City Council is a fundamental change in the manner in which the City will conduct its business and affairs; and

WHEREAS, as a result of such a reduction, it is necessary that the functions and purposes of certain city boards and commissions be consolidated and streamlined; and

WHEREAS, such consolidation will result in the more efficient and effective conduct of City business and affairs.

NOW, THEREFORE, BE IT ORDAINED BY THE CITY COUNCIL OF THE CITY OF EVANSTON:

SECTION 1: That resolution 68-R-75 which established the Police Services Committee is hereby repealed;

BE IT FURTHER RESOLVED, that the Human Services Committee is hereby assigned the responsibility and the power to review the disposition of all complaints filed with the Police Department.

BE IT FURTHER RESOLVED, that the Administration and Public Works Committee is hereby assigned the responsibility and power to:

a) keep the City Council aware and abreast of police policies and problems; and

b) to keep the City Manager and Chief of Police aware and abreast of council and citizens attitudes, concerns, and problems with law enforcement activity.

BE IT FURTHER RESOLVED, that in carrying out their respective responsibilities, the Administration and Public Works Committee and the Human Services Committee, shall have access to any information and assistance it deems necessary. The City Manager shall comply with the request of the respective committee and make available such information and assistance that may be requested; and

BE IT FURTHER RESOLVED, that in carrying out their respective functions, the committee shall at all times accord deference to the privacy interests of persons affected and their rights under the law;

BE IT FURTHER RESOLVED, that nothing contained herein nor any activity of the Human Services Committee or the Administration of Public Works Committee shall restrict the Civil Service Commission, the City Manager, the Chief of Police or any other body in the rightful exercise of their lawful powers and responsibilities.

SECTION 2: This Resolution shall be in full force and effect from and after the date of

Document No. 10

Flint, Mich.

Annual Report '89

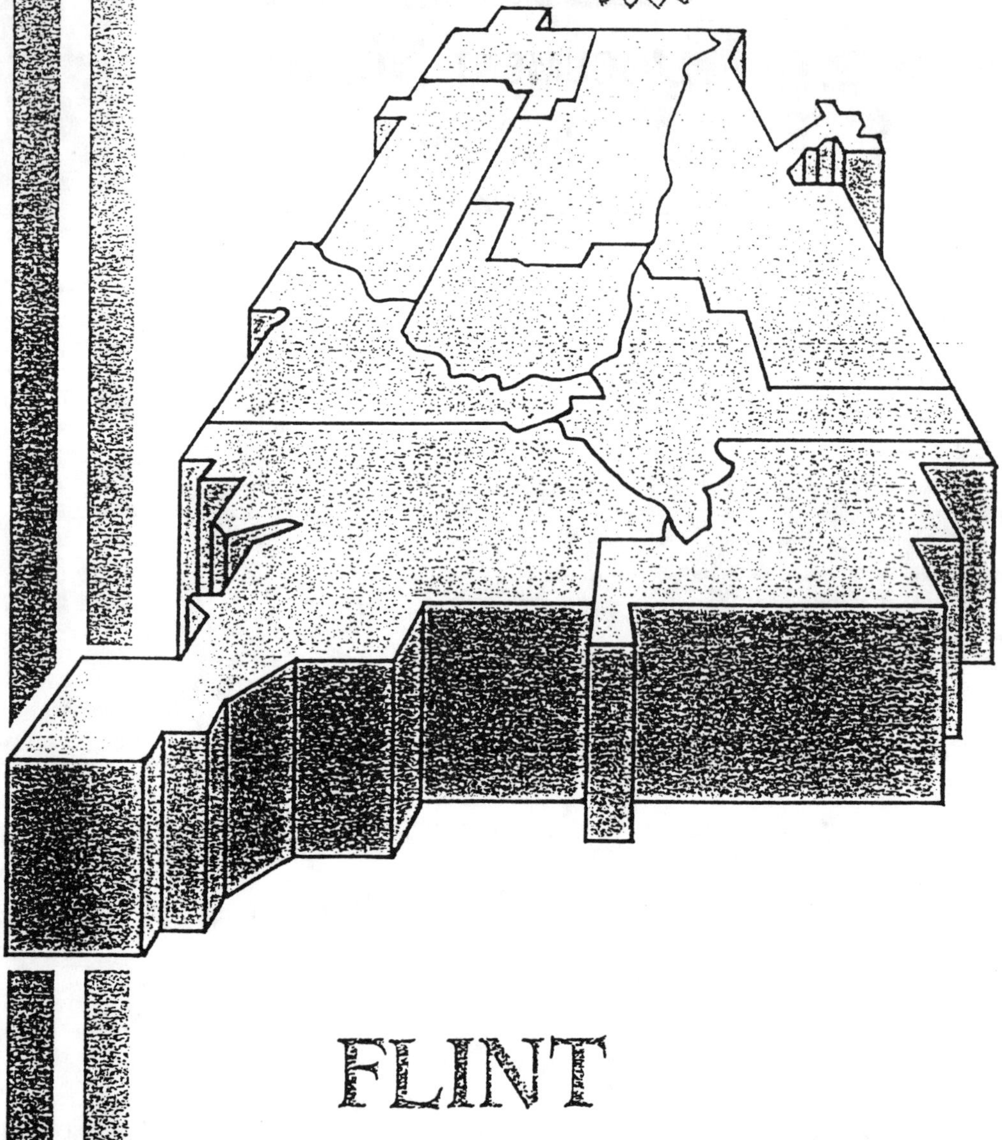

FLINT OMBUDSMAN

Ombudsman's Statement

To the City Council and Citizens of Flint:

The rising tide of drug-related crime has gripped our community. The police department has responded to the outcry from citizens by stepping up its enforcement of anti-drug laws.

While we support a reduction in the drug terror holding our community hostage, we share the founding fathers' concern that the *innocent* should not be swept away by a torrent of civil rights abuses in the name of law and order.

We have seen an increase in the number of complaints against the police department over the past year. Much of the increase is attributed to this new anti-drug effort. We believe the department has taken steps to reduce the opportunity for abuse by officers on the street. We have made several suggestions on this topic to Police Chief Fay Peek and he has agreed to consider our recommendations. We believe a professional working relationship exists between our office and the police department and more progress can be made in this area.

To deal with the increase in police complaints, we realigned staff assignments in October after it became apparent the usual summer increase was going to continue through the fall. We now have three investigators assigned exclusively to complaints concerning the police department.

Since we took office in 1987, we have attempted to share some of the information our office collects with the city's administrators and policy makers. We believe complaint information is a useful feedback system managers can use to pinpoint systemic problems. To further that objective, we continue to provide monthly summary reports of the complaints we receive.

We have also instituted a process of notifying department directors and central administration when a citizen has been referred by our office to another city agency to resolve a complaint.

There are a number of people who have supported this office and given of their time when we need advice. A group of individuals to which we wish to extend a special acknowledgement is our advisory committee. We have had several important issues to resolve this year, and this group has served as a sounding board to consider a number of alternatives. They have also made many helpful suggestions and provide an important link between our office and the community we serve.

The advisory board members are:

Rev. Avery Aldridge
Melvyn Brannon
Inez Brown
Dr. Nate Burtley
Rob Jewell
Michael Joliat
Richard Jordan
David Leyton
Larry Roehrig
Dan Sain
Rev. Leroy Shelton
Charles Wells
Joe Wilson

Ombudsman's Statement
(Continued)

Each year, we are called upon to assist citizens with a variety of complaints. The single largest segment, about 60 percent of the total, is with the police department. Others are based on allegations of wrongdoing by city employees and officers, or violations of the city charter.

But we receive many other types of complaints. They range from neighborhood nuisances to health and safety issues to problems with income tax refunds. We also assist citizens with water and cable television bill problems, weed complaints and abandoned vehicles. In addition to responding to complaints, we receive about 1,000 telephone calls annually from citizens seeking information about how to contact other government agencies.

We entered 1990 determined to uphold the integrity of our office and to continue to advocate for the citizens, especially those who are disadvantaged or disenfranchised. To achieve this objective, we plan to continue our community out-reach program. Since 1987, our staff has spoken before more than 100 community and school groups to let them know they can get help at city hall.

We also plan to continue to keep open the lines of communication we have developed with the various ethnic and religious communities that make up the mosaic of our city.

Our top priority remains ferreting out the systemic problems within city government which lead to recurring problems. The reports contained in this report reflect the priorities outlined above. We hope the public notice we have given these problems has contributed in some way to their resolution.

We could not have achieved these objectives without the strong support and professionalism provided daily by our staff members. They are dedicated in their pursuit of helping those who come to our office for support and information. It is truly gratifying to see their commitment to public service.

In summary, we believe 1989 was a year that presented many challenges and many opportunities. With the continued support of those who believe in this office, we can continue our fight to make Flint a better city in which to live and work.

Respectfully submitted,

Terry R. Bankert
Ombudsman

Casework Analysis

The number of citizen complaints leading to investigations was up over 1988. Last year, we instituted a total of 688 investigations. In 1988, there were 601 investigations. We attribute the increase to more complaints involving the police department. (See page 5 for a breakdown of the number of investigations by department.)

The number of investigations also was greater than the total recorded for 1987. The increase has put a strain on office resources as the seriousness of police-related complaints has increased, as well.

The graph below shows the distribution of investigations instituted by our office into police department complaints over the course of 1989. The month-to-month fluctuations generally follow the weather and temperature patterns in our area. You will note that the anticipated fall reduction in police casework did not approach mid-winter levels as was the case in previous years.

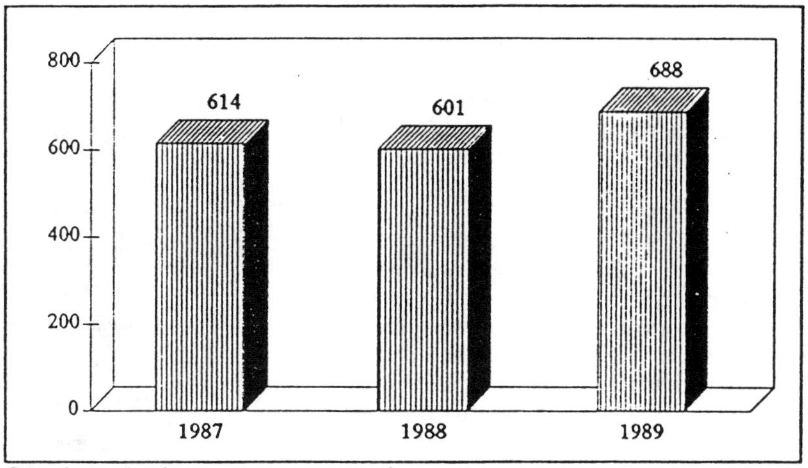

Complaints leading to investigations by year

It is difficult to identify the cause of the increase in police-related complaints. One possible explanation is that it is a reaction to increased drug-enforcement efforts.

When it became apparent the increase was not a temporary phenomenon, we realigned staff assignments to accommodate the changing patterns. We entered 1990 with three of our four investigators dedicated solely to police complaints.

We also made changes in our referral process this past year. We now notify each department in writing that a citizen has been referred to file a complaint with a supervisor. This is in accord with our philosophy of permitting the administrative department to solve the problem before our office becomes involved.

A copy of the notice is also sent to the central administration. Our office also continues the practice of providing monthly summaries of allegations citizens have filed concerning complaints about city services and the conduct of its employees.

Complaint data are important tools managers can use to evaluate the delivery of service within the various systems in city government.

Many of the complaints we receive are systemic in nature and long-range solutions call for system changes. Our goal is to provide reasonable solutions.

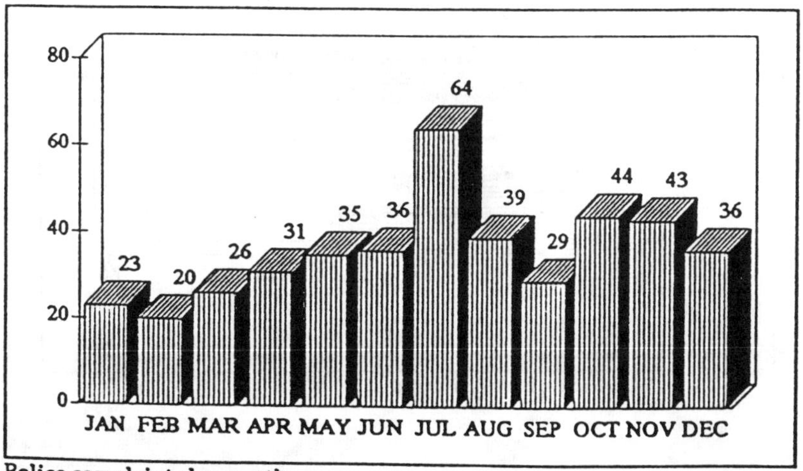

Police complaints by month

Casework Analysis
(Continued)

Approximately 80 percent of the 688 complaints leading to investigations in 1989 were from Flint residents. The remaining 20 percent came from those who reside outside of Flint, or were complaints filed anonymously and no address can be determined.

The graph on the top right shows the distribution of investigations from Flint citizens. As you can see, we receive complaints from all areas of the city. The geographic distribution of complaints from within the city leading to investigations varies from ward to ward.

Ward 1 generated the greatest number of complaints, with 83. Ward 7 was second highest with 73. Wards 3 and 5 each generated 65 investigations. The fewest complaints came from Wards 2 and 9.

These numbers are similar to those recorded in prior years. Ar examination of the number of police complaints by ward (bottom right) provides some insight to the overall increase recorded last year. These totals lend some support to the argument that the increase in overall casework was in part the result of stepped-up anti-drug activity in the police department.

As the police department represents about 61 percent of our overall caseload, it is logical that the comparison of police complaints by ward parallels the overall total investigations shown above. Wards 1, 3, 5 and 7 account for the greatest number of investigations into police complaints.

We intend to keep monitoring these figures to determine what patterns may be presented.

It is our goal to remain flexible enough to respond quickly to changes in our casework as expressed in the complaints we receive.

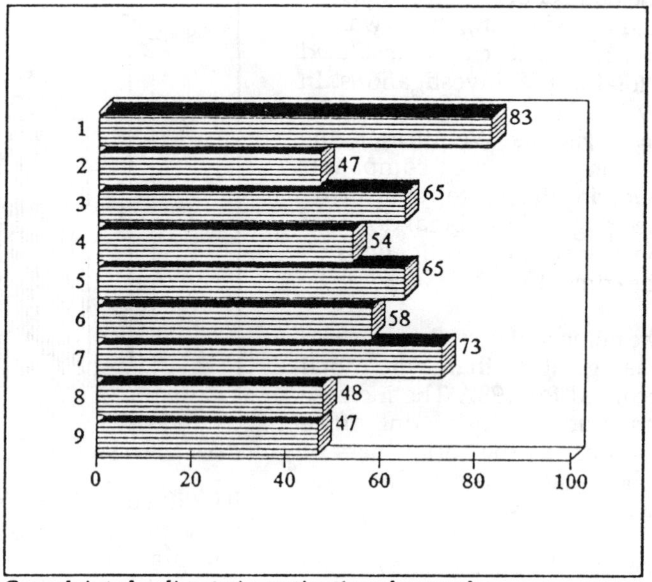

Complaints leading to investigations by ward

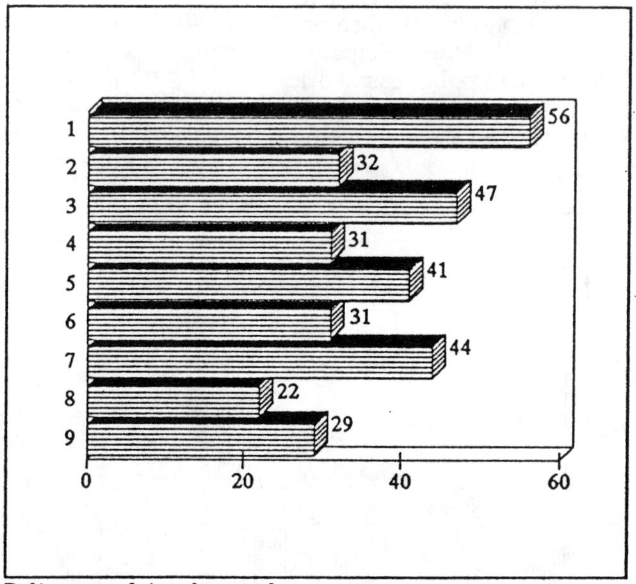

Police complaints by ward

Investigations by department

There was a substantial increase in the number of complaints against the police department that led to investigations last year. The number of investigations was up from 325 in 1988 to 426 last year. We attribute part of that increase to stepped-up anti-drug activity within the police department. As we could see the number of police-related complaints increasing, we began to plan to devote more resources in that direction. As a result of changes in staff assignments made in the fourth quarter of 1989, we now have three investigators devoted to handling police department complaints.

The table below also shows a drop in the number of water department complaints, from 76 in 1988 to 60 in 1989. This was due in large part to a trial program established jointly between the ombudsman and the water department to handle bill-related complaints. We judged the program to be successful in resolving some of the disputed bills. However, the program was terminated and there are no plans to re-establish the joint effort.

There was an increase in the number of complaints directed at the treasurer and many appeared to be related to new tax collection efforts. Some of the additional complaints were concerning delays in receiving income tax refunds. Others were because the department withholds of refunds from those who may not have filed income tax returns in prior years.

Agency	1988	1989
Building Inspections	65	52
Cable	7	3
Clerk	3	1
Council	3	3
Community Development	4	7
Downtown Development	0	1
Finance	0	2
Fire	12	5
Forestry	8	7
Housing	4	14
Human Relations	1	1
Hurley	0	3
Mayor	3	5
NIPP	3	0
Other	36	28
Parks	8	9
Personnel	1	1
Police	325	426
Public Works	23	33
Purchasing	1	1
Risk Management	3	0
Treasury	14	23
Waste	9	4
Water	76	60
Total	**601**	**688**

Ombudsman Reports/Criticisms - 1989

A report concerning suspected illegal activity by city employees.

Investigator: R. MacIntosh
Filed: April 5, 1989

FINDING

The city has no specific policy requiring its employees to report to law enforcement officials evidence they uncover of suspected criminal activity by other municipal workers or officers.

We believe this is a glaring oversight and we recommend the mayor immediately rectify this situation by instituting a strict policy for all city departments.

Further, there appears to be a lack of knowledge on the part of some supervisors that they must report any suspected illegal activity to the ombudsman.

BACKGROUND

The instance that brought this matter to the ombudsman's attention was an anonymous complaint filed in October 1987. Evidence had been uncovered within the Flint Housing Commission suggesting one of its managers had pocketed rents.

When the complaint was received by the ombudsman, the matter was being handled within the housing commission as a personnel matter. The employee had been dismissed, but the discipline was reduced to a five-day suspension through negotiations with her union.

Ultimately, the former housing commission employee pleaded guilty in U.S. District Court in October 1988 to embezzling $7,300. She never returned to work and now is on permanent layoff, according to Kenneth Simmons, housing commission director.

Simmons had informed a U.S. Department of Housing and Urban Development administrative agent of the possible embezzlement in the late summer of 1987. But the HUD agent, who has since retired, advised Simmons to wait until completion of the housing commission's annual audit before alerting HUD's criminal investigative arm.

The criminal investigation was the result of informal discussions within HUD about the matter and not the result of any direct action on the part of housing commission officials to involve law enforcement officials.

An auditor hired by the Flint Housing Commission did inform HUD of the apparent discrepancies in the books after the commission's 1987 annual audit. Nearly $13,000 in collections were never posted, or suspected of never being posted, to commission accounts. An additional $3,000 in questionable credit adjustments and credits were also documented in the annual audit.

Since documenting the losses, the housing commission has made a number of changes suggested by HUD to reduce the opportunity for misuse of funds.

Investigators in the HUD Inspector General's Office confirmed they were informed of the discrepancies by the outside auditor retained by the housing commission.

Before HUD was informed, the ombudsman referred the matter to the Flint police in November 1987, as required by the City Charter.

Chief Fay Peck, then the detective bureau command officer, made one inquiry of Simmons.

Simmons told Peck that an audit was underway and that he would forward the results when the audit was completed. But Simmons never provided any information to the local police. He told the ombudsman he forgot.

Peck did not follow up, as well. While there has been a conviction on a federal charge, we could find no evidence of a local investigation in the ensuing year to determine if any state or city laws have been violated.

There are a number of local ordinances governing the conduct of city employees. They are codified in section 1-131 through 1-138 and are referenced in the City Charter as "ordinances in the public interest."

Section 1-134 prohibits city employees from using city property for "personal gain or benefit." Furthermore, section 1-138 requires city officers or employees who become aware of conduct that violates any of the public interest ordinances to "furnish that information forthwith to the office of the ombudsman."

We could find no evidence the housing commission intended to comply with this ordinance before our inquiry, which was prompted by the October 1987 complaint.

These "public interest" restrictions were intended by the charter framers to be taken seriously by city employees. The penalty for violation of sections 1-131 thought 1-138 is forfeiture of office.

RECOMMENDATIONS

1. A clear policy should be articulated by the mayor requiring all city employees to report immediately to all appropriate law enforcement agencies evidence that illegal conduct may have occurred. Discipline for failure to follow this policy should be in accord with the charter-mandated public interest ordinances.

2. The Flint police should establish a mechanism to accept, document and process these complaints. As there may be several law enforcement agencies involved, a tracking system should be developed so all areas of potential inquiry can be covered.

3. Supervisors and city employees should be informed that failure to report illegal conduct to law enforcement agencies and to the ombudsman appears to be a misdemeanor violation of city ordinance section 1-138 and that forfeiture of office could be the penalty.

4. The Flint Housing Commission continue to work with HUD to develop accounting and cash-handling practices that will provide safeguards against embezzlement.

A report concerning management of the city's cable television franchise.

Investigator: T. Bankert
Filed: April 19, 1989

FINDING

The present failure to properly monitor Flint's cable television franchise agreement with Comcast may prohibit future action by the city to enforce the terms of the contract.

The responsibility for monitoring falls to the mayor's city administrator and the mayor's cable television advisory committee. However, a recent review by our office found a shocking lack of organization and commitment on the part of the city to carry out those responsibilities.
This failure may shackle the city and prevent us from joining the on-rushing global communications revolution that could help diversify our economy.

BACKGROUND

The city has no obligation under federal law to spend any portion of the $292,000 annual cable franchise fee on oversight of this agreement. However, we believe it is a disservice to the taxpayers if it does not devote a reasonable portion.

The lack of commitment is obvious. For example, we could find no complete central file of documents relating to the franchise and the performance of Comcast.

The current lack of documentation and activities of the cable advisory committee have the potential of eliminating any chance of changing cable companies, should the city wish to in the future. It also may prohibit negotiating a significantly different agreement to give Flint new technologies in the future.

As a result of this, Flint stands to miss out on technologies such as fiber optic that may be important to commerce, industry and Flint's citizens.

Unfortunately, we must conclude the lack of adequate documentation of past service problems has hurt significantly the city's chances of correcting future problems. It may prevent a future city council from changing cable companies, even if it believed a change was justified and desired.

The city may already have acquiesced through inaction to problems previously identified, but not corrected or pursued.

The member of the mayor's staff assigned to the cable advisory committee said that his principal job as the mayor's press secretary prevents him from spending more that 4-5 hours per month on cable related activities.

A consultant hired by the city in 1987 suggested we need someone to spend a minimum of 36 to 40 hours a month on cable matters.

We recommend the city council and the city administrator review with the cable advisory committee its role and needs. A review and compilation of past documentation is also needed. A file of relevant documents should be centralized. Among the documents to be collected should be written descriptions of issues that have come before the cable advisory committee. Written responses from Comcast to advisory committee inquiries should also be located and filed. The recommendations and critique of the third-year (1987) performance evaluation, along with this year's evaluation, should also be pursued.

The city administrator is identified in the city code as the person responsible for the administration and enforcement of the cable franchise agreement. He may delegate those responsibilities to a staff member. We suggest a professional should be assigned who can give more time to this project or the council should consider changing the cable ordinance and give this responsibility to another department.

Historically, the mayor's public relations director was delegated this task. The demands of this position may be too great and we recommend consideration of assigning cable television responsibilities to another administrative staff member.

During our review, a number of issues were raised. We have reviewed the franchise agreement, federal and state laws and the city code. Below we discuss several of these issues.

Does the city of Flint have an obligation to utilize a portion of its cable franchise fee for the oversight of the cable franchise agreement?

Conclusion: There are no provisions in the "Cable Franchise Policy and Communications Act of 1984" requiring any specific level of expenditure. Section 622 (b) of this act states "the fee need not be tied as a matter of federal law to the cost of regulation."

But there are important functions that a city must do in order to be in a position to change or influence a cable company during renewal. Among the most important is documentation of past problems. These functions of documentation and franchise agreement oversight can only be done by assigned staff and should not be expected of the volunteer citizens cable advisory committee.

In brief, if the city cannot document problems with the present cable company, it will never be in a position to change companies later.

Why would the possibility of changing cable companies in the future be important?

Communications organizations, including some telephone companies, have developed fiber optic technology. Installing such a system may be something our present company is unwilling to do. A fiber optic cable system may have the potential to attract new business or retaining existing ones that will want to tap into it. But this emerging new technology will be lost if the city does not act today to effectively monitor, and administer, its existing cable franchise agreement.

We can't speculate on the full range of technological options, or even what will be permitted under future cable TV regulations. But today we know that fiber optic could be the information highway of the future. Why should the city give up this option to leverage this technology in the future because of poor documentation and administration today?

Under the terms of the franchise agreement and federal law, it is imperative that a city notify the cable operator in writing of any violation of the contract.

The franchise agreement and the city code also give direction as to how our cable franchise agreement should be monitored. These documents then establish the process that the city council has established for the administration to oversee the cable franchise.

The Flint City Code Section 15, entitled cable

communications systems, combined with the cable franchise agreement, are the tools the city has to monitor its cable agreement.

City code section 15-42 establishes a cable advisory committee to assist the city administrator in the oversight duties.

Under the code this body has the following duties:

a. Investigate, research and otherwise stay abreast of all developments in the technology of cable communications and advise the city council when such technology is such that there are potential uses and benefits to the citizens of the city which have not been heretofore contemplated or dealt with in this chapter, in an effort to insure that the citizens of the city are, and will be, receiving the finest and widest range of benefits from any cable communications system.

b. Advise the city council from time to time on proposed amendments to this chapter to insure that the citizens of the city are and will be receiving the finest and widest range of benefits from any cable communications system licensed under this chapter and at least services which are comparable to those provided by the cable communications systems in other political subdivisions of similar size.

c. Assist, whenever possible, in coordinating the efforts of cable communications systems, educators, government agencies and other interested citizens to provide the finest and widest range of benefits from any cable communications system licensed under this chapter to the citizens of the city.

d. Study, research and investigate any other permitted matters upon the request of the city council and make any reports and recommendations to the mayor and the city council as the mayor and/or city council may from time to time request.

e. Meet and confer with the city administrator and the equal opportunity officer to review the performance of the licensee and to report to the city council and the mayor any serious or repeated infractions of the terms and conditions of this chapter.

Section 15-43 of the code states, "All necessary and actual expenses incurred by the panel in the conduct of its business, research and investigation shall be paid from funds budgeted for that purpose by the city council."

The cable communications systems franchise agreement, adopted by the Flint City Council on March 26, 1984, gives additional direction to the advisory committee.

Section 7 of that agreement states, "Within a reasonable time, to be determined by the franchisee and the cable panel, each cable system shall be upgraded so that it is no less advance than any other system of comparable size, excepting only systems which are experimental, pilot or demonstration."

Section 9 of the agreement states "(the) franchisee shall explore with the city and the panel the expansion of services to provide for auxiliary services, including, but not limited to, fire alarm, security alarm, civil defense warning, meter reading data, or other electronic transmission services, home shopping, interactive, two-way service, and facsimile reproduction services."

Section 14 states, "(the) franchisee shall make such facilities (studio and mobile production) available for the production and presentation of community access programs by responsible community groups and citizens under access rules and regulations approved by the cable communications advisory panel."

Section 15: Relationship with the Flint Cable Communications Advisory Panel.

A. The franchisee will work closely with the panel in all areas of mutual franchisee-community concern; particularly in the following:

1. Establishment and revision of the schedule of services to subscribers and other users of the system.

2. Establishment of rules governing use of facilities, equipment, channels, studios and services of the system.

3. Resolution of conflicts not adequately covered by established rules.

> A. A representative of the franchisee shall attend regularly scheduled panel meetings.
>
> B. The franchise shall annually provide the city council and Cable Advisory Panel within 120 days following the close of its fiscal year, an audited financial statement of Comcast Cablevision for the preceding year.

C. The panel and the franchisee shall hold scheduled performance evaluation sessions within 30 days of the third, fifth, tenth and fourteenth anniversary dates of the execution of this agreement. ...Topics which may be discussed at any scheduled or special evaluation session may include, but not limited to, service rates structures, franchisee fee, penalties, free or discounted services, application of new technologies, system performance, services provided, programming offered, customer complaints, judicial and FCC ruling and city rules.

During the third-year system review, several recommendations were made by the consulting firm hired to conduct the review. The fifth-year review scheduled this spring will be a public hearing.

It does not appear that cable oversight duties are being discharged in a planned managed process. The cable advisory panel seems un-focused in its deliberations. The city does not provide staff and resources to this oversight body or other active support which results in unfocused execution. The city has provided little support for its activities and there seems to be little documentation concerning Comcast's implementation of the current franchise agreement.

We recommend the city council and the mayor review these recommendations and consider making improvements to protect the citizens' interest.

A report concerning the tragedy on Grace Street.

Investigators: T. Bankert & D. Buchanan
Filed: May 12, 1989

FINDING

Police call screening personnel mishandled several urgent pleas from citizens for aid as more than a hundred drunken teenagers congregated in Grace Street.

The birthday party that drew these youths was the scene of a tragedy as an errant bullet killed a 16-year-old innocent bystander.

The neighbors' calls for assistance were improperly classified as a loud party, and not a loud party and a fight, making it a lower priority. The calls were a low priority for nearly a half hour.

The first call was logged at 10:32 p.m. and the shooting occurred at 11:05 p.m. There is no way to know whether the arrival of a police car prior to the shooting would have saved the life of the innocent girl.

A cruiser check on a routine loud party would have possibly been a brief stop for a car on patrol. But this was not a routine party. Several hundred loud and drinking teenagers had transformed a Flint neighborhood into a nightmare for a number of families.

When central dispatch did alert the patrol bureau at 10:55 p.m., it was for cars to check on a large party with traffic problems. Several patrol cars were available at that time. However, none responded until dispatch issued a shooting alert at 11:05 p.m. Better departmental monitoring and supervision can resolve the problem of patrol cars not checking back into service shortly before a shift change.

The party was openly promoted by a flyer at several, if not all, Flint high schools and at a basketball game. At least one Flint Board of Education employee may have seen the flyer being distributed. The flyer promoted a 50 cents all-you-can-drink party.

Once the 11:05 p.m. call of a shooting was received, the police did an appropriate job of responding to the call, carrying out the homicide investigation and the subsequent arrests of suspects.

No Flint resident should have to endure a 45-minute wait for police while several hundred loud and drunken high school youths are invading their neighborhood, yards and driveways. The call screening policy, or interpretation by the call screening personnel, was not adequate to handle the severity of this event as described by the Flint citizens calling for assistance.

We are also troubled by the opinions expressed by some to the ombudsman during the course of this investigation that police response time is intentionally slow in minority communities. This issue should be studied.

The Flint police chief has made some policy changes. They are designed to address some of the systemic problems that appear to have led to the slow response to this particular incident. We believe those changes are a responsible administrative response and should be monitored closely to determine if they meet the stated objectives.

The policy changes instituted by the chief are:

1) Roll calls for all shifts have been broken into two segments and adjusted to spread shift changes over an hour instead on one-half hour.

2) Shift changes for radio operators also will be staggered to allow an hour in between so incoming dispatchers can be briefed by the previous shift.

The chief has also given verbal assurances he plans to change policies to permit the immediate reassignment of an officer who is on a low-priority call if more serious calls are received. We recommend these changes be put into writing.

Flint citizens deserves the best police protection possible. We can not permit there to be a perception the city lacks police patrol coverage during shift change.

BACKGROUND

On December 2, 1988 a young Flint man organized a birthday party for his sister on Grace Street.

A Northwestern High School student who attended the party told the ombudsman a lady at the door was frisking everyone for weapons. He said a disk jockey was in the basement. People were drinking alcohol at the party and drugs were also present, the witness said.

Another student said they went to the party after the Northern basketball game and paid 50 cents to enter. He said the basement was crowded.

Another student said when they got to Grace, cars lined both sides of the street.
At least five of the high school-age witnesses questioned by the ombudsman said they learned of the event through flyers distributed at school.

One student indicated that she had distributed flyers at school until a school employee told her to put them away.

A number of other witnesses say they had heard of the party at a local fast food restaurant that night.

This birthday party had several hundred high school students present in a one-block area snarling traffic and creating a disturbance. Most had bought the 50-cent drink ticket entitling them to all the alcohol they could consume.

One witness said, "at 10:30 a fight broke out and I called Flint Police Department. ... I was told a cruiser would be sent. The cruiser did not come until after the ambulance. If Flint Police Department had come when I first called them, she would still be alive today."

He also said, "they (the police) don't like to come into our neighborhood. ... In this neighborhood, we always have trouble getting the Flint Police Department to come out when we call for help."

RECOMMENDATIONS

1. The Flint Board of Education should work closely with the Flint Police Department to establish a policy to bring these parties immediately to the attention of the police department.

2. Policy changes instituted for roll call and dispatch should be monitored closely.

3. A study should be conducted to substantiate or refute fears that response differs based on the racial make-up of a neighborhood.

A report concerning a violation of the city's emergency purchasing procedures.

Investigator: R. MacIntosh
Filed: December 6, 1989

FINDING

The Flint Parks and Recreation Department may have violated the city's charter and purchasing ordinance in its haste to open the Kennedy and Whaley pools last summer.

Substantial costs were incurred without obtaining the

appropriate approval from the purchasing director, as required by the ordinance, or the city council and finance director, as required by the charter.

Further, because the repairs were not bid and the city had no written contract, there is little recourse now but to pay the bill, which is 340 percent of the original estimate.

BACKGROUND

The parks department decided in the spring to open the pools. Recreation Supervisor Steven Waller told the ombudsman that the decision to open the pools was made in late May. In a later written response to a draft of this report, the recreation department said the decision was made in late March.

Traditionally, the boilers and pumps need repairs after a winter of inactivity. Waller said it was apparent after the pools were filled that damage to the pumping and heating systems was greater than anticipated. It was decided the repairs were beyond the expertise of city crews.

In early June, a licensed heating and plumbing contractor was retained at a cost of $1,900 to survey the damage and estimate the cost of repairs. Waller said the firm was selected because it had serviced the pool system in the past.

Purchasing Director Thomas McCabe told the ombudsman that a purchase order for approximately $1,900 was issued in June to cover the cost of the survey. This is consistent with the purchasing code. The city code does not require competitive bidding or city council approval for purchases of less than $2,000.

Waller said the company returned a short time later, and estimated repairs would total $15,000, an amount well over the competitive bid limit.

Parks Director Dr. James Makokha said waiting to obtain bids and to let a contract would have delayed the pool openings a month or more, and that was unacceptable. Further, he said, this firm would likely be awarded any contract based on its experience with the system.

It is at this point the department apparently went ahead without: obtaining the appropriate approval from the purchasing director and finance director, competitive bids, a written contract or council approval, according to McCabe.

In his response, Makokha disputed McCabe's contention and said the parks department believed it had his approval to use the emergency purchasing procedure. But there were no memoranda attached to the parks department response to support this claim.

The purchasing director reiterated in his written response that he did give his approval to hire the heating firm initially "to look into the cost" of opening the pools. (See attached.) However, he did not provide any support for the parks department's position that subsequent approval was granted to have the repairs completed.

An executive of the heating firm said the parks department gave his company verbal instructions to carry out the repairs as quickly as possible. However, this approval was based on the $15,000 estimate, Waller said.

The heating contractor said he was told to complete the repairs promptly using whatever resources required and to work through the July 4th holiday, if necessary.

He told the ombudsman the estimate submitted was "only an estimate" and that the extent of the damage was not apparent until the systems were disassembled.

The work was completed and the pools opened in early July. The total bill was $51,762, or about three and a half times the estimate.

Makokha told the ombudsman his staff initially refused to pay the bill because they thought it was inflated. Makokha believes the company padded the bill by assigning unnecessary workers who stood idle most of the time.

Several months of discussions were held between the company and the parks department. In November, a decision was made to pay $51,088, despite doubts held by Makokha and his staff about some portions of this bill.

The city code permits the purchase by a department director, without competitive bidding, in "case of (an) emergency which may result in the loss of life or property."

The code requires a written explanation of the circumstances be filed immediately with the city clerk, entered into the city council minutes and available for public inspection (Sec. 18-21.10).

We could find no such explanation on file. In addition, we could find no evidence that loss of life

or property was imminent.
Neither response from the administrative departments addressed the charter requirement that "no purchase may be made...unless the chief finance officer advises that there is an unencumbered balance in the appropriation against which the purchase is to be charged to pay for the purchase." (Sec. 8-301 B).

When asked, the recreation department challenged a suggestion that this unfortunate situation could have been avoided by better planning.

It is the recreation department's position that the heating systems cannot be repaired until the pools are filled with water. There is a reluctance on the part of the department to fill the pools too far in advance of the opening. It may subject the city to unwanted liability if a tragedy should occur as the pools sit unattended, Makokha said.

It is also the parks department's position that no amount of forward planning could have prevented this situation. Therefore, it may be reasonable to conclude that the city could be in a similar position in the future.

RECOMMENDATIONS

1. A review should be carried out to determine if the city charter or city code was violated.
2. Review the procedures used by other cities in planning for and obtaining pool maintenance services.

A report concerning illegal dumping along Gilkey Creek.

Investigator: B. Burdette
Filed: December 7, 1989

FINDING

The city and the state Department of Natural Resources need to develop a process for the enforcement of laws prohibiting dumping and filling along floodplains.

It appears that enforcement of these laws could be strengthened by a coordinated effort in which the responsibilities of the two agencies are spelled out clearly.

This lack of strong coordination between the city and the DNR was revealed in an investigation into a complaint by an eastside Flint business situated next to Gilkey Creek.

BACKGROUND

Universal Lift Parts is located at 3752 and 3800 Robert T. Longway, between Center Road and Averill Street in the City of Flint. Gilkey Creek runs on the south border of the property.

Universal Lift President Kenneth Ayres contends that beginning in 1981, a number of parties have been involved in illegal filling and dumping within the floodplain area of Gilkey Creek between Center Road and Averill Street.

Ayers contends that this illegal activity has contributed to excessive flooding of its property and caused damage to his buildings. He also contends his property value has declined considerably because of these conditions and his business has been disrupted unduly.

A review of the law conducted by outside counsel at the ombudsman's request shows the state has primary legal responsibility for protection of the waterways (see appendix I).

While it appears the dumping and filling is illegal, it is not clear whether it is the cause of Universal Lift's problem. The DNR has estimated its impact on flooding would be minor. Consequently, it is difficult to speculate whether formal enforcement under state law would be successful.

The city does, however, have some authority in these matters. The Flint Building and Safety Inspection Division issued notices of violations in 1986 to property owners in the area. They were notified of violations in the floodway and given specific instructions for corrective measures to be taken to avoid the issuance of appearance tickets.

However, it appears that an appearance ticket was issued to only one of these property owners and final disposition of that ticket is unclear at this time.

Records obtained by the ombudsman indicate that the violation notices issued in March 1986 expired on July 1, 1986. At that time, because the problem had not been corrected, the matter was turned over to the city attorney.

The ombudsman contacted the DNR about this problem in 1986 and was advised that the owners in question were in violation by dumping in the floodplain and that the DNR was staying in contact with the city about the problem.

The state DNR had issued a violation notice to another property owner on Aug. 2, 1982. The DNR estimates that the filling and dumping in the floodplain would increase the water level during a severe storm by about 1.25 inches.

DNR officials said they forwarded this information to the state attorney general for prosecution in 1982. But no action has been taken.

Officials with the DNR said they believed the attorney general has not prosecuted because the scientific evidence shows the illegal fill has a minor impact on the creek. They surmise that prosecution, based on the estimated impact, did not meet a cost/benefit test.

The ombudsman was later informed by the city attorney in 1986 that the matter was under review to determine what legal action would be taken.

In 1988, Ayres held a meeting for various city, county, and state officials to review the complaint because nothing had been done to correct the problem.

CONCLUSION

Based on the law, it appears that the state DNR is the best entity to attack this problem and the city should seek its assistance.

However, the city's failure to finally address this problem cannot be ignored. While the city may be commended for issuing comprehensive violation notices, one can only speculate why comprehensive appearance tickets were not issued.

In order to avoid the diffusion of responsibility that results when different departments and divisions have jurisdiction of the same problem, it is incumbent upon the city to formulate a policy to attack problems such as that suffered by Universal Lift.

When a complaint arises to the level of endangering the public health, safety and welfare or large amounts of private property, it appears that a comprehensive review would be in order. It should assess the impact of the problem and to determine if, in fact, a public nuisance exists.

A report concerning the enforcement of domestic violence laws.

Investigators: P. Huber-Davis & B. Burdette
Filed: December 7, 1989

FINDING

The Flint Police are not properly utilizing the state's spouse abuse law designed to protect female victims of domestic violence.

The intent of the law was to separate the man and woman. Studies have shown that failure to remove the male combatant from the scene increases dramatically the immediate likelihood of further violence.

Investigations into several complaints filed with our office reveal the intent of the law has not been fulfilled.

We recommend the department review its implementation of the law and the training given to officers who must enforce it.

Police Chief Fay Peek has indicated that he will accept this recommendation. His first step in this process is to establish a domestic violence case summary that is required to be filed for every call in which domestic violence is suspected.

We believe this is a responsible administrative response and evidence of intent to deal with the problems outlined below.

BACKGROUND

The police chief has established a policy, consistent with state law, that requires an arrest when officers have reasonable cause to believe a domestic assault has occurred.

He has told his officers they do not have to witness the assault. Physical evidence, such as bruises or blood, is sufficient. This differs from the evidence necessary for an arrest in a simple assault case.

In several instances of domestic violence the required arrests have not been made. Nor has there been sufficient follow-up by supervisors when arrests are not made in domestic violence cases.

Further, there appears to be a misunderstanding that the domestic violence law applies a different standard for arrests and criminal complaints when compared with the simple assault law.

Several complaints we have received about police response to domestic violence demonstrate these problems.

In one instance, a Flint woman complained that she wished to file an assault complaint against her live-in companion after he injured her in the parking lot of a local service agency on March 13.

According to the victim, an argument erupted as they were headed for a counseling session at the agency. Along the way, he grabbed her by the head and jerked her around.

He put his arm around her throat and hand over her mouth, she said. She fought back by sticking him in the face with a wooden stick. He accelerated the car and continued to restrain her.

Upon arrival, the argument continued with the man adamant about not attending the counseling session, according to the woman. She managed to get out of the car and headed for the building. The man stopped the car and pursued, catching up with her as she neared the building.

He grabbed her and dragged her away from the building, back toward the car. She screamed for help. Someone in the building responded to her plea. The man released her and she fell to the pavement.

Police were called to the scene and the man was taken to the station by patrol car. The woman traveled in another vehicle.

Once at the station, the woman was discouraged from attempting to file a complaint and warned that if she did, a cross complaint would be filed against her because the incident constituted "mutual combat."

When questioned about this by the ombudsman, Sgt. Karen Pizzala of the criminal sexual conduct investigations squad responded:

> "The only injury that I observed on (the woman) was a very small scratch on her. I believe it was on her arm. She told me she had a bump on her head, which I did not observe. (The man's) injuries, although minor, were more noticeable than (the woman's). His right ear was red from where she grabbed it and twisted it. (The woman) admitted to jabbing in the area of his eye with a wooden ice cream stick. She also stated that she was just fooling around when she tried to jump out of the car.
>
> "Because of the counter complaint and the information obtained from both complainants, it appeared that both were equally at fault. Therefore, neither was booked..."

A medical examination that day by a doctor revealed the woman had a bruise on her left arm and scrape on her scalp. The doctor also reported the woman lost a large clump of hair.

In his version of events given to police, the man said an argument erupted over money as they were traveling. He said she tried to jump from the moving auto. He grabbed and restrained her. He said the argument escalated and she jabbed him in the right temple with a fingernail file until it broke in half.

Based on these accounts, Sgt. Pizzala concluded there would be no booking. In response to an earlier draft of this report, Sgt. Pizzala said she did not take further action after interviewing both the man and the woman because she received conflicting stories.

Sgt. Pizzala said she decided to release both of them until a further investigation could be conducted by the assigned officer (her response is attached).

We concede that it would be difficult to take action based on the incident in the automobile. However, the aggressive act of the man in the parking lot of trying to drag the woman away from the building is the type of incident the law is designed to avoid and punish.

Another woman complained to our office that she called police to file a spouse abuse complaint against her husband at approximately 10 a.m. on Feb. 26.

When the police arrived, her husband had left. A felonious assault complaint was taken in which she charged he hit her across the back with a broom handle and a set of window blinds. The officers reported seeing the bruises.

She also charged her husband pushed her from the house without shoes or a coat.

Police were called to the scene about 12 hours later by the husband. Upon arrival, the police did not take the man into custody based on the earlier complaint.

The woman felt her husband should have been arrested at that time.

The officers who responded to the second call, which was placed by the husband, said they did not arrest him because of the time that had elapsed and because of the lack of physical evidence.

When questioned about this by the ombudsman, the officer reported:

> "When (the woman) mentioned she had filed a spouse abuse complaint on first shift, we advised her to let the detective assigned to the case handle the matter. This was done because of the time lapse and the lack of physical evidence."

We recommend the department establish a policy to deal with the subsequent arrest in cases when the alleged perpetrator returns to the home.

In another complaint received by our office, a woman, who was separated, said she called central dispatch on March 1 because her husband was at her house threatening her.

She said the officer told her they would not send anyone to her house because she was still married and there was nothing they could do.

Sgt. Carolyn Sims, who served on the patrol desk that day, told us she received a telephone call from the mayor's office concerning this plea for help.

The sergeant was told by the mayor's staff a woman was on the line complaining the police refused to respond to her home. The sergeant instructed the mayor's staff member to have the woman telephone her at the patrol desk.

The woman called Sgt. Sims, who instructed the dispatcher to send a cruiser to the woman's address.

In this case there was no injury. But the husband would not leave the premises until the police arrived. It is reasonable to wonder if family violence calls are a high priority when it took a call from the mayor's office to get a car dispatched.

In another incident, police said they were flagged down on June 11 by a man who told them his wife was in the house with a large butcher knife and that she had tried to attack him with it.

She admitted she did do so, but only after her husband had attacked her with a tennis racket.

The officer said he advised both parties involved they could make complaints against each other. However, the officer told us she did not want to make a complaint because the husband was not going to file one against her.

The police left the scene, but later received another call to the same house regarding a family fight. During this response a complaint was taken from the husband but not the woman.

The woman was treated for her injuries the next day. Her doctor reported:

> "Domestic violence. The patient was beaten by her husband. She currently has pain in the right side of her head where she was hit with a plastic tumbler. He hit her on the left side of the head, also the back of her neck, and kicked her in the buttocks."

We felt this action by the police department could have been more sensitive to the condition of the woman and that medical attention should have been suggested to her. The husband was arrested 10 days later for this assault.

In addition to the problems outline above, it is not clear whether officers comply consistently with the policy requiring them to provide written information about protection available under the domestic violence law.

The departmental policy requires:

> "Police officers after interviewing in a domestic violence dispute must provide the victim with the information mandated by MCL 764.15c. This law states that the victim must be provided with the following information:
>
> a. Listing of phone numbers of various shelters;
> b. A statement indicating that the victim can ask the prosecutor to file a criminal complaint;
> c. That the victim can individually go to court and obtain various injunctive orders.
>
> Cards containing this information will be available to the officers for distribution to the victims of domestic disputes. Officers shall indicate in their report that this information was provided to the victims."

RECOMMENDATIONS

1. Officers be properly instructed about the differences between the domestic violence and assault laws.

2. The department establish tighter monitoring of officer response when answering calls for domestic violence.

3. Dispatchers should be instructed to send a patrol car as soon as one is available for all calls concerning domestic violence. These calls should be considered a high priority.

4. Establish a policy to deal with the arrest of those accused of domestic violence when they return to the home.

5. Establish a dialogue between the police department, city attorney and county prosecutor to clarify how the state domestic violence and the felonious assault laws can be coordinated so enforcement of one does not restrict enforcement of the other law.

A report concerning police physical abuse.

Investigator: R. MacIntosh
Filed: December 21, 1989

FINDING

We have referred to the U.S. Department of Justice for further investigation a complaint from a Flint man who said Officer Shawn Stimac kicked him in the ribs as he laid on the ground on July 11, 1989.

Officer Stimac has denied the allegation, as has another police officer who was also at the scene.

Our referral was based on the testimony of someone who said she is an independent eyewitness. She directly contradicts Officer Stimac's version of events.

This referral to the justice department is done to fulfill our obligation under the city charter. We are required to forward to the appropriate law enforcement agency any evidence we uncover suggesting laws may have been broken.

We have also informed the chief of police of the evidence and recommended he institute an internal investigation. The chief has indicated he will accept that recommendation.

BACKGROUND

Police had been called to the intersection of Josephine and Touraine in the vicinity of Carpenter School at about 8 p.m. because a gang of youths were fighting.

Officers said the fight had apparently ended by the time they arrived as the scene was quiet.

Jimmy Story Jr. of Cecil Drive said he was walking by the scene with another man and was ordered by police to stop and submit to a search.

Story said he protested that he was merely passing by, but put his hands on the back of the squad car to permit a pat-down by the officer. Story said he continued to protest and was kicked in the buttocks by Officer Stimac, then thrown to the ground.

While on the ground, Story said, he was kicked several times in the left ribs.

A witness who lives across the street from the scene said she saw a white officer kick Story two or three times in the left side.

Stimac indicated he was the only white officer at the scene.

Officer Stimac said prior to arriving at the scene he had received a radio call to check for a man with a gun. As the Story and the other man passed their position, one appeared to reach inside his coat as if he were going to draw a weapon. That is the action that precipitated the frisk, Stimac said.

Stimac denied that he kicked Story or used force. He said Story and his companion were removed from the area because a crowd had gathered and they were released unharmed at Carpenter School.

The officer said he shook hands with Story when he was released and that he appeared to be without injury.

Medical records provided by St. Joseph Hospital give some support to Story's allegation, but this evidence is not conclusive.

The records show that Story came to the emergency room shortly after noon the next day.

The radiologist concluded that x-rays showed a questionable undisplayed fracture involving the left 10th rib. When questioned by the ombudsman about his finding, the doctor said the evidence from the x-ray and tenderness in the area indicated the rib was probably broken.

Story also complained of a wrist injury, but none was found, the medical report shows.

The medical report said Story told the doctors he was injured while handcuffed by police and kicked in the left rib cage. Slight swelling was noted on his right arm.

No bruises were noted at the rib cage but he told doctors it was tender to the touch.

A report concerning barriers to filing complaints about police misconduct.

Investigator: B. Burdette & T. Bankert
Filed: December 22, 1989

FINDING

There are barriers in the process of accepting complaints from citizens about the behavior of police officers that may prevent some legitimate grievances from entering the system.

Specifically, this report addresses the policy of requiring complainants to sign a form acknowledging that giving false information to police is a misdemeanor.

The department does not require this form be completed by citizens who file a complaint about another civilian. The form is required only when the complaint is directed at a police officer.

We believe this may be perceived as a subtle form of intimidation. Further, we question its effectiveness. We could find no evidence of a single successful prosecution for providing false information in a complaint against a police officer.

BACKGROUND

A citizen complained to our office several months ago that she found it very difficult to file a complaint with the police department about the conduct of an officer.

The woman said she telephoned the police department shortly after the incident to find out how to file such a complaint.

The officer she spoke with told her that he needed details of the complaint. She explained what had occurred and the officer asked several questions. The woman said she got the impression that he was screening the information in an attempt to determine whether or not to accept the complaint. They both became angry and ended the call.

The citizen said she called back and spoke to someone who said he was a supervisor. This officer also asked her for the details. He advised her that she would have to come into the station with witnesses to file the complaint and that she would have to sign a form.

He read her the law (false reports to police) and told her that they were trying to cut down on the number of complaints that they receive because many people complain to get back at the police.

The ombudsman attempted to obtain reports from these officers. However, no one can remember talking with this citizen.

An April 1988 memorandum from Chief Fay Peek to the bureau commanders outlines the procedures for handling complaints.

This memorandum said that it is mandatory that complaints be made in person so that the complainant can read and sign the "false reports to police" form.

This form contains Section 31-19 of the Flint City Code which states that it is unlawful to knowingly give false information to the police department. The form states that the complainant acknowledges that they have read it and been cautioned that prosecution is a consequence of its violation. The form must be signed by the complainant and two witnesses.

In 1987, the ombudsman issued a report outlining the value citizen complaints can have when used as a management tool to evaluate service delivery.

We also called upon the city to develop a centralized complaint handling system to provide accurate feedback to the administrative departments.

This report further underscores the continuing need to open the lines of communication between the citizens and the government.

Complaints, requests and suggestions are an important part of the day-to-day communication between local government and the public.

Researchers say participation in government by complaining allows citizens to behave responsibly, intelligently, perhaps even creatively in their daily lives. Better citizens and better government will tend to follow from increased participation.

A large portion of participation in government happens in the form of complaints to a governmental unit.

From the perspective of Flint's citizens, effective complaint handling will be achieved when the citizen feels he or she has been treated fair.

This view implies fair treatment for all citizens, even those with complaints that seem irrelevant or unjustifiable. Fair treatment includes appropriate referrals for matters beyond the department's or the city's jurisdiction and thorough explanations when unreasonable requests must be refused.

RECOMMENDED GOALS

An effective complaint handling system should achieve four goals:

1) It should increase satisfaction citizens receive from the organization's responses to complaints.

2) It should improve the quality of the treatment received from government complaint-processing personnel as it is reflected in response time, courteousness, helpfulness and fairness.

3) It should increase the willingness and ability of citizens to make their complaints known to governmental officials.

4) It should provide meaningful information to policy makers to monitor and change municipal service delivery.

Complaint intake is an important form of citizen participation in a democratic society.

Complaint resolution is an important component of ensuring local government accountability.

Complaint monitoring is a means to identify early economic or racial inequities that may be introduced when municipal services are altered.

Complaint evaluation is a tool for the effective management of municipal service delivery.

An approach to effective complaint handling is to view it as an insurance policy that does not allow local government to fail those it is supposed to serve.

RECOMMENDATIONS

We recommend the police department discontinue requiring complainants to sign the "false reports to police" form. We believe this procedure could discourage people from making complaints.

Chief Fay Peek has indicated he will review this policy and consider our recommendation.

Some people may be prevented from making a complaint because they do not have transportation to the station. Others may believe that they will be arrested if they provide incorrect or inaccurate information about the complaint.

Many of the people who file complaints against the police department have already had a negative experience with police officers. They should not feel discouraged or threatened when they attempt to resolve the problem by filing a complaint.

Document No. 11
Houston

INTRODUCTION

CITIZEN REVIEW COMMITTEE

In 1990, it was recognized by many that there was a need to create a review process wherein citizens of the city of Houston were given an opportunity to review internal police investigations. Thus, the Citizen's Review Committee (CRC) was created.

The Citizen Review Committee is comprised of three panel groups (Panel A, Panel B and Panel C). Each panel consists of seven members with one member elected by the panel as chairperson. Panel member's length of service ~~with~~ will be determined by the drawing of lots for one, two or three year terms.

The original committee member selection was made by the Mayor from a group of fifty individuals who expressed an interest in a commitment to serving on the committee. Committee members are required to meet the following qualifiers and disqualifiers.

<u>Qualifiers</u>

- U. S. Citizen
- Reside in city limits for three years
- Willing to spend four to five hours a week reviewing cases and attending meetings
- Willing to make up to a three year commitment
- Willing to attend a training session at the Houston Police Department Training Academy

Disqualifiers

- Prior felony convictions
- Class A or B convictions within the last five years
- Holding any political office
- Working for another law enforcement agency
- A current City of Houston employee
- An immediate family member of any Houston Police Department personnel

Once selected, the committee members are obligated to attend a two-and-half day training session. Houston Police Department employees instruct committee members about the HPD disciplinary process, policy, procedures, self defense techniques, "Shoot don't Shoot" situations and Internal Affairs Division (IAD) procedures.

The Citizen Review Committee is placed in the review process as the **last step** before the Chief of Police. In this fashion, the Citizen Review Committee will have an opportunity to not only review the completed investigations, which have been reviewed by various levels of the Police Department, but an opportunity to review the recommended discipline as well. The committee will review internal investigations which meet the following criteria:

- Use of Force
- Discharge of firearms

- Incidents resulting in serious bodily injury or death
- Any other investigations requested and approved for review by the Chief of Police

The committee's purpose is to review the entire internal affairs investigation to determine if the investigation was sufficient, the conclusions correct, and that proper discipline, is issued. The committee passes along a recommendation on each and every case it reviews to the Chief of Police.

CRC panels meet weekly to review and discuss IAD cases. CRC panels review an average of twenty cases per month. The CRC chairperson from each of the three panels also serves as a member of the Administrative Disciplinary Committee (ADC). Each chairperson has one full vote on all disciplinary matters.

CRC members hold their meetings in a conference room located in the Internal Affairs Division Building at 1415 N. Loop West, Suite 501. They have available staff support consisting of the IAD Captain, IAD Lieutenant, and a CRC Senior Secretary. The CRC members have fourteen days to complete their review of each investigation. There are currently twenty members on the CRC.

a:CRC.INTRO

Document No. 12

Iowa

CITIZENS' AIDE[141]
(OMBUDSMAN)

[Prior to 3/30/94, see Citizens' Aide(210)]

[Rules published 3/30/94 exempt from Iowa Code chapter 17A pursuant to Iowa Code section 2C.9(5). These rules were also published in the 3/30/94 IAB as authorized by the ARRC pursuant to Iowa Code section 17A.6(1)"c."]

CHAPTER 1
ORGANIZATION

1.1(2C) Authority and function
1.2(2C) Location and access
1.3(2C) Composition and duties of staff

CHAPTER 2
PROCEDURES

2.1(2C) Definitions
2.2(2C) Intakes
2.3(2C) Institutional contacts
2.4(2C) Preliminary review and inquiry
2.5(2C) Criteria for investigation
2.6(2C) Decision not to investigate
2.7(2C) Decision to investigate
2.8(2C) Investigations
2.9(2C) Subpoenas
2.10(2C) Hearings to examine witnesses
2.11(2C) Disposition after investigation
2.12(2C) Investigative reports
2.13(2C) Annual reports
2.14(2C) Referral for disciplinary or criminal action
2.15(2C) Privileges and immunities
2.16(2C) Penalties for obstruction

CHAPTER 3
INFORMATION PRACTICES

3.1(2C,22) Definitions
3.2(2C,22) Statement of policy
3.3(2C,22) Requests for access to records
3.4(2C,22) Access to confidential records
3.5(2C,22) Requests to treat record as confidential
3.6(2C,22) Additions, dissents or objections to records
3.7(2C,22) Notice to suppliers of information
3.8(2C,22) Release to subject
3.9(2C,22) Consensual disclosure of confidential records
3.10(2C,22) Disclosure without consent of subject
3.11(2C,22) Availability of records
3.12(2C,22) Personally identifiable information
3.13(2C,22) Other groups of records
3.14(2C,22) Data processing systems
3.15(2C,22) Applicability

CHAPTER 4
RULE MAKING

4.1(2C) Applicability
4.2(2C) Adoption of rule
4.3(2C) Contents, style, and form of rule

CHAPTER 5
PETITIONS FOR RULE MAKING

5.1(17A) Petition for rule making
5.2(17A) Agency consideration

CHAPTER 6
DECLARATORY RULINGS

6.1(17A) Petition for declaratory rulings
6.2(17A) Agency consideration
6.3(17A) Refusal to issue ruling
6.4(17A) Declaratory rulings

CHAPTER 1
ORGANIZATION

[Prior to 3/30/94, see 210—Chapter 1]

141—1.1(2C) Authority and function. The office of the citizens' aide/ombudsman was established by the general assembly in 1972 and is charged with the responsibility to investigate complaints from any persons regarding administrative actions of Iowa state or local governmental agencies and to render objective opinions or recommendations on the complaints, in the interests of resolving complaints and improving administrative processes and procedures. In addition to the powers and duties specified in Iowa Code chapter 2C, the office of citizens' aide/ombudsman shall investigate complaints received pursuant to Iowa Code section 23A.4 and serve on the child support enforcement program advisory committee pursuant to Iowa Code section 252B.18.

141—1.2(2C) Location and access. The office of citizens' aide/ombudsman is located at the Capitol Complex, 215 E. Seventh Street, Des Moines, Iowa 50319. The office can be reached at the following numbers: telephone (515)281-3592, Iowa WATS 1-800-358-5510, TDD/TTY (515)242-5065, and fax (515)242-6007. Office hours are 8 a.m. to 4:30 p.m., Monday through Friday, except designated state holidays.

141—1.3(2C) Composition and duties of staff.

1.3(1) The office of citizens' aide/ombudsman is composed of the following staff positions:

a. Citizens' aide/ombudsman. The citizens' aide/ombudsman is appointed by the legislative council pursuant to Iowa Code section 2C.3. The citizens' aide/ombudsman shall meet the qualifications specified in Iowa Code section 2C.4 and serve for the term of office provided in Iowa Code section 2C.5. The citizens' aide/ombudsman employs and supervises all staff in the positions and at the salaries authorized by the legislative council.

b. Deputy citizens' aide/ombudsman. The citizens' aide/ombudsman shall designate one of the members of the staff as the deputy citizens' aide/ombudsman. The deputy citizens' aide/ombudsman shall act as the citizens' aide/ombudsman when the citizens' aide/ombudsman is absent from the state or becomes disabled, or when the position of citizens' aide/ombudsman is vacant, until the vacancy is filled by the legislative council.

c. Legal counsels. The legal counsels shall provide legal advice, assistance, and representation to the citizens' aide/ombudsman and members of the staff in matters pertaining to their authority and duties and shall perform other assigned duties.

d. Assistant for corrections. The assistant citizens' aide/ombudsman for corrections is primarily responsible for investigating complaints relating to penal and correctional agencies, and performs other assigned duties.

e. Assistants. The assistant citizens' aide/ombudsmen receive intakes, investigate complaints, and perform other assigned duties.

f. Support staff. The support staff performs secretarial, clerical, and other assigned duties.

1.3(2) Delegation of authority or duties. The citizens' aide/ombudsman may delegate to any staff member any authority or duties of the citizens' aide/ombudsman, except the duty of making formal recommendations to agencies or reports to the governor or the general assembly.

These rules are intended to implement Iowa Code section 2C.9(5).

[Filed 12/15/75, Notice 10/20/75—published 12/29/75, effective 2/2/76]
[Filed 8/26/81, Notice 7/22/81—published 9/16/81, effective 10/21/81]
[Filed 8/1/84, Notice 6/20/84—published 8/29/84, effective 10/3/84]
[Adopted and published 3/30/94 pursuant to Iowa Code §2C.9(5), effective 5/1/94]

CHAPTER 2
PROCEDURES

[Prior to 3/30/94, see 210—Chapter 2, 6.1(601G) and 7.1(601G)]

141—2.1(2C) Definitions. As used in this chapter:

"Administrative action" means any action, decision, omission, policy, practice, procedure, or rule of an agency or any failure of an agency to act pursuant to law.

"Agency" means all governmental entities, departments, boards, commissions, councils or institutions, and any officer, employee or member thereof acting or purporting to act in the exercise of official duties. It does not include:

1. Any court or judge or appurtenant judicial staff;
2. The members, committees, or permanent or temporary staffs of the Iowa general assembly;
3. The governor of Iowa or the governor's personal staff;
4. Any instrumentality formed pursuant to an interstate compact and answerable to more than one state; and
5. Any agency, official or employee of the federal government.

"Employee" means any employee of any agency.

"Officer" means any officer of any agency.

"Person" means an individual, aggregate of individuals, corporation, partnership, or unincorporated association.

"Records" or *"documents"* means any writings, drawings, graphs, charts, photographs, phonorecords, audiotapes, videotapes, and any other data or information stored or preserved in any medium.

141—2.2(2C) Intakes.

2.2(1) *Persons who may contact office.* Any person may contact the citizens' aide/ombudsman concerning an administrative action by an agency. If a person contacts the citizens' aide/ombudsman on behalf of another person whose specific right or interest is directly affected by an administrative action, the citizens' aide/ombudsman may request that the affected person contact the citizens' aide/ombudsman as the complainant or obtain the consent of the affected person before considering the complaint.

2.2(2) *Methods of contact.* The citizens' aide/ombudsman may be contacted at the office of citizens' aide/ombudsman or at the site of an agency or other location specified by the citizens' aide/ombudsman. No appointment is needed for the initial office visit. Contact may be made by mail, telephone, fax machine, office visit, or any other method deemed acceptable by the citizens' aide/ombudsman, except as provided in subrule 2.2(3). Contact may also be made indirectly by the receipt of a person's correspondence which is referred or forwarded to the office of the citizens' aide/ombudsman.

2.2(3) *Written complaints.* The citizens' aide/ombudsman may require certain types of complaints to be submitted in writing or on a form prescribed by the citizens' aide/ombudsman.

2.2(4) *Assistance by citizens' aide/ombudsman.* If a person is incapable of submitting a written complaint or has difficulty communicating with the citizens' aide/ombudsman because of a disability or language barrier, the citizens' aide/ombudsman shall assist that person in completing the complaint or make accommodations to facilitate communication with that person.

2.2(5) *Self-initiated complaints.* An investigation into an agency's administrative action may be initiated on the citizens' aide/ombudsman's own motion, if the citizens' aide/ombudsman determines it is an appropriate subject for investigation.

2.2(6) *Anonymous complaints.* The citizens' aide/ombudsman may accept a complaint from an anonymous person. However, if the citizens' aide/ombudsman at any time determines the complainant's identity is needed to pursue an investigation of the complaint, the citizens' aide/ombudsman may request that the complainant's identity be disclosed. If the identity of the complainant is not disclosed as requested, the citizens' aide/ombudsman may decline to pursue investigation of the complaint.

2.2(7) *Information requests.* If a person who contacts the citizens' aide/ombudsman requests information, the citizens' aide/ombudsman may provide such information, if it relates to state and local government, or refer the person to another agency or to any other appropriate entity or source for the information.

2.2(8) *No fee or charge.* The citizens' aide/ombudsman shall not assess any monetary or other charge against any person who contacts the office of citizens' aide/ombudsman for assistance.

141—2.3(2C) Institutional contacts.

2.3(1) *Correspondence.* Any correspondence from a person confined or residing in an institution or facility under the control of an agency shall be forwarded, unopened and without undue delay, to the office of citizens' aide/ombudsman by the institution or facility. Any correspondence from the office of the citizens' aide/ombudsman to such a person shall be delivered, unopened and without undue delay, by the institution or facility to that person.

2.3(2) *Telephonic communication.* A telephonic communication between a person confined or residing in an institution or facility under an agency's control and any staff member of the office of citizens' aide/ombudsman shall not be monitored by any officer or employee of that agency.

141—2.4(2C) Preliminary review and inquiry.

2.4(1) *Review of complaint.* The citizens' aide/ombudsman shall review and consider each complaint to determine if it is within the citizens' aide/ombudsman's jurisdiction, if it is an appropriate subject for investigation, and if it warrants an investigation, under the criteria in rule 2.5(2C).

2.4(2) *Preliminary inquiry.* The citizens' aide/ombudsman may make a preliminary inquiry to obtain information for the purpose of making the determination required in subrule 2.4(1). A preliminary inquiry may utilize any of the methods available for investigations under subrule 2.8(1). However, a preliminary inquiry shall not be considered an investigation.

2.4(3) *Resolution without investigation.* If, in the course of a preliminary inquiry on the complaint, an agency provides an explanation or response, or takes an action which resolves the complaint, the citizens' aide/ombudsman may decline to investigate the complaint. The citizens' aide/ombudsman shall inform the complainant regarding the resolution of the complaint. However, the resolution of a complaint during a preliminary review and inquiry does not preclude the citizens' aide/ombudsman from conducting an investigation into the complaint.

141—2.5(2C) Criteria for investigation.

2.5(1) *Jurisdiction.* The citizens' aide/ombudsman has jurisdiction to investigate any administrative action of an agency, except that the citizens' aide/ombudsman shall not investigate the complaint of an employee of an agency in regard to that employee's employment relationship with the agency.

2.5(2) *Subjects for investigation.* An appropriate subject for investigation includes any administrative action which the citizens' aide/ombudsman has reason to believe might be:

1. Contrary to law or regulation;
2. Unreasonable, unfair, oppressive, or inconsistent with the general course of an agency's functioning, even though it is in accordance with the law;
3. Based on a mistake of law;
4. Arbitrary in ascertainments of fact;
5. Based on improper motivation or irrelevant consideration; or
6. Unaccompanied by an adequate statement of reasons.

The citizens' aide/ombudsman may also inquire into an agency's policy, practice or procedure if the citizens' aide/ombudsman has reason to believe improvements can be made to the policy, practice or procedure which lessen the risk that objectionable administrative actions will occur.

2.5(3) *Reasons to decline investigation.* The citizens' aide/ombudsman may decline to investigate a complaint if the citizens' aide/ombudsman finds substantiating facts that:

a. The complainant has available another remedy or channel of complaint which the complainant could reasonably be expected to use;

b. The grievance pertains to a matter outside the citizens' aide/ombudsman's power;

c. The complainant has no substantive or procedural interest which is directly affected by the matter complained about;

d. The complaint is trivial, frivolous, vexatious, or not made in good faith;

e. Other complaints are more worthy of attention;

f. The resources of the citizens' aide/ombudsman are insufficient for adequate investigation;

g. The complaint has been delayed too long to justify present examination of its merit;

h. The complainant does not provide or refuses to provide, without good reason, information in the complainant's possession or knowledge which is requested by the citizens' aide/ombudsman;

i. A previous determination has been made by the citizens' aide/ombudsman regarding the subject matter of the complaint; or

j. The complaint has been resolved due to a change in the complainant's circumstances or the law, or an action taken by the agency during a preliminary review and inquiry on the complaint.

141—2.6(2C) Decision not to investigate.

2.6(1) *Notice of decision.* If, after preliminary review and consideration of a complaint, the citizens' aide/ombudsman decides not to investigate the complaint, the complainant shall be informed of the decision and the reasons for the decision. The citizens' aide/ombudsman may also inform the agency involved of the decision, if such notice is deemed appropriate.

2.6(2) *Referral of nonjurisdictional complaint.* If the citizens' aide/ombudsman does not have jurisdictional authority to investigate a complaint, the complainant may be referred to an agency or other appropriate entity or person for assistance.

2.6(3) *Effect of declining investigation.* A decision to decline investigation of a complaint under subrule 2.5(3) does not preclude the citizens' aide/ombudsman from inquiring into the complaint or a related subject matter in the future.

141—2.7(2C) Decision to investigate.

2.7(1) *Notice of decision.* If, after preliminary review and inquiry and consideration, the citizens' aide/ombudsman decides to investigate a complaint, the complainant and the agency involved in the complaint shall be notified of the decision.

2.7(2) *Notice to agency.* A notice of investigation to an agency shall be directed to the head or director of the agency and any other officer or employee of the agency who is a subject of the complaint, as determined by the citizens' aide/ombudsman. Such notice may be given simultaneously or in conjunction with any investigative action that is initiated under rule 2.8(2C).

141—2.8(2C) Investigations.

2.8(1) *Methods.* The citizens' aide/ombudsman may use any one or more of the following methods in conducting an investigation:

a. Review applicable laws, rules, regulations, and policies;

b. Request a statement from an agency providing reasons for taking an administrative action;

c. Make informal verbal or written inquiries to an agency and other persons for assistance or information;

d. Examine and copy records or documents of an agency;

e. Enter and inspect without notice any premises within an agency's control;

f. Attend administrative hearings or proceedings;

g. Issue a subpoena to compel a person to provide sworn testimony or to produce relevant records or documents;

h. Hold private hearings as provided under rule 2.10(2C);

i. Convene a public hearing as a forum to obtain public input or comment on a subject of general or broad public concern;

j. Any other method determined appropriate by the citizens' aide/ombudsman.

2.8(2) *Ex parte communications.* A communication or receipt of information by the citizens' aide/ombudsman or any person in the course of an investigation shall not be considered an ex parte communication as described in Iowa Code section 17A.17.

2.8(3) *Status reports.* The citizens' aide/ombudsman shall report the status of an investigation to the complainant upon request of the complainant or whenever it is deemed appropriate.

141—2.9(2C) Subpoenas.

2.9(1) *Issuance.* Pursuant to Iowa Code section 2C.9(4), the citizens' aide/ombudsman has power to issue a subpoena to compel any person to appear, give sworn testimony, or produce documentary or other evidence relevant to a matter under inquiry.

2.9(2) *Notice.* The citizens' aide/ombudsman shall give reasonable notice of the date, time, place, and purpose for the taking of testimony or the production of documentary or other evidence. Notice shall be served in accordance with the law applicable to the service of subpoenas in civil actions.

2.9(3) *Fees.* A person required to give testimony or produce documentary or other evidence is entitled to payment of the same fees and travel allowances as are payable to a witness whose attendance has been required in a district court of this state.

2.9(4) *Enforcement.* If a person fails or refuses to obey a subpoena, the citizens' aide/ombudsman may file a petition with the district court having jurisdiction for an order directing obedience to the subpoena under Iowa Code section 2C.9(4).

141—2.10(2C) Hearings to examine witnesses.

2.10(1) *Purpose.* The citizens' aide/ombudsman has authority to conduct private hearings under Iowa Code section 2C.8. A private hearing is the taking of testimony from any person, with or without the issuance of a subpoena. A hearing is not a contested case proceeding under Iowa Code chapter 17A. The purpose of a hearing is not to adjudicate the substantive rights of a complainant or an agency, but to discover and gather factual information relevant to a subject matter of a complaint.

2.10(2) *Notice.* The citizens' aide/ombudsman shall provide reasonable notice to the person whose testimony is sought of the date, time, and place for taking that person's testimony. If the citizens' aide/ombudsman issues a subpoena compelling a person to give testimony, notice shall be provided in the subpoena.

2.10(3) *Location.* The citizens' aide/ombudsman has discretion to take testimony from a person at the office of the citizens' aide/ombudsman or at another location as deemed appropriate by the citizens' aide/ombudsman, or by telephone conference call.

2.10(4) *Rights of witnesses.* A person who gives testimony is accorded the same privileges and immunities as are extended to witnesses in the courts of this state. The witness is entitled to be accompanied and advised by counsel or other representative while being questioned, but only counsel may speak or raise objections to questions on behalf of the witness. Objections to questions shall be noted but the witness shall answer all questions, except when a privilege or immunity accorded to the witness has been asserted.

2.10(5) *Conduct of hearings.* The citizens' aide/ombudsman, deputy citizens' aide/ombudsman, and assistants may administer oaths to persons giving testimony before them. The citizens' aide/ombudsman determines the order for the taking of testimony and may sequester witnesses or examine a witness privately. Questions will be posed by the citizens' aide/ombudsman. At the conclusion of the citizens' aide/ombudsman's examination of a witness, counsel for the witness may be permitted to question the witness, after which the citizens' aide/ombudsman may inquire further into any matters raised during the examination. The scope of the questions shall be decided and may be limited by the citizens' aide/ombudsman.

2.10(6) *Evidence.* Strict rules of evidence shall not apply. Irrelevant, immaterial, or unduly repetitious evidence may be excluded. The probative value and weight of any evidentiary matter shall be determined by the citizens' aide/ombudsman.

2.10(7) *Record.* The citizens' aide/ombudsman may record the testimony on audiotape or videotape or by use of a certified court reporter and may have the testimony transcribed.

a. A witness is permitted to record any testimony that the witness may give, if such recording will not interfere unduly with the taking of the testimony in an orderly manner.

b. A witness is entitled to obtain a copy of the audiotape, videotape, or transcription of the witness's testimony upon request and payment of a reasonable fee for producing the copy.

c. Audiotapes and videotapes of testimony shall be preserved for a period not less than 60 days from the date they were recorded.

141—2.11(2C) Disposition after investigation.

2.11(1) *Complaint unsubstantiated.* If, after completing an investigation, the citizens' aide/ombudsman determines the complaint is not substantiated, based upon a preponderance of the evidence, the citizens' aide/ombudsman shall inform the complainant and the agency involved of such determination.

2.11(2) *Complaint indeterminate.* If, after completing an investigation, the citizens' aide/ombudsman is unable to conclusively determine, based upon a preponderance of the evidence, whether the complaint is substantiated or unsubstantiated, the citizens' aide/ombudsman shall inform the complainant and the agency involved of such conclusion.

2.11(3) *Complaint substantiated.* If, after completing an investigation, the citizens' aide/ombudsman determines the complaint is substantiated, based upon a preponderance of the evidence, the citizens' aide/ombudsman shall inform the complainant and the agency involved of the findings of fact and conclusions. If appropriate, the citizens' aide/ombudsman shall also inform the agency of any recommendation that:

1. The matter be further considered by the agency;
2. The administrative action be modified or canceled;
3. A rule on which an administrative action is based be altered;
4. Reasons be given for an administrative action; or
5. Any other action be taken by the agency.

2.11(4) *Agency response to recommendations.* If the citizens' aide/ombudsman requests, the agency shall notify the citizens' aide/ombudsman within 20 days in writing of any action taken or to be taken on the recommendations or the reasons for not complying with the recommendations.

2.11(5) *Legislative action.* If the citizens' aide/ombudsman believes that a law resulted in administrative action which was unfair or otherwise objectionable, the citizens' aide/ombudsman shall notify the general assembly of desirable statutory change. Notification may be given by submitting a legislative proposal or by presenting testimony or statements to the general assembly or one of its committees or members regarding the statutory change.

2.11(6) *Referral for disciplinary or criminal action.* The citizens' aide/ombudsman shall refer a public official, employee or other person for disciplinary or criminal proceeding, if such referral is warranted under rule 2.14(2C).

141—2.12(2C) Investigative reports.

2.12(1) *Issuance of reports.* The citizens' aide/ombudsman may prepare a report of the findings of fact, conclusions, and recommendations relevant to an investigation.

a. Critical reports. If the citizens' aide/ombudsman determines as a result of an investigation that an administrative action of an agency, officer or employee warrants criticism, the citizens' aide/ombudsman may issue a critical report containing the findings, conclusions and recommendations relevant to that investigation.

b. Special reports. A special report may be issued if the findings of fact, conclusions, or recommendations are not critical of an agency, or an officer or employee of an agency, but are of significant interest to the public.

2.12(2) *Publication of reports.* The citizens' aide/ombudsman may publish and send a critical report or a special report to the governor, the general assembly or any of the committees of the general assembly. Any published report sent to the governor, the general assembly or any of its committees becomes public information and may be disseminated to the news media and to any interested members of the general public upon request.

2.12(3) *Prepublication procedure for critical reports.* Before publishing a critical report or announcing a conclusion or recommendation which criticizes an agency, officer or employee, the citizens' aide/ombudsman shall consult with that agency, officer or employee.

a. The citizens' aide/ombudsman shall transmit a copy of the critical report to the agency and each officer or employee who is a subject of the criticism and allow the agency, officer or employee a reasonable opportunity to reply to the report in writing.

b. Reply to report. The agency, officer or employee shall notify the citizens' aide/ombudsman within 7 days from the date the critical report is received of any decision by that agency, officer or employee to make a reply. The agency, officer or employee shall be allowed 30 days from the date of receipt of the critical report to submit a written reply to the citizens' aide/ombudsman. The citizens' aide/ombudsman may for good cause extend the time allowed to submit the reply, if an extension is requested by the agency, officer or employee.

c. Comment to reply. The citizens' aide/ombudsman may comment on any reply from an agency, officer or employee. The comments may include modifications by the citizens' aide/ombudsman to any findings, conclusions, or recommendations in the critical report. The citizens' aide/ombudsman shall transmit in writing any comments to the replying agency, officer or employee.

d. Reply or comment attached to report. Any unedited reply made by an agency, officer or employee and any written comments by the citizens' aide/ombudsman shall be attached to every critical report which is published, sent, or disseminated by the citizens' aide/ombudsman, unless inclusion of the reply is waived by the agency, officer or employee.

e. Confidential information not published. The citizens' aide/ombudsman may not publish any confidential information which the citizens' aide/ombudsman is not authorized to disclose or is prohibited from disclosing by law. The citizens' aide/ombudsman may prepare, for the purpose of publication, an edited version of the critical report, from which confidential information has been deleted or excluded. The citizens' aide/ombudsman shall transmit the edited version of the critical report to the agency, officer or employee and consult with that agency, officer or employee to ensure the report does not contain confidential information that may not be disclosed. Any reply or comment which is attached to this report and which contains confidential information that may not be disclosed shall likewise be edited to delete or exclude the confidential information.

141—2.13(2C) Annual reports.

2.13(1) *When and to whom submitted.* Pursuant to Iowa Code section 2C.18, the citizens' aide/ombudsman shall by April 1 of each year submit an economically designed and reproduced annual report to the general assembly and to the governor concerning the activities and work performed during the preceding calendar year.

Document No. 13
Kansas City, Mo.

KANSAS CITY, MO. POLICE DEPARTMENT

PROCEDURAL INSTRUCTION

DATE OF ISSUE	EFFECTIVE DATE	NO.
5-19-93	5-20-93	93-1

SUBJECT	AMENDS
Citizen Complaint Policy and Procedure	

REFERENCE	RESCINDS
	Procedural Instruction 91-23

I. PURPOSE

To provide policies and procedures for processing and investigating citizen complaints.

II. CATEGORIES OF CITIZEN COMPLAINTS

A. Category I Complaints - All citizen complaints or allegations lodged against members which involve:

1. Unauthorized use of force.

2. Abuse of authority.

3. Discourtesy, or abusive and/or insulting language.

4. Ethnic slurs, i.e., language, conduct, or behavior which tends to degrade a person's race, religion, creed, or nationality.

* B. Category II Complaints - All other citizen complaints involving citizen's dissatisfaction with an officer's action, including but not limited to failure to follow department procedures.

III. THE OFFICE OF CITIZEN COMPLAINTS

A. The Office of Citizen Complaints, hereinafter referred to as the "Office," was established by the Board of Police Commissioners as a service agency for the community and the department.

B. The functions of the Office Director, assisted by Office staff members, are to:

1. Receive all citizen complaints.

2. Refer complaint investigations to the Internal Affairs Unit.

3. Objectively review all complaint circumstances and/or investigations.

4. Submit memorandum reports to the Board of Police Commissioners on Category I complaints, and the Chief of Police on both categories of complaints. The reports should summarize evidence and conclusions, and advise an appropriate classification.

5. Complete required notifications.

* 6. Maintain a comprehensive Central Complaint File on citizen complaints received by the Office.

IV. POLICY

A. The department shall perform the following functions as they relate to the Office:

1. Accept complaints from citizens in person and forward them to the Office for disposition.

2. Investigate complaints.

B. The Office shall accept Category I and Category II complaints filed within sixty days after the date of occurrence.

* C. Complaint classifications of conciliated, substantiated, unsubstantiated, exonerated, or closed, as determined by the Office, are advisory when submitted to the Board of Police Commissioners and the Chief of Police. Only the Chief of Police shall have the authority to prescribe discipline in accordance with §84.500 R.S.Mo.

D. Upon request by a citizen, members shall identify themselves by name and identifying number, e.g., badge, serial, etc.

* E. The citizen lodging the complaint or the co-complainant parent or guardian shall be required to sign the complaint.

* F. Members shall be provided an opportunity to respond to the allegations of the complaint.

G. Any department member who interferes with, discourages, or delays the making or the investigation of such complaints shall be subject to appropriate disciplinary action.

V. PROCEDURE

This directive has been arranged in annexes for easy reference.

Steven C. Bishop
Chief of Police

DISTRIBUTION: Law Enforcement Personnel
Civilian Supervisory Positions
Department Element Manuals
Post on bulletin board for two weeks.

TABLE OF ANNEXES

Annex A	Receiving Citizen Complaints
Annex B	Processing Citizen Complaints
Annex C	Investigation of Citizen Complaints
Annex D	Determination of Complaint Classifications
Annex E	Disposition of Complaints
Annex F	Access to Central Complaint Investigation File

RECEIVING CITIZEN COMPLAINTS

A. Signed Complaints

* 1. ANY CITIZEN COMPLAINT, regardless of category, can be lodged at any police facility or at the Office (306 East 12th Street, Room 913). The Office of Citizen Complaints Statement must be signed by the complainant.

* 2. Statements require the complainant to be eighteen years of age or older. Any complainant under eighteen years of age must be accompanied by a parent or legal guardian who will be a co-complainant and will sign the statement.

3. The officer in charge of a police facility will be notified of any complaint made at the facility, and may interview the complainant.

* 4. The member receiving the complaint at a police facility will immediately call the Office at extension 5005. (During non-business hours, the information will be recorded on the telerecorder system attached to the Office telephone.) This telephone notification creates a control mechanism against lost reports. The following information will be transmitted:

   a. A citizen complaint was received and a Form 337 P.D. was completed.

   b. Time complaint was received.

   c. Name and address of complainant.

   d. Rank, name, serial and/or badge number, and element of assignment of the member about whom the complaint was filed, if identified.

   e. Rank, name, and element of assignment of the member transmitting the information.

* 5. Unsigned forms will be accepted and immediately forwarded to the Office. However, a member accepting a citizen complaint must ensure the citizen understands the complaint **will not** be investigated unless identification of the complainant is made as required by the Board of Police Commissioners.

B. Complaint Made in Person

1. The member accepting a citizen complaint made in person will furnish the complainant with two blank copies of the Form 337 P.D. and one sheet of carbon paper. The member will also explain the proper positioning of the carbon paper, and the Forms 337 P.D., if continuation of the complaint on the reverse side of the form is necessary.

   a. The complainant will be instructed to complete and sign the Form 337 P.D. in the complainant's own handwriting and to leave the "Department Member Receiving Complaint" block blank.

   b. Upon request, the complainant may have whatever assistance is necessary in completing the Form 337 P.D. If given assistance, the person assisting will include, under "Details of Complaint," a brief statement as to why such assistance was given. The complainant and any other person assisting will sign the Form 337 P.D. The member will sign in the receiving member's block.

   c. After the complainant has completed the Form 337 P.D., the member will review the contents for legibility. If a word is not legible, the member will print the proper word directly above the complainant's handwritten word and ask the complainant to initial the correction.

* 2. If the complainant refuses to sign, the member will enter "Refused to Sign" on the complainant's signature line and mail the Form 337 P.D. to the Office.

3. When it appears to the member that the complainant is apparently under the influence of an intoxicant/drug, suffering from a mental disorder, or exhibits any other trait or condition bearing on his credibility, the member will note these conditions on the reverse side of the original of the Form 337 P.D. The member will include observations as to the physical condition of the complainant, specifically noting any visible marks or injuries relative to the alleged complaint. Statements to be noted on the reverse side of the Form 337 P.D. will be made only after the complainant has either signed or refused to sign the statement. All such remarks and statements will be followed by the signature of the member making the remarks.

4. The member will notify the Office as outlined in Annex A, Section A, 4.

5. The original of the Form 337 P.D. will be placed in a sealed interdepartment envelope and immediately mailed to the Office. The carbon copy of the Form 337 P.D. will be given to the complainant as a receipt of the complaint.

6. **The copy given to the complainant shall not contain the observations of the member receiving the complaint.**

C. Complaint by Mail

1. A member receiving a citizen complaint through the U.S. Mail will: (1) notify the Office by telephone or telerecorder phone and (2) place the correspondence and envelope in a sealed interdepartment envelope and immediately mail it to the Office.

2. The Office will arrange for the completion of the Form 337 P.D.

D. Complaint by Telephone

Any department member contacted via telephone by a citizen requesting to file a complaint will inform the complainant that they must respond to the nearest police facility or to the Office, 306 East 12th Street, Room 913 to initiate complaint procedures. Complaints will not be accepted over the phone.

E. Complaint as a Duty Obligation

1. In maintaining the purpose of the Code of Ethics, a member who observes another member's misconduct toward a citizen will initiate a complaint or inform the citizen of the complaint procedure.

   a. This duty obligation of members does not include those acts or omissions of duty which are strictly internal incidents which will be reported on the Incident Report, Form 387 P.D., only.

   b. Complaints of an internal nature, reported on the Form 387 P.D., will be not received, processed, or investigated by the Office.

* 2. A member initiating a complaint will complete the Form 337 P.D. The report will be completed to the extent of the member's personal knowledge and what the member is able to obtain from persons involved in or witnessing the incident. A statement of the member's initiation of complaint shall appear in the "Details of Complaint" section. The

member initiating the complaint will enter the words "Police Initiated" in the complainant's signature block and complete the "Department Member Receiving Complaint" block at the bottom of the form. After preparing the report, the member will place it in a sealed interdepartment envelope and immediately mail it to the Office. The member will also notify the Office as outlined on Annex A, Section A, 4.

ANNEX B

PROCESSING CITIZEN COMPLAINTS

* A. All Category I and Category II citizen complaints will be forwarded to the Office as outlined in Annex A. The Internal Affairs Unit will make prompt notification to the Chief of Police. The notification may be satisfied by mailing a typed copy of the Form 337 P.D. in a sealed envelope. The Chief of Police shall retain such information for the sole purpose of determining whether immediate administrative action should be taken against the officer. The Office will make prompt notification to the subject member of the date, time, location, and name of complainant or co-complainants. This notification shall be satisfied by mailing a typed list of the above required information to the subject member in the sealed envelope. A copy of the Form 337 P.D. shall not be forwarded to the subject member.

B. The Office Director will forward both categories of citizen complaints to the Internal Affairs Unit, when inappropriate for preinvestigation conciliation.

C. The Office will have ten working days to complete processing of each citizen complaint after receipt of the completed investigation file from the Internal Affairs Unit. If unable to complete the processing within the allotted time, the Office Director will notify members of the Board of Police Commissioners on Category I complaints, and the Chief of Police on all complaints stating the reason for a delay. The notification will establish a new date(s) for the Board members, and/or the Chief of Police to receive the Office report.

The complainant will be notified of the delay and the anticipated final disposition date in a letter prepared by the Office Director.

INVESTIGATION OF CITIZEN COMPLAINTS

A. Internal Affairs Unit

1. The Internal Affairs Unit will investigate all Category I and Category II complaints received from the Office. If the Internal Affairs Unit is unable to conduct investigations of Category II complaints, e.g., workload, etc., the Internal Affairs Unit commander may request the Chief of Police to reassign the investigation.

2. Upon receipt of a citizen complaint from the Office, the Internal Affairs Unit will:

   a. Enter the complaint in the Citizen Complaint Tickler File.

   b. Use all recognized investigative methods consistent with existing departmental policy.

   c. Enter the results of the investigation in the Citizen Complaint Investigation File.

   d. Forward the results of the investigation to the Office.

3. The Internal Affairs Unit will complete an investigation within **thirty working days** of receipt of a complaint. If unable to complete the investigation within the allotted time, the unit commander will notify the Office Director.

* 4. The Office will maintain a file containing all substantiated, unsubstantiated, exonerated, and closed findings.

B. Other Department Elements

1. When notified by the Internal Affairs Unit of its inability to investigate a Category II citizen complaint, the Chief of Police shall assign the investigation, via the chain of command, to the proper division for handling.

2. The division assigned to the investigation of Category II complaint shall use any recognized investigative method, consistent with existing departmental policy.

3. Upon completion, the commander of the division conducting the complaint investigation will forward the results to the Chief of Police. Only the results, not recommendations, of the investigation will be forwarded.

* 4. Upon receipt of a completed complaint investigation conducted by a division other than the Internal Affairs Unit, the Chief of Police will forward the results to the Office which shall enter the results in the Citizen Complaint File.

DETERMINATION OF COMPLAINT CLASSIFICATIONS

A. The Office will determine which classification, outlined in the following sections, is appropriate upon receipt of the completed complaint investigation. The Office Director will report the classification determination to each member of the Board of Police Commissioners and the Chief of Police on all Category I complaints. Only the Chief of Police will receive reports on Category II complaints, unless a specific request is made by a Board member.

1. <u>Conciliated</u>

a. Preinvestigation conciliation

A conciliation discussion between the Office Director and the complainant may occur before investigation. A file of these conciliated complaints will be maintained in the Office. If a complaint is conciliated in this manner, no further investigation is required.

b. Post-investigation conciliation

(1) The complainant and the subject member met at the request of the Office Director to discuss the incident, and arrived at a mutual understanding.

(2) The citizen has misunderstood the actions, duty, or authority of the member, or if investigation of the complaint indicates that conciliation is appropriate.

(3) The conciliation procedure is conducted by the Office Director in a non-investigatory atmosphere. This enables the parties to honestly and freely discuss the incident without counsel, media, or personal representative present.

(4) Letters requesting a conciliation conference will be signed by the Office Director and forwarded to the complainant and member(s) concerned.

(a) A member receiving a letter will respond to the notification by checking the appropriate statement block at the bottom of the letter and returning it to the Office Director within forty-eight hours of receipt.

(b) A member volunteering to participate will be contacted by the Office during the member's normal duty hours to arrange a time for a conference.

(5) If a proper settlement of the complaint has occurred, the Office Director will make all notifications and recommend this be accepted as final disposition of the complaint. The Office Director will also indicate whether there was any misconduct on the part of the member(s).

2. Substantiated - The subject member acted in violation of the Code of Ethics, Rules of Conduct, or a written directive.

3. Unsubstantiated - The investigation of the complaint produced insufficient information to clearly prove or disprove the allegation. A proper determination of "unsubstantiated" may be justified by lack of witnesses, absence of objective and persuasive proof, or lack of cooperation.

4. Exonerated - Either the action complained about did occur but was found to be justified, legal, and proper; or there is no dispute the alleged action did not occur.

5. Closed - Either the complaint was withdrawn, or the complainant could not be contacted during the investigation.

B. The completed investigation of each citizen complaint will be reviewed thoroughly by the Office. The Office Director will prepare a memorandum summarizing evidence, conclusions, and the determination of an appropriate classification.

1. A copy of the report on all Category I complaints will be forwarded to each member of the Board of Police Commissioners. If, after fifteen days, no notice has been received by the Office indicating a Commissioner's disagreement, the complaint file and report will be forwarded to the Chief of Police.

2. The complaint file and report on Category II complaints will be forwarded directly to the Chief of Police. The Board of Police Commissioners will not be notified on Category II complaints, unless specifically requested by a Board member.

C. After receiving the Office Director's memorandum on the appropriate classification, members of the Board of Police Commissioners may:

1. Approve the classification as advised and do nothing else.

Following the fifteen-day expiration date, the Office Director may assume that the Board has approved classification.

2. Disapprove the classification as advised.

If a Commissioner disagrees with the classification, the Commissioner will so notify the Board Attorney and the Office Director. The Office will then withhold further action pending review and consideration by the Board. The Board Attorney will promptly notify the other Commissioners and will arrange for a meeting of the dissenting Commissioner, the Office staff, Board Attorney, and any other Commissioner who may wish to attend. A determination will be made by the majority of the Commissioners present as to whether the initial classification of the Office should be changed as requested by the dissenting Commissioner.

D. If the Chief of Police disagrees with the Office on a Category I complaint classification, he will promptly notify the Board Attorney. The Board Attorney will convene a meeting with the following persons: the Board Attorney, the Chief of Police, the Office Director, and any Commissioner who wishes to attend. The Board Attorney will notify the entire Board of the results of the meeting.

E. If the Chief of Police disagrees with a Category II complaint classification, he and the Office Director will meet and come to a decision.

F. While processing the citizen complaint, additional evidence may be offered for the Office's consideration. The Office may request further investigation, review the investigative file, and reconsider its determination based on the additional evidence. The procedure, listed in Annex D, Sections A through C, will then be repeated.

DISPOSITION OF COMPLAINTS

A. Recommendations

After a classification has been agreed upon by the Board of Police Commissioners, the Office Director will forward a copy of the completed complaint investigation file to the Chief of Police. Judging each case on its individual merit, the Chief of Police may, at his discretion, direct the respective chain of command to recommend a disposition, which may include appropriate discipline in accordance with the current Personnel Policy titled, Disciplinary Actions. Members of the chain of command will forward their recommendations to the Chief of Police within **fifteen working days**. They will not contact the Office for reinvestigation or change of complaint classification.

B. Final Disposition of Citizen Complaints and Notification

1. <u>Substantiated cases</u>

a. If the Chief of Police concurs with the recommendation that the complaint is substantiated, the Office Director will close the case in the Central Complaint File. Notifications prepared by the Office and signed by the Chief of Police or his designee will be distributed to the bureau commander, who will notify the appropriate division/unit commander.

* b. For all Category I complaints, the complainant will be notified by a letter prepared by the Office for the signature of the Secretary-Attorney of the Board of Police Commissioners. The Secretary-Attorney shall review the letter and either modify and sign or merely sign the letter. The letter shall be signed and mailed within **ten working days.**

c. For all Category II complaints, the complainant will be notified by a letter prepared by the Office and signed by the Chief of Police or his designee. The letter will be signed and mailed within **ten working days.**

d. Within ten working days, the Chief of Police will notify the department member(s) by letter of the disposition and any related disciplinary action. The letter will be disseminated through the appropriate chain of command in accordance with current policy.

2. Unsubstantiated, exonerated, and closed cases

   a. If the Chief of Police concurs with the recommendation that a complaint be classified as unsubstantiated, exonerated, or closed, the Office Director will close the case. Notifications will be handled as outlined in Annex E, Section B, 1, a-c.

   b. For both Category I and Category II complaints, the member will be notified by letter prepared by the Office and signed by the Chief of Police or his designee. The letter will be signed and mailed within ten working days.

3. After final disposition, new or previously undisclosed evidence may become available. The member via chain of command, or the complainant may request the Office Director or the Secretary-Attorney of the Board, to reconsider the decision of the Office. This request for reconsideration is limited to the findings of the Office and does not pertain to disciplinary actions.

ACCESS TO CENTRAL COMPLAINT INVESTIGATION FILE

A. Access to the Central Complaint Investigation File will be strictly controlled by the Office Director. The Office Director may remove any information from a Complaint Investigation File which the Chief of Police believes is reasonably necessary to protect confidentiality or security.

B. The subject member of the complaint, the member's attorney, the complainant's attorney have the right to review, but not photocopy, the completed investigation file.

C. Access to completed investigative files will be limited to behavioral performance evaluations by commanding officers.

D. Records, files, subpoenas, documents, and materials compiled and maintained in the Office of Citizen Complaints, pertaining to internal investigations resulting from citizen complaints, shall not be subject to disclosure, except as described above.

E. The Legal Advisor will be contacted in regard to any request for the reproduction of any part of the investigative file.

Document No. 14

Minneapolis

Minneapolis Civilian Police
Review Authority

Administrative
RULES

Approved by the Board of Directors of the
Minneapolis Civilian Review Authority

Wednesday, October 31, 1990

TABLE OF CONTENTS

Source of Authority 1

Effective Date 1

Purpose 1

Application 2

Scope of Authority 2

Period of Limitation 2

Interpreters 2

Assistance and Information from Authority 3

Severability 3

Collection and Dissemination of Data 3

- Responsible Authority 3
- Types of Data 3
  - Investigative Data 4
  - Criminal Data which is Confidential 4
  - Public Data 4
- Request for Access to Data 5
- Denial of Access to Data 5
- Charge for Providing Requested Data 5

Liability of Board Members 5

Amendment of Rules 5

Definitions 6

Standing to File a Complaint 11

- Information Required 12

Amendment of Complaint 12

Withdrawal of Complaint 13

Initial Intake 13

(Table of Contents Continued)

Notice of Receipt of Signed Complaint 13
Preliminary Review 14
Dismissal 14
Mediation 15
Investigation 16
Conclusion of Investigation 18
No Probable Cause Determination 18
Evidentiary Hearing 19
Duties of Hearing Panel 19
Personal Bias or Prejudice 20
Discretionary Withdrawal by Panel Member 20
Request for Withdrawal by Hearing Panel Member 20
Pre-Evidentiary Hearing Conference 21
Consolidation 22
Rules of Evidence 23
Burden and Standard of Proof 23
Affirmative Defense 23
Failure to Appear at the Evidentiary Hearing 23
Order of Procedure 24
Continuance 26
Record of Hearing 27
Disposition 27
    Time Limit 27
    Findings of Fact and Determination 28
    Reconsideration 28
Submission to Chief for Disciplinary Action 28

MINNEAPOLIS CIVILIAN POLICE REVIEW AUTHORITY
ADMINISTRATIVE RULES

1.0 Source of Authority

1.01 The Minneapolis Civilian Police Review Authority, hereinafter referred to as the "Authority," was established by Ordinance of the City of Minneapolis January 26, 1990. The Authority includes a Board of seven members, an Executive Director, Investigators, and Administrative Staff. (Minneapolis Code of Ordinances, Title 9, Chapter 172.)

1.1 Effective Date

1.11 The effective date of the following Rules is January 1, 1991.

1.12 Purpose

1.121 The purpose of the following Rules of Procedure is to facilitate and guide the independent civilian police review process in Minneapolis, Minnesota. This process shall be based on due regard for the Constitutional and Legal Rights of all persons, and shall promote the highest possible degree of mutual respect between the Minneapolis Police Department and the Community.

1.122 To achieve this purpose, the Authority shall receive, consider, investigate and make a determination regarding complaints or grievances brought by the Public against any Minneapolis Police Officer. These Rules provide for the impartial, independent and prompt investigation and disposition of complaints and grievances in a manner which protects the Public and Individual Officers of the Minneapolis Police Department who may become involved in such complaints.

1.123 The Authority shall encourage members of the Public to bring forward legitimate complaints concerning abuse and improper conduct. The desired result of the Authority and of these rules is to strengthen public confidence and to assure that the highest standards of professionalism are observed in the handling and disposition of allegations of abuse of authority.

1.124 The provisions of these Rules shall be liberally construed to achieve these objectives.

1.13 **Application**

1.131 The following Rules shall be employed by the Authority to govern the receipt and processing of Complaints. The Authority shall provide information concerning its findings of fact, determinations and other relevant information, subject to the provisions and limitations of the law.

1.14 **Scope of Authority**

1.141 The Authority shall receive complaints that allege misconduct by an individual police officer or officers acting in their own discretion, including, but not limited to the following:

a. use of excessive force;
b. inappropriate language or attitude;
c. harassment;
d. discrimination in the provision of police services or other discriminatory conduct on the basis of race, color, creed, religion, ancestry, national origin, sex, affectional preference, disability or age;
e. theft;
f. failure to provide adequate or timely police protection. (Ord. §172.20)

1.142 Under the above provision, (d) and (f) constitute misconduct only if the activity involved is within the individual officer's control, as opposed to a failure to provide services or protection based on a system failure.

1.15 **Period of Limitation**

1.151 A complaint must be filed with the Authority within one (1) year of the time of the alleged misconduct. (Ord. §172.160)

1.16 **Interpreters**

1.161 The Executive Director shall have discretionary authority to provisionally qualify, utilize and compensate interpreters. Each party in need of an interpreter shall give notice to the Authority within seven (7) days of receipt of the Notice of Hearing so that appropriate arrangements may be made.

1.162 The Rules of Confidentiality shall apply to an interpreter utilized in any stage of the review process including, but not limited to a mediation session, interview or evidentiary hearing. The interpreter shall not have had any personal or professional involvement with any of the issues of the particular case prior to the hearing.

1.17 **Assistance and Information From Authority**

1.171 If any party desires assistance or information, which can legally be made public, he or she may request such from the Authority. This may include, but is not limited to: assistance in filling out forms; having rules read, explained and/or interpreted; distributing of public information; and keeping the parties to a Complaint regularly informed on the progress of their particular case, in accordance with the provisions of the Minnesota Government Data Practices Act and §1.2 of these Rules.

1.18 **Severability**

1.181 If any provision of this set of Rules or the application thereof to any person or circumstance is held to be invalid, such invalidity shall not affect other provisions of the rule or application of any other part of this regulation which can be given effect without application of the invalid provision. To this end the provisions of all sections, subsections, or subdivisions herein and the various applications thereof are declared to be severable.

1.2 **Collection and Dissemination of Data**

1.21 **Responsible Authority**

1.211 The Executive Director is the "Responsible Authority" and as such is responsible for assuring that the Authority complies with the Minnesota Government Data Practices Act, of the Minnesota Code, and applicable Ordinances of the City of Minneapolis and applicable provisions of these Rules.

1.22 **Types of Data**

1.221 All data collected by the Authority shall be considered personnel data and, as such, is private data, as defined by Minnesota Government Data Practices, §13.43, except for that data described in the following sections of these Rules: §1.222, §1.223, §1.23, §1.24 and §1.25.

1.222 Some personnel and, therefore, private data shall become public upon final disposition of a disciplinary case, as defined by the Minnesota Government Data Practices Act, §13.43 Sub. 2(b).

1.223 Investigative data and certain criminal data shall be considered confidential, in accordance with these Rules (§1.23 and §1.24) and as defined by Minnesota Government Data Practices Act (§13.02 and §13.82).

1.23 **Investigative Data**

1.232 Data created or collected by the Authority which is part of an active investigation is confidential data until the Executive Director makes a Probable Cause Determination or No Probable Cause Determination, as described in these Rules below (§6.161), at which point the data collected in the investigation and the summary thereof shall become private or nonpublic data. Nothing in this subsection shall be construed to make nonpublic that data that is already designated as public by law and these Rules.

1.24 **Criminal Data which is Confidential**

1.241 The Executive Director may, in consultation with the Chief and the City Attorney and/or County Attorney, classify as confidential certain data created and collected by the Authority in the course of the investigation of a complaint and which the Executive Director determines are or probably will be material in a criminal case.

1.25 **Public Data**

1.251 The following data created and collected by the Authority shall be public:

a. The name and address of the Complainant;
b. The name, rank and job description of the Officer;
c. The fact that a complaint has been filed against the Officer;
d. The status of a Complaint. The following shall be considered status information:
    1. The fact that a Complaint has been withdrawn by the Complainant;
    2. The fact that a Complaint has been dismissed;
    3. The fact that a Complaint is in mediation;
    4. The fact that a mediation agreement has been reached;
    5. The fact that a Complaint is being investigated;
    6. The fact that a Complaint has been referred to an Evidentiary Hearing Panel;
    7. The fact that the Officer has been exonerated:
    8. The fact that a Complaint has been referred to the Chief;
e. The final disposition of any disciplinary action, together with the specific reasons for the action and data documenting the basis of the action, excluding data that would identify confidential sources who are employees of the City of Minneapolis.

1.26 **Request for Access to Data**

1.261 Upon request to the Executive Director, a person shall be permitted to inspect and/or copy public data at reasonable times and places. Upon request, a person shall be informed of the data's meaning.

1.27 **Denial of Access to Data**

1.271 If the Executive Director determines that the requested data is classified so as to deny the requesting person access, the Executive Director or his or her designee shall inform the requesting person of the determination either orally at the time of the request, or in writing as soon after that time as possible, and shall cite the specific statutory section, temporary classification, or specific provision of law on which the determination is based. Upon the request of any person denied access to data, the responsible authority or designee shall certify in writing that the request has been denied and cite the specific statutory section, temporary classification, or specific provision of law upon which denial was based.

1.28 **Charge for Providing Requested Data**

1.281 If a person requests data for the purpose of inspection, the responsible authority may not assess a charge or require the requesting party to pay a fee to inspect the data. However, if a person requests copies, or electronic transmittal of the data to the person, the Authority may require the requesting person to pay the actual costs of searching for and retrieving government data, but may not charge for separating public from not public data. If the Authority is not able to provide copies at the time a request is made, copies shall be supplied as soon as reasonably possible.

1.3 **Liability of Board Members**

1.30 No member of the Board of the Authority shall be liable to any person for damages or equitable relief by reason of any action taken or recommendation made by a Board member or by the Authority, if the action taken was within the scope of the functions of the Authority and if the Board member acted in the reasonable belief that such member's action was warranted by the facts known to such member after reasonable effort to obtain the facts of the matter.

1.31 **Amendment of Rules**

1.311 These Rules may be altered or amended at any regular or special meeting of the Authority by vote of the full Board, but only after appropriate notice and public hearing, consultation with the Minneapolis Chief of Police and others, and subject to approval by the Minneapolis City Council.

2.001 Whenever used in these Rules, unless plainly evident from the context that a different meaning is intended, the following terms mean:

2.01 ***Adequate and timely***

2.011 Such length of time as may fairly, properly, and reasonably be allowed or required, having regard to the nature of the act or duty, or of the subject-matter, and to the attending circumstances.

2.02 ***Authority***

2.021 The Minneapolis Civilian Police Review Authority. The Authority includes a Board of seven members, an Executive Director, Investigators and Administrative Staff. (Minneapolis Code of Ordinances, Title 9, Chapter 172.)

2.03 ***Board***

2.031 The Board of Directors of the Minneapolis Civilian Police Review Authority, which consists of seven members.

2.04 ***Chief***

2.041 The Chief of Police in the City of Minneapolis.

2.05 ***Clear and Convincing***

2.051 The standard of proof in the evidentiary hearings.

2.052 "Clear and Convincing" means that measure or degree of proof which will produce in the mind of the trier(s) of fact a firm belief or conviction as to allegations sought to be established; it is intermediate, being more than mere preponderance, but not to the extent of such certainty as is required by beyond a reasonable doubt.

2.06 ***Complainant***

2.061 The person filing a complaint with the Minneapolis Civilian Police Review Authority who alleges that he/she has been aggrieved by the conduct of a sworn Officer or Officers of the Minneapolis Police Department.

2.07 ***Complaint***

2.071 The allegation, signed and sworn, by a complainant regarding an Officer or Officers of the Minneapolis Police Department.

2.08 ***Conference***

2.081 The Pre-evidentiary Hearing Conference. This conference will he held prior to the evidentiary hearing, with the Hearing Panel Chairperson, the Officer and/or his/her representative, the Complainant, and the Executive Director in attendance, for purposes of planning for the orderly, expeditious and fair conduct of the evidentiary hearing.

2.09 ***Confidential Data***

2.091 The Minnesota Government Data Practices Act defines "confidential data on individuals" as data which cannot be made public and is inaccessible to the individual subject of that data.

2.10 ***Day***

2.101 Monday through Friday, except holidays recognized by the City of Minneapolis, during regular business hours.

2.11 ***Department***

2.111 The Minneapolis Police Department.

2.12 ***Deputy Chief***

2.121 The appropriate deputy chief assigned to the division of the accused officer.

2.13 ***Discrimination***

2.131 Disparate treatment of persons because of their race, color, creed, religion, ancestry, national origin, sex, affectional preference, disability or age.

2.14 ***Executive Director***

2.141 A person hired by the Authority, required to be an Attorney-at-Law, to manage the ongoing operation of the Authority and to execute functions to aid the Authority in carrying out its purpose.

2.15 ***Excessive Force***

2.151 The officer's particular use of force was not "objectively reasonable" in light of the facts and circumstances confronting the Officer without regard to the officer's underlying intent or motivation. The "reasonableness" of a particular use of force must be judged from the perspective of a reasonable officer on the scene, and its calculus must embody an allowance for the fact that police officers are often forced to make split-second decisions abut the amount of force necessary in a particular situation. Factors to be considered include the following: 1) The severity of the crime at issue; 2) whether the suspect posed an immediate threat to the safety of officers or others, and 3) whether the subject was actively resisting arrest or attempting to evade arrest by flight. (Graham v. Connor, 109 S. Ct. 1865, 104 L. Ed. 2d 443, 1989.)

2.16 ***Family***

2.161 Relation to Complainant because of immediate family status, adoption, or by being a significant other.

2.17 ***Final Disposition***

2.171 A final disposition occurs when the Chief makes a final disciplinary decision, regardless of the possibility of any later proceedings or court proceedings. In the case of proceedings before the Minneapolis Civil Service Commission or arbitration proceedings arising under collective bargaining agreements, a final disposition occurs at the conclusion of the Civil Service Commission or arbitration proceedings.

2.18 ***Garrity Warning***

2.181 Under <u>Garrity v. New Jersey</u>, 385 U.S. 493 (1967), and <u>Gardner v. Broderick, Police Commissioner of New York</u>, 392 U.S. 273 (1968), a police officer can be ordered to give a statement regarding actions taken by him/her while employed with the Minneapolis Police Department. The failure to answer such questions, pertaining only to the scope of their duty, may form the basis of an officer's dismissal or result in disciplinary proceedings against that officer. The rights of an officer in regard to this warning are that any statements given under this warning, or the fruits thereof, compelled as a condition of employment, cannot then be used in any subsequent criminal proceeding against the employee except in cases of alleged perjury by the employee giving the statements where the criminal charge is based upon the falsity of the statement given.

2.19 ***Harassment***

2.191 Inappropriate words, gestures, and other actions which are intended to annoy, alarm or abuse another person.

2.20 ***Hearing Panel***

2.201 The evidentiary hearing panel, consisting of one (1), three (3), five (5) or seven (7) persons, appointed by the Authority Chairperson to conduct the hearing and make Findings of Fact and Determinations.

2.21 ***Inappropriate language or Conduct***

2.211 That language or action, which under the circumstances may be rendered inappropriate. This may include, but is not limited to such conduct as racial, sexual or ethnic slurs (i.e., the use of any common or slang terms, which are generally perceived to be derogatory in nature to refer to any member of a racial, ethnic, religious group, or to refer to any person's nationality, sex or sexual preference, or which may constitute sexual harassment).

2.22 ***Investigator***

2.221 A person, hired by the Authority, who is a civilian with prior experience or training as an investigator, to conduct the Authority's complaint investigations. A civilian, for purposes of this provision, is a person who is not now, nor has ever been a sworn officer of the Minneapolis Police Department.

2.23 ***Mediation***

2.231 An informal dispute resolution process, facilitated by a neutral third party, whereby the Complainant and the Officer mutually agree to amicably come together to try to resolve the issue(s) of the Complaint.

2.24 ***Mediator***

2.241 A neutral third party in contract with the Authority to mediate disputes between Complainants and Officers.

2.25 ***Order to Cooperate***

2.251 The Minneapolis Police Department and all other City of Minneapolis employees and officials, by ordinance shall, except as expressly prohibited by any other law, respond promptly to any and all reasonable requests for information, for participation in evidentiary hearings, and for access to data and records for the purposes of enabling the Authority to carry out its responsibilities. The failure by any official or employee of the Minneapolis Police Department or by any other City of Minneapolis employee or official to comply with such requests for information, participation, or access shall be deemed an act of misconduct.

2.26 ***Officer***

2.261 A sworn Officer or Officers of the Minneapolis Police Department against whom an allegation of misconduct has been made in a Complaint.

2.27 ***Perjury***

2.271 The willful assertion as to a matter of fact, opinion, belief or knowledge, made by a witness in an Authority proceeding as part of his/her evidence, either upon oath or in any form allowed by law to be substituted for an oath, whether such evidence is given in person in an evidentiary hearing, or in an affidavit, or otherwise, such assertion being material to the issue or point of inquiry and known to such witness to be false.

2.272 A person is guilty of perjury if in any official proceedings s/he makes a false statement under oath or equivalent affirmation, or swears or affirms the truth of a statement previously made, when the statement is material and s/he does not believe it to be true.

2.28 ***Person***

2.281 One who may file a Complaint: an adult, a minor with an adult's assistance, an adult filing on behalf of a minor, or a vulnerable adult with assistance from a family member, a guardian or other court appointed representative.

2.29 ***Personal Knowledge***

2.291 Direct knowledge of the allegations or incident from which the allegations arose, namely the victim of the alleged misconduct by an Officer or a witness to that alleged misconduct.

2.30 ***Private Data***

2.301 The Minnesota Government Data Practices Act defines "private data on individuals" as data that is not public and is accessible to the individual subject of that data.

2.31 ***Public Data***

2.311 The Minnesota Government Data Practices Act defines "public data not on individuals" and "public data on individuals" as data which is accessible to the public.

2.32 ***Review Panel***

2.321 A Panel of Board members appointed, when the Executive Director makes a No Probable Cause determination, to review and determine the adequacy of the investigation in the case and/or the appropriateness of the No Probable Cause determination.

2.33 ***Tennessen Warning***

2.331 "Tennessen Warning" is the title given to the notice which the Minnesota Government Data Practices Act requires the Department to give to an individual when the Department asks the Officer to provide private or confidential data about him/herself. In this "Warning," individuals must be informed of the following:

a. Why the data is being collected and how it will be used within the Authority and the Department collecting it;
b. Whether the individual is legally required to provide the data or may refuse to do so;
c. What the consequences are to the individual of either providing or not providing the data; and
d. The identities of other persons and agencies who have a legal right to have access to the data being provided.

2.332 The Authority and the Department must then take appropriate steps to ensure that the data is only used and only disseminated consistent with what has been stated in the "Warning."

2.33 ***Tolled***

2.331 When time limitations established within these rules are suspended or temporarily stopped because of other procedures.

2.34 ***Vulnerable Adult***

2.341 Vulnerable adult" means any person 18 years of age or older:

a. Who is a resident or inpatient of a facility (a hospital or other entity required to be licensed pursuant to sections 144.50 to 144.58 of Minn. Stat.; a nursing home required to be licensed to serve adults pursuant to section 144A.02 of Minn. Stat.; an agency, day care facility or residential facility licensed to serve adults pursuant to sections 245.781 to 245.812 of Minn. Stat.; or a home care provider licensed under section 144A.46);
b. Who receives services at or from a facility required to be licensed under sections 245.781 to 245.812, except a person receiving outpatient services for treatment of chemical dependency or mental illness;
c. Who receives services from a home care provider licensed under section 144A.46 of Minn. Stat.; or
d. Who, regardless of residence or type of service received, is unable or unlikely to report abuse or neglect without assistance because of impairment of mental or physical function or emotional status. (Minn. Stat. §626.557.)

3.0 **Standing to File a Complaint**

3.01 Any person who has personal knowledge of alleged misconduct on the part of an Officer may file a complaint with the Authority by submitting a complaint either by telephone, in writing, or in person at locations to be determined by the Authority.

3.02 No complaint will be deemed filed with the Authority until it has been reduced to writing and signed by the Complainant. Until a complaint is reduced to writing and signed by the complainant, the Complaint shall be treated as a tentative complaint and held in a "pending" file until a formal complaint is made.

3.03 Complaint forms will conclude with the following words: "I hereby certify that to the best of my knowledge, and under penalty of perjury, the statements made herein are true." No criminal charges of perjury will be brought without the concurrences of the Chief and the Authority.

3.04 At least one of the above-mentioned locations will not be affiliated with the Department, nor staffed by Department employees.

3.05 "Person" means a victim of the alleged misconduct or a witness of the alleged misconduct, as referenced in §3.01 of these Rules.

3.06 Exceptions to §3.05 are:

a. In the case of a minor, the parent or legal guardian may file a complaint on behalf of the minor.
b. In a case involving the death of a person, a family member may file a complaint on behalf of the deceased.
c. In the case of a vulnerable adult, a family member, conservator or legal guardian may file a complaint on behalf of the vulnerable adult.

3.1 **Information Required**

3.11 The Complainant must provide, at a minimum, the following information:

a. Name, address, telephone number, date of birth; if pursuant to §3.06, a complaint has been filed on behalf of someone else, this information concerning the minor, deceased person or the vulnerable adult must also be filed.
b. Alternate means of contact; if pursuant to §3.06, a complaint has been filed on behalf of someone else, this information concerning the minor or the vulnerable adult must also be filed;
c. Written statement setting forth the allegation(s), including: date, time and location of the alleged misconduct and any other pertinent details;
d. Identification of police officer (badge and/or name and/or description).

3.12 **Amendment of Complaint**

3.121 A signed complaint may be amended until thirty (30) days after its initial filing.

3.122 Circumstances under which a Complainant may amend his/her Complaint include, but are not limited to, new evidence having been obtained such as a new witness coming forward or the recollection of pertinent information.

3.123 This amendment must also be in written form and signed under penalty of perjury.

3.13 **Withdrawal of Complaint**

3.131 A Complainant may withdraw from the review process at any point in the proceedings by submitting a written, dated and signed notice to the Authority of the complainant's intentions to withdraw. The signed withdrawal statement must include an affirmation that the Complainant has not been coerced or intimidated into withdrawing the Complaint.

3.132 In the case of such withdrawal, the Executive Director may give the case file to the Chief, if:

a. The Executive Director determines that the file contents could be material in a criminal case; or
b. `The Chief makes a request for the file.

3.2 **Initial Intake**

3.21 Complaints will be gathered by the Authority staff from all intake areas from the previous working day.

3.22 A file will be opened for each Complainant as of the date the complaint is received in the office of the Authority.

3.23 If a signed complaint is not received at the office of the Authority within fifteen (15) days of the initial receipt, the Authority will close the file until such time as the Complainant submits a signed complaint.

3.24 This stopping of the complaint process does not prevent the Complainant from filing another complaint within the prescribed limitations period of the Minneapolis Code of Ordinances, Title 9, Chapter 172, §172.160, and these Rules.

3.25 In unusual circumstances, the Executive Director may authorize an investigation to begin prior to the end of the fifteen (15) day period for receiving a signed complaint. However, at the end of the fifteen (15) day period, the investigation must stop and the file will be closed.

3.3 **Notice of Receipt of Signed Complaint**

3.31 The Complainant shall receive written notice of receipt of their signed complaint. This Notice shall be mailed no later than five (5) business days from the date of the receipt of the signed Complaint in the Office of the Authority.

3.32 Notice of the filing of a signed complaint and of the specific allegations contained therein will be forwarded to the Officer, the Deputy Chief, and the Chief of Police, within five (5) days of the filing of a signed complaint.

3.33 A copy of the Authority Rules delineating the procedures will be forwarded to all parties along with the Notice of Receipt of the Complaint.

3.4 Preliminary Review

3.41 In the interest of expediting the processes of the Authority, and without compromising any parties' claim(s), the Authority has delegated to the Executive Director the authority to make an initial decision based upon a Preliminary Review.

3.411 Within thirty (30) days of the date that a signed complaint is filed, the Executive Director shall make one of the following three (3) decisions:

a. recommend the case for mediation;
b. that no further action warranted (dismissal); or
c. forward the case to investigation.

4.0 Dismissal

4.01 The reasons for Dismissal of a Complaint may include but are not limited to the following:

a. No dispute as to material fact exists. And, no reasonable person could sustain a complaint based upon such facts;
b. Even if all of the complainant's alleged statements are true, no act of misconduct exists;
c. The alleged facts are so unbelievable that no reasonable person could sustain the complaint based on such facts;
d. Failure of the complainant to cooperate.

4.02 Upon dismissal of a complaint, the Executive Director shall prepare a written report stating his/her reason(s), which report shall be sent to the Chairperson of the Authority and to the Complainant and the Officer.

4.03 If the Complainant disagrees with the dismissal, he/she may submit a written appeal to the Board for review of the Executive Director's decision.

4.031 The Board, at its next regular meeting, shall either:

a. ratify the Executive Director's decision; or
b. refer the case back to the Executive Director for a decision regarding mediation or investigation.

4.032 The Complainant and the Officer shall receive written notice of the Board's decision.

5.0 Mediation

5.11 The Authority shall inform all Complainants and Officers of the possibility of mediation as an alternative to the Authority's processes. Mediation is an informal process, held before a neutral third party, attended by the Complainant and the Officer for the purpose of fully, thoroughly, and frankly discussing the alleged misconduct and attempting to arrive at a mutually agreeable resolution of the Complaint.

5.12 In cases in which the Executive Director decides not to dismiss the complain, he/she may decide that the case is appropriate for mediation.

5.13 The Executive Director shall inform the Chief of this decision to proceed to mediation.

5.14 Mediation shall not be available to an Officer who has participated in mediation, under the auspices of the Authority, for a serious similar misconduct allegation or a similar misconduct allegation within the previous 12 months.

5.15 This determination shall be communicated to the Complainant and the Officer. Both the Complainant and the Officer must agree to mediation, within ten (10) days of receiving notice of the Executive Director's referral to mediation, for it to proceed, otherwise, the case shall be referred to investigation.

5.16 If the Complainant and the Officer agree, the Authority shall schedule a mediation session at the earliest convenient time. Written notice of the time, date and location of the first mediation session shall be provided each party.

5.17 The mediation session(s) will consist of the Complainant, the Officer, and the Mediator. In the case of a minor, a parent or legal guardian must be present. In the case of a vulnerable adult, a family member, conservator or legal guardian must be present. If an interpreter is requested, arrangements will be made to have one present upon request by either party. No other person may be present. No record of the proceeding will be taken.

5.18 Procedures and guidelines for mediation will be established at the beginning of the mediation process through agreement of all participants.

5.19 The mediation session(s) will continue as long as the mediator and the parties feel progress is being made in the resolution of the issues. The mediation process shall terminate when either party announces its unwillingness to continue mediation or when the parties sign an agreement setting forth the resolution of the disputed issue(s).

5.20 However, in no case shall the time for mediation extend beyond thirty (30) days from the date the Authority has received notice of willingness to participate in mediation from both the Complainant and the Officer. In order to facilitate and encourage mediation, the Authority time limitations and deadlines will be tolled during mediation.

5.21 The Authority or its designated agent shall monitor the mediation process and the implementation of a mediation agreement. If one party fails to abide by this agreement, the aggrieved party may pursue a hearing before the Authority.

5.22 No record will be made of the mediation proceedings, and no information discussed will be used in subsequent proceedings. (Minn. Stat. §595.02, Subd. 1(k) (1989)).

5.23 A copy of the mediation agreement will not be sent to the Chief.

6.0 Investigation

6.01 Upon a determination that there is reason to believe that a violation may have occurred in accordance with the City of Minneapolis Code of Ordinances, Title 9, Chapter 172, §172.20, the Authority shall proceed with an investigation of the complaint.

6.1 Time Limit

6.11 The investigation shall be completed within one-hundred and twenty (120) days of the date a signed complaint was filed. The Authority may once extend this deadline by an additional sixty (60) days with written explanation of the reason(s) for the extension. (Ord. §172.90)

6.12 Consultation with the Chief

6.121 Before beginning the investigation, the Executive Director shall consult with the Chief on all pertinent matters regarding the pending investigation. The Executive Director and the Chief shall discuss the possibility of a criminal investigation and charge.

6.13 Criminal Investigation and/or Charges

6.131 The Executive Director shall also consult with the City Attorney and the County Attorney to determine if there is a related current criminal investigation.

6.132 After the above-mentioned consultations, the Executive Director has the discretion to hold its process in abeyance, if such investigation might impede or harm a criminal investigation. If the Authority's investigation is held in abeyance, the Authority time constraints shall be tolled. (Ord. §172.90)

6.133 During such time as the Authority may hold its proceedings in abeyance, the Authority shall request the Chief to take the appropriate steps to assure preservation of the following items of evidence:

a. The original Emergency Communications Center ("ECC") tapes relevant to the complaint;
b. All police reports, records, evidence and any other documentation relevant to the case;
c. Names, Addresses, Telephone Numbers, and any Statements or other information from Witnesses.

6.14 Notice to Chief of Police

6.141 Once a decision has been made by the Executive Director or the Board to proceed with an investigation, a "Notice to Give Garrity Warning" shall be sent, by the Executive Director, to the Chief requesting him/her to order the Officer(s) to cooperate with the investigation. With this order to cooperate, the Chief shall give a Garrity Warning.

6.15 Requirement of Cooperation in Investigation

6.151 The Minneapolis Police Department and all other City of Minneapolis employees and officials shall, except as expressly prohibited by law, respond promptly to any and all reasonable requests for information, for participation in evidentiary hearings, and for access to data and records for the purpose of enabling the Authority to carry out its responsibilities under this Chapter. The failure by an official or employee of the Minneapolis Police Department or by any other City of Minneapolis employee or official to comply with such requests for information, participation, or access shall be deemed an act of misconduct, unless such failure to comply is pursuant to the Officer's or employee's statutory or constitutional rights. (Ord. §172.120)

6.152 If the Chief fails to cooperate with the Authority in giving the order to cooperate, and the Garrity Warning, the Chief shall, in writing, state his/her reasons for doing so and submit said reasons to the Mayor. The Mayor shall either sustain the Chief's decision, or order the Chief to cooperate.

6.16 Copies of Sworn Statements

6.161 The Officer, Complainant and any witnesses, shall, upon their request, be given a true and correct copy of their own signed, sworn statement(s) without unnecessary delay.

6.171 At the conclusion of the Investigation, the Investigator shall forward the file with a report of findings to the Executive Director. The Executive Director shall then make one of two determinations:

a. There is Probable Cause to believe that a violation of Minneapolis City Ordinance, Title 9, Chapter 172, §172.20 has occurred and therefore the matter shall proceed to an Evidentiary Hearing; or
b. There is No Probable Cause to believe that a violation of Minneapolis City Ordinance, Title 9, Chapter 172, §172.20 has occurred and the Complaint shall be dismissed as:
   1. Officer exonerated, for one of two reasons:
      (a) The facts alleged in the complaint are true but do not constitute misconduct by the Officer; or
      (b) The facts alleged in the complaint are not true; or
   2. Insufficient evidence to sustain the complaint.

6.18 No Probable Cause Determination

6.181 If there is a No Probable Cause determination by the Executive Director, the Complainant, the Officer, and the Police Chief shall be notified in writing within five (5) days.

6.182 If the Complainant disagrees with the No Probable Cause determination, s/he may, in writing petition the Authority Chairperson to appoint a Review Panel. The petition shall specifically state:

a. the inadequacies of the investigation; and
b. how these inadequacies should be remedied.

6.183 In response to this petition from the Complainant, the Chairperson of the Authority may, upon review of the merits of the petition, appoint a Review Panel of no more than three members of the Board.

6.184 The purpose of a Review Panel is not to receive evidence, but merely to assess whether additional investigation is warranted. The Executive Director shall make a presentation to the Review Panel on how the investigation has been conducted (e.g., who was interviewed, what documents have been obtained, etc.). The Complainant may very briefly present arguments on additional persons who should be interviewed and/or additional documents and materials to be collected.

6.185 The Review Panel shall either

a. Sustain the No Probable Cause determination;
b. Refer the case back to the Executive Director for specific additional investigation; or
c. Make a Probable Cause determination and refer the case for Evidentiary Hearing.

7.0 Evidentiary Hearing

7.01 When the Executive Director makes a Probable Cause determination, he/she shall inform the Chairperson of the Authority. Within five (5) days, he/she shall give notice to the Complainant, the Officer and the Chief. The notice to the Officer shall include the specific findings of the Probable Cause Determination.

7.011 The Authority shall make reasonable efforts to commence and complete an evidentiary hearing within forty-five (45) days, but no longer than sixty (60) days, of the Executive Director giving notice of a Probable Cause determination.

7.012 The Chairperson of the Authority shall appoint a Hearing Panel, within five (5) days of receipt of the Probable Cause determination, of one, three, five, or seven members of the Board to conduct an evidentiary hearing.

7.013 The Authority Chairperson shall designate a Chairperson for each Panel.

7.014 Notice of the membership of the Hearing Panel shall be given, within five (5) days of the appointment of the Panel, to the Complainant and the Officer.

7.015 The Authority Chairperson may appoint a Hearing Panel of one member in cases in which the evidence is not significantly controverted and in which the Authority's processes will be expedited by the appointment of one-member Panel.

7.016 If a written objection to a one-member Panel is filed within five (5) days of receipt of the "Notice of the Appointment of the Hearing Panel," by either the Complainant, or the Officer, the Authority Chairperson shall appoint a Hearing Panel of at least three members.

7.1 Duties of Hearing Panel

7.11 It shall be the duty of each Hearing Panel member to conduct a fair and impartial hearing, to assure that the facts are fully elicited, and to adjudicate all issues and avoid undue delay.

7.12 Subject to the Rules and Regulations of the Authority and laws of the City of Minneapolis and the State of Minnesota, the Hearing Panel shall have the following authority with respect to the cases between the time the cases are assigned to it and the time it makes its findings of fact and determination.

a. Administer Oaths and Affirmations;
b. Rule on Evidentiary Issues;
c. Regulate the course of the Hearing;
d. If appropriate or necessary, expel persons from the hearing for contemptuous conduct;
e. Examine witnesses;
f. Adjourn the hearing as the needs of justice and good administration require;
g. Take other action as necessary, as authorized by the Rules and Regulations of the Authority.

7.13 **Personal Bias or Prejudice**

7.131 A Hearing Panel Member shall be disqualified from sitting on that Hearing Panel if he/she has a demonstrated personal bias or prejudice, or the appearance thereof, in the outcome of the Complaint. This does not include holding or manifesting any political or social attitude or belief which does not preclude objective consideration of a case on its merits.

7.132 Examples of personal bias or prejudice include, but are not limited to:

a. Familial relationship, close friendship or close working relationship with parties material to the Complaint;
b. Witnessing events material to the inquiry;
c. Being a party to the Complaint;
d. Holding a bias for or against a particular party that is sufficient to impair the Panel member's impartiality;
e. Having a financial interest in the outcome of the Hearing.

7.14 **Discretionary Withdrawl by Hearing Panel Member**

7.141 A member of a Hearing Panel may withdraw from that panel whenever that member deems himself or herself to be disqualified.

7.15 **Request for Withdrawl by a Party to the Case**

7.151 Within five (5) days of receipt of the notice of membership of the Hearing Panel, either the Executive Director, the Complainant or the Officer may file with the Chairperson of the Authority, a written challenge, for cause, to a member of the Hearing Panel.

7.152 Cause is limited to those definitions of personal bias or prejudice delineated in § 7.132 above. When a challenge for cause is filed, the Chairperson shall contact the challenged Hearing Panel Member as soon as possible. If the Authority Chairperson and the challenged Hearing Panel Member agree that the challenge is for good cause, then the member shall withdraw and the Chairperson of the Authority shall appoint another board member as a replacement.

7.153 If the challenged Panel Member does not agree that the challenge is for good cause, the Chairperson shall decide the merits of the challenge and replace the Member or not. If a challenge to a Panel Member is rejected, the written challenge and the Chairperson's written response shall be incorporated into the record.

7.2 **Pre-Evidentiary Hearing Conference**

7.201 The Authority, after designation of the Hearing Panel, shall direct the Officer and his/her counsel, by written notice, to appear, along with the Executive Director, at a specified time, date and location for a Conference.

7.202 A Conference held under this section shall be held at such time as the Hearing Panel Chairperson may specify, in no case, more than fifteen (15) days from either the Notice of membership of the Hearing Panel or the resolution of all challenges to members of the Hearing Panel.

7.203 This Conference is not for presentation of evidence, but for the exchange of relevant information. The Conference shall be conducted by the Hearing Panel Chairperson for the following purposes:

a. simplification, clarification, and specification of the issues;
b. obtaining of stipulations, any agreed upon admissions of fact, the contents and authenticity of any and all documents to avoid unnecessary proof, and any known, subsequent requests for subpoenaed information;
c. identification of any and all witnesses known to the parties at that time, any known, subsequent requests for witness subpoenas, and the limitation of the number, if any, of expert witnesses;
d. sharing of pertinent information, whether inculpatory or exculpatory, including exchanging summaries expressing the nature of witness(es) testimony;
e. other steps necessary to expedite the presentation of evidence;
f. The time, date and setting of the evidentiary hearing; notice of which will be sent to each party, at least ten (10) days prior to the scheduled hearing. This scheduling shall be conducted with due regard for the work schedules of the Officer and the Complainant; and
g. Such matters as may aid in the orderly disposition of the proceeding.

actions taken at the Conference. This shall control the subsequent course of proceedings unless modified for good cause.

7.2051 If settlement is reached at this Conference, the Hearing Panel Chairperson shall draft a written settlement agreement and have it signed by both parties. This agreement shall then be entered into the file. The implementation of this settlement will be monitored by the Authority.

7.2052 In order for a settlement to be reached, the Executive Director shall have received from the Complainant a signed authorization to attempt a settlement. Such settlement requires the subsequent agreement of the Complainant.

7.21 **Failure to Appear at Prehearing Conference**
7.211 The failure of a party to appear at the Conference may result in a decision against that party. The Officer may, in advance, request that his/her presence be waived if they choose to have a representative at the Conference.

7.212 Requests for a new Conference must be made, in the absence of extraordinary circumstances, within five (5) days after the scheduled Conference date. The Hearing Panel Chairperson, upon showing of good cause, may excuse such failure to appear. In such event, the Conference will be rescheduled.

7.3 **Requirement of Cooperation in the Evidentiary Hearing**
7.31 The requirement of the Officer to cooperate delineated in Minneapolis Code of Ordinances, Title 9, Chapter 172, §172.120 and above in these Rules (§6.12) and the Order to Cooperate (with the appropriate Garrity warning) earlier given by the Chief shall continue in effect for the Evidentiary Hearing.

7.4 **Consolidation**
7.41 Whenever two or more separate complainants have arisen from the same incident or event, the Chairperson of the Authority may, in his/her discretion and on his/her own initiative or in response to a request from any of the parties, move to consolidate the cases into one Evidentiary Hearing.

7.42 If a party should object, and is able to show with good cause that his/her case will be prejudiced by the consolidation, that party may remain severed.

7.51 The Executive Director and the Officer or his/her representative, shall have the right to present his/her case or defense by oral and documentary evidence, to submit rebuttal evidence and to conduct such cross-examination as may be required for a full and true disclosure of the facts. The Hearing Panel may admit all evidence which possesses probative value, including reliable hearsay, if it is the type of evidence on which reasonable persons are accustomed to rely in the conduct of their serious affairs. Evidence which is incompetent, irrelevant, immaterial, or unduly repetitious shall be excluded.

7.52 **Burden and Standard of Proof**
7.521 The burden shall be on the Executive Director to prove that the misconduct alleged in the Probable Cause determination did occur. The standard of proof shall be "Clear and Convincing" evidence.

7.53 **Affirmative Defense**
7.531 It shall be an affirmative defense for the Officer that he/she acted in accordance with the rules, regulations and training of the Department.

7.54 **Exhibits**
7.541 All evidence to be considered in the case, including, but not limited to, all records and documents in the possession of either party, or a true and accurate photocopy, shall be marked as that party's exhibit and offered and made a part of the record.

7.55 **Objection to Conduct of Hearing**
7.551 Any objection, including grounds for such objection, with respect to the conduct of the hearing, may be stated orally or in writing, and shall be included in the record. No such objection shall be deemed waived by further participation in the hearing.

7.56 **Failure to Appear at the Evidentiary Hearing**
7.561 The failure of the Officer, and/or his/her representative, or the Executive Director to appear at the Evidentiary Hearing, without good cause, may be considered by the Hearing Panel in weighing the evidence before it.

7.562 The failure of the Complainant to appear at the Evidentiary Hearing, without good cause, shall require the Hearing Panel to decide either:

a. To proceed with the Evidentiary Hearing and consider the failure to appear in weighing the evidence before it; or
b. Dismiss the complaint.

7.563 Requests to reschedule the Hearing, after a failure to appear, must be made, in the absence of extraordinary circumstances, within two (2) days after the previously scheduled hearing date. Notice of the request must be provided all parties. The Hearing Panel Chairperson upon showing of good cause, may excuse such failure to appear. In such event, the Hearing will be rescheduled.

7.57 **Order of Procedure:** Opening the Hearing, Opening Statement, Presentation of Evidence, Closing Statements, Closing of the Hearing.

7.571 **Opening the Hearing**

7.5711 The Hearing Panel Chairperson shall open the hearing by briefly stating the name and case file number of the case. A short statement of the facts as they are alleged in the Probable Cause determination will be given by the Chairperson.

7.5712 The Chairperson shall state the major points of the Prehearing Conference agreement and place that agreement in the record. Any other stipulations, settlements, or agreements entered into by the parties prior to the hearing shall be entered into the record.

7.5713 The Chairperson shall state additional procedural rules of the hearing if so requested and/or it seems appropriate.

7.5714 The Chairperson shall swear in any witnesses, individually, prior to their giving testimony at the hearing.

7.572 **Opening Statement**

7.5721 The Complainant, Executive Director and the Officer will be provided time for Opening Statements. The Executive Director shall first present his/her version of the facts to the Panel in an opening statement. The Officer, or his/her representative may follow the Executive Director with Opening Statement.

7.573 **Witnesses**

7.5731 The Executive Director shall call his/her witnesses first. The Officer or his/her representative may cross examine the witnesses. Any other evidence by the Executive Director may then be presented orally or in written form.

7.5732 The Officer may then call his/her witnesses. An opportunity for the Executive Director to cross-examine will then be provided. Any other evidence by the Accused officer may then be presented orally or in written form.

7.5733 Cross examination of witnesses shall be conducted in a sequence and in a manner determined by the Hearing Panel Chairperson to expedite the hearing while ensuring a fair hearing. The Chairperson shall make rulings as are necessary to prevent argumentative, repetitive, or irrelevant questioning and to expedite the cross-examination to the extent consistent with the disclosure of all relevant testimony and information.

7.5734 All evidentiary testimony presented to prove or disprove a fact at issue shall be under oath or affirmation. Testimony in written form shall be signed and sworn by the affiant.

7.5735 Any witness, including the Complainant and the Officer, may be represented and counseled by personal legal counsel during that witness' testimony. This personal legal counsel shall only be present during that witness' testimony and may not participate in the process.

7.5736 If the Complainant or the Officer refuses to testify in the Evidentiary Hearing, the Panel may, along with other facts and circumstances of the case, draw an adverse inference from that failure to testify.

7.58 **Complainant's Role in the Evidentiary Hearing**

7.581 In accordance with the provisions of the Minnesota Government Data Practices Act, the Complainant may not be present during the evidentiary hearing, except when he or she is testifying as a witness.

7.582 If the Executive Director does not call the Complainant as a witness, therefore subject to cross examination, the Officer may call the Complainant as a witness for cross examination.

7.583 Upon completion of the Complainant's direct testimony and while still under oath, may make additional comments.

7.59 **Closing Statements**

7.591 At the close of the presentation of evidence, the Hearing Panel shall provide the Executive Director and the Officer with opportunities for closing statements. The Executive Director shall proceed first, reserving time for rebuttal if he/she so chooses, followed by the Accused Officer or his/her representative.

7.60 **Closing of the Hearing**

7.601 After the closing statements, the Hearing Panel Chairperson shall either:

a. Close the hearing;
b. Continue the hearing, by setting up another hearing date, time and setting; or
c. With the agreement of both parties, leave the record open to provide further documentation or evidence for the record.

7.7 **Continuance**
7.71 The granting of a continuance will be allowed for just cause.

7.712 A request for continuance of the hearing shall be submitted to the Hearing Panel Chairperson, in writing, at least ten (10) days prior to the scheduled hearing date and shall be served upon all parties to the Complaint.

7.713 If time does not permit, the party requesting the continuance shall notify the Hearing Panel Chairperson and the other parties by telephone regarding the circumstances and the need for a continuance.

7.714 If a continuance is granted, a new hearing date will be established in consultation with all parties.

7.715 In determining whether just cause exists, due regard shall be given to the ability of the party requesting the continuance to effectively proceed without a continuance.

a. Just Cause shall include, but is not limited to: death or incapacitating illness of a party, representative, or attorney of a party; a court order requiring a continuance; lack of proper notice of a hearing; unavailability of a material witness; a substitution of the representative or attorney of a party if the substitution is shown to be required; an order from an accused police officer's commanding officer to report to duty during the time of the hearing because of an emergency or lack of others in the same capacity to take the officer's place; an agreement for a continuance by all parties provided it is shown that more time is clearly necessary to complete preparation for the hearing and the parties and the Hearing Panel Chairperson have agreed to a new date, or the parties have agreed to a settlement of the case which has or will likely be approved by the final decision maker.
b. Just Cause shall not include: intentional or avoidable delay; failure of a representative or attorney to properly utilize time limitations authorized by ordinance.

7.716 During the hearing, if it appears in the interest of justice that further testimony should be received and sufficient time does not remain to conclude the testimony, the Hearing Panel Chairperson may, by agreement of both parties, either:

a. order that additional testimony or information be submitted in written form; or
b. continue the hearing to a future date and oral notice on the record shall be sufficient.

7.8 **Record of Hearing**

7.81 **Maintaining the Record**
7.811 The Hearing Panel Chairperson shall maintain the official record of the case until the issuance of the Findings of Fact and Determination.

7.812 **Content**
7.8121 The Record shall contain:

a. Any and all notices or other procedural matters that have been reduced to writing;
b. All evidence received or considered;
c. An audiomagnetic recording of the hearing;
d. All memoranda or data submitted by any party in connection with the case;
e. A transcript of the hearing, if one was prepared.

7.813 **Closing of the Record**
7.8131 The record of the hearing shall be closed upon the completion of the testimony, or receipt of the final written memorandum, if any, or late-filed exhibits which the parties and the Hearing Panel Chairperson have agreed should be received into the record.

7.814 **Transcript**
7.8141 The audiomagnetic recording of the hearing shall be transcribed if requested by a party or if ordered by the Hearing Panel Chairperson. If a transcript is made, the Authority shall require the requesting party who request copies of the transcript from the Authority to pay a reasonable charge therefor.

8.0 **Disposition**

8.1 **Time Limit**
8.11 Within thirty (30) days of the closing of the record of an evidentiary hearing, the Hearing Panel shall make Findings of Fact and a Determination of the complaint.

8.12 **Findings of Fact and Determination**

8.121 For the Determination, the Hearing Panel shall make one of the following decisions:

a. Officer exonerated, for one of two reasons:
   1. The facts alleged in the complaint are true but do not constitute misconduct by the Officer; or
   2. The facts alleged in the complaint are not true;

b. Insufficient evidence exists to sustain the complaint; or

c. Complaint sustained.

8.13 The Authority shall immediately send notice of the Hearing Panel's Findings of Fact and Determination to the Complainant and the Officer.

8.2 **Reconsideration**

8.21 Within five (5) days of receipt of the Hearing Panel's Findings of Fact and Disposition, either the Complainant or the Officer may submit a written Request for Reconsideration to the Authority. The Request for Reconsideration must state the reasons for review and any other special circumstances, including but not limited to the availability of new evidence that was not known to the party or could not have been discovered by that party by the exercise of due diligence.

8.22 The Request for Reconsideration shall be distributed to the members of the Hearing Panel. Within ten (10) days of receipt of the Request for Reconsideration, the members of the Hearing Panel shall be polled by the Chairperson of the Hearing Panel to determine if the decision should be reconsidered.

8.23 If there is a decision to reconsider, then a reconsideration hearing will be scheduled to receive any new evidence, or a Panel meeting held to sustain or reject the prior decision regarding the complaint.

9.0 **Submission to Chief for Disciplinary Action**

9.01 When a complaint is sustained, and after the period for reconsideration, the Findings of Fact and Determination shall be submitted to the Chief, who shall make a disciplinary decision based upon this information. The Chief, within thirty (30) days of the receipt of the record, shall provide the Authority and the Mayor with a written explanation of the reason(s) for his/her disciplinary decision. (Ord. §172.130)

Document No. 15

New Orleans

No. 50

CITY OF NEW ORLEANS
CHIEF ADMINISTRATIVE OFFICE

POLICY MEMORANDUM June 12, 1984

TO: All Departments, Boards, Agencies and Commissions

FROM: Erroll G. Williams, Chief Administrative Officer

SUBJECT: OFFICE OF MUNICIPAL INVESTIGATION

1. PURPOSE.

This memorandum is revised in order to incorporate a copy of the Policies and Procedures Manual for the Office of Municipal Investigation (OMI).

2. JURISDICTION OF OMI.

The Office of Municipal Investigation was established by Councilmanic Ordinance No. 8130 M.C.S., a copy of which is attached for reference. OMI has exclusive jurisdiction to investigate complaints of alleged illegal or improper conduct which may result in the suspension, dismissal or prosecution of the accused municipal employee.

3. OMI POLICIES AND PROCEDURES MANUAL.

Attached for reference is a copy of the Policies and Procedures Manual for OMI. A review of the manual will be beneficial to understanding the responsibilities and authority of the agency.

4. REFERRING COMPLAINTS.

Departments receiving a citizen complaint of alleged illegal or improper conduct shall immediately refer the complaint to the Office of Municipal Investigation. The Citizen Action Center shall also refer complaints of alleged illegal or improper conduct to OMI.

5. INVESTIGATION BY OMI.

When OMI receives a complaint directly, it shall investigate, provided that the complaint involves illegal or improper conduct. Complaints involving "minor discrepancies" will be referred to the appropriate department for administrative action. If a citizen is not satisfied after the affected department has completed its investigation of a "minor discrepancy", OMI may investigate or refer the complaint to the Citizen Action Center for mediation. When OMI's inquiry is completed, the affected department and the Chief Administrative Officer will be notified of the findings.

6. INQUIRIES.

All inquiries shall be referred directly to OMI at 587-1613 or Room 401, at 2400 Canal Street.

Erroll G. Williams
Chief Administrative Officer

EGW:KS:ch
attachment

POLICIES AND PROCEDURES MANUAL

OF THE

OFFICE OF MUNICIPAL INVESTIGATION

I. INTRODUCTION

A. PURPOSE

The Office of Municipal Investigation (OMI) is a division of the Chief Administrative Office, authorized to investigate complaints of misconduct involving city employees. OMI's powers and duties are described in City Ordinance No. 8130 M.C.S., as amended. The head of the division is the Chief Investigator who reports directly to the Chief Administrative Officer.

B. DEFINITIONS:

(1) "Formal Notice to Appear" - written notice requiring a mandatory appearance before the Chief Investigator.

(2) "Informal Request to Appear" - a request, oral or written, for a voluntary appearance before the OMI.

(3) "Misconduct" - includes, but is not limited to bribery, theft of city property, improper discharge of firearms, coercion, and/or excessive use of physical force by an employee in the conduct of official duties, the performance of a lawful, official action in an illegal or improper manner or the violation of a law, rule, or regulation which may be considered as a reasonable cause for reprimand, suspension, or dismissal from public employment. (See Section D of Proposed Ordinance)

(4) "Person" - any natural person, proprietorship, corporation, government, partnership, trust, joint venture, group association, organization or other business or enterprise of any kind or nature and any division, department or other suborganizational unit.

(5) "Supervisor" - department head, division head, section chief, and/or other city official who hires, terminates, promotes and/or disciplines city employees.

(6) "Minor Infractions" - is anything that is not "misconduct" as hereinabove defined.

II. POWERS AND DUTIES

A. POWERS AND DUTIES:

(1) Upon the filing of a complaint OMI shall:

(a) Determine immediately whether the subject matter of the complaint concerns an allegation of employment misconduct or only minor discrepancies.

(b) Begin a complete investigation if the subject matter of a complaint concerns an allegation related to employee misconduct.

(c) Refer the complaint immediately to the proper city agency if the complaint does not concern an allegation of employee misconduct.

(2) The OMI shall have the responsibility and power to investigate and inquire into any alleged misconduct by any city employee, classified or unclassified, other than elected municipal officials.

(3) The OMI may review the processes and decisions of internal investigations conducted by other City Departments, except the Department of Law and the City Civil Service Commission.

(4) OMI personnel shall have the right to administer oaths, subpoena witnesses and compel the production of books and papers.

B. LIMITATIONS:

All investigations must be completed or otherwise disposed of within ninety (90) days from the receipt of the complaint. However, an extension of time may be granted on any given complaint upon written request by the Chief Investigator of OMI to the Chief Administrative Officer. Each extension shall not exceed more than sixty (60) days and shall not be granted more than twice for any given complaint. The maximum time a case can remain open, after receipt of a complaint, is seven (7) months.

III. COMPLAINTS

A. COMPLAINTS:

(1) Any person may file a complaint with the OMI, except an employee of OMI.

(2) The identity of a complainant will be confidential upon the request of the complainant.

(3) An individual may also file an anonymous complaint.

(4) Any individual may file a complaint or grievance against OMI. Complaints of this type should be given directly to the Chief Administrative Officer or his designee who shall determine the appropriate manner of investigation or response. The complainant shall be informed of the conclusions or

decisions resulting from the investigation of complaint.

B. DUTY OF AGENCY HEADS TO NOTIFY OMI OF MISCONDUCT:

All city agency heads are required to report immediately all particulars of any complaint of misconduct to OMI. Notification by oral or written correspondence is acceptable.

C. DUTY OF OMI TO NOTIFY AGENCY HEADS:

Upon receipt of a complaint of misconduct against a city employee, the OMI shall notify the employee's agency head of the complaint as long as such notification will not prejudice or compromise the inquiry.

D. DETERMINATION OF MISCONDUCT:

The Chief Investigator shall determine what constitutes misconduct as defined by the ordinance.

E. SUBJECT MATTER:

The subject matter of a complaint must allege employee misconduct in the performance of official city responsibilities.

F. METHOD OF FILING COMPLAINT:

(1) A complaint may be filed with the OMI in the following manners:

(a) telephone or any other telegraphic medium;
(b) written letter, request or memorandum;
(c) personal visit to OMI, or
(d) personal visit by OMI to the potential complainant.

(2) All complainants are entitled to receive a copy of their complaint upon request and notification of final disposition.

(3) No other party shall receive a copy of the complaint.

G. TIME:

Normal business hours of the OMI shall be 8:45 a.m. to 6:00 p.m., Monday through Friday, except for City holidays.
OMI Business Phone: (504)587-1613.

H. INVESTIGATION OF FIREARM DISCHARGES:

(1) The discharge of a firearm by a city employee occuring in Orleans Parish shall be immediately investigated by the OMI without the necessity of a prior complaint as

elsewhere provided herein.

(2) In all cases of firearm discharges by city employees occuring in Orleans Parish, the Police Department shall notify OMI and OMI shall respond and proceed to the scene of the discharge of firearm incident.

(3) The New Orleans Police Department Homicide Division shall have the sole responsibility and supervisory authority for criminal investigations of all firearm discharge incidents.

(4) The OMI investigator, upon arriving at the scene of a firearm discharge incident, shall first contact the New Orleans Police Department Officer-In-Charge and shall not interfere with the criminal investigation.

(5) The OMI may be present during the New Orleans Police Department questioning of the City employee believed to have discharged his weapon. However, the OMI shall not have authority to question the City employee until the New Orleans Police Department concludes its criminal investigation.

(6) The OMI may interview witnesses to the firearm discharge incident following the termination of the New Orleans Police Department criminal investigation.

(7) The OMI may view evidence at the scene of the incident together with the Officer-In-Charge. However, the OMI shall not touch evidence where such touching may interfere with the admissibility of the evidence in a criminal prosecution. The New Orleans Police Department shall supply the OMI with the serial number of the discharged weapon, if the serial number is readily ascertainable, at the scene of the incident.

(8) Upon request of the Chief Investigator, the New Orleans Police Department shall supply the Chief Investigator with the report of its criminal investigation. The Chief Investigator shall be solely responsible for preserving the confidentiality of this report.

I. INTERFERENCE:

No person shall interfere with, bar or in any way hinder an investigation, and any attempt to interfere with, bar, or hinder an investigation shall be reported immediately to the OMI Chief Investigator by the OMI investigator involved.

J REFERRALS:

Complaints determined by OMI to be minor infractions shall be referred immediately to the proper agency for appropriate action. Once notified of the minor infraction, the agency shall have thirty (30) days in which to take appropriate action and thereafter to provide written notification to OMI of its action.

K. RETALIATION PROHIBITED:

Any employee who suffers any retaliatory action by a supervisor or other employee as a result of filing a complaint with the OMI and/or cooperating with an OMI investigation, may file a complaint of retaliation with OMI.

L. OMI REVIEW OF AGENCY ACTION ON INVESTIGATIVE CONCLUSIONS:

After receiving OMI's investigative report, the city agency head shall report in writing to the OMI what action, if any was taken against the employee(s) involved within thirty (30) days, with extensions to be granted by the Chief Administrative Officer or Chief Investigator. Upon receipt of the agency's report, the OMI Chief Investigator may:

(1) Review the final action taken, except that of the Department of Law or City Civil Service Commission, if it appears that:

(a) The decision was not supported by the facts, or
(b) new or additional evidence has been discovered, or
(c) the investigation appears on its face to have been unfair and/or biased.

(2) If a determination is made not to review the internal investigation and/or final decision of the city agency, such a determination shall be reported by OMI to the complainant within a reasonable period of time.

(3) If the Chief Investigator of OMI, upon review of the action and final decision of a city agency head, concludes that any item in paragraph (1) of this subsection, then this conclusion shall be reported to the Chief Administrative Officer.

IV. INVESTIGATORY PROCESS

A. PARALLEL INVESTIGATION:

Since the OMI is not to replace any other city investigatory body, an employee may be the subject of parallel administrative investigations by both a city agency and the OMI. The Chief Administrative Officer shall review any OMI investigative report and thereafter make any necessary recommendations to the city agency head involved. The recommendations of the Chief Administrative Officer shall supercede any contrary investigative conclusions reached by a city agency head or OMI.

B. INVESTIGATIVE METHOD:

(1) Without prior written approval, OMI shall use only the following investigatory methods: interviews, review of records and/or documents and normal surveillance activities. Polygraph tests shall be used only in accordance with city policy.

(2) Use of any other investigatory method or methods shall be approved in writing by the Chief Administrative Officer and the City Attorney's Office.

(3) The Chief Administrative Officer, upon the written recommendation of the Chief Investigator, may grant to any city employee full or partial immunity from administrative disciplinary action in exchange for his/her sworn testimony pertaining to misconduct of another city employee.

C. SUSPENSION OF INVESTIGATIONS:

Any OMI investigation may be suspended if at any time during the course of the investigation it appears likely that the employee who is under investigation will be arrested in connection with the specific charge of the OMI investigation. The Director of OMI shall consult with the Chief Administrative Officer to determine whether or not the investigation should proceed to completion or be delayed until the pending criminal investigation or arrest has been completed.

V. APPEARANCE

A. NOTIFICATION:

(1) A copy of the "Notice to Appear" (an example of which is attached hereto as Exhibit A) will be mailed by certified mail to the residence of the employee or to any place where the employee is located. A "Notice To Appear" will also be mailed to any employee's work place.

(2) An employee shall be released from normal duties to attend an interview.

(3) The "Notice" is confidential, unless actions by the employee cause it to be disclosed; then the confidentiality of the "Notice" is deemed waived.

(4) Upon receipt of the "Notice", an employee may call OMI for additional information.

(5) A notice to the subject of an investigation shall briefly state the nature of the charge, the date, the location of the interview and the status of the employee to be investigated.

(6) A notice to any other employee shall briefly state the date and the location of the interview.

(7) A written "Notice To Appear" to the employee is a formal notice, and penalties shall be attached for failure of the employee to respond to questions in accordance with R.S. 33:2426.

B. <u>REPRESENTATIVE BEFORE OMI INTERVIEW SESSION:</u>

(1) An employee may be represented at the interview by an attorney or by any other designated individual.

(2) The representative must be designated by the employee before the representative is entitled to receive information from OMI.

(3) A representative may be designated by appearing with employee before OMI or upon oral or written notice to OMI by the employee.

(4) The representative is entitled to know the nature of the charges against the employee.

C. <u>INTERVIEW:</u>

(1) The Office of Municipal Investigation may require the appearance of any employee during that employee's scheduled work shift. If an appearance is not possible during the work shift, OMI may require any employee to appear no earlier than six hours after the completion of the employee's tour of duty unless prudence and judgement dictate otherwise. Time and place of the interview shall be determined by OMI.

(2) If an employee is required to attend an interview outside of regular working hours, the employee shall be compensated for the appearance according to standard payment practices.

(3) Prior to the interview, the employee shall be advised of all statutory and constitutional rights appropriate to the nature of the interview and shall be provided a form for his/her signature with those rights enumerated thereon to be used as verification of the fulfillment of this requirement.

(4) An employee who fails to answer the questions from OMI is subject to disciplinary action. The OMI investigator shall forward the complaint of failure to answer to the Chief Administrative Officer who shall commence disciplinary proceedings. The Chief Administrative Officer shall instruct the employee's city agency head to proceed with disciplinary action as defined by departmental rules, Civil Service rules and applicable laws.

(5) Statements made by an employee during an OMI interview shall not be forwarded to or alluded to in any OMI report to any city, state or federal agency for criminal prosecution.

D. TAPE RECORDING:

OMI shall tape all employee investigative interviews. An employee may bring his own tape recorder and tapes to the interview. Any employee who fails to tape the interview may come to the OMI office or send his designated representative to listen to the tape of his interview. Also, the employee who fails to tape his interview is entitled to receive, upon request, a copy of the tape at the employee's expense. All transcriptions of their personal interviews will be made available to employees for their review and verification for accuracy.

E. POSTPONEMENT:

Upon request to and at the discretion of the Chief Investigator, if good cause is shown, postponement of appearances may be granted.

VI. REPORTS

A. PUBLICATION:

(1) All reports prepared by OMI shall be confidential in nature. A copy of the report shall be provided only

to the city agency head involved in the investigation and the Chief Administrative Officer. The employee shall be given a copy of the conclusions contained in the investigative report.

B. DEPARTMENTAL DISCIPLINARY HEARINGS:

At the request of the city agency head, the OMI investigator shall attend all departmental disciplinary hearings for the sole purpose of presenting the facts developed by the investigation. However, at no time will the OMI investigator discuss with or recommend to the city agency head, his deputy, or his designated representative, disciplinary action for any employee who is or has been the subject of an OMI investigation.

C. CONFIDENTIALITY OF REPORTS:

(1) All data, documents, and files received or established by OMI are confidential and shall not be disclosed, if such data, documents and files contain:

(a) Records pertaining to pending criminal litigation or any criminal litigation which can be reasonably anticipated until such litigation has been finally adjudicated or otherwise settled; or

(b) Records containing the identify of a confidential source or information or records which would tend to reveal the identify of a confidential source of information; or

(c) Records containing security procedures, investigative training information or aids, investigative techniques, investigative technical equipment or instruction on the use thereof, or internal security information; or

(d) Records containing the identify of an undercover police officer or records which would tend to reveal the identify of an undercover police officer.

(2) Notwithstanding the foregoing, upon request a witness or a party shall have a copy of his/her statement made during an OMI interview.

(3) Any request for files or statements shall be made directly to the Chief Investigator.

D ACCESS TO CITY RECORDS:

(1) The OMI shall have access to all city records and documents, including employee personnel records, as authorized by law. The OMI shall have access to all such documents, city records, and personnel records as would be available to any duly authorized law enforcement officer of the City of New Orleans. It shall have the right to administer oaths, subpoena witnesses and compel the production of books and paper pertinent thereto.

(2) OMI shall make request to any city agency head for the delivery or review of any files held by the agency. However, if the city agency head is unavailable, OMI shall contact the Chief Administrative Officer and request that the files be removed from the agency into the custody and control of OMI. If the files are voluminous and protected, then OMI may request to review them at the agency.

(3) Upon OMI's request to the proper agency, all records shall be made available immediately.

(4) If a city agency head refuses to provide the requested documents, the refusal shall be reported immediately to the Chief Administrative Officer.

(5) Until released by the Chief Investigator, records or files shall remain in the custody of OMI.

(6) Upon completion of an investigation, the OMI shall immediately return all records or files to the agency from which they came.

VII. CARRYING OF FIREARMS

While on duty OMI officer shall be allowed to carry only those firearms prescribed by NOPD regulations.

VIII. BADGES

OMI officers shall carry identification badges which are unique in design from any other local law enforcement agency.

IX. STATISTICS

The OMI shall maintain timely and comprehensive statistics of its activities that are easily accessible for review by the public.

ATTACHMENT

ORDINANCE
(AS AMENDED)
CITY OF NEW ORLEANS

CITY HALL: JUNE 19, 1980

CALENDAR NO. 9356

NO. 8130 MAYOR COUNCIL SERIES

BY: COUNCILMAN SINGLETON (BY REQUEST)

An Ordinance to amend Chapter 2 of Ordinance Number 828 M.C.S., known as the Code of the City of New Orleans, by adding thereto a new Article to be designated as Article XI relative to the establishment of an Office of Municipal Investigation of the City of New Orleans.

SECTION 1. THE COUNCIL OF THE CITY OF NEW ORLEANS HEREBY ORDAINS, that Article XI of Chapter 2 of Ordinance Number 828 M.C.S., known as the Code of the City of New Orleans, be and the same is hereby ordained to read as follows:

ARTICLE XI. OFFICE OF MUNICIPAL INVESTIGATION

Section 2-74. Establishment and functions.

(a) There is hereby established within the Chief Administrative Office an Office of municipal investigation (OMI) subject to the control and supervision of the Chief Administrative Officer. The OMI shall have such assistants and staff as may be authorized by the city budget.

(b) Staff on the OMI shall be in the classified service, shall be bonded, shall not have arrest powers other than those afforded any other citizen and shall be delegated authority as given by the Chief Administrative Officer, pursuant to Section 4-302 (4) of the Home Rule Charter of the City of New Orleans.

(c) The OMI shall have the responsibility and power to investigate and inquire into any alleged misconduct of any city employee, including the Mayor and his appointees but not including any other municipal elected official or persons appointed directly by and serving at the pleasure of said official. When so authorized by the Chief Administrative Officer (or the Mayor if the Chief Administrative Officer is the object of an investigation), the OMI may request assistance from other city departments and/or outside consultants to aid its investigations.

(d) For purposes of this ordinance, "misconduct" shall include; but not be limited to, bribery, theft of city property, improper discharge of firearms, coercion, and/or excessive use of physical force by an employee in the conduct of official duties, the performance of a lawful, official action in an illegal or improper manner, or the violation of a law, rule, or regulation which may be considered as reasonable cause for dismissal from public employment.

(e) Allegations of minor discrepancies may be handled at departmental levels. Such complaints should follow other normal channels. However, all other complaints must be investigated unless otherwise provided for herein.

(f) Investigations shall commence upon the receipt of a complaint. The complainant need not be the actual victim of the alleged misconduct.

(g) Investigations are the be conducted according to acceptable, prudent procedures that are subject to review by the City Attorney and Chief Administrative Officer. Polygraph tests shall only be used pursuant to City policy.

(h) The OMI shall have access to all city records and documents, including employee personnel records, as authorized by law. The Office of Municipal Investigation shall have access to all such documents, city records, and personnel records as would be available to any duly authorized law enforcement officer of the City of New Orleans. It shall have the right to administer oaths, subpoena witnesses and compel the production of books and paper pertinent thereto.

(i) The OMI shall have the authority to require the appearance of any city employee during the employee's employment hours if possible and to question such employee regarding matters specifically relating to the allegations of misconduct. Employees failing to testify or answer questions may still be subject to administrative disciplinary action. No promise of reward shall be offered as an inducement to answering questions. The imposition of use immunity shall not be considered as a reward or inducement for answering questions. If an employee is likely to be placed under arrest subsequently, the OMI shall seek the counsel of the Chief Administrative Officer and determine whether the administrative process should be delayed until the criminal action is completed.

(j) Should a complainant refuse to cooperate with OMI, the OMI shall determine if alternative investigation techniques are applicable before considering such refusal as sufficient cause to close the investigation.

(k) All investigations are to proceed promptly after receipt of a complaint. Provision must be made for receipt of a complaint on a 24-hour basis.

(l) All investigations must be completed or otherwise disposed of within 90 days of receipt of the complaint and the complainant is to be notified of the conclusion by first-class mail. Under unusual circumstances, an extension of time may be permitted by the Chief Administrative Officer for completion of the investigation.

(m) All OMI personnel shall be available to participate as a witness and to present testimony and evidence to those tribunals, administrative or criminal, that retain jurisdiction after a complaint if sounded.

(n) Investigative conclusions are to be reported to the complainant, the employee accused, the appropriate department director, and the Chief Administrative Officer. Where criminal prosecution is recommended, a copy shall also be sent to the City Attorney and appropriate federal or state officials. An employee shall be disciplined only through the regular processes provided by law.

(o) The OMI is not to replace any other city investigatory body. The OMI shall provid- an additional point at which citizens or employees may register misconduct complaints. The OMI and other city departments shall promptly notify each other on receipt of misconduct complaints. Parallel investigations may take place between OMI and other city investigatory bodies. The OMI shall be administered by a Chief Investigator who shall be in the classified Civil Service. The Chief Investigator shall have not less than five years experience in conducting investigations related to law enforcement, military or civilian. An advisory committee shall be appointed by the Chief Administrative Officer. This committee shall include three citizens of the City of New Orleans, the Director of the City Civil Service, and three members of the City Council appointed by the President of the Council. Said committee shall provide to the City Civil Service Commission for its consideration recommendations relating to job description and specifications for all OMI investigative positions.

SECTION 2. If any portion of the Ordinance be held unconstitutional or invalid by a Court of competent jurisdiction, such holding shall not affect the validity of the remaining portion of the Ordinance, but such remainin- portion shall be and remain in full force and effect.

SECTION 3. All Ordinances or parts of Ordinances in conflict herewith are hereby repealed.

SECTION 4. All the provisions of this Ordinance shall expire on June 1, 1983. The Council shall begin reviewing the provisions of this Ordinance on April 1, 1983 for the purpose of determining the effectiveness of the

Ordinance and determining whether the Council at that time wishes to introduce legislation to continue any or all of the provisions of this Ordinance.

ADOPTED BY THE COUNCIL OF THE CITY OF NEW ORLEANS MAY 14, 1981

SIDNEY J. BARTHELEMY
PRESIDENT OF COUNCIL

Delivered to the Mayor on MAY 14, 1981

Approved:
MAY 18, 1981

ERNEST N. MORIAL
MAYOR

Returned by the Mayor on MAY 18, 1981 at 1:30 P.M.

JOSEPH C. PETERSON
CLERK OF COUNCIL

EXHIBIT A

OFFICE OF MUNICIPAL INVESTIGATION

In re: CASE NO.

To

SUBPOENA

YOU ARE HEREBY NOTIFIED that an inquiry will be conducted on the __________ day of ______________, 1984, at ____________ ____________________ in the Office of Municipal Investigation, 2400 Canal Street-Suite 401, acting by virtue of the authority vested in it by Section 2-74, Article XI, Chapter 2, of Ordinance Number 828 M.C.S., known as the Code of the City of New Orleans, Louisiana 1956, and commanded to appear to testify in the above case.

WARNING: Willful failure to appear and give testimony before the OMI or its authorized agents at the date, time and location specified in this notice will subject you to possible forfeiture of your city position as provided by the provisions of Louisiana Revised Statutes 33:2426.

This subpoena is issued upon application of ______________ ______________, Special Agent. Twenty-four Hundred Canal Street, Suite 401, New Orleans, Louisiana, 70119, telephone number (504) 587-1613.

CITY OF NEW ORLEANS
OFFICE OF MUNICIPAL INVESTIGATION

________________, 19__. ____________________________
OMI DIRECTOR

RETURN

CERTIFIED MAIL ON: __________
Date

ON HIS/HER PERSON: __________
Date

BY: ____________________________
Special Agent

BY: ____________________________
Special Agent

EXHIBIT B

Date of Transcription __________

ADMINISTRATIVE STATEMENT

It is now __________ AM/PM, ____________________, 19__, ____, I hereby advise you that this Office of Municipal Investigation (OMI) inquiry is regarding allegations of misconduct made against ______________ ____________________ by ____________________________, in that you/he/she ____, which was documented under ____________________________________.

I hereby advise you, ____________________________, that Louisiana Revised Statute, Title 33, Article 2426, requires all Civil Service Employees to answer questions in official inquiries and that refusal to comply results in job forfeiture as well as a two (2) year ineligibility period as to appointment to any city Civil Service job. I further advise you that any statement you make or answers you give in this OMI Administrative Investigation, since required by law under the penalty of job forfeiture, cannot be introduced in any criminal proceeding against you.

***

"I understand that any and all statements I make are for purposes of administrative action only. I further understand that no part of any statement I have to the OMI will be forwarded to any local, state or federal enforcement agency for criminal prosecution. I further understand that failure to answer any or all questions propounded to me by OMI may subject me to disciplinary action, including possible discharge from City employment. It is only upon the aforesaid representations that I give this statement."

______________________________ CITY EMPLOYEE

______________________________ DATE

AN ORDINANCE to establish a Code of Ethics for the government of the City of New Orleans.

WHEREAS, in the public interest, a Code of Ethics for the conduct of the government of the City of New Orleans is to be established herewith, to promote integrity in City Government; to protect the public from overt acts contrary to public interest by public officials, employees and members of public boards and commissions and their agents; to protect City officials, employees and members of public boards and commissions and their agents from unwittingly performing such acts by defining improper and/or prohibitive activities, conflicts of interest and propriety, and extent of receiving gifts by such persons, and to provide penalties for violations of the provisions hereof.

SECTION 1. THE COUNCIL OF THE CITY OF NEW ORLEANS HEREBY ORDAINS that there shall be established a Code of Ethics for the government of the City of New Orleans.

SECTION 2. The Code of Ethics shall apply to all officials of the government of the City of New Orleans, whether elected or appointed; to all employees, whether classified or unclassified; and to members and/or employees of all boards, agencies and commissions which have a direct or indirect interest in any business or professional activity involving public funds or public trust.

SECTION 3. The following shall be considered as general prohibitions applicable to all persons coming within the purview of this ordinance:

A. Participation in any business or profession, contract or agreement, or the acceptance of any employment which conflicts with the discharge of assigned public duties;

B. Disclosure of confidential information for personal gain or advantage;

C. The use of influence to secure special privileges for self or others;

D. Investment or representation in any financial transaction or enterprise in which profit to self or others would depend in any way upon public position or authority;

E. Sale or rental of goods, services or concessions to the City or any of its agencies by any person, firm or corporation in which one or more City officers, employees or board members hold or control the majority financial interest therein;

F. Acceptance of any gift of currency, cash certificate, stock or bonds from any person, persons, firms, corporation and/or agencies doing business with the City except that gratuities given to laborers and parking attendants and political campaign contributions are not prohibited;

G. Participation in official action by vote or by use of influence on the part of an official where such activities, if successful, would result in a grant of compensation, contracts, privileges or advantages to any individual or business in which such official has a personal interest;

H. Use of public office to procure preferential treatment, whether of employment, contract, business, fee or service with the City or any of its governmental agencies for any member of immediate family, client or business associate;

I. Use of City-owned properties or facilities for factional political purposes, meetings or furtherance of factional political interests;

SECTION 4. The following shall be considered as specific prohibitions and applicable to City officials and/or employees and/or board members, as the case may be:

A. No City official or employee shall have dual employment, except employment elsewhere than with the City, and only when such official or employee is off duty or on authorized leave from public duties, and such employment in no way conflicts with public duties;

B. No City official or employee shall accept fees for himself or for anyone other than himself for services which are within the scope of his duty and for which he is being compensated by the City;

C. No officer or employee of the City shall have a financial interest in any contract with the City, and no contract for professional or other services shall be awarded on the basis of fee kickbacks;

D. No attorney employed by the City or its agencies shall prosecute or defend litigation contradictorily with the City;

E. No officer or employee of the City shall participate in insurance commissions on City-owned properties.

F. The members of all boards and commissions of the City shall be held to the standards of a prudent administrator;

G. No members or officer of a board shall borrow money or receive anything of value from any contractor doing business with the board; no member, officer, or employee of any board shall have any interest in any contract let by the board; any member or officer of any board may have a financial interest in any activity or enterprise which is not subject to regulation of the board of which he is a member, but any member of any board who is a director or stockholder in any corporation, or is an agent or attorney for any person who is financially interested in any subject before the board, shall reveal such interest to the board and shall not discuss or vote on the subject at any meeting of the board or any of its committees;

H. Any member of a board, except ex-officio board members, who shall qualify as a candidate for any public elective office, or who shall accept an appointive office or position of public employment for which compensation is paid, shall forfeit his membership on the board;

I. Nothing herein shall deprive City officials or employees from having a financial interest in any activity or enterprise which is not in conflict with their respective positions or with any provisions of this ordinance, the City Code or the City Charter.

SECTION 5. The following shall be considered matters of public information:

A. Duties and hours of employees.

1. Full time employees shall perform a full day's work each and every working day.

2. Job descriptions shall be provided for all employees.

B. Members of City boards and commissions shall file with the Mayor and Clerk of the Council within sixty (60) days after this ordinance becomes effective, an affidavit revealing the amount of their financial interest in any activity or enterprise subject to regulation by the board or commission of which they are members; should such interest be acquired subsequent to sixty (60) days after the effective date of this ordinance, said affidavit must be filed upon the date of said acquisition.

SECTION 6. With regard to employees in classified service, the provisions of Section 4-1504 and 8-112 of the City Charter are adopted herein by reference.

Any qualified elector of the City of New Orleans may file written complaints in the form of an affidavit with the Civil Service Commission concerning violations of this Section involving appointed officials, classified and unclassified employees, and members of City boards, commissions and agencies.

All complaints shall be held as confidential information, unless, in the case of classified employees, the Commission decides that a complaint warrants a public hearing, or in the case of appointed officials, unclassified employees or members of boards and agencies and commissions, the City Council decides that a complaint warrants a public hearing.

City officials, employees, and members of boards, agencies, and commissions shall cooperate with the Commission in providing information on any complaint.

On complaints involving classified employees, the Commission shall determine guilt or innocence and fix penalties.

On complaints involving any person appointed to the unclassified service, including officials and employees, the Civil Service Commission, after investigation, if deemed necessary, shall make recommendations to the City Council. The City Council shall then proceed in accordance with Section 3-125 of the City Charter.

On complaints involving members of City boards, agencies and commissions, the Civil Service Commission, after investigation, if deemed necessary, shall make recommendations to the City Council. The City Council shall then proceed in accordance with Section 9-104 of the City Charter.

SECTION 7.

A. Any qualified elector of the City of New Orleans may file a written complaint in the form of an affidavit with any member of the City Council concerning violations of this Section involving members of the City Council.

B. Members of the Council receiving complaints in said form may request an executive conference of all members of the City Council to consider the complaints and may proceed in accordance with the City Charter.

C. Complaints concerning the Mayor involving violations of this Section shall follow the same procedure as for Councilmen, as authorized under Section 3-124 of the City Charter, except that a majority vote of the elected membership of the Council shall be required to call a public hearing and to adopt a resolution of censure for violations under this Section.

SECTION 8. Penalties for violation of the above shall be as follows:

A. Classified employees shall be suspended or dismissed in accordance with Section 8-113 of the City Charter;

B. Employees and appointed officials shall be suspended or dismissed in accordance with Section 3-125 of the City Charter;

C. Members of boards, commissions and agencies shall be removed and/or shall forfeit their appointment in accordance with Section 9-104 of the City Charter;

D. Elected officials shall be subject to censure by City Council Resolution;

E. None of the above action shall preclude the instituting of criminal prosecution wherever warranted.

SECTION 9. The effective date of this ordinance establishing the Code of Ethics for the government of the City of New Orleans shall be thirty (30) days after its adoption.

ADOPTED BY THE COUNCIL OF THE CITY OF NEW ORLEANS MAY 16, 1963.

Document No. 16

New York City

CIVILIAN COMPLAINT INVESTIGATIVE BUREAU

1990

ANNUAL REPORT

LEE P. BROWN
POLICE COMMISSIONER

SANDRA M. MARSH
DEPUTY COMMISSIONER /
EXECUTIVE DIRECTOR

WILLIAM F. CARNEY
DEPUTY CHIEF
COMMANDING OFFICER

STATISTICAL TABLES

The following tables and graphs outline statistical data developed in the reporting and investigative process by the Civilian Complaint Investigative Bureau staff. The tables also list final data resulting from the review by the Civilian Complaint Review Board.

TABLE 1

The following table is a comparison of complaints and allegations for calendar years 1989 and 1990.

	1989	1990	CHANGE	% CHANGE
COMPLAINTS	3515	3377	- 138	- 3.9
ALLEGATIONS				
Force	2417	2376	- 41	- 1.7
Abuse of Authority	1201	1140	- 61	- 5.1
Discourtesy	1724	1618	- 106	- 6.1
Ethnic Slur	380	420	+ 40	+ 10.5
TOTAL ALLEGATIONS*	5722	5554	- 168	- 2.9

* Each complaint contains one or more allegation of misconduct. Therefore, there will always be a greater total number of allegations than complaints.

TABLE 2

FORCE ALLEGATIONS DISTRIBUTION

	# of Allegations		% of Allegations	
	1989	1990	1989	1990
Gun Fired	3	3	0.1	0.1
Beat	361	355	14.9	15.0
Mace	1	5	0.1	0.2
Drag/Pull	100	109	4.1	4.6
Push/Shove	656	614	27.1	25.9
Nightstick	206	203	8.5	8.5
Gun Pointed	79	84	3.3	3.5
Gun as Club	55	38	2.3	1.6
Radio as Club	36	36	1.5	1.5
Punch/Kick	453	506	18.8	21.3
Slap	135	140	5.6	5.9
Other	332	283	13.7	11.9
Total	2,417	2,376	100.0	100.0

TABLE 3

ABUSE OF AUTHORITY ALLEGATIONS DISTRIBUTION

	# of Allegations		% of Allegations	
	1989	1990	1989	1990
Person Searched	194	185	16.2	16.2
Vehicle Searched	44	37	3.7	3.3
Detention	10	9	0.8	0.8
Summons, Other	7	0	0.6	0.0
Arrest, D.A.T.	5	3	0.4	0.3
Property Damage	140	149	11.7	13.1
Premise Searched	45	32	3.7	2.8
Threat of Force	434	397	36.1	34.8
Property Seized	23	30	1.9	2.6
Threat to Property	9	13	0.8	1.1
Threat of Arrest	101	102	8.4	8.9
Other	189	183	15.7	16.1
Total	1,201	1,140	100.0	100.0

TABLE 4

DISCOURTESY ALLEGATIONS DISTRIBUTION

	# of Allegations		% of Allegations	
	1989	1990	1989	1990
Curse	1,311	1,213	76.0	75.0
Nasty Words	313	323	18.2	20.0
Profane Gesture	8	2	0.5	0.1
Rude Gesture	21	13	1.2	0.8
Rudeness	2	0	0.1	0.0
Sexist Remark	8	8	0.5	0.5
Gay Slur	18	25	1.0	1.5
Other	43	34	2.5	2.1
Total	1,724	1,618	100.0	100.0

TABLE 5

ETHNIC SLUR ALLEGATIONS DISTRIBUTION

	# of Allegations		% of Allegations	
	1989	1990	1989	1990
Black	247	241	65.0	57.4
Hispanic	48	66	12.6	15.7
Jewish	6	16	1.6	3.8
Asian	9	7	2.4	1.7
Italian	5	5	1.3	1.2
White	17	19	4.5	4.5
Other	48	66	12.6	15.7
Total	380	420	100.0	100.0

TABLE 6

WHERE AND HOW CIVILIAN COMPLAINTS WERE REGISTERED

1990

LOCATION	In Person	By Telephone	By Letter	Total
C.C.I.B.	139	1,034	102	1,275
P.D. Field Unit	1,266	794	38	2,098
P.C.'s Office	0	1	3	4
Totals	1,405	1,829	143	3,377

1989

LOCATION	In Person	By Telephone	By Letter	Total
C.C.I.B.	155	1,139	95	1,389
P.D. Field Units	1,301	793	28	2,122
P.C.'s Office	0	2	2	4
Totals	1,456	1,934	125	3,515

TABLE 7

HOW INDIVIDUALS LEARNED ABOUT THE CIVILIAN COMPLAINT REVIEW BOARD

The following is a recapitulation of the way that complainants told us they learned about the Civilian Complaint Review Board.

HOW LEARNED	1989	1990	PERCENTAGES 1989	PERCENTAGES 1990
Police Personnel	1,544	1,357	59.8	64.0
911 Operator	319	228	12.3	10.8
Family/Friend	286	249	11.1	11.7
Telephone Company	70	45	2.7	2.1
Media	102	35	4.0	1.7
Community Groups	54	43	2.1	2.0
Mayor's Office	16	8	0.6	0.4
District Attorney's Office	29	15	1.1	0.7
Attorney	164	140	6.3	6.6
Sub-Total	2,584	2,120	100.0	100.0
Unknown *	931	1,257		
TOTAL	3,515	3,377		

* Refers to those instances in which the complainant declined to provide the information.

TABLE 8

NUMBERS AND TYPES OF INCIDENTS THAT GENERATED CIVILIAN COMPLAINTS

	1989	1990
Traffic Incident/Traffic Summons	641	630
Demonstration	23	21
Aided Case	28	43
Emotionally Disturbed Person	19	14
Past Crime or Crime in Progress	251	262
Dispute	395	378
Patrol Incidents - General	805	712
Stop/Question/Frisk	144	181
Reported Disturbance/Noise	64	66
Vehicle Stop & Check	115	91
Compl. witnessing incident	52	61
Total Patrol Incidents	1,180	1,111
At Station House	52	38
Call to Police Department Facility	25	15
Arrest/Desk Appearance Tickets		
Arrest of complainant	244	219
Arrest/Not complainant	229	237
Total Arrest/Desk Appear. Tickets	473	456
Summons (Non-Traffic)	70	81
Other	357	274
Undetermined *	1	53
Total	3,515	3,377

* As of the closing date of this report, the investigation of these cases has not been finalized, or the generating incident was unknown.

TABLE 9

FORCE ALLEGATIONS/DOCUMENTED INJURY REPORT

This table reflects the actual number and type of injuries documented during the course of investigation into allegations of unnecessary or excessive force reported during the years indicated.

TOTAL FORCE ALLEGATIONS

1989	1990
2,417	2,376

INJURIES DOCUMENTED BY INVESTIGATION

	1989	1990
Gun Shot Wound	0	0
Bruises	53	71
Lacerations/Stitches	85	92
Fractures	20	30
Internal Injuries	4	6
Swelling	17	22
Redness	0	5
Other (strains, sprains, etc.)	133	41
Total	312	267

PERCENTAGE OF DOCUMENTED INJURIES/FORCE ALLEGATIONS

1989		1990	
312 / 2,416	12.9 %	267 / 2,328	11.5 %

Note: The total number of injuries documented by investigation for 1989 and 1990 is based on those cases in which the investigation has been completed as of the date of this report. Upon completion of the remainder of 1989 and 1990 force complaints, the number of documented injuries may rise.

TABLE 10

DISCIPLINARY ACTIONS RECOMMENDED BY THE CIVILIAN COMPLAINT REVIEW BOARD

	1989	1990
Substantiated-Charges	47	69
Substantiated-Command Discipline	39	64
Substantiated-Instructions	9	10
Substantiated *	121	0
Other Misconduct Noted-Charges	5	13
Other Misconduct Noted-Command Discipline	5	23
Other Misconduct Noted-Instructions	5	23
Other Misconduct Noted *	35	0
Total Disciplinary Actions **	266	202

TABLE 11

DISPOSITIONS OF COMPLAINTS RECEIVED IN 1989 AND 1990

	1989	1990 ***
Substantiated	157	81
Unsubstantiated	813	931
Unfounded	89	92
Employee Exonerated	105	49
Sub-total of complete investigations	1,164	1,153
Complaint Withdrawn	274	234
Victim Unavailable	44	47
Complainant Unavailable	422	397
Victim Uncooperative	82	91
Complainant Uncooperative	598	566
Department Employee Unidentified	75	70
Sub-total of cases closed as other than full investigations	1,495	1,405
Conciliated	687	606
Miscellaneous	168	160
Open ****	1	53
Grand Total	3,515	3,377

* In these cases, the Board did not recommend a specific disciplinary action to the Police Commissioner.

** Includes all disciplinary actions preferred in calendar year, which also includes actions stemming from prior year's complaints which were not closed until the current year.

*** This number will continue to change until all 1990 cases have been reviewed by the Board.

**** Includes all District Attorney holds and cases awaiting completion of investigation.

TABLE 12

COMPARISON BETWEEN CCIB RECOMMENDATIONS AND BOARD FINDINGS IN CIVILIAN COMPLAINTS FOR CALENDAR YEAR 1989 AND 1990

CCIB RECOMMENDATIONS	1989	1990	BOARD FINDINGS	1989	1990
Substantiated	4	10	Unsubstantiated	3	7
			Exonerated	1	0
			Unfounded	0	1
			Miscellaneous	0	2
Unsubstantiated	107	65	Substantiated	43	28
			Unfounded	41	23
			Exonerated	16	9
			Compl. Withdrawn	1	0
			Vict. Unavailable	1	1
			Vict. Uncoop.	0	1
			Referred to I.A.D.	0	1
			Miscellaneous	5	2
Unfounded	15	4	Unsubstantiated	11	3
			C. Unavailable	1	0
			C. Uncooperative	0	1
			Dept. Empl. Unid.	1	0
			Miscellaneous	2	0
Exonerated	3	6	Substantiated	0	1
			Unsubstantiated	3	4
			C. Uncooperative	0	1
Complaint Withdrawn	2	1	Unfounded	2	1
Complainant Unavailable	13	4	Unfounded	2	1
			C. Uncooperative	11	2
			Miscellaneous	0	1
Victim Uncooperative	3	0	C. Uncooperative	1	0
			Compl. Withdrawn	1	0
			Miscellaneous	1	0
Complainant Uncoop.	11	6	Unfounded	0	1
			Exonerated	1	1
			Compl. Withdrawn	2	1
			Victim Uncoop.	1	0
			C. Unavailable	7	0
			Miscellaneous	0	3
Dept. Employee Unid.	11	2	Substantiated	3	0
			Unsubstantiated	1	0
			Unfounded	2	1
			C. Uncooperative	2	0
			Miscellaneous	3	1
Grand Total	169	98		169	98

TABLE 13

TENURE OF SUBJECT OFFICERS IDENTIFIED IN CIVILIAN COMPLAINTS

1989			1990		
YRS OF SERVICE	NO. OF COMPLAINTS	PERCENTAGE	YRS OF SERVICE	NO. OF COMPLAINTS	PERCENTAGE
1	4	0.14	1	7	0.26
2	152	5.43	2	105	3.89
3	558	19.95	3	272	10.10
4	613	21.92	4	591	21.94
5	424	15.16	5	499	18.52
6	327	11.69	6	385	14.29
7	189	6.76	7	267	9.91
8	181	6.47	8	183	6.79
9	113	4.04	9	144	5.35
10	15	0.53	10	67	2.49
11	19	0.68	11	13	0.48
12	0	0.00	12	20	0.74
13	0	0.00	13	0	0.00
14	1	0.04	14	0	0.00
15	0	0.00	15	1	0.04
16	25	0.89	16	0	0.00
17	64	2.29	17	28	1.04
18	1	0.04	18	50	1.86
19	7	0.25	19	5	0.19
20	15	0.54	20	4	0.15
21	32	1.14	21	6	0.22
22	22	0.78	22	13	0.48
23	5	0.18	23	10	0.37
24	9	0.32	24	2	0.07
25	7	0.25	25	1	0.04
26	5	0.18	26	8	0.30
27	1	0.04	27	0	0.00
28	0	0.00	28	2	0.07
29	1	0.04	29	1	0.04
30	0	0.00	30	3	0.11
31	2	0.07	31	0	0.00
32	0	0.00	32	1	0.04
33	4	0.14	33	0	0.00
34	0	0.00	34	3	0.11
35	0	0.00	35	3	0.11
36	0	0.00	36	0	0.00
37	0	0.00	37	0	0.00
38	0	0.00	38	0	0.00
39	1	0.04	39	0	0.00
TOTALS	2,797	100.00		2,694	100.00
Ongoing/ Undetermined	718			683	
TOTAL	3,515			3,377	

TABLE 10

COMPARISON OF COMPLAINTS RECEIVED REGARDING OFFICERS LIVING WITHIN AND OUTSIDE THE CITY OF NEW YORK FOR 1990

OFFICERS RESIDING WITHIN THE CITY (12/31/90)	OFFICERS RESIDING OUTSIDE THE CITY (12/31/90)
15,850	10,727
COMPLAINTS AGAINST OFFICERS* RESIDING WITHIN THE CITY	**COMPLAINTS AGAINST OFFICERS* RESIDING OUTSIDE THE CITY**
1,696	998
COMPLAINT EXPERIENCE FOR OFFICERS RESIDING WITHIN THE CITY	**COMPLAINT EXPERIENCE FOR OFFICERS RESIDING OUTSIDE THE CITY**
10.70 per 100 officers	9.30 per 100 officers

* First identified officer only.

Note: These totals do not include 683 cases in which the subject officer(s) have not yet been identified.

TABLE 20

COMPARISON OF RACE OF COMPLAINANT AND RACE OF SUBJECT OFFICER

1990

	No. of Compls	% of Compls	No. of Subject Officers	% of Subject Officers	Overall Racial Distribution of Dept. Members
White	767	26.3	2,009	74.6	75.2%
Black	1,307	44.8	270	10.0	11.3%
Hispanic	757	26.0	380	14.1	12.6%
Others	84	2.9	35	1.3	0.8%
Sub-total	2,915	100.0	2,694**	100.0	100.0%
Unknown*	462		683		
Total	3,377		3,377		

1989

	No. of Compls	% of Compls	No. of Subject Officers	% of Subject Officers	Overall Racial Distribution of Dept. Members
White	827	26.7	2,120	75.6	76.7%
Black	1,386	44.8	283	10.1	11.0%
Hispanic	778	25.2	375	13.4	11.5%
Others	103	3.3	24	0.9	0.8%
Sub-total	3,094	100.0	2,802**	100.0	100.0%
Unknown*	421		713		
Total	3,515		3,515		

* The complainant declined to answer questions pertaining to race, or the subject officer has not been identified.

** First identified officer only.

TABLE 21

CROSS-TABULATION OF RACE OF COMPLAINANT AND RACE OF SUBJECT OFFICER

1990

COMPLAINANT'S RACE	SUBJECT OFFICER'S RACE					
	White	Black	Hispanic	Others	Unknown	Total
White	494	53	73	8	139	767
Black	786	139	130	9	243	1,307
Hispanic	438	46	120	5	148	757
Others	50	4	11	7	12	84
Unknown	241	28	46	6	141	462
TOTAL	2,009	270	380	35	683	3,377

1989

COMPLAINANT'S RACE	SUBJECT OFFICER'S RACE					
	White	Black	Hispanic	Others	Unknown	Total
White	543	45	85	9	146	828
Black	829	139	120	9	288	1,385
Hispanic	452	65	131	3	126	777
Others	60	5	16	1	21	103
Unknown	236	29	23	2	132	422
TOTAL	2,120	283	375	24	713	3,515

TABLE 22

COMPARISON OF SEX OF COMPLAINANT AND SEX OF SUBJECT OFFICER

1990

	Sex of Compl	% of Compls	Sex of Subject Officer	% of Subject Officers	% of Sex of Dept. Members Overall
Male	2,226	67.0	2,513	93.3	86.6
Female	1,095	33.0	181	6.7	13.4
Sub-Total	3,321	100.0	2,694*	100.0	100.0
Unknown	56		683		
Total	3,377		3,377		

1989

	Sex of Compl	% of Compls	Sex of Subject Officer	% of Subject Officers	% of Sex of Dept. Members Overall
Male	2,226	64.7	2,624	93.6	87.4
Female	1,214	35.3	178	6.4	12.6
Sub-total	3,440	100.0	2,802*	100.0	100.0
Unknown	75		713		
Total	3,515		3,515		

* First identified officer only.

TABLE 23

CROSS-TABULATION OF SEX OF COMPLAINANT AND SEX OF SUBJECT OFFICER

1990

COMPLAINANT'S SEX	SUBJECT OFFICER'S SEX			
	Male	Female	Unknown	Total
Male	1,715	95	416	2,226
Female	770	86	239	1,095
Unknown	28	0	28	56
TOTAL	2,513	181	683	3,377

1989

COMPLAINANT'S SEX	SUBJECT OFFICER'S SEX			
	Male	Female	Unknown	Total
Male	1,700	99	427	2,226
Female	880	77	257	1,214
Unknown	44	2	29	75
TOTAL	2,624	178	713	3,515

Document No. 17
Omaha, Neb.

P. J. Morgan

EXECUTIVE ORDER OF THE MAYOR
M-01-93

RECEIVED JUL 8 1993 LAW DEPT.

SUBJECT: Creation of the Citizen Review Board (CRB)

I. PURPOSE

To establish a mechanism through which certain complaints and disciplinary decisions made against sworn members of the Omaha Police and Fire Departments are reviewed.

II. ESTABLISHMENT:

The Citizen Review Board (C.R.B.) shall be composed of nine individuals appointed in the following manner:

A) Two sworn members of the Omaha Police Department selected from a list submitted by the Omaha Police Union Local 101, and one sworn member of the Fire Department selected from a list submitted by the Professional Firefighters Association of Omaha, Local No. 385. Neither the representatives of the Police Department or the Fire Department who are selected pursuant to this subsection shall be elected or appointed officials of either Union. The individuals appointed pursuant to this subsection shall hold ranks subordinate to either the rank of Major/Deputy Chief in the Police Department or the rank of Assistant Fire Chief in the Fire Department.

B) Three citizens of the City of Omaha shall be appointed all of whom shall be members of a protected class by virtue of that individuals race, national origin or sex. At least one member appointed pursuant to this subparagraph shall be a woman and at least two members shall be a protected class member by virtue of their race or national origin.

C) Three citizens of the City of Omaha shall be appointed who are not members of a protected class by virtue of their race or national origin. At least one member appointed pursuant to this subparagraph shall be a woman.

D) All individuals, excluding sworn police and fire personnel, who are proposed appointees to the CRB shall be subject to a back ground check prior to their appointments. This back ground check shall include, but not necessarily be limited to, a check of that proposed appointee's criminal record history. The Mayor shall take into account the results of the background check in making appointments to CRB.

PLAINTIFF'S EXHIBIT 6

1819 Farnam, Suite 300 Omaha, Nebraska 68183-0300 Telefax (402) 444-6059 (402) 444-5000

III. TRAINING:

With the exception of sworn personnel who are members of the CRB each member appointed by the Mayor to the CRB shall be provided with a four week orientation session which shall include police and fire practices, procedures and policies. The nature and extent of the orientation provided herein shall be determined by the administration of the Omaha Police Department and Omaha Fire Department should be made available to all appointees as soon as is practicable following that individuals appointment to the CRB.

It is the intent of this Executive Order that the membership of the CRB shall be reflective of the social, ethnic and economic components that generally comprise the Omaha Community at large. Recommendations regarding the appointment of members to the CRB may be based on, but not necessarily limited to, recommendations from the following agencies: the Omaha Police Union, the Omaha Fire Union, the Native American Coalition, the Urban League, the League of Women Voters, the Hispanic Coalition, the National Association for the Advancement of Colored People, National Council of Jewish Women, National Conference of Christians and Jews Council and the Interdenominational Ministerial Alliance.

IV. TERM:

The first persons appointed by the Mayor shall serve for terms of one (1), two (2) or three (3) years respectively. Thereafter, all appointments shall be for three (3) year terms. The length of terms of the initial appointees shall, to the extent practicable, be evenly distributed through the three groups of appointments outlined in paragraph I., A, B, and C.

V. RULES OF PROCEDURE:

The CRB shall elect its chairperson, vice chairperson and secretary from its membership. Individuals elected to these positions shall hold them for one year. The vice chair person shall serve in the absence of the chairperson. ROBERTS RULES OF ORDERS shall govern the proceedings of the CRB in all cases in which said rules are not inconsistent with Charter, applicable City ordinances, the collective bargaining agreements applicable to police and fire personnel and any rules of procedure duly adopted by the CRB. Due to the provisions of the collective bargaining agreements, and pursuant to Section 23-25 of the Omaha Municipal Code, the proceedings of the CRB are considered confidential and, therefore, not open to the public or the media.

VI. QUORUM AND MEETINGS:

A quorum of the CRB shall be five of the nine members. Meetings shall be held on no less than a monthly basis.

VII. <u>OPERATIONS</u>:

The CRB may request by two-thirds majority vote of its nine members appropriate office equipment, material and personnel assistance be provided to it through the Mayor's office. Provision for any equipment, personnel or material granted pursuant to this provision shall be at the sole discretion of the Mayor.

VII. <u>JURISDICTION</u>:

The Police and Fire Departments shall have initial original jurisdiction on all complaints against sworn Police or Fire employees and such complaints shall be processed in accordance with the Standard Operating Procedures of the applicable division, and any relevant portions of a labor agreement which may be applicable to the processing of such complaints.

Department

VIII. <u>PURPOSE</u>:

The general purpose of the CRB shall be:

A. Make recommendations regarding the establishment of appropriate criteria for recognizing sworn members of the Police and Fire Departments to identify high standards in the performance of their sworn duties and functions.

B. After completion of an investigation by the Office of Professional Standards and decision made as a consequence thereof by the Chief of Police or Fire a citizen or civilian employee may request in writing the initiation of a complaint with the CRB which shall fully and completely review any such complaint. The complaint may allege one or more of the following:

1. Police harassment

2. Excessive use of force

3. Use of language likely to demean the inherent dignity of any person to whom it was directed and/or to trigger disrespect for law enforcement officers.

4. A violation of the Standard Operating Procedures or rules or regulations codified by the Nebraska Commission on Law Enforcement and Criminal Justice.

In conducting its review the CRB may request that the Chief of the proper Department order any sworn law enforcement officer or firefighting personnel to be present at said review process. The CRB shall via the Chief's office be allowed access to investigative material developed by the Office of Professional Standards or the Fire Department internal investigation, as applicable. The CRB shall render its recommendation regarding a proper disposition of a citizen's complaint. Each such disposition and recommendation shall be reduced to writing.

IX. EFFECTIVE DATE:

For the purposes of considering appointments to the CRB and conducting certain preliminary endeavors, such as orientation, this Executive Order shall become effective immediately. On and after August 1, 1993, the CRB shall commence receiving and reviewing any complaint which is the subject of a written request. During the interim between the execution of this Executive Order, and the effective date for considering and reviewing complaints, the Mayor's Advisory Board shall continue to function as necessary through and including July 31, 1993.

X. RECOMMENDATIONS:

All written recommendations shall be forwarded directly to the Mayor and where appropriate either the Chief of the Police Department or the Chief of the Fire Department. Additionally, the CRB shall make monthly reports which shall be submitted to the Mayor, the City Council and other appropriate entities or individuals.

BY THE POWER VESTED IN ME BY SECTION 3.04 AND 8.06 OF THE OMAHA HOME RULE CHARTER OF 1956, I SET MY HAND TO THIS ORDER ON THIS 9th DAY OF JUNE, 1993.

P.J. Morgan

P.J. Morgan, Mayor

8636F

Document No. 18

Phoenix

3. **DISCIPLINARY REVIEW BOARD**: This board is established to provide the Police Chief with an advisory board to assist in giving stability, consistency, fairness and timely information to the department's disciplinary process. The board is authorized to review disciplinary reports, refer such reports back to unit commanders for further investigation and to recommend the degree and severity of disciplinary action to the Police Chief. The board will not conduct hearings or investigations. Employees responsible for a Performance Achievement Plan will not appear before the Disciplinary Review Board. *

3. A. The board for a sworn employee will consist of an assistant chief, two captains, two employee peers, and two citizens of Phoenix. The board for a civilian employee will consist of an assistant chief, a civilian administrator, one captain, two employee peers, and two citizens of Phoenix. An assistant chief will chair the board.

B. The board will review all disciplinary reports in which a suspension, demotion or dismissal has been approved by a division commander and all reports of an employee being cited for driving a vehicle while under the influence, as well as all sustained reports in which an employee has committed a criminal act. However, when an employee is involved in a serious violation of the law or the rules and regulations of the department to the extent that the violator could be immediately dismissed from employment, a supervisor may, through the chain of command, immediately and directly refer the matter to the Police Chief, or his designee, for action. Such a referral will bypass the Disciplinary Review Board. [52.2.6; 52.3.3]

(1) The involved employee shall have the right to appear before the departmental Disciplinary Review Board when the disciplinary matters brought before the board may lead to demotion, suspension or dismissal.

(a) The purpose of such appearance is to give the employee an opportunity to respond to any sustained assertions made against him.

(b) The department shall notify the employee ten calendar days prior to the board meeting. The notification shall contain the date, time, violation(s), and basis of each violation that has been sustained.

(c) The employee may meet with his immediate supervisor along with his second level supervisor, or the employee's bureau/precinct commander to discuss the matter being reviewed by the board. The employee may be accompanied by a unit representative at the meeting.

(d) If the immediate supervisor conducted the investigation, the employee may meet with the next supervisor in his chain of command. Such a request shall be made in writing to the employee's immediate supervisor. The employee may be accompanied by a unit representative at the meeting.

(e) The employee may appear before the board, with a unit representative of his choosing, to state his reasons why the proposed action is unjustified.

(f) The employee may submit relevant written matter in support of his position.

(g) Any appearance before the board during the employee's regular work shift shall be counted as time worked. Employees are not eligible for overtime pay when appearing before the board during other than regular work shift hours.

C. After review, the board will arrive at a recommendation, including the number of hours in cases of suspension, and submit it to the division commander.

(1) Such recommendations are advisory only.

3. C. (2) If the board disagrees with the recommendations submitted by the division commander and feels the disciplinary actions should be less severe than a suspension, demotion or dismissal, it will return the report to the division commander, who may proceed with action as provided under paragraph 2.I or submit the matter directly to the Police Chief for further consideration.

(3) The recommendations of the board will be included in the permanent record of the disciplinary report.

Document No. 19

Pittsburgh

(employees' and citizens' guides)

City of Pittsburgh

DEPARTMENT OF PUBLIC SAFETY
Office of Professional Standards
(412) 255-2804

Carla M. Gedman, Civilian Asst. Chief

MISCONDUCT COMPLAINTS

An Employee's Guide to the Office of Professional Standards

What Is the Office of Professional Standards?

OPS investigates and helps resolve complaints about Public Safety Department employees--including police, fire, EMS, building inspection and administrative employees. Our office conducts pre-employment background investigations on candidates for Public Safety jobs. OPS is completely independent of the Public Safety bureaus; its authority is drawn from the Public Safety Director, to whom it reports. The office is staffed by a civilian Assistant Chief, civilian Coordinator, Police Sergeant and four Detectives.

How Does OPS Operate?

The Office of Professional Standards acts solely as a fact-finder, and does not make disciplinary decisions or recommendations. OPS relies on city work rules, union contracts, civil service regulations, city code and state laws to define illegal and inappropriate conduct and rules of investigation. By remaining independent from any Public Safety Department bureau, and removed from the disciplinary process, OPS ensures citizens and employees of fair, thorough investigations. OPS also identifies problem areas where policy development or retraining may be necessary.

Who May File a Complaint with OPS?

Any person directly involved in an incident who questions the appropriateness of a Public Safety employee's conduct may file a complaint with OPS. "Third party" complaints are not accepted except for parents or guardians of minors or developmentally delayed persons. Because OPS is required to conduct a full investigation in every case, complaints must be filed in writing. Anonymous complaints are considered unfounded unless corroborative evidence is obtained.

BACKGROUND INFORMATION

Public employees are held to a higher standard of conduct because of the public trust in government. The City, as an employer, may establish work rules that must be job related and may also utilize a disciplinary system to enforce rules.

That system must also be job related. On a related matter. there is a public policy responsibility to investigate failure to comply with work rules. The City has a duty to take responsible steps to assure that jobs are performed appropriately. Accordingly, public personnel must answer questions specifically, narrowly, directly related to the performance of their official duties. This includes related off-duty conduct that is job related. Prior to the actual interview, employees will be informed whether the investigation is administrative or criminal in nature. Employees may not refuse to cooperate in an administrative interview; failure to comply in this setting may result in disciplinary action.

The benefits to an internal investigation are: a certain amount of protection in outside inquires, that is, an official department decision is on record. This "freezes" the testimony of witnesses who may pursue other avenues, civil and federal court, for example.

This meets the public trust responsibility of a public employee fairly, and is much better for the employee (and the public) than sweeping a complaint "under the rug".

EMPLOYEE RIGHTS

Check your specific collective bargaining agreement, department procedural orders, and civil service regulations.

In general:

- "Accused" employees may review the complaint and are entitled to a copy of their own statement upon request.

- Closing letters will be sent which provides the employee the opportunity to review the OPS case report. "Sustained" cases in the Police Bureau only are not included here. The disciplinary process has its own review procedures.

- Any interview may result in disciplinary action depending on the outcome of the total investigation. An employee will always be informed of the possible work rule violations prior to the interview.

Possible closing categories are sustained, not sustained, exonerated, unfounded, and closed by memo.

If an employee wishes to check their OPS history, they may request a review through the civilian Assistant Chief.

If you have any questions regarding an OPS related matter, please call 255-2804, Monday through Friday, 8:30 A.M. until 4:30 P.M.:

Civilian Assistant Chief Carla Gedman
Civilian Coordinator Roy Dean
Sergeant James Hayes
Detective Robert Mathews
Detective Marianne Polk
Detective William Myers
P.O. Leslie Woods
P.O. John Abrams
Clerk-Steno Sally Bronson

MISCONDUCT COMPLAINTS

A CITIZENS GUIDE TO USING THE OFFICE OF PROFESSIONAL STANDARDS

OFFICE OF PROFESSIONAL STANDARDS

Public Safety Building, 7TH Floor
Pittsburgh PA 15219

255-2804 / 255-2805

What is the Ofiice of Professional Standards ?

OPS investigates and helps resolve complaints about Public Safety Department employees - including police, fire, EMS, building inspection and administrative employees. It conducts pre-employment background investigations on candidates for Public Safety jobs. OPS is competely independent of the five Public Safety bureaus; it's authority is drawn from the Public Safety Director, to whom it reports.

How does OPS operate?

The Office of Professional Standards acts soley as a fact finder, and does not make disciplinary decisions or recommendations. OPS relies on city work rules, union contracts, civil service regulations, city code and state laws to define illegal and inappropriate conduct and rules investigation, By remaining independent from any Public Safety Department bureau, and removed from the disciplinary process, OPS ensures citizens and employees of fair, thorough investigations. OPS also itentifies problem areas where policy development or retraining may be necessary. OPS is staffed by a Civilian Assistant Chief, Civilian Coordinator, Detectives and a clerical staff.

How do I file ?

You should contact OPS as soon after the incident as possible. Some union contracts have a 90 day statute of limitations on most cases of misconduct. You may call OPS for information and assistance, but formal complaints cannot be made over the phone. You may file in person at the OPS office, or send a letter describing the complaint, including your name, address, daytime phone and signature.

You can reach the Office of Professional Standards by calling 255-2804, Monday through Friday 8:30 a.m. to 4:30 p.m.. You may file your complaint in person at the offices Monday through Friday 8:30 a.m.. to 3:30 p.m.

Who may file a complaint with OPS ?

Any person directly involved in an accident who questions the appropriateness of a Public Safety employee's conduct may file a complaint with OPS. "Third party' complaints are not accepted, except for parents or guardians of monors or developmentally delayed persons. Because OPS is required to conduct a full investigation in every case, including questioning complainants, no anonymous complaints can be investigated without corroborative evidence.

What happens to my complaint after it's filed

Your complaint will be reviewed by an intake officer at OPS. All pertinent information will be sought - - witness names and phonr numbers, photos of injuries or damage, medical records - - anything that will shed light on the case. Shortly after filing your complaint, you'll receive a letter providing you with a case number and the investigator's name. When the case is closed, you will receive a closing letter informing you of the disposition.

Cases are reviewed by the employee's supervisors and the Public Safety Director. Discipline procedures are well-defined and carried out by the bureau supervisors with approval from the Public Safety Director.

What if I have other questions?

The OPS staff is happy to help you determine if you have a complaint that should be handled by them or if it could be more appropriately handled in another way. They will insist in identifying the agency best able to meet your needs. Call at 255-2804 for any questions you may have.

Document No. 20

Pittsburgh

(functions and procedures)

CITY OF PITTSBURGH

DEPARTMENT OF PUBLIC SAFETY

TO: Mayer A. DeRoy, Chief
Bureau of Police

FROM: GLENN M. CANNON, Director
Department of Public Safety

DATE: April 8, 1991

SUBJECT: OPR FUNCTIONS AND PROCEDURES RELATING TO THE BUREAU OF POLICE

The Office of Professional Responsibility (OPR) is responsible for conducting investigations into matters relating to employees or employment in the Department of Public Safety. OPR is also responsible for reviewing all disciplinary action taken against Public Safety employees.

OPR has department-wide jurisdiction and functions under the authority of the Director of Public Safety. The Assistant Chief is responsible for the office operations and answers to the Director. The office consists of one civilian investigator and four police officers.

There are four major types of police cases handled by OPR which originate from a number of different sources. Those cases consist of public complaints investigated by OPR, (OPR investigation), public complaints reviewed by OPR, (Director Referrals), Bureau complaints initiated by Bureau officers and supervisors which are reviewed and if necessary, investigated by OPR (Bureau Investigation), and Special Investigations (SI) that are either initiated by OPR on its own or as a result of information received from other sources. Each of the above areas are explained in detail below.

In addition to the above, OPR is also responsible for reviewing policies or procedures that may be subject to abuse for misuse by employees. This function primarily relates to matters effecting employee accountability for disciplinary purposes. OPR is also responsible for preparing cases for Fire Bureau Trial Boards, arbitrations and other proceedings, facilitating the hearings themselves and retaining records of hearings and disciplinary actions.

OPR will also review and make recommendations to the Director regarding cases that have been initiated and investigated by the Police Bureau itself.

Finally, OPR is responsible for post disciplinary functions such as making sure that the discipline imposed is carried out.

Following are detailed explanations of specific OPR functions.

1. PUBLIC COMPLAINT INVESTIGATED BY OPR

Public complaints directed at members of the Bureau of Police will be investigated by OPR in all cases in which physical abuse or excessive force is alleged.

The office will also investigate allegations of wrongful detention and verbal abuse, or any other alleged violation of a General Order; if the severity of the complaint dictates OPR involvement or if matters beyond the particular facts may be of concern, i,e., the accused officers employment history, similar allegations by others, etc.

Allegations of less serious offenses will be referred to the Assistant Bureau Chief for investigation and recommendation.

When a public complaint is received by OPR and the decision is made for OPR to investigate the matter, the complaint will be chronologically assigned a P-OPR number which will indicate that the complaint involves the Police Bureau, state the OPR case number and the year the action was filed, (P-OPR #50-86).

When an OPR investigation is completed, a "P-OPR Final Report," will be prepared containing a procedural summary of the investigation, a factual summary, a factual analysis, OPR findings and recommendations and an appendix containing all documents, statements, reports, etc., relied upon in the investigation.

The report will be sent to the Chief of Police for his review and recommendations. At the Chief's discretion, the report will be routed to other members of the Bureau of Police.

Following the review by the Bureau of Police, the report will be returned to OPR with the Chief's recommendation on the appropriate action to be taken and the basis for such recommendation, if necessary.

OPR will forward the report along with the Chief's recommendation to the Director at which time, the Director will approve, disapprove or modify the action recommended. No disciplinary action can be imposed without first obtaining the Director's approval.

Routing of Public Complaints Investigated by OPR
(P-OPR Final Reports)

PUBLIC COMPLAINTS channeled to:

OPR	- accept complaint - decision to investigate

OPR (Continued)	- OPR number assigned - investigation & final report - recommendation
CHIEF OF POLICE	- review report - recommends action - recommend further investigation
DIRECTOR/OPR	- recommendation approved - disciplinary action ordered - recommendation disapproved or modified - further investigation ordered

Once the disciplinary action is approved, OPR is responsible for monitoring the discipline. OPR will send a letter to the complainant informing them of the result of the investigation and action taken. Accused officers will receive a closing notice as well for all dispositions except sustained. The grievance procedure and current disciplinary process has its own guidelines for case reviews. OPR will also prepare termination and suspension letters for the Director's signature and will file and retain copies of letters of reprimand written by the Chief of Police or his designates.

OPR will calculate and set suspension dates through the Bureau of Police to ensure that seniority adjustments for periods of suspension are made. OPR will work with the Personnel Section in order to accomplish the above.

2. PUBLIC COMPLAINT REVIEWED BY OPR

As discussed above, certain public complaints will be investigated by the Police Bureau and reviewed by OPR. The types of cases investigated by the Bureau of Police will be ones alleging verbal abuse, rudeness or the use of foul language on the part of the police officer.

Although such cases may be less significant compared to other OPR cases, they are extremely significant to the complaining party and have a damaging impact on the many positive accomplishments of the Bureau. Such complaints have a devastating impact on the public's perception of the Bureau's professionalism.

When OPR decides that a particular case is proper for Bureau investigation, it will be assigned a Police Director Referral number, reflecting the case number and year, (P-DR #5-86).

The P-DR will then be sent to the Assistant Chief of the Police Bureau in which the employee is assigned. The case is routed to a member of the Bureau for investigation, normally the Commander. The person assigned to conduct the investigation will be expected to interview all witnesses, both civilian and police, take statements when possible, and review all reports or other physical evidence. The investigating officer will prepare a report analyzing the facts and making recommendations which will be reviewed, approved and commented on by all persons in the chain of command up to and including the Chief. The reports should include all relevant facts and the source of such facts. If witnesses are unavailable or uncooperative, that should be noted in the report.

If OPR feels the investigation is incomplete, it will be returned to the Chief for further investigation. Officers should be instructed that they are expected to make complete and thorough investigations and failue to do so could result in disciplinary action. In every case an investigation should not be returned to OPR if all apparent witnesses, including the complainant, have not been interviewed.

Upon the completion of the Bureau investigation and approval of the findings, OPR will send a letter to the complainant identifying the investigating officers and notifying the complainant of the results of the investigation and the action taken.

Once the discipline is appoved by the Director, OPR will assume the same type of post investigative duties as those described in #1 above.

Below is a routing chart for public complaints investigated by the Police Bureau and reviewed by OPR.

Routing of Public Complaints Investigated
by Police Bureau

PUBLIC COMPLAINTS channeled to:

OPR	- accept complaint - decision to D.R. - D.R. number
ASSISTANT CHIEF OF POLICE	- assigns investigation - reviews report - recommends action
OPR	- recommend action - reviews report - further investigation

DIRECTOR - disciplinary action approved, disapproved or modified

3. POLICE BUREAU

P-BI (Police-Bureau Investigation) investigatins are investigations conducted by Police Bureau personnel or OPR personnel, and often involve complaints based on charges filed by a supervising officer against someone under their command or in some cases by one police officer against another. They require the Police Bureau or OPR to investigate the charges, interview witnesses and review other evidence in preparation for possible disciplinary action.

When received by OPR, such cases will be assigned a P-BI number (P-BI #1-87). Such number will be used to identify the case during the course of the investigation.

Following review and approval of the P-BI by OPR, the matter will be submitted to the Director for approval.

Below is a routing chart for P-BI cases conducted by the Police Bureau. P-BI cases handled by OPR are routed in the same manner as P-OPR cases. See #1.

BUREAU CHARGES	- DAR prepared
CHIEF OF POLICE	- review charges - approves charges - recommend action
OPR	- P-BI number assigned - review charges - recommend action - further investigation
DIRECTOR	- discipline action approved, modified or disapproved

Post investigation duties performed by OPR in #1 above will also be performed following BI cases.

4. POLICE SPECIAL INVESTIGATIONS

Special investigations will involve the commitment of manpower to specific projects or investigations. Such projects or investigations may originate from a number of sources. Special investigations will be routed from OPR to the Director. Such investigations will be assigned a Police Special Investigation number (PSI).

In addition to the matters described above, OPR is available to assist all Bureaus on any employee related matter.

CG:sab

cc: D/Director Ralph D. Pampena
A/Chief Carla Gedman

Document No. 21
Portland, Ore.

ORDINANCE NO. **167276**

Adopt report entitled, "Police/Citizen Accountability Initiative;" adopt amendments to City Code Section 3.21, Police Internal Investigations Committee; adopt amendments to Police Internal Investigations Audit Committee and Citizen Advisors Rules; adopt Schedule of Appointment for Citizen Advisors and authorize IID complaint neighborhood intake sites. (Ordinance; amend Code Section 3.21)

The City of Portland ordains:

Section 1. The Council finds:

1. Community policing is premised on a cooperative relationship between police and neighborhoods;

2. Citizen oversight of police conduct and practices is a component of accountability to the community;

3. The accessibility of a review process, including a citizen's ability to initiate a complaint, is key to its credibility and success;

4. Policy makers and managers should benefit from regular citizen reports on trends and policy issues raised by the police Internal Investigations process;

5. The Mayor attended numerous meetings of the PIIAC Citizen Advisors throughout 1993 to assess the current system;

6. The PIIAC Citizen Advisors, the Mayor, and members of the public have contributed suggestions for changes to the existing system for oversight of police conduct designed to increase its effectiveness, resulting in the report attached as Exhibit A; and

7. The attached Exhibits B, C, and D, and ordinance directive e implement the report attached as Exhibit A.

NOW, THEREFORE, the Council directs:

a. Exhibit A entitled "Police/Citizen Accountability Initiative" dated December 15, 1993 is accepted.

b. Exhibit B entitled, Chapter 3.21, Police Internal Investigations Audit Committee is adopted.

c. Exhibit C entitled "Police Internal Investigations Audit Committee and Citizen Advisor Rules" is adopted.

d. Exhibit D entitled "Appointments Schedule for Appointment of Citizen Advisors to Police Internal Investigations Audit Committee" is adopted.

ORDINANCE No. 167276

e. The Commissioner in Charge of Police shall have the authority to work with the Office of Neighborhood Associations and the Bureau of General Services to identify and establish neighborhood sites where citizens can file IID complaints with assistance from non-Police Bureau personnel.

f. Section 3.21.080 shall take effect on July 1, 1994. Until that time, the Auditor shall be responsible for the duties under this section.

Passed by the Council, JAN 12 1994

Mayor Katz
Adrianne Brockman
Dec. 29, 1993

BARBARA CLARK
Auditor of the City of Portland
By Britta Olson Deputy

Document No. 22
Rochester, N.Y.

Rochester Police Department
General Order

effective date:	subject:	G.O. 320
May 15, 1993	CIVILIAN REVIEW BOARD	
rescinds: G.O. 320 Dated June 1, 1987	reference standard(s): CALEA: 1.3.15; 26; 54 NYS: 8.12; 14.4	

I. CIVILIAN REVIEW BOARD MEMBERSHIP

Civilian Review Board (CRB) shall consist of the following:

Three citizen panelists from the Rochester community (selected on a rotating basis) as designated by the Center for Dispute Settlement (CDS) and certified by the American Arbitration Association. One of the panelists will be designated as the Chairperson.

II. CRB FUNCTIONS AND RESPONSIBILITIES

The CRB will be convened to review one or more investigations at any given session. The functions and responsibilities of the CRB will include the following:

A. Receive completed investigation(s) from the Commanding Officer of the Professional Standards Section on all investigations where a citizen or Departmental complaint against a police officer would, if proven, constitute a crime or constitute unnecessary force.

B. Review other selected cases as requested by the Chief of Police.

C. Review the fairness, thoroughness, completeness, and timeliness of these completed investigations and identify possible shortcomings.

D. Conduct voluntary interviews of officers, complainants or witnesses involved in the case being reviewed.

E. Return to the commanding officer of the Professional Standards Section any investigation which any member of the Board feels is deficient, giving reasons therefor. If the Board remains dissatisfied, subsequent appeals may be made to the Chief, the Mayor and City Council.

F. Vote as a group on the Professional Standards Section conclusion and prepare a report of findings for the Chief of Police with dissenting opinions if a unanimous conclusion is not reached.

G. Recommend changes or review of policy, procedures, or training for forwarding to the Chief of Police who will forward to the Internal Investigation Advisory Committee.

H. Maintain the strict confidentiality of all information contained within the Professional Standards Section reports and all matters discussed by the Board.

III. COMMANDING OFFICER OF THE PROFESSIONAL STANDARDS SECTION

A. Notify the Center for Dispute Settlement of the time and place that panelists are needed to serve on a CRB and supply CDS with the name(s) of the complainant and the police employee and the nature of the complaint for review. (This will allow any panelist who may have knowledge of the case to be disqualified or to disqualify himself.)

B. Prepare the designated location of the Board review. Provide to each member of the Committee a copy of the completed investigation(s) to be reviewed. Ensure that all copies of the Professional Standards reports remain in the room provided for the use of the CRB during their review.

C. Provide equipment for viewing a video-taped complainant, witness or officer interview as required. Provide equipment for listening to audio tapes as required.

D. Ensure all copies of the Professional Standards reports at the end of each session are secured until the CRB reconvenes, should more than one session be required to complete the review of the case(s).

E. Arrange on behalf of CRB interviews between them and police or civilian witnesses.

F. Retrieve from the CRB all copies of investigations after Board review, maintaining the original in the Professional Standards Section files.

G. Request that the Professional Standards Section conduct further investigation into any case returned as incomplete by the CRB.

H. Forward the results of the Professional Standards Section investigation and the CRB findings to the Chief of Police.

• • •

CIVILIAN REVIEW BOARD

CRB RESPONSIBILITIES:

1. REVIEW the submitted investigative package for timeliness, thoroughness, and fairness.

2. DETERMINE if there are any significant areas within the package that necessitate additional follow-up prior to the committee's recommending a finding.

3. QUESTION PSS investigative officer if any aspect of the investigation is unclear. Question advising captain regarding procedural questions.

4. RETURN to the PSS Commanding Officer, without finding, any package determined to need follow-up. Indicate the specific area believed to be deficient.

5. RECOMMEND a specific finding based on a review of the complete package for each allegation addressed by the investigation as follows with dissenting opinions as applicable (see 8):

   UNFOUNDED - act complained of did not occur

   UNPROVABLE - there is insufficient evidence to prove or disprove the allegation

   SUSTAINED - the act occurred and amounts to misconduct or misjudgment

   EXONERATED - the act did occur but the personnel's conduct was justified, lawful, and proper

6. ARTICULATE the specific reasoning for each recommended finding (ie., the justification for that recommendation).

7. EXPRESS any concerns that may have arisen during the course of a case review:

   1. Procedural: a change in departmental policy is warranted

   2. Remedial: either oral remedial instruction or a memorandum of record be drawn up

   3. Training: a refresher course or additional training

8. When the results of the CRB's findings are not unanimous, each CRB member will identify themselves along with their recommended findings (see 5).

9. The CRB or a CRB member who recommends a finding other than that reached by PSS or a finding resulting from an issue raised for the first time by the CRB, will support that finding with specific references to the material in the investigative package and a statement of rationale.

NOTE: CRB MEMBERS ARE OBLIGATED TO MAINTAIN THE STRICT CONFIDENTIALITY OF ALL INFORMATION CONTAINED WITHIN THE INVESTIGATIVE AND ALL RELATED MATTERS DISCUSSED.

III. PROCEDURE FOR CIVILIAN REVIEW BOARD (C.R.B.) CASE REVIEW

The Civilian Review Board is a panel consisting of three civilian personnel.

The three civilian members for a C.R.B. are chosen by the Center for Dispute Settlement selection process. A chairperson and two panelists will be selected on a rotating basis.

The C.R.B. purpose or function and its responsibilities are specifically outlined in General Order 320.

CASES THAT WILL BE REVIEWED BY THE C.R.B. PANEL WILL BE ALL USE OF FORCE COMPLAINTS AND COMPLAINTS THAT ALLEGE CRIMINAL CONDUCT BY AN OFFICER/EMPLOYEE. IN ADDITION, ANY CASE SO DESIGNATED BY THE CHIEF OF POLICE WILL BE PRESENTED TO A C.R.B.

The arrangements for setting up a case review for a C.R.B. panel are as follows:

Step 1 Obtain the completed case package from the investigating sergeant. (A completed case is one that has been reviewed by the Commanding Officer of the Professional Standards Section.)

Step 2 Put the following information in the C.R.B. notebook log sheet (Attachment 2):

A. Time and date of C.R.B.
B. P.S.S. case number
C. Respondent (names of police personnel complained about)
D. Name of complainant
E. C.D.S. members on panel (usually filled in on the day of the case review
F. Initial type of complaint:
   UF = Use of force
   P = Procedural
   MP = Missing property

G. Case disposition (filled in after panel reports their findings)

H. Date notified

Step 3 After the police portion of the C.R.B. is scheduled, notify the Center for Dispute Settlement "intake person" of the date and request two civilian members for the panel (by phone). Then, give the C.D.S. "intake person" the following information:

A. Date of the C.R.B.

B. Time of the C.R.B.

C. P.S.S. case number

D. Respondent (names of police personnel complained about)

E. Complainant's name

F. Type of complaint the panel will review:

1. Use of force
2. Procedural
3. Missing property

Step 4 Put scheduled C.R.B. date on the calendar in the secretary's office.

Step 5 Turn the investigative package over to the P.S.S. secretary for the following steps:

A. Secretary will make three (3) copies of the case package (each member has a copy to read). The original case package will be included in the copies to be reviewed.

B. All four (4) copies will be kept in the Commanding Officer's file cabinet (bottom drawer) until the date of the C.R.B.

Step 6 Date of the C.R.B. Review

A. The investigator will prepare the meeting room with the appropriate materials needed for the review. The material list includes the case packages, video/audio tapes and playback equipment, writing tablets and pens and any other materials necessary to facilitate the review process.

The allegation sheet, C.R.B. cover sheet, and the four (4) case summaries will be set aside from the four (4) packages. The investigative findings on the allegation sheet will remain blank until after the C.R.B. has concluded their review and placed their findings on the sheet (Attachment 4).

The investigator will remain within the building during the initial meeting of the C.R.B. in the event any panel member has a question concerning the investigation.

B. Introduce the complaint and present the investigative package with a brief explanation to the C.R.B. at their City Hall meeting room.

C. Instruct all panel members not to mark on the case packages in the event further hearings are necessary.

Step 7 Instruct the panel members that after the case review, one of the panel members will dictate the findings to the P.S.S. stenographer via telephone, tape record, or handwrite the findings. Any dissenting opinions should be dictated by the dissenting panelist(s). Any finding not consistent with the investigator's findings must be fully and thoroughly explained on the record in order to assist the Chief in reaching a final decision.

Step 8 The case packages are then returned to the P.S.S. investigating sergeant with the findings attached. All four copies are kept by P.S.S. at this time in the event:

A. Further information or investigation is requested by the C.R.B. panel;

B. Chief of Police designates that charges be placed against the involved police personnel;

C. In case of either A or B above, the investigative package will be reused by panel members or the Hearing Board members.

Additional Notes

1. In the event a civilian panelist is absent, contact C.D.S. for a replacement prior to cancelling the C.R.B.

2. If additional investigation is required, select a feasible adjournment date for the panel to reconvene as the SAME MEMBERS MUST BE RESCHEDULED TO FINISH THE C.R.B. REVIEW.

3. Try to arrange the C.R.B. reviews on a date when the sergeant that conducted the investigation is working in the event any questions need to be answered by the C.R.B. panel.

Document No. 23

San Diego

CITY OF SAN DIEGO
Proposition G

(This proposition will appear on the ballot in the following form.)

G AMENDS THE CHARTER OF THE CITY OF SAN DIEGO BY AMENDING SECTION 43.

SECTION 43 ADVISORY BOARDS AND COMMITTEES

No changes in subsection (a), (b) and (c).

(d) CITIZENS' REVIEW BOARD ON POLICE PRACTICES. Notwithstanding any other provision of this Charter, the City Manager shall have the exclusive authority to create and establish a citizens' review board on police practices to review and evaluate citizens' complaints against members of the San Diego Police Department and the San Diego Police Department's administration of discipline arising from such complaints. The City Manager shall establish such rules and regulations as may be necessary for this board to carry out its functions; provided, however, that such rules and regulations shall be consistent with the laws of the State of California concerning citizens' complaints against peace officers. Nothing in such rules and regulations shall interfere with the board's authority to independently refer a completed citizen complaint investigation to the grand jury, district attorney, or any other governmental agency authorized by law to investigate the activities of a law enforcement agency. The board shall submit semiannual reports to the City Manager and City Council concerning its evaluation of the San Diego Police Department's investigation of citizens' complaints; provided, however, that such reports shall not disclose any information required to be kept confidential by law.

The City Council voted 5-4 to place this measure on the ballot. Councilmembers **Roberts, McColl, Struiksma, Henderson** and **McCarty** cast votes in favor. Mayor **O'Connor** and Councilmembers **Wolfsheimer, Pratt** and **Filner** voted in opposition.

Amends the Charter of the City of San Diego by adding Subsection (d) to Section 43 of Article V, to read as follows:

SEC. 43 ADVISORY BOARDS AND COMMITTEES

No changes in subsection (a), (b) and (c).

<u>(d)CITIZENS' REVIEW BOARD ON POLICE PRACTICES. Notwithstanding any other provision of this Charter, the City Manager shall have the exclusive authority to create and establish a citizens' review board on police practices to review and evaluate citizens' complaints against members of the San Diego Police Department and the San Diego Police Department's administration of discipline arising from such complaints. The City Manager shall establish such rules and regulations as may be necessary for this board to carry out its functions; provided, however, that such rules and regulations shall be consistent with the laws of the State of California concerning citizens' complaints against peace officers. Nothing in such rules and regulations shall interfere with the board's authority to independently refer a completed citizen complaint investigation to the grand jury, district attorney, or any other governmental agency authorized by law to investigate the activities of a law enforcement agency. The board shall submit semiannual reports to the City Manager and City Council concerning its evaluation of the San Diego Police Department's investigation of citizens' complaints; provided, however, that such reports shall not disclose any information required to be kept confidential by law.</u>

N 368-89

CITY ATTORNEY'S IMPARTIAL ANALYSIS

The San Diego City Council has authorized the placement on the ballot of two (2) propositions dealing with the subject of the review of police practices. Proposition F is a proposal to amend the San Diego City Charter by creating a "Police Review Commission" consisting of nine (9) members appointed by the Mayor and confirmed by the City Council. Utilizing its own executive director and subpoena power, the Commission is charged with reviewing allegations of police misconduct and reporting its findings to the Chief of Police and City Manager. Proposition G is a proposal to amend the San Diego City Charter by creating a "Citizens' Review Board on Police Practices" created and established solely by the City Manager. Utilizing rules and regulations established by the City Manager, the Board will review complaints arising from the Police Department and may independently refer its investigations to the grand jury, district attorney or other authorized agency.

To facilitate the comparison of these two (2) proposals by the voters, the City Council directed the City Manager to provide the estimated financial impact of each proposal. The City Manager has supplied the City Attorney with the following estimates for each proposal.

1. **PROPOSITION F: POLICE REVIEW COMMISSION.**

   Until the Board Members are appointed and establish their own rules and regulations, precise administrative costs are impossible to establish. However, a cost comparison utilizing the cities of San Francisco, Kansas City, Washington, D.C., Miami and Detroit, which utilize police review formats, ranges in costs from $244,763 to $2,021,000 for an annual average cost of $988,858.

2. **PROPOSITION G: CITIZENS' REVIEW BOARD ON POLICE PRACTICES.**

   Since this Board would be similar to the existing citizens' advisory panel on police practices, the estimated costs of this Board would be approximately $48,000 per year.

JOHN W. WITT
City Attorney

Document No. 24

San Diego County

(citizen complaint form)

SAN DIEGO COUNTY
CITIZENS LAW ENFORCEMENT REVIEW BOARD
CITIZEN COMPLAINT FORM

INSTRUCTIONS FOR COMPLETING CITIZENS COMPLAINT FORM:

Please describe the incident that led to this complaint, telling what happened from beginning to end. Be as clear and specific as you can be. Please describe the problem with what happened. How could it be solved to your satisfaction? Please print your responses. If you do not know the officer's name or badge number, try to describe the officer. If you need more space, attach added sheets.

Your statement must be a true and accurate account of the incident to the best of your knowledge, and you must sign and attest to its accuracy. If you have questions or need help, please call the Review Board at (619) 685-2200 between 8:00 AM and 5:00 PM weekdays, or leave a message at that number after hours.

In accordance with the County Administrative Code, a copy of the complaints received by the Review Board shall be transmitted to the Sheriff or the Chief Probation Officer. Complaints which are in the possesson of the Review Board or it's staff, shall be confidential and shall not be disclosed to any member of the public, except in accordance with applicable law.

Your complaint will be investigated. If you move or change phone numbers, remember to let the Review Board know.

==

INSTRUCCIONES PARA LLENAR LA FORMA DE QUEJAS:

Por favor describa el incidente que motivó esta queja, explicando que pasó desde el principio hasta el fin, y lo más detalladamente que pueda. Describa lo que pasó, y lo que usted considere una solución. Por favor, presente su repuesta por escrito. Si no sabe el nombre del oficial o el número de su placa, trate de describirlo. Sí necesita más espacio, adjunte más hojas.

Su declaración sobre el incidente tiene que ser verdadera y precisa, hasta donde sea de su conocimiento. Usted debe firmar y dar fe de la veracidad del contenido de su declaración. Si tiene preguntas, necesita ayuda, o si prefiere esta forma en Inglés, por favor llame a la oficina del Consejo de Revision al (619) 685-2200 entre 8:00 AM Y 5:00 PM durante la semana, o deje un mensaje después del horario de oficina.

De acuerdo con el codigo administrativo del Condado, copias de todas las quejas recibidas por el Consejo de Revision, deberan ser transmitidas al Sheriff o al jefe de la oficina de Libertad Vigilada--Probacion. El Consejo de Revision y su personal son responsables de mantener confidenciales todas las quejas en su posesion. No seran dadas a conocer a ninguna persona, salvo en caso de ser requeridas por la ley vigente.

Su queja será investigada. Si cambia su número de teléfono o su domicilio, por favor avise al Consejo de Revision.

1. COMPLAINANT: ____

Last Name First Name Middle Name

____

Home Address Street Apt # City State Zip

____

Work Address Street Ste # City State Zip

____

Telephone Number Home Work Message

Optional: ____

Date of Birth Sex Ethnicity

2. INCIDENT CAUSING THIS COMPLAINT: Location: ______________________

____

Address or Description of Location; Type of place

Date and Time of Incident ______________________________ AM or PM

Aggrieved Person (If Not Complainant) ______________________________

If Complainant and/or Aggrieved Person is in Custody, list release date, out-of-custody address & phone: ______________________________

____

Optional: ____

Date of Birth Sex Ethnicity

Name(s) and/or Badge Number(s) of Officer(s) Involved if Known ____________

____

DESCRIPTION OF INCIDENT: ______________________________________

____

____

____

____

____

____

____

Witness(es) ______________________________

Include name/address/phone for each witness; attach added sheets if needed

3. SWORN STATEMENT OF COMPLAINANT: I hereby certify that, to the best of my knowledge, and under penalty of perjury, the statements made herein are true.

Signature | Print name | Date

CLERB staff use only:

A. DATE COMPLAINT RECEIVED: ______________________________

COMPLAINT INTAKE BY ______________________________

Circle How Received: Person Letter Dept Phone Other

Injuries Claimed? Yes [ ] No [ ] Injuries Visible? Yes [ ] No [ ]

Drug/Alcohol Related? Yes [ ] No [ ] Medical Release Signed? Yes [ ] No [ ]

Photos taken? Yes [ ] No [ ] By: ______________________________

B. COMPLAINT ASSIGNED TO ______________________________

PRELIMINARY RECOMMENDATION: ______________________________

Circle COMPLAINT CATEGORY: I. II. III. IV. V.

Circle Complaint Against: Personnel Policy Procedure

C. FINAL RECOMMENDATION ______________________________

DISPOSITION Unfounded [ ] Not Sustained [ ] Action Justified [ ] Sustained [ ]

After you have completed this form, return it to the Citizens' Law Enforcement Review Board by folding it along the lines below so that the address shows on the outside. Drop in any mailbox.

Despues de completar la forma, doblela sobre las lineas marcadas y depositela en el buzon.

C.L.E.R.B.
600 Pacific Hwy. Rm 602
San Diego, CA 92101

Place Stamp Here

County of San Diego
Citizens' Law Enforcement Review Board
1600 Pacific Hwy. Rm. 602
San Diego, Ca 92101

Document No. 25

San Diego County

(rules and regulations)

CITIZENS LAW ENFORCEMENT REVIEW BOARD
RULES AND REGULATIONS

TABLE OF CONTENTS

SECTION 1: PURPOSE — Page 1

SECTION 2: DEFINITIONS — Page 1

SECTION 3: ORGANIZATION AND MEETINGS — Page 2

3.1 Compositions of the Review Board — Page 2
3.2 Term of Membership — Page 2
3.3 Vacancies on the Review Board — Page 2
3.4 compensation — Page 2
3.5 Officers of the Review Board — Page 2
3.6 Orientation and Training — Page 3
3.7 Transaction of Business — Page 3
3.8 Special meetings of the Review Board — Page 4
3.9 Review Board Staff — Page 4

SECTION 4: AUTHORITY, JURISDICTION, DUTIES AND RESPONSIBILITIES OF REVIEW BOARD — Page 5

4.1 Citizens Complaints: Authority — Page 5
4.2 "Misconduct" Defined — Page 5
4.3 Citizen Complaints: Pre-requisite — Page 5
4.4 Citizen Complaints: Jurisdiction — Page 5
4.5 Citizen Complaints: Notification of Disposition — Page 6
4.6 Citizen complaint Not Required: Jurisdiction with Respect to Actions involving Death — Page 6
4.7 Other Duties and Responsibilities — Page 6

SECTION 5: PROCEDURES REGARDING COMPLAINTS — Page 6

5.1 Policy — Page 6
5.2 Lodging and Filing of Complaints — Page 7
5.3 Who May File Complaint — Page 7
5.4 Time Limitations for Filing Complaints — Page 7
5.5 Complaint Form — Page 8
5.6 Recording of Complaints — Page 8
5.7 Withdrawal of Complaints — Page 8
5.8 Termination, Resignation or Retirement — Page 8

SECTION 6: COOPERATION AND COORDINATION — Page 8

SECTION 7: SUBPOENAS: OATHS — Page 8

SECTION 8: CONFIDENTIALITY OF RECORDS — Page 8

SECTION 9: INVESTIGATION OF COMPLAINT — Page 9

9.1 Transmittal of Complaints — Page 9
9.2 Screening of Complaints — Page 9
9.3 Scope of Investigation — Page 9
9.4 Investigative Report — Page 10
9.5 Review Board Options After Receipt of Investigative Report — Page 10
9.6 Disposition by Review Board without a Hearing — Page 10
9.7 File Accessibility — Page 10
9.8 Notification to Parties — Page 10

SECTION 10: DETERMINING WHEN A HEARING IS NECESSARY — Page 11

10.1 Request for Investigative Hearing — Page 11
10.2 When is a Hearing necessary — Page 11
10.3 Scope of the Investigative Hearing — Page 11

SECTION 11: NO CONTEST RESPONSE — Page 11

SECTION 12: INVESTIGATIVE HEARING PANELS — Page 11

12.1 Composition of Hearing Panel — Page 11
12.2 Selection of Three-Person Hearing Panels — Page 11
12.3 Challenges of Board Members — Page 12
12.4 Public Comments — Page 12

SECTION 13: INVESTIGATIVE HEARING PROCEDURES — Page 12

13.1 Schedule of Investigative Hearing — Page 12
13.2 Notice Requirements — Page 12
13.3 Hearings Open to Public — Page 12
13.4 Authority to Compel Appearance — Page 12
13.5 Conduct of the Investigative Hearing — Page 12
13.6 Deliberation — Page 13

SECTION 14: EVIDENCE — Page 13

14.1 What Evidence May be Considered — Page 13
14.2 Representatives — Page 13
14.3 Interpreters — Page 14
14.4 Authority to Compel Appearance — Page 14
14.5 Failure to Appear — Page 14
14.6 Confidentiality of Review Board Records — Page 14
14.7 Discovery — Page 14
14.8 Record of Investigative Hearing — Page 14
14.9 Standard of Proof — Page 14

SECTION 15: SUMMARY DISMISSAL — Page 14

SECTION 16: REVIEW BOARD FINDINGS AND RECOMMENDATIONS — Page 14

16.1 Finding and Report by Three-Member Hearing Panel — Page 14
16.2 Submission to full Review Board — Page 15
16.3 Consideration by full Review Board — Page 15
16.4 Investigative Hearings before entire Review Board — Page 15
16.5 Final Report by Review Board
16.6 Conclusions in Final Report — Page 15
16.7 Consideration of Subject Officer's Disciplinary History — Page 15
16.8 Transmittal of Final Report
16.9 Reconsideration of Final Report — Page 15

SECTION 17: PROCEDURES WHEN NO CITIZEN COMPLAINT REQUIRED — Page 16

SECTION 18: DELEGATION OF FUNCTIONS TO EXECUTIVE OFFICER — Page 16

SECTION 19: AMENDMENTS TO RULES AND REGULATIONS — Page 16

CITIZENS LAW ENFORCEMENT REVIEW BOARD
PROPOSED RULES AND REGULATIONS
(Adopted by the C.L.E.R.B. on March 9, 1992
Revised by the C.L.E.R.B. on October 21, 1992
Adopted by the C.L.E.R.B. on April 12, 1994)

SECTION 1: PURPOSE.

The purpose of these rules and regulations is to facilitate the operation of the Review Board, including the review of citizen complaints filed against peace officers or custodial officers employed by the County of San Diego in the Sheriff's Department or the Probation Department, as authorized by San Diego County Ordinance #7880, as amended (Article XVIII, Section 340-340.15 of the Administrative Code of the county of San Diego). Complaints subject to review are those which allege improper or illegal conduct of peace officers or custodial officers arising out of the performance of their duties or the exercise of peace officer authority, within the jurisdiction of the Review Board, as more fully described in Section 4 below.

In order that this purpose can be achieved, the Citizens Law Enforcement Review Board, hereafter referred to as the Review Board, shall receive, review, investigate and report on citizen complaints in accordance with these rules and regulations. These rules are to provide for the fair, impartial, independent and prompt investigation of citizen complaints in a manner which a) protects both the public and the Departments, Sheriff and Probation, which are involved in such complaints, and b) enhances the relationship and mutual respect between the Departments and the public they serve.

The Review Board shall publicize the review process in a manner which encourages and gives the public confidence that they can come forward when they have a legitimate complaint regarding the conduct of peace officers or custodial officers designated above. The Review Board shall also make every effort to ensure public awareness of the seriousness of the process, and that fabricated complaints will neither be tolerated nor reviewed. The statutory and constitutional rights of all parties shall be safeguarded during the review process.

SECTION 2: DEFINITIONS.

Wherever used in these rules, unless plainly evident from the context that a different meaning is intended, the following terms mean:

2.1 "Subject Officer: "The peace officer or custodial officer employed by the County of San Diego in the Sheriff's Department or the Probation Department against whom has been filed a Citizen complaint alleging improper or illegal conduct as set forth in sections 4.1 and 4.2 or about whom an investigation is undertaken without the filing of a complaint as set forth in section 4.6.

2.2 "Aggrieved Person:" Any person who appears from a complaint to have suffered injury, harm, humiliation, indignity, or any other damage as a result of actions by a peace officer or custodial officer in the performance of his or her official duties or the exercise of peace officer authority.

2.3 "Citizen Complaint" A complaint received from any person without regard to age, citizenship, residence, criminal record, incarceration, or any other characteristic of the complainant alleging an improper act or misconduct, as further defined in sections 4.1 and 4.2 below, of a peace officer or custodial officer in the performance of his or her official duties or the exercise of peace officer authority.

2.4 "Chair:" The Chairperson of the Citizens Law Enforcement Review Board, or the Vice Chairperson if the Chairperson is not able to preside.

2.5 "Complainant:" Any individual who files a complaint regarding the conduct of a peace officer or custodial officer in the employ of the Sheriff's Department or the Probation Department arising in the performance of his or her official duties or the exercise of peace officer authority and who files a complaint with the Review Board.

2.6 "County:" County of San Diego, California

2.7	"Ordinance:"	County Ordinance #7880, as amended, Article XVIII (commencing with Section 340) of the Administrative Code of the County of San Diego adopted by the Board of Supervisors of the County of San Diego, California, which became effective on May 2, 1991.
2.8	"Review Board:"	The eleven (11) members of the Citizens Law Enforcement Review Board nominated and appointed in accordance with the provisions of the Ordinance.
2.9	"Hearing Panel:"	A three (3) member subcommittee of the Review Board selected to conduct an investigative hearing of a citizen complaint, and make appropriate findings and recommendations to the Review Board based on the hearing.
2.10	"Presiding Member:"	The member of a three person Hearing Panel appointed by the Chair to preside at an investigative hearing.

SECTION 3: ORGANIZATION AND MEETINGS.

3.1 Composition of the Review Board. The Review Board shall consist of eleven (11) members nominated by the Chief Administrative Officer and appointed by the Board of Supervisors. Each Review Board member shall be a qualified elector of San Diego County and shall possess a reputation for integrity and responsibility and have demonstrated an active interest in public affairs and service.

3.2 Term of Membership. Each member shall serve a term of three (3) years. A member shall serve on the Review Board until a successor has been appointed. A member shall be appointed for no more than two (2) Consecutive full terms. Appointment to fill a vacancy shall constitute appointment for one term. The term for all members shall begin on July 1 and end on June 30. The terms for all persons who are the initial appointees to the Review Board shall be deemed to commence on July 1, 1991.

Members of the Review Board serve at the pleasure of the Board of Supervisors and may be removed from the Review Board at any time by a majority vote of the Board of Supervisors.

3.3 Vacancies on the Review Board. A vacancy shall occur on the Review Board on the happening of any of the following events before the expiration of the member's term:

(a) Death of the incumbent,

(b) Resignation of the incumbent,

(c) Ceasing of the incumbent to be a resident of the County of San Diego,

(d) Absence of the member from three consecutive regular meetings of the Review Board, or,

(e) Failure to attend and satisfactorily complete the required training course within three months of the beginning of a member's term or of the member's appointment to fill a vacancy.

When a vacancy occurs the Board of Supervisors and, where appropriate, the member shall be notified of the vacancy by the Chair. Vacancies shall be filled within forty five (45) days for the balance of the unexpired term, and in the same manner as the position was originally filled.

3.4 Compensation. Members of the Review Board shall serve without compensation, except that they shall be reimbursed for necessary expenses incurred in performing their duties in accordance with provisions of the County Administrative Code.

3.5 Officers of the Review Board. The members of the Review Board shall elect annually from its membership a Chair, a Vice Chair and a Secretary. The term of office shall be for one year or until the successor has been elected. The duties of the Officers shall be as follows:

A. Chair: The Chair shall preside over all meetings of the Review Board and shall have the right to vote on all questions. The Chair shall ensure that the laws of the County pertaining to the activities of the Review Board and the rulings of the Review Board are faithfully executed. The Chair shall act as the spokesperson in all matters pertaining to the Review Board.

The Chair shall sign all documents on behalf of the Review Board after the same have been approved by the Review Board and shall perform such other duties and delegated responsibilities as may be imposed upon him or her by the Review Board. The Chair shall appoint all subcommittees, and, ex-officio, be a member of all subcommittees.

B. <u>Vice-Chair</u>: In the absence of the Chair, the Vice-Chair shall perform all the duties of the Chair with the same force and effect as if performed by the Chair.

C. <u>Chair Pro Tem</u>: If both Chairs are absent at any meeting of the Review Board and have not selected a Chair Pro Tem, the Review Board shall select a Chair Pro Tem who shall perform all the duties of the Chair.

D. <u>Secretary</u>: The Secretary shall keep a true and correct record of all proceedings of the Review Board. The Secretary shall have custody of all reports, books, papers, and records of the Board.

E. <u>Secretary Pro Tem</u>: In the absence of the Secretary, the Review Board may appoint a Secretary Pro Tem.

3.6 <u>Orientation and Training</u>. The Chief Administrative Officer is responsible for the establishment of an orientation and training program for the members of the Review Board. Each member of the Review Board shall attend and satisfactorily complete a training course within three months of the beginning of the member's term, or of the member's appointment to fill a vacancy. Failure to attend and satisfactorily complete the course within the prescribed time shall result in the member's removal from the Review Board and automatically create a vacancy.

The orientation and training program includes familiarization with the following:

(a) County Government structure and the Review Board;

(b) County Charter, Brown Act and State Law pertaining to the Review Board;

(c) State Law relating to Peace Officers' rights and privacy;

(d) Operations of the Sheriff's Department and the Probation Department;

(e) Disciplinary process for Deputy Sheriffs and Probation Officers;

(f) Sheriff and Probation Departments' training programs;

(g) Community perspective on Law Enforcement;

(h) Constitutional and civil rights law relating to police misconduct and citizen's rights.

(i) Memoranda of Agreement between the County of San Diego and the Deputy Sheriff's Association or San Diego Probation Officers' Association.

3.7 <u>Transaction of Business</u>. The Review Board shall establish a regular meeting schedule and shall give public notice of the time and place of the meetings. The official address of the Review Board will be:

Citizens Law Enforcement Review Board
1600 Pacific Hwy., Room 602
San Diego, CA 92101

All regular and special meetings of the Review Board shall be held at the official address, or at any other public place as designated by the Chair.

The meetings and business of the Review Board will be conducted in accordance with the following:

(a) The agenda for each meeting will normally be provided to all members in time to be received at least one week prior to the regularly scheduled meeting.

(b) The agenda for each meeting will be posted, distributed, and otherwise made public in accordance with the requirements of State and County law applicable to advisory boards.

(c) All meetings shall be held in accordance with the requirements of the Ralph M. Brown Act, Section 54950 et seq., of the California Government Code.

(d) A majority of members currently appointed to the Review Board shall constitute a quorum.

(e) The affirmative vote of the majority of the members currently appointed to the Review Board shall be required to carry a motion or proposal.

(f) The Review Board's legal counsel will normally be present for all meetings of the Review Board.

(g) In all procedures not provided for by these Rules, or the enabling Ordinance #7880, as amended, the Review Board shall be governed by Robert's Rules of Order, Newly Revised.

(h) The Review Board shall keep written minutes of all meetings and a copy shall be filed with the Clerk of the Board of Supervisors.

(i) Subcommittees may be established by the Review Board as appropriate, however, no more than five (5) members of the Review Board (including the Chair as an ex-officio member) shall serve on any one subcommittee.

(j) Members and the Chair of each subcommittee shall be designated by the Chair of the Review Board.

(k) As noted in Section 3.3 above, a member's absence from three (3) consecutive regular meetings of the Review Board shall result in the member's automatic removal from the Review Board.

(l) Normally, the order of business for the Review Board meetings shall be as follows:

1. Roll Call.
2. Approval of Minutes.
3. Special order of business; announcements; communications.
4. Public comment.
5. Executive Officer's report.
6. General policy items.
7. Subcommittee reports.
8. Unfinished business.
9. New business.
10. Discussion and consideration of complaints and reports.
11. Recess to closed session, if appropriate.
12. Adjourn.

3.8 Special Meetings of the Review Board. Special meetings may be held at the call of the Chair, or the vice-Chair in the absence of the Chair. Upon petition of six (6) members of the Review Board, the Chair shall call a meeting of the Review Board within one (1) week. Review Board members will be given at least twenty-four (24) hours notice prior to any special meeting. The notice and agenda for any special meeting will be distributed in accordance with Section 54956 of the Government Code. No business other than that specified in the special meeting agenda shall be considered.

3.9 Review Board Staff. The Review Board shall appoint personnel in support of the Review Board as may be authorized by the Board of Supervisors. Currently, the following four (4) positions have been authorized: An Executive Officer, a Special Investigator, an Administrative Secretary II, and an Intermediate Clerk Typist. The Board of Supervisors has also authorized the hiring of outside, independent legal counsel for the Review Board.

The Executive Officer shall recommend to the Review Board the filling of any staff position for approval by the Review Board; and shall supervise the administrative, clerical, investigative and other personnel as necessary to discharge the functions of the Review Board. The Executive Officer shall promulgate internal office procedures and prepare necessary standardized forms for the conduct of the investigations and the receipt of citizen complaints. The daily operations of the Review Board, including the conduct of investigations, shall be managed by the Executive Officer who shall oversee the regular functioning of the staff assigned to help carry out the duties of the Review Board.

SECTION 4: AUTHORITY, JURISDICTION, DUTIES AND RESPONSIBILITIES OF REVIEW BOARD.

4.1 Citizen Complaints: Authority. Pursuant to Ordinance #7880, as amended, (Article XVIII, Section 340-340.9 of the San Diego County Administrative Code), the Review Board shall have authority to receive, review, investigate and report on citizen complaints filed against peace officers or custodial officers employed by the County in the Sheriff's Department or the Probation Department, which allege:

(a) Use of excessive force;

(b) Discrimination or sexual harassment in respect to members of the public;

(c) The improper discharge of firearms;

(d) Illegal search or seizure;

(e) False arrest;

(f) False reporting:

(g) Criminal conduct; and/or

(h) Misconduct.

4.2 "Misconduct" Defined. "Misconduct", as referred to in section 4.1 (h) above, is defined to mean and include any alleged improper or illegal acts, omissions or decisions directly affecting the person or property of a specific citizen arising out of the performance of the Peace officer's or custodial officer's official duties or the exercise of Peace officer authority by reason of:

(a) An alleged violation of any general, standing or special orders or guidelines of the Sheriff's Department or the Probation Department; or,

(b) An alleged violation of any county ordinance or state or federal law; or,

(c) Any act otherwise evidencing improper or unbecoming conduct by a peace officer or custodial officer employed by the Sheriff's Department or the Probation Department.

4.3 Citizen Complaints: Pre-requisite. The Review Board shall have no authority with respect to alleged improper activities and misconduct, as set forth in sections 4.1 and 4.2 above, to take action in regard to incidents for which no citizen complaint has been filed with the Review Board.

4.4 Citizen Complaints: Jurisdiction. The Review Board shall have jurisdiction in respect to all citizen complaints arising out of incidents occurring on or after November 7, 1990; provided, however, that the Review Board shall not have jurisdiction to take
any action in respect to complaints received more than one year after the date of the incident giving rise to the complaint, except that if the person filing the complaint was incarcerated or physically or mentally incapacitated from filing a complaint following the incident giving rise to the complaint, the period of incarceration or incapacity shall not be counted in determining whether the one year period for filing the complaint has expired.

The complainant shall bear the burden of demonstrating that he/she was incarcerated or physically or mentally incapacitated from filing a complaint within one year from the incident giving rise to the complaint by submitting a written statement to the Review Board. Prior to determining whether it has jurisdiction over the complaint, the Review Board will notify the subject officer, provide him/her with a copy of the complaint and the complainant's statement, and give him/her the opportunity to submit a statement limited solely to the issue of whether there was such an incarceration or physical or mental incapacity. This matter shall be scheduled for consideration by the Review Board at its regular meeting and the agenda materials distributed prior to the meeting shall include the written statments submitted by the complainant and subject officer.

The written statement submitted to the Review Board pursuant to this section shall be attested to under penalty of perjury as provided by Section 5.5 of these rules.

4.5 Citizen Complaints: Notification of Disposition. The Review Board shall have authority to notify in writing any citizen having filed a complaint with the Review Board of the disposition of his or her complaint. The Chief Administrative Officer shall also receive appropriate notification of the disposition of citizen complaints. Such notifications shall be in writing and shall contain the following statement: "In accordance with Penal Code section 832.7, this notification shall not be conclusive or binding or admissible as evidence in any separate or subsequent action or proceeding brought before an arbitrator, court or judge of California or the United States."

4.6 Citizen Complaint Not Required: Jurisdiction with Respect to Actions involving Death. The Review Board shall have authority to review and investigate the death of any individual arising out of or in connection with actions of peace officers or custodial officers employed by the County in the Sheriff' s Department or the Probation Department, arising out of the performance of his or her
official duties or the exercise of peace officer authority, regardless of whether a citizen complaint regarding such death has been filed with the Review Board. The Review Board shall have jurisdiction in respect to all deaths of individuals coming within the provisions of this subsection occurring on or after November 7, 1990; provided however, that the Review Board may not commence review or investigation of any death of an individual coming within the provisions of this subsection more than one year after the date of the death, unless the review and investigation is commenced in response to a complaint filed within the time limits set forth in section 4.4.

4.7 Other Duties and Responsibilities. The Review Board shall have authority to:

(a) Prepare reports, including at least the Sheriff or the Chief Probation Officer as recipients, on the results of any investigations conducted by the Review Board in respect to the activities of peace officers or custodial officers, including recommendations relating to any trends in regard to employees involved in citizen complaints. The Review Board is not established to determine criminal guilt or innocence.

(b) Prepare an annual report to the Board of Supervisors, the Chief Administrative Officer, the Sheriff and the Chief Probation Officer summarizing the activities and recommendations of the Review Board including the tracking and identification of trends in respect to all complaints received and investigated during the reporting period.

(c) Review and make recommendations on policies and procedures of the Sheriff and the Chief Probation Officer to the Board of Supervisors, the Sheriff and the Chief Probation Officer.

(d) Annually inspect county adult detention facilities and annually file a report of such visitations together with pertinent recommendations with the Board of Supervisors, the Presiding Judge of the Superior Court, the Sheriff, the Board of Corrections and the Attorney General. Inspections shall be concerned with the conditions of inmate employment, detention, care, custody, training and treatment on the basis of, but not limited to, the minimum standards established by the Board of Corrections.

(e) Establish necessary rules and regulations for the conduct of its business, subject to approval of the Board of Supervisors.

SECTION 5: PROCEDURES REGARDING COMPLAINTS.

5.1 Policy. The following shall provide a framework for the receipt, screening, processing, and disposition of citizen complaints regarding alleged illegal or improper conduct (set forth in Sections 4.1 and 4.2) by employees of the County of San Diego in the Sheriff' s Department and the Probation Department:

(a) It is the policy of the Review Board to encourage citizens who have complaints concerning the conduct of peace officers or custodial officers employed by the County in the Sheriff's Department or the Probation Department to bring the same to the attention of the Review Board. The Review Board will attempt to assist and accommodate complainants regarding the complaint filing process.

(b) The investigation of complaints shall be conducted in a fair, impartial, objective and ethical manner.

(c) Complaints will be considered, investigated (where appropriate), and disposed of in accordance with the procedures set forth herein.

(d) As promptly as possible, citizen complaints received by the Review Board shall be transmitted by the Executive Officer to the Sheriff or the Chief Probation Officer.

(e) The Review Board will make every effort to ensure that no adverse consequences will result to any person or witness as a result of having brought a complaint or having provided information in any investigation of a complaint.

(f) The Review Board will make every effort to consider and to respond to citizens' complaints against peace officers or custodial officers, and, where investigation is necessary, will conduct an impartial and fair investigation into any such complaints in accordance with the procedures set forth herein.

(g) The right of any complainant to bring a complaint shall be absolute and unconditional. The reluctance or refusal of the complainant to prepare a complaint form shall not impair his or her right to lodge a complaint. No complaint shall be investigated, however, until a complaint signed by or on behalf of the person aggrieved has been received by the Review Board or a member of its staff.

(h) The investigation of a complaint will be conducted in a manner designed to avoid unnecessary inconvenience or embarrassment to the complainant, the aggrieved person, the witnesses, the subject officer, and any agency or instrumentality of the County.

(i) To the extent possible consistent with its duties and responsibilities, the Review Board shall coordinate its activities with other public officers, such as the Sheriff, the District Attorney, the Grand Jury, the U. S. Attorney, and the Public Defenders Office, so that the other public officers and the Review Board can fully and properly perform their respective duties.

5.2 Lodging and Filing of Complaints. Complaints may be lodged in writing, in person, by telephone or by any other means of Communication. A complaint may be lodged with the Review Board on behalf of oneself or on behalf of another person by any interested person or group. A complaint shall be considered received by the Review Board at the time it is lodged.

No complaint will be deemed to have been filed with the Review Board unless and until it has been reduced to writing, and signed by the complainant or his/her representative, in accordance with the following procedures:

(a) If the complaint is lodged in person, the Review Board employee shall furnish the complainant with a blank complaint form. The complainant shall be asked to fill out the form and to sign the form in the space provided. A copy of the completed form shall be given to the complainant to serve as a record of the filing of the complaint.

(b) If the complaint is lodged by mail, the complaint form shall be completed by the Review Board staff on the basis of the information contained within the correspondence. The Review Board staff shall mail a copy of the completed complaint to the complainant as a record of the lodging of the complaint, together with a request that the complainant review the complaint form for accuracy, and if accurate, sign the same and return it to the Review Board office.

(c) If the complaint is lodged by telephone, the Review Board staff shall fill out an original complaint form and prepare one duplicate copy of the complaint form as a record of the lodging of the complaint. The Review Board employee taking the complaint shall give his or her name to the complainant. The Executive Officer shall furnish the complainant with a copy of the completed form, together with a request for verification of the accuracy and a signature.

(d) In those cases where the complainant is incarcerated in a detention facility in the County of San Diego, the complaint will be handled as outlined in (b) or (c) above.

5.3 Who May File Complaint. Citizen complaints shall include complaints received from any person what so ever without regard to age, citizenship, residence, criminal record, incarceration, or any other characteristic of the complainant.

5.4 Time Limitations for Filing Complaints. All complaints shall be received within one year after the date of the incident giving rise to the complaint, except that if the person filing the complaint was incarcerated or physically or mentally incapacitated from filing a complaint following the incident giving rise to the complaint, the time duration of such incarceration or physical or mental incapacity shall not be counted in determining whether the one year period for filing the complaint has expired, subject to the provisions of Section 4.4 of these Rules and Regulation, pursuant to the provisions of Section 4.4 of these rules.

5.5 Complaint Form. The Review Board shall cause all complaints received by it to be reduced to writing on the complaint form. Unless the Review Board has received another writing setting forth the substance of the complaint and signed by the complainant, the completed form shall be furnished to the complainant advising that the complaint will not be deemed to have been filed with the Review Board until and unless it is reduced to writing. The truthfulness of a written complaint shall be attested to under penalty of perjury in the following manner, or by words of similar effect: "I hereby certify that, to the best of my knowledge, and under penalty of perjury, the statements made herein are true".

5.6 Recording of Complaints. The Review Board shall cause a central register of all complaints filed with it to be maintained in its office. The central register shall record actions taken on each complaint. The central register shall contain the following:

(a) Name of the Complainant, the Aggrieved Party, and the Subject Officer,

(b) Number of complaint,

(c) Date complaint was filed,

(d) A brief description of the subject matter of the complaint,

(e) Date the complaint was transmitted to the Sheriff's Department or the Probation Department,

(f) Results of the Review Board's consideration and/or investigation, if any,

(g) Date and content of the final disposition of the complaint.

5.7 Withdrawal of Complaints. A complaint may be withdrawn from further consideration at any time by a written notice of withdrawal signed and dated by the complainant. The effect of such withdrawal will normally be to terminate any further investigation of the complained of conduct, unless the Executive Officer or a Review Board member recommends that the investigation continue and the Review Board, in its discretion, concurs.

5.8 Termination, Resignation or Retirement of Subject Officer. The Review Board shall have the discretion to continue or terminate an investigation, if, after a complaint is filed and before the Review Board completes its investigation, the subject officer terminates employment with the Sheriff's Department or the Probation Department. The Sheriff or the Chief Probation Officer or the subject officer shall notify the Review Board when the subject officer's employment is terminated.

SECTION 6: COOPERATION AND COORDINATION.

In the discharge of its duties, the Review Board shall receive complete and prompt cooperation from all officers and employees of the County. The Review Board and other public officers, including the Sheriff, the District Attorney, and the Grand Jury, shall coordinate their activities so that the other public officers and the Review Board can fully and properly perform their respective duties.

Such cooperation shall include appearing at and answering questions during interviews, appearing at and answering questions during hearings, assisting with access to physical evidence, and cooperation with any other relevant investigation procedures.

The Review Board shall attempt to avoid contacting any subject officer at his or her home. The Review Board shall attempt to get the subject officer's work schedule prior to scheduling an interview or investigative hearing. The Review Board shall attempt to avoid scheduling interviews or investigative hearings on an officer's regular days off, scheduled vacation or authorized leave of absence.

SECTION 7: SUBPOENAS: OATHS.

The Review Board shall, pursuant to the Charter of the County of San Diego, section 6C6(d), have the power to subpoena and require the attendance of witnesses and the production of documents and papers pertinent to its investigations; and shall have the power to administer oaths.

SECTION 8: CONFIDENTIALITY OF RECORDS.

Any personnel records, citizen complaints against County personnel in the Sheriff's Department or the Probation Department, and information obtained from these records, which are in the possession of the Review Board or its staff, shall be confidential and shall not be disclosed to any member of the public, except in accordance with applicable law. Copies of records and complaints of the Review Board shall be made available to the Sheriff or the Probation Officer upon completion of the investigation of the Review Board unless prohibited by applicable law.

SECTION 9: INVESTIGATION OF COMPLAINTS.

9.1 Transmittal of Complaints. Citizen complaints filed with the Review Board shall be transmitted forthwith to the Sheriff or the Chief Probation Officer.

9.2 Screening of Complaints.

(a) Complaints shall be referred to the Executive Officer for investigation. Each complaint will be initially screened by staff and classified as follows:

1. "Category I" Complaint against a peace officer or custodial officer employed by the County in the Sheriff's Department or the Probation Department which requires an immediate and thorough investigation.

2. "Category II" Complaint which does not warrant an immediate and full investigation, and/or is appropriate for deferral.

3. "Category III" Miscellaneous. Essentially a request for information -- complainant needs satisfied after explanation of County Sheriff's Department or Probation Department operations.

4. "Category IV" Complaint not within the jurisdiction of the Review Board. Such complaints will be referred to the Review Board for Summary Dismissal.

5. "Category V" Complaints not alleging facts establishing a prima facie showing of misconduct. Such complaints may be referred to the Review Board for Summary Dismissal.

(b) The classification of each complaint, as set forth in section 9.2(A) (1)-(5), must be reviewed and approved by the Review Board before significant further action is taken by staff with respect to such complaint.

(c) The Executive Officer shall periodically advise the Review Board as to the progress and status of each complaint.

(d) The Executive Officer may periodically advise the complainant and the subject officer(s) as to the status of a complaint.

9.3 Scope of Investigation. The investigation of a citizens complaint may include, but need not be limited to, the following:

(a) Interviews with the Complainant, the aggrieved party, each Subject Officer, and witnesses or other persons likely to have information concerning the complaint; examination of the scene of the incident; viewing and analyzing physical evidence, if any, associated with the alleged incident; review, analysis and preservation of other physical evidence, if any. Such investigations must be conducted in a manner that will not obstruct the criminal investigations conducted by the Sheriff, District Attorney, or other law enforcement agencies. In the event that the Subject Officer is compelled to cooperate in an investigation, the Subject Officer shall be provided the "Lybarger warning" when required under the appropriate circumstances.

(b) It shall be the responsibility of the investigator to record each step in the investigation and the result thereof in an investigation report which shall be made a part of the complaint file.

(c) The Review Board investigators shall attempt to secure written statements under oath from all participants in and witnesses to the alleged incident. Where any witness or participant is unwilling to make a signed written statement, the assigned investigator shall prepare a verbatim transcript or written summary of the oral statement, if any, provided by such participant or witness. Where a written statement is given and signed by a participant or witness, the assigned investigator shall provide the person making such statement with a copy of the statement.

(d) Interviews and statements may be tape-recorded by the investigator. Such recordings shall be kept and preserved until the case is finally disposed of by the Review Board and its findings reviewed by the Board of Supervisors or other appropriate agency or official, or for such longer period as may be required by law.

(e) The general policy of the Review Board will normally be to defer its investigation of a complaint for the period of time during which formal criminal proceedings relating to the subject matter of the complaint are pending against the subject officer. The Review Board reserves the right to commence immediate investigations, or to defer investigations, in all other cases depending upon Review Board priorities and available resources.

9.4 Investigation Report. At the conclusion of the (pre-hearing) investigation, the investigator shall complete an appropriate written report setting forth the names of the complainant, the aggrieved party, and the subject officer; and summarizing what investigation was conducted and what information was disclosed by the investigation. The report shall also contain a procedural recommendation by the Executive Officer to the Review Board as to what further action should be taken by the Review Board, such as whether an investigative hearing before a three-member Hearing Panel is appropriate, or before the full Review Board, or whether the case is appropriate for Summary Dismissal, or any other appropriate action or disposition.

The Investigative Report shall be submitted to the Chair of the Review Board who may attach his or her own recommendation and submit the entire report to the Review Board, either orally or in writing, or both.

9.5 Review Board Options After Receipt of Investigative Report. After receipt of the Investigative Report, the Review Board shall take whatever further action it deems appropriate for disposition of the allegations of the Complaint, including the following options:

(a) Conduct an investigative hearing or hearings, pursuant to Sections 10-16; or

(b) Review and determine the Complaint based on the Investigative Report and the evidence in the investigative file, but without an investigative hearing, pursuant to Section 9.6; or

(c) Summarily dismiss the Complaint, in whole or in part, pursuant to Section 15; or

(d) Refer the Complaint back to staff for further investigations; or

(e) Defer further action on the Complaint; or

(f) Any other appropriate action or disposition, consistent with the Ordinance.

9.6 Disposition By Review Board without a Hearing. If the Review Board decides to review and determine a Complaint based on the Investigative Report and investigative file evidence, but without an investigative hearing, the Review Board shall apply the standard of proof set forth in Section 14.9 and shall follow the Final Report process set forth in Sections 16.5-16.8. If the Executive Officer recommends that the Review Board make a determination on a Complaint without an investigative hearing, the subject officer and representative shall have an opportunity to: (a) review the Investigative Report and; (b) submit additional evidence prior to the determination of the Complaint by the Review Board.

9.7 File Accessibility. Every member of the Review Board shall have full access to all complaints and files maintained by the Review Board or its staff.

9.8 Notification to Parties. Upon completion of the Investigative Report, the Chair shall provide the Complainant, aggrieved party, and each Subject Officer the following:

(a) Written notice that the Complaint will be considered by the Review Board; and an explanation of the process to be utilized by the Review Board.

(b) Any recommendations dealing solely with summary disposition or procedural matters.

(c) A copy of the Investigative Report and the summary supplied to the Review Board. A notification that all additional statements, records, reports, exhibits, and other items contained in the file will be available on request; except for any evidence that can not be so made available because its disclosure is prohibited by law.

(d) Written notice that the parties may consult an attorney if desired, and that an attorney or other representative may represent him/her at any hearing, but that an attorney or other representative is not mandatory.

(e) A summary or copy of these rules and regulations, and any other similar informational items appropriate to the individual case.

SECTION 10: DETERMINING WHEN A HEARING IS NECESSARY.

10.1 Requests for Investigative Hearing. The Complainant, Subject Officer, Executive Officer, or a member of the Review Board may request an investigative hearing (as set forth in Sections 12-14) for some or all of the allegations of a complaint.

10.2 When is a Hearing Necessary. An investigative hearing will be conducted, in accordance with the procedures for such hearings set forth in Sections 11-15, when the Review Board determines that such a hearing may facilitate the fact-finding process.

An investigative hearing may be deemed to facilitate the fact- finding process when:

(a) There has been an undue lapse of time since the occurrence of the incident which is the subject of the Complaint; or

(b) There are additional witnesses, evidence, or information that contradicts or supplements, or is not disclosed by the Investigative Report; or

(c) There is reason to question the conclusion of the Investigative Report; or

(d) A hearing would advance public confidence in the Complaint process; or

(e) An appearance in person by the parties would facilitate the fact finding process.

10.3 Scope of the Investigative Hearing. The scope of an Investigative Hearing may vary. It may consist of a single, narrowly drawn issue; of multiple issues; or of the entire complaint. The scope should be determined by the Review Board when authorizing a hearing; and all interested parties to the complaint shall be informed of any limitation in scope when notified of the hearing.

SECTION 11: NO CONTEST RESPONSE.

A Subject Officer may enter a written response of "no contest" at any time before a hearing. A response of "no contest" indicates that the Subject Officer accepts the allegations of the Complaint as substantially true in fact and interpretation.- The Subject Officer shall be bound by the terms of the no contest response in any further consideration of the Complaint by the Review Board.

SECTION 12: INVESTIGATIVE HEARING PANELS.

12.1 Composition of Hearing Panel. A Hearing Panel of the Review Board shall normally consist of three (3) members of the Review Board, selected pursuant to Section 12.2 below, with one member designated as the Presiding Member. In cases involving the death of a person, and in such other cases as the Review Board shall decide, the Review Board will sit as a Board of the Whole with a minimum of six (6) Board members present.

12.2 Selection of Three-Person Hearing Panels.

(a) Selection of three-person Hearing Panels under this section shall be made by rotation among the Review Board members, as appointed by the Chair using any basis (including lottery) that balances the workload among Board members. A Review Board member may request that he or she be temporarily excused to equalize caseload, avoid conflicts of interest, or for other good cause. In the event a Review Board member is so excused, another Board member shall be reassigned by the Chair.

(b) If a Hearing Panel is unable to meet to convene a hearing on a scheduled date due to the unavailability for any reason of one or more of its members, or if a Panel agrees to reschedule a hearing due to the unavailability for any reason of the complainant(s) or subject officer(s) or legal counsel for either, the case or cases assigned to such panel may be re-assigned to another Hearing Panel. However once a hearing of a case has been convened by a Hearing Panel, the same Panel shall consider the case to final disposition.

12.3 Challenges of Board Members.

(a) Challenge for Conflict of Interest or Bias. A Board member sitting on a Hearing Panel shall consider all complaints in a fair and impartial manner. A Board Member who has a personal bias or prejudice, or the appearance thereof, in the outcome of a complaint shall not sit on the Hearing Panel hearing that complaint. Personal interest in the outcome of a complaint does not include holding or manifesting any political or social attitude or belief, where such belief or attitude does not preclude objective consideration of a case on its merits. Examples of personal bias include, but are not limited to:

1. Familial relationship or close friendship with parties material to the inquiry;

2. Witnessing events material to the inquiry from a non-neutral perspective;

3. Being a party to the inquiry;

4. Having a financial interest in the outcome of the inquiry;

5. Holding a bias against a particular party that is sufficient to impair the Board member's impartiality.

(b) Procedure for Challenges. Within five (5) calendar days after the date on which the Review Board furnishes notice of a Hearing, including the names of the Board Members constituting that Panel, either party to the complaint may file a written challenge for cause to any Board Member hearing the complaint. Challenges for conflict of interest or bias must substantiate the challenge in terms of the standard set forth in Section 12.3 (a) above.

When a challenge for cause is filed, the Chairperson shall contact the challenged Board Member as soon as possible, and if the Member agrees that the challenge is for good cause, or otherwise agrees, the Chairperson shall ask another Board Member to serve. If the challenged Board Member does not agree that the challenge is for good cause, the Chairperson shall poll the other members of the Panel, and if both agree that the challenge is for good cause the Chairperson shall so notify the challenged Board member and ask another to serve. If a challenge to a Board member is rejected and the member serves, the written challenge and the Board member written response shall be incorporated in the investigative packet as part of the record of the Complaint.

(c) Replacement of Challenged Board Member. Any Board member removed, or who removes him/her self, from the Hearing Panel due to a challenge for cause shall be replaced by the Chair with another Board member.

12.4 Public Comments. Board members shall avoid public comment on pending complaints, investigations, and hearings.

SECTION 13: INVESTIGATIVE HEARING PROCEDURES.

13.1 Schedule of Investigative Hearings. Investigative hearings may be scheduled by the Chair for any regular or special meeting of the Review Board; or, as to hearings before a Hearing Panel, by the Presiding Member for any other appropriate time.

13.2 Notice Requirements. Ten (10) days notice of an investigative hearing shall be given to the Complainant, each Subject Officer, and any other person whose attendance the Review Board deems appropriate. The notice shall state the date, time and place of the investigative hearing, and the names of the Hearing Panel.

13.3 Hearings Open to Public. All hearings shall be open to the public, to the extent permitted by law.

13.4 Authority to Compel Appearance. The authority of the Review Board's subpoena may be used to compel the appearance of witnesses, including Subject Officers, and/or the production of documents. Subpoenas may be requested through the Chair of the Review Board.

13.5 Conduct of the Investigative Hearing. Hearings should be informal, and should be conducted in the following manner unless the Chair or Presiding Member orders otherwise:

(a) The Presiding Member will conduct the investigative hearing subject to being overruled by a majority of the Hearing Panel. Members of the Board shall be primarily responsible for obtaining testimony. One Board member may be assigned by the Chair or Presiding Member to do the initial questioning of witnesses when a complaint is called for investigative hearing. Additional questions may be asked by any Board member, or by a party or party's representative, or by an assigned staff members.

(b) At the discretion of the Review Board, opening statement(s) may be made on behalf of the Complainant and the Subject Officer(s) involved.

(c) The investigative hearing will generally then proceed as follows: The Complaint will be presented, and witnesses, if any will be introduced. The Board may assign a staff member or counsel to assist in the presentation of a complaint where such assistance appears necessary to facilitate a fair and orderly hearing of the complaint. The Subject Officer may then respond to the Complaint, and introduce witnesses, if any. Each person testifying, and each party to the Complaint, may be questioned by the Board and by the parties or their attorneys. In the event that the Subject Officer is compelled to cooperate in an investigative hearing, the Subject Officer shall be provided the "Lybarger warning" when required under the appropriate circumstances. After the Board has taken all relevant evidence, each party may, in the discretion of the Presiding Member, be given an opportunity to make a closing statement.

(d) At the conclusion of any witness' testimony, either the complainant or the officer involved may request that the Hearing Panel cover any additional areas of inquiry they feel need to be covered. The Presiding Member shall determine whether any further questions will be asked.

(e) Unless otherwise ordered by the Chair or Presiding Member, the entire investigative hearing on a given complaint should be conducted on one occasion. However, if the Hearing Panel determines that additional evidence is necessary to reach its findings, it will continue the investigative hearing to a future date unless the parties agree to allow the Hearing Panel to receive such material in writing without reconvening.

13.6 Deliberation. After obtaining evidence, the Hearing Panel will deliberate in closed session. The Hearing Panel shall not consider any information not received as part of the investigative hearing. The Hearing Panel may reconvene in the presence of all parties to ask further questions, and each party shall have the opportunity to respond to any such questions.

SECTION 14: EVIDENCE.

14.1 What Evidence May be Considered. The investigative hearing need not be conducted according to technical rules relating to evidence and witnesses. Any relevant evidence shall be admitted if it is the sort of evidence on which responsible persons are accustomed to rely in the conduct of serious affairs, regardless of the existence of any common law or statutory rule which might make improper the admission of such evidence over objection in civil actions.

Hearsay evidence may be used for the purpose of supplementing or explaining other evidence.

Evidence shall be taken in accordance with the following provisions:

(a) Each party shall have these rights: to call and examine witnesses; to introduce exhibits; to cross-examine opposing witnesses on any matter relevant to the issues even though that matter was not covered in the direct examination; to impeach any witness regardless of which party first called the witness to testify; and to rebut the evidence against the party. If the Subject Officer does not testify in his/her own behalf he/she may be called and examined as if under cross-examination.

(b) Oral evidence shall be taken only under oath or affirmation.

(c) Upon the request of either party or a Board member, witnesses may be excluded from the hearing until they are called to testify.

(d) Irrelevant and unduly repetitious evidence shall be excluded.

(e) The rules of privilege shall be effective to the extent that they are otherwise required by constitution or statute to be recognized at hearings before the Review Board.

14.2 Representatives. The Complainant, aggrieved party, Subject Officer, and any witness shall have the right to have a representative of his or her choice present at all times during his/her own fact-finding interviews or investigative hearings conducted by or on behalf of the Review Board. The representative shall not be a witness or a person subject to the same investigation.

14.3 Interpreters. The Chair shall have discretionary authority to provisionally qualify and utilize interpreters. Each party in need of an interpreter shall give notice to the Chair within seven (7) days of receipt of the notice of hearing so that appropriate arrangements can be made.

14.4 Authority to Compel Appearance. The authority of a Review Board subpoena may be used to compel the production of documents and/or the appearance of witnesses, including the Subject Officer.

14.5 Failure to Appear. When either the Complainant or the Subject Officer fails to appear, the Board Panel may receive statements from those persons present and relying on the evidence received, continue with the investigative hearing.

14.6 Confidentiality of Review Board Records. The Review Board shall not disclose to the general public any reports, statements, files, records, documents, tapes or other items whose confidentiality is protected by law. This confidentiality may be waived in accordance with applicable law, statute, ordinance, or legal proceedings. Moreover, evidence contained in a Review Board's investigative file may be disclosed to the Complainant and the Subject Officer, but only to the extent and in the manner authorized by these Rules and Regulations.

14.7 Discovery.

(a) By the Review Board. The Review Board, through its staff and agents, may utilize whatever formal or informal methods for the discovery of evidence as are authorized and available under federal, state, ~~or local~~ law.

(b) By the Parties. Prior to a hearing, the Complainant and each Subject Officer may have access to or receive copies of evidence contained in the Review Board's investigative file for the complaint, except for any evidence that can not be so made available because its disclosure is prohibited by law. Parties seeking such discovery must give at least forty eight (48) hours advance notice to the Review Board, either in writing or by telephone.

14.8 Record of Investigative Hearing. All hearings shall be tape- recorded by the Review Board. At the option of the Chair, a stenographic record may be kept, and, if kept, shall be available upon payment of the cost of duplicating or transcribing the same, to a Complainant or Subject Officer requesting a transcript. Any record of the investigative hearing shall become part of the case file.

14.9 Standard of Proof. No finding with respect to an allegation of a complaint shall be sustained unless it is proven by a preponderance of the evidence presented at the hearing(s) or otherwise contained in the investigative record. "Preponderance of the evidence" means evidence that has more convincing force than that opposed to it.

SECTION 15: SUMMARY DISMISSAL.

After reviewing the Investigative Report and records, the Review Board may summarily dismiss a Complaint by majority vote, upon recommendation of the Executive Officer, its own motion, or that of the Subject Officer. Parties to the Complaint shall be notified of a proposed summary dismissal, and may appear to argue for or against summary disposition. Summary dismissal will be appropriate in the following circumstances:

(a) The Review Board does not have jurisdiction over the subject matter of the Complaint.

(b) The Review Board does not have jurisdiction because the Complaint was not timely filed.

(c) The Complaint is so clearly without merit that no reasonable person could sustain a finding based on the facts.

SECTION 16: REVIEW BOARD FINDINGS AND RECOMMENDATIONS.

16.1 Finding and Report by Three-Member Hearing Panel. At the conclusion of an investigative hearing before a Hearing Panel, the Panel members shall deliberate in closed session and, by majority vote, adopt a recommended finding with respect to the Complaint. The Panel shall then prepare a written report summarizing the evidence, the recommended finding, the reasons for the recommended finding, any dissenting opinion, and any other information that may be useful to the full Review Board in its consideration of the case. The Panel shall take into account any rule, regulation, or policy of the subject officer's employing department brought to its attention by the subject officer or representative that the Panel determines to be pertinent to the complaint being investigated

16.2 Submission to full Review Board. The written Panel report referred to in Section 16.1 shall be forwarded to all members of the Review Board, and the matter placed on the next scheduled regular or special meeting of the Review Board.

A copy of the written Panel report referred to in section 16.1, above, shall be forwarded to each Complainant and Subject Officer, together with a notice of the time and place of the Review Board meeting at which the complaint will be considered. All Complainants and Subject Officers shall be notified that the Review Board may accept written objections to the panel report within ten (10) days of the date of the report.

16.3 Consideration by full Review Board. The Review Board shall consider the report of the Hearing Panel and any other information that may be brought to its attention at the meeting. Thereafter, the Review Board may:

(a) Vote to conclude the matter without further investigation, review, or hearings;

(b) Request further information or review by staff, by the Hearing Panel, or through other appropriate means

(c) Vote to conduct further proceedings on the matter before the entire Review Board;

(d) Take such other or additional action as it deems necessary and appropriate, such as the making of recommendations regarding policy or rule changes, referral to appropriate governmental agencies, or other appropriate action.

(e) Accept the Panel report as the Final Report of the Review Board.

16.4 Investigative Hearings before entire Review Board. In cases that are initially heard before the entire Review Board, the interim steps required when a case is heard before a three-member Hearing Panel are inapplicable.

16.5 Final Report by Review Board. At the conclusion of a matter before the entire Review Board, the Board shall deliberate and, by majority vote, shall adopt and prepare a final report with respect to the complaint or matter under consideration. This report shall include findings as to the facts relating to any complaint, as well as an overall conclusion as to any complaint as specified in Section 16.6 below. Dissenting members may set forth reasons for their dissent in writing and any such dissent(s) shall be included in the final report.

16.6 Conclusions in Final Report. The Final Report of the Review Board shall contain an overall finding as to each allegation of the complaint in the following manner:

(a) If the investigation shows the alleged act did not occur, the finding shall be "Unfounded".

(b) If the investigation fails to support the allegations but the allegations cannot be shown as false, the finding shall be "Not Sustained".

(c) If the investigation shows the alleged act did occur but was lawful, justified and proper, the finding shall be "Action Justified".

(d) If the investigation supports the allegations and the action is not justified, the finding shall be "Sustained".

A finding of "Sustained" should include an explanation of the finding of improper conduct; recommendations relating to the imposition of discipline, including the facts relied on in making such recommendations, and recommendations relating to any trends in regard to employees involved in citizen complaints; and/or recommendations for remedial changes in policies or practices where appropriate.

16.7 Consideration of Subject Officer's Disciplinary History. Only after a finding of "sustained" with respect to an allegation of improper or illegal conduct by a Subject Officer, should the Review Board consider the Subject Officer's disciplinary history in determining the appropriate recommendation for discipline. The details of the Subject Officer's disciplinary history will be held confidential by the Review Board and will not be made a part of the Final Report.

16.8 Transmittal of Final Report. The final report adopted by the Review Board shall be immediately forwarded to the Board of Supervisors, the Sheriff or Chief Probation Officer, the Complainant, and each Subject Officer.

16.9 Reconsideration of Final Report. Upon request by the complainant, subject officer or their representatives, the Final Report may be re-opened for reconsideration by the Review Board provided that: (a) previously unknown relevant evidence is discovered which was not available to the Review Board before it issued its Final Report, and; (b) there is a reasonable likelihood the new evidence will alter the findings and recommendations contained in the Final Report. A Final Report may also be re-opened for reconsideration by the Review Board at the request of the Board of Supervisors or upon initiative of the Review Board when such reconsideration is in the public interest.

Every party to the proceeding or their representative(s) shall be notified of any request or proposal for reconsideration and shall be given the opportunity to respond to the Review Board before the request or proposal is acted upon.

SECTION 17: PROCEDURES WHEN NO CITIZEN COMPLAINT REQUIRED.

In cases involving death arising out of or in connection with activities of peace officers or custodial officers employed by the County, and in such other matters where the Review Board is authorized to act pursuant to Ordinance #7880, as amended (Article XVIII, Sections 340.9(c)-(h) of the San Diego County Administrative Code), the Review Board has authority to review and investigate regardless of whether a citizen complaint has been filed. In such cases:

(a) The Review Board will undertake such review and investigation when a Board member requests the action and a majority of the Review Board then votes to initiate the review and investigation.

(b) The review and investigation, including the investigative hearing procedures for such cases, shall otherwise proceed in the same manner, pursuant to these rules as regulations, and in cases initiated by a citizen complaint.

SECTION 18: DELEGATION OF FUNCTIONS TO EXECUTIVE OFFICER.

The Review Board may, in its discretion, from time to time delegate to the Executive Officer certain of the procedural and administrative functions or duties assigned to the Review Board by these Rules and Regulations. The Review Board shall not, however, delegate to the Executive Officer any functions, duties or responsibilities which are required by the Ordinance to be performed by the Review Board.

SECTION 19: AMENDMENTS TO RULES AND REGULATIONS.

These Rules and Regulations are subject to approval by the Board of Supervisors of the County of San Diego, as required by the Ordinance. Once approved, these Rules and Regulations may only be amended by a majority vote of the Review Board, and any such amendments are subject to approval by the Board of Supervisors.

Document No. 26

San Francisco

(annual report)

THE POLICE COMMISSION
OFFICE OF CITIZEN COMPLAINTS
CITY AND COUNTY OF SAN FRANCISCO

ALFREDA DAVIS PORTER
DIRECTOR

555 SEVENTH STREET
ROOM 252
SAN FRANCISCO
CALIFORNIA
94103-4732
FAX: (415) 553-1192
(415) 553-1407

1993 STATISTICAL REPORT

YEAR END SUMMARY

THE POLICE COMMISSION

OFFICE OF CITIZEN COMPLAINTS

CITY AND COUNTY OF SAN FRANCISCO

February 16, 1994

ALFREDA DAVIS PORTER
DIRECTOR

555 SEVENTH STREET
ROOM 252
SAN FRANCISCO
CALIFORNIA
94103-4732
FAX: (415) 553-1192
(415) 553-1407

Harry W. Low, President
The Police Commission
850 Bryant Street
San Francisco, CA 94103

Re: 1993 Annual Statistical Report

Dear President Low:

The Office of Citizen Complaints is pleased to present to the Commission the 1993 Annual Statistical Report. This report includes year end comprehensive complaint statistics; comparative charts and graphs; policy recommendations already presented, or to be presented; and a sustained case status report for cases received and sustained since January 1, 1990.

District Stations registering an increase in complaints are: Central +24%; Southern +67%; and Tenderloin Task Force +14%. Stations registering a decrease of 20% or more are: Mission -27%; Park -20%; and Richmond -24%.

There has been an across the board increase in specific allegations, except for Discourtesy, which decreased 10%. Of significance are: Unnecessary Force +5%; Conduct Reflecting Discredit +37%; Racial Slurs +43%; and Sexual Slurs +325%.

The OCC has found Policy Failure in 11 cases during 1993. Three of the 11 cases stemmed from the same failed policy, and resulted in the issuance of a corrective Department Bulletin prior to the OCC submitting a recommendation for change. Other policy recommendations pending will be calendared for public input in the near future, after the OCC holds discussions with Department representatives.

Of continuing importance to the OCC is the dramatic rise in cases pending within the agency over the previous year. As stated when the third quarter report was issued, this number is directly attributed to the loss of OCC staff. I am concerned that if critical staff positions are not restored, the pending case numbers will rise to a level from which recovery will be difficult, if not impossible. This matter is calendared before the Board of Supervisor's Budget Committee on February 23, 1994.

My staff and I look forward to discussing this report in depth after it is calendared for public discussion.

Very truly yours,

Alfreda Davis Porter
Director

TABLE OF CONTENTS

Cases Pending, Five year trend (Graph)	1
Comprehensive Statistical Report	2
How Cases Are Received	2
Complaint Totals By Station Comparison (Graph)	3
Complaints and Allegations By Unit	4
Allegations By Percentage (Chart)	5
Total Allegations Closed	6-7
Policy Recommendations	8-18
Sustained Case Status Report	19-24
Resolution Summary - 1993 Sustained Cases	24
Definitions of Allegations	25
Definitions of Findings	26
District Map	27

OCC Pending Case Level
5 Year Comparison

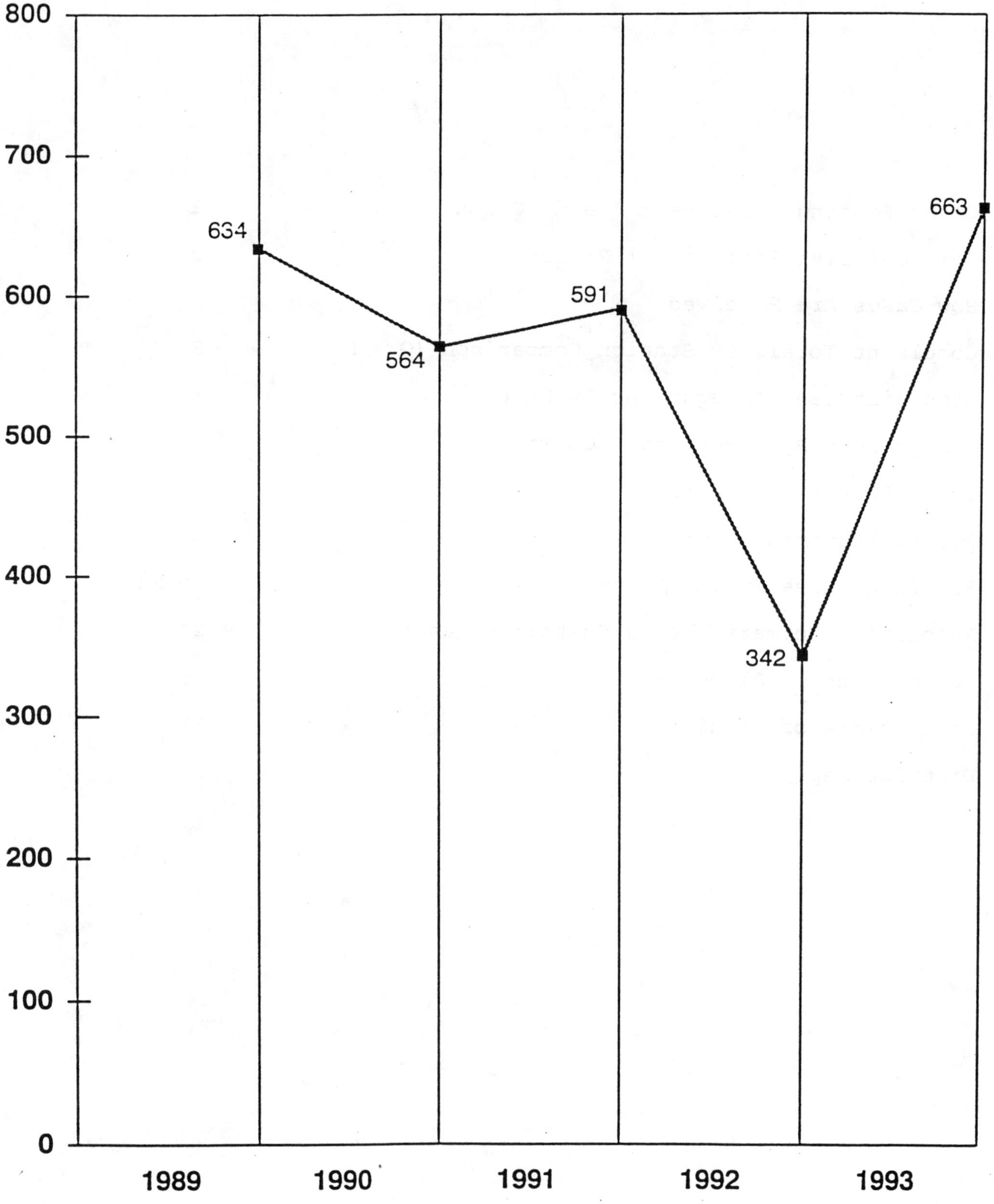

Comprehensive Statistical Report
from Jan. 1, 1993 through Dec. 31 1993

Year to date totals 01/01/1993 to 12/31/93	FIRST QUARTER	SECOND QUARTER	THIRD QUARTER	FOURTH QUARTER	YTD TOTAL
Number of Cases Received	238	289	273	237	1037
Number of 1992 Cases Pending	--	--	--	--	25
Number of 1993 Cases Pending	--	--	--	--	638
Total Number of Cases Pending	--	--	--	--	663
Number of 1992 Cases Closed	154	59	38	22	273
Number of 1993 Cases Closed	50	76	197	76	399
Total Number of Cases Closed	204	135	235	98	672
Total Mergers/Voids 1993	--	--	--	--	11
Total Info. Only 1993	--	--	--	--	54
Number of Cases Sustained	21	19	15	23	78
% Sustained Vs Closed Cases (Includes 11 Policy Recommendations)	--	--	--	--	11.6%

HOW COMPLAINTS ARE RECEIVED
DATE: 01/01/1993 TO 12/31/1993

MONTH	IN PERSON	PHONE	MAIL	SFPD	MAYOR	OTHER	TOTALS
January	41	16	14	2	0	8	81
February	29	16	14	1	0	10	70
March	31	20	20	3	0	13	87
TOTAL 1ST QUARTER	101	52	48	6	0	31	238
April	39	29	30	5	0	11	114
May	31	21	12	3	0	7	74
June	32	20	37	7	0	5	101
TOTAL 2ND QUARTER	203	122	127	21	0	54	289
July	35	17	28	7	0	9	96
August	27	21	22	3	0	12	85
September	32	14	21	15	0	10	92
TOTAL 3RD QUARTER	297	174	198	46	0	85	273
October	32	14	20	8	0	13	87
November	22	21	17	6	0	11	77
December	27	21	13	4	0	8	73
TOTAL 4TH QUARTER	378	230	248	64	0	117	237
YEAR TO DATE TOTAL	378	230	248	64	0	117	1037

Complaints by District Station
1992, 1993 Comparison

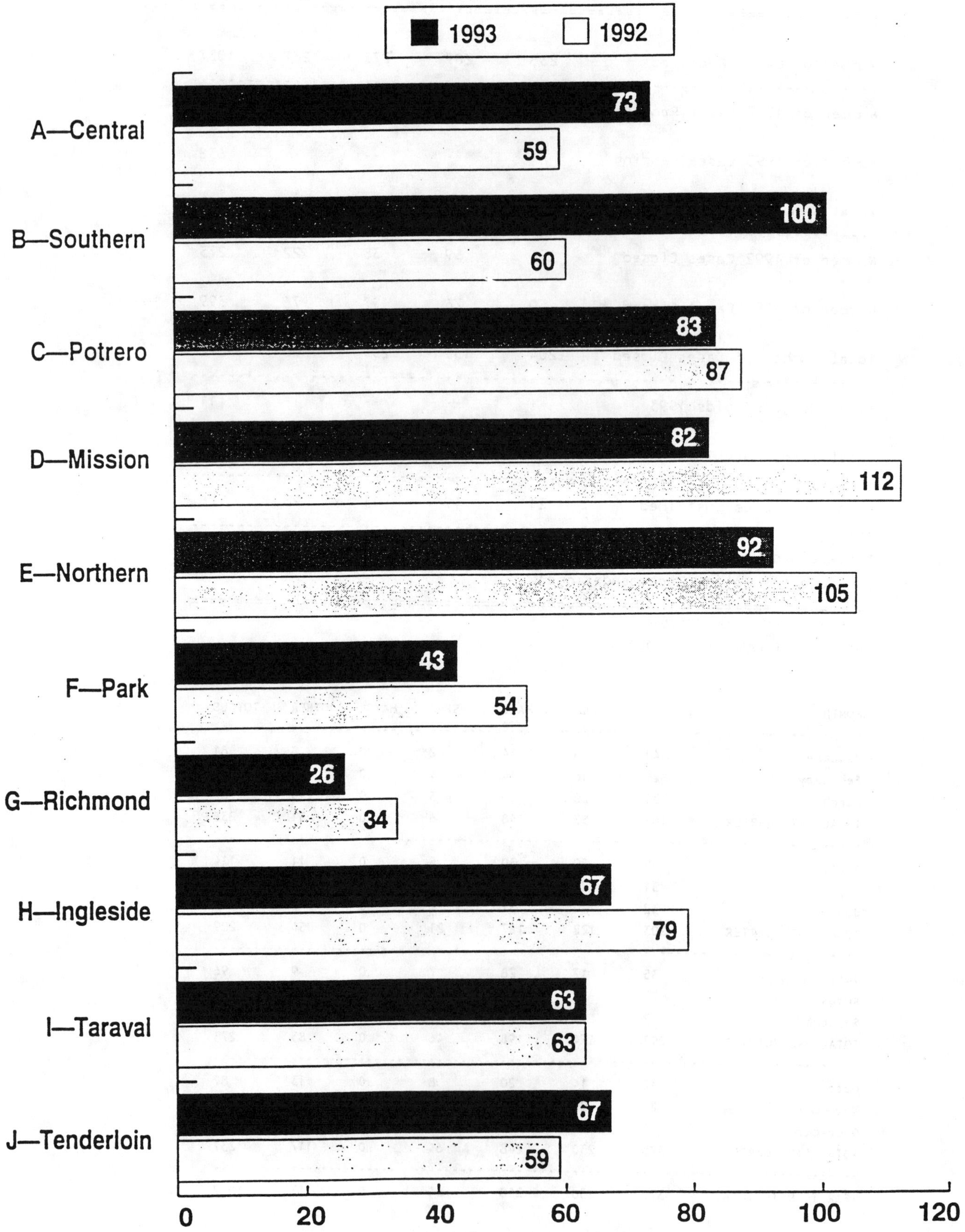

OFFICE OF CITIZEN COMPLAINTS
Complaints and Allegations by Unit
DATE: 01/01/1993 TO 12/31/1993

ALLEGATION NUMBERS

UNIT	Complaint Count	Unnecessary Force	Unwarranted Action	Conduct Reflecting Discredit	Neglect of Duty	Racial Slur	Sexual Slur	Discourtesy	Procedure	Policy	Training Failure	Total Allegations	Total Officers
-Unknown Assignment	276	60	133	52	81	3	2	32	12	6	0	381	372
1A -Chief's Office	3	0	0	3	1	0	0	1	0	0	0	5	3
1J -Tenderloin Task Fo	67	48	57	15	36	9	7	16	0	0	0	188	75
1Z -Housing Police	2	0	1	2	2	1	0	1	0	0	0	7	2
2R -Communications	9	0	0	1	5	0	0	6	0	0	0	12	7
3A -Central Station	73	21	70	17	47	2	1	14	0	0	0	172	92
3B -Southern Station	100	28	74	39	50	6	0	20	0	0	0	217	89
3C -Potrero Station	83	29	72	42	36	5	0	19	0	0	0	203	74
3D -Mission Station	82	57	57	27	48	3	2	20	0	0	0	214	109
3E -Northern Station	92	47	82	30	54	2	4	21	0	0	0	240	110
3F -Park Station	43	26	41	18	27	1	0	12	0	0	0	125	50
3G -Richmond Station	26	7	27	10	12	1	0	8	0	0	0	65	36
3H -Ingleside Station	67	30	89	25	33	0	0	19	0	0	0	196	83
3I -Taraval Station	63	10	65	20	32	3	1	20	0	0	0	151	62
3U -Field Operations II	3	0	3	0	0	0	0	1	0	0	0	4	2
4A -Traffic Administra	3	1	1	0	2	0	0	2	0	0	0	6	3
4B -Solo Motorcycle	24	1	11	7	6	1	0	9	0	0	0	35	17
4K -Special Motorcycle	4	0	2	0	1	0	0	2	0	0	0	5	4
4M -Muni Transit Detai	7	1	5	2	3	2	0	3	0	0	0	16	9
4T -Headquarters Compa	23	7	22	3	11	0	0	8	0	0	0	51	24
5A -Night Investigatio	4	0	3	2	1	0	0	1	0	0	0	7	3
5B -Hit & Run	1	0	0	2	0	0	0	0	0	0	0	2	2
5C -Auto	9	0	14	2	3	0	0	1	1	0	0	21	12
5D -Burglary	3	1	1	2	1	0	0	0	0	0	0	5	3
5F -Fraud	7	1	2	2	5	0	0	1	0	0	0	11	6
5G -General Works	10	2	9	0	6	0	0	1	0	0	0	18	11
5H -Homicide	4	0	0	2	4	0	0	3	0	0	0	9	5
5I -Sex Crimes	1	0	0	0	1	0	0	0	0	0	0	1	1
5N -Narcotics	13	3	15	0	1	0	0	2	0	0	0	21	16
5S -S Squad	5	2	9	1	2	1	0	2	0	0	0	17	9
5T -Juvenile	4	0	1	0	3	0	0	1	0	0	0	5	5
5V -Vice Crimes/Prosti	5	1	5	3	1	0	0	3	0	0	0	13	4
101-Info only (Referral)	17	4	6	4	7	0	0	4	0	0	0	25	0
102-Info only	9	2	2	0	5	0	0	0	0	0	0	9	0
TOTAL	1142	389	879	333	527	40	17	253	13	6	0	2457	1300

NOTE: 1) Complaint count varies due to multiple units being involved.
2) Allegation count is larger than complaint count due to multiple allegations in some complaints.

Allegations by Percentage 1992, 1993 Comparison

1993

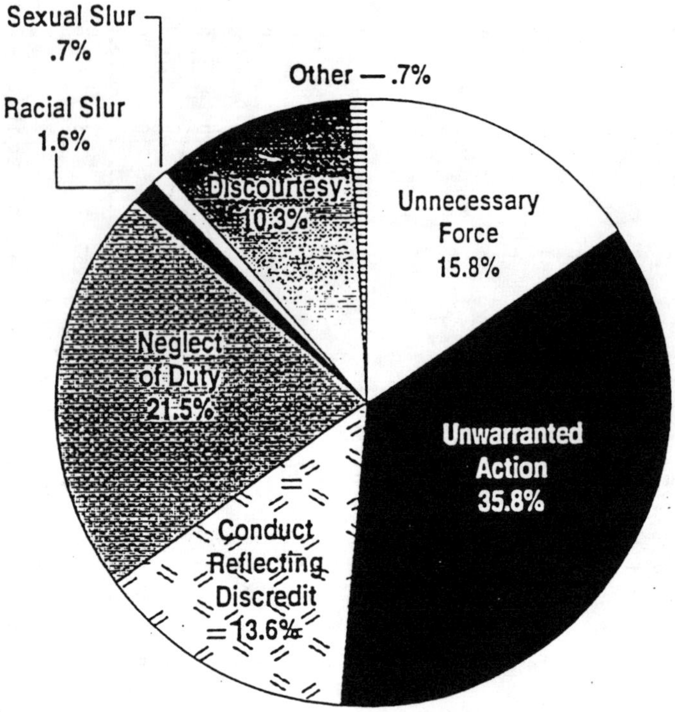

1992

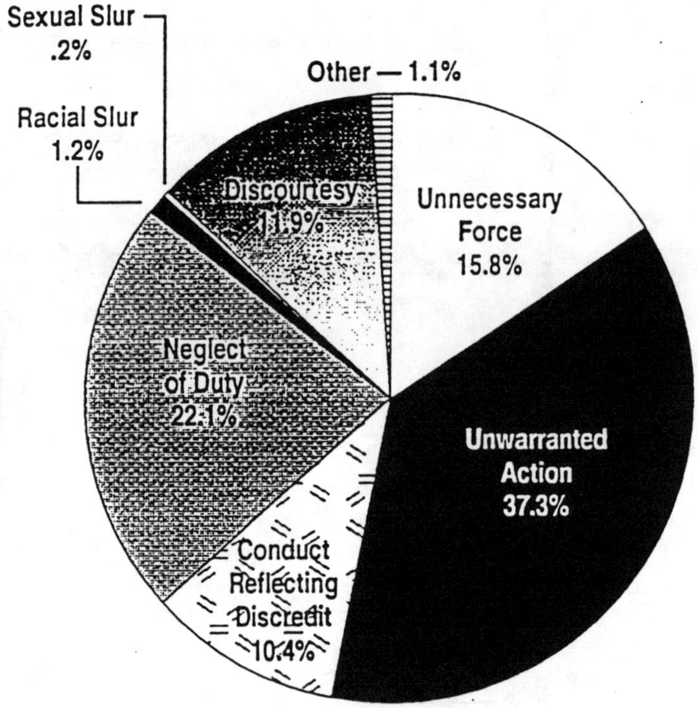

OFFICE OF CITIZEN COMPLAINTS

TOTAL ALLEGATIONS CLOSED FROM 01/01/1993 TO 12/31/1993

ALLEGATIONS SUSTAINED

	UF	UA	CRD	ND	RS	SS	D	SUBTOTAL	POLICY PROCEDURE	TRAINING FAILURE	TOTAL
TOTAL FIRST QUARTER	2	1	3	20	0	0	2	28	3	0	31
TOTAL SECOND QUARTER	2	3	5	5	0	0	2	17	0	1	18
TOTAL THIRD QUARTER	0	7	4	4	0	0	3	18	3	0	21
TOTAL FOURTH QUARTER	0	1	4	9	1	1	1	17	1	0	18
YEAR TO DATE TOTAL	4	12	16	38	1	1	8	80	7	1	88

ALLEGATIONS NOT SUSTAINED

	UF	UA	CRD	ND	RS	SS	D	SUBTOTAL	POLICY PROCEDURE	TRAINING FAILURE	TOTAL
TOTAL FIRST QUARTER	42	59	40	39	3	1	37	221	0	0	221
TOTAL SECOND QUARTER	31	24	30	26	5	0	20	136	0	0	136
TOTAL THIRD QUARTER	42	60	42	74	3	2	44	267	0	0	267
TOTAL FOURTH QUARTER	68	54	53	67	7	1	52	302	0	0	302
YEAR TO DATE TOTAL	183	197	165	206	18	4	153	926	0	0	926

ALLEGATIONS UNFOUNDED

	UF	UA	CRD	ND	RS	SS	D	SUBTOTAL	POLICY PROCEDURE	TRAINING FAILURE	TOTAL
TOTAL FIRST QUARTER	12	15	21	36	3	0	3	90	1	0	91
TOTAL SECOND QUARTER	14	19	10	19	1	0	8	71	1	0	72
TOTAL THIRD QUARTER	9	21	23	31	6	0	9	99	1	0	100
TOTAL FOURTH QUARTER	21	22	11	31	1	2	10	98	2	0	100
YEAR TO DATE TOTAL	56	77	65	117	11	2	30	358	5	0	363

ALLEGATIONS FOUND TO BE PROPER CONDUCT

	UF	UA	CRD	ND	RS	SS	D	SUBTOTAL	POLICY PROCEDURE	TRAINING FAILURE	TOTAL
TOTAL FIRST QUARTER	8	81	3	35	0	0	2	129	2	0	131
TOTAL SECOND QUARTER	5	46	0	9	0	0	0	60	3	0	63
TOTAL THIRD QUARTER	7	98	4	19	0	0	2	130	3	0	133
TOTAL FOURTH QUARTER	27	144	6	19	0	0	1	197	0	0	197
YEAR TO DATE TOTAL	47	369	13	82	0	0	5	516	8	0	524

ALLEGATIONS IN WHICH NO FINDING WAS THE DISPOSITION

	UF	UA	CRD	ND	RS	SS	D	SUBTOTAL	POLICY PROCEDURE	TRAINING FAILURE	TOTAL
TOTAL FIRST QUARTER	13	20	11	11	0	0	8	63	1	0	64
TOTAL SECOND QUARTER	6	11	6	6	0	2	6	37	0	0	37
TOTAL THIRD QUARTER	14	17	9	10	4	0	9	63	0	0	63
TOTAL FOURTH QUARTER	13	8	3	10	1	1	3	39	0	0	39
YEAR TO DATE TOTAL	46	56	29	37	5	3	26	202	1	0	203

OFFICE OF CITIZEN COMPLAINTS
TOTAL ALLEGATIONS CLOSED FROM 01/01/1993 TO 12/31/1993

ALLEGATIONS IN WHICH NO FINDING WAS THE DISPOSITION

	UF	UA	CRD	ND	RS	SS	D	SUBTOTAL	POLICY PROCEDURE	TRAINING FAILURE	TOTAL
TOTAL FIRST QUARTER	13	20	11	11	0	0	8	63	1	0	64
TOTAL SECOND QUARTER	6	11	6	6	0	2	6	37	0	0	37
TOTAL THIRD QUARTER	14	17	9	10	4	0	9	63	0	0	63
TOTAL FOURTH QUARTER	13	8	3	10	1	1	3	39	0	0	39
YEAR TO DATE TOTAL	46	56	29	37	5	3	26	202	1	0	203

ALLEGATIONS IN WHICH NO FINDING DISPOSITION WAS WITHDRAWN

	UF	UA	CRD	ND	RS	SS	D	SUBTOTAL	POLICY PROCEDURE	TRAINING FAILURE	TOTAL
TOTAL FIRST QUARTER	5	12	7	2	0	0	4	30	1	0	31
TOTAL SECOND QUARTER	0	3	4	2	0	2	2	13	0	0	13
TOTAL THIRD QUARTER	5	9	5	5	3	0	5	32	0	0	32
TOTAL FOURTH QUARTER	4	1	2	2	0	0	2	11	0	0	11
YEAR TO DATE TOTAL	14	25	18	11	3	2	13	86	1	0	87

POLICY RECOMMENDATION
OCC CASE NO. 829-91

SUBJECT: DISABLED PERSONS AT DEMONSTRATIONS

Recommendation:

It is recommended that the San Francisco Police Department develop written policies to formalize its procedures used in the arrest of disabled persons at demonstrations and crowd control situations. Further, it is recommended that the specific issue of the handling of the medical paraphernalia of disabled arrestees and detainees be addressed.

Background:

As the result of regular demonstrations by advocacy groups for disabled persons, the San Francisco Police Department has recently developed procedures and training related to how officers handle crowd control situations attended by disabled persons. However, the procedures are not written as policies. During the arrest of a disabled woman at a demonstration in 1991, an officer confiscated a catheter in her fanny pack. While the officer did not break any known department policies, this demonstrator's allegation of unwarranted action gives notice of the need for an articulation of specific procedures.

Diana Christensen — 3-25-93

Prepared by:
DIANA CHRISTENSEN
Investigator
Date

3/25/93

Reviewed by:
BARBARA ATTARD
Sr. Investigator
Date

Alfreda Davis Porter — 3/25/93

Approved by:
ALFREDA DAVIS PORTER
Director
Date

THE POLICE COMMISSION
OFFICE OF CITIZEN COMPLAINTS
CITY AND COUNTY OF SAN FRANCISCO

ALFREDA DAVIS PORTER
DIRECTOR

555 SEVENTH STREET
ROOM 252
SAN FRANCISCO
CALIFORNIA
94103-4732
FAX (415) 553-1192
(415) 553-1407

POLICY RECOMMENDATION

OCC CASE NO. 147-92

Recommendation:

The Office of Citizen Complaints is recommending that the Department conduct a specialized training session, as part of the Community Awareness and Sensitivity Training course at the Academy, instructing officers to respond sensitively to persons whose gender may not be immediately apparent or whose gender may be mistaken by the officer. It is recommended that the Department instruct officers to refer to persons in the gender that they identify themselves to the officer, when such self identification is made. OCC recommends that this training be a part of the initial Academy training for new recruits, and that a Department Bulletin be issued for all officers who are currently on the force regarding this issue.

Background:

In the present case, the complainant was referred to with the pronoun "Sir" during a traffic stop. Although the complainant explained to the officer that she is a woman, the officer continued to address her with the masculine pronoun.

In a city as culturally and sexually diverse as San Francisco, it is important that officers have clear guidelines for addressing members of the public in a polite and sensitive manner. In the Investigative Hearing conducted at the Office of Citizen Complaints, the representative for the involved officer stated that there are no specific Department guidelines advising officers how they should refer to a person when gender identification is in question.

Submitted by:

Barbara Attard, Sr. Investigator — Date: 3/4/93

Approved by:

Alfreda Davis Porter, Director — Date: 3/5/93

TRAINING FAILURE
OCC Case Number 351-92

Recommendation:

> That the Department train all officers in crowd control techniques and reporting requirements regarding use of force during crowd control situations on a regular basis. If officers not normally assigned to crowd control are utilized in unusual situations, that their supervising officers advise them regarding reporting responsibilities.

Background:

During the investigation of OCC Case #351-92, one of the complaints resulting from the Rodney King demonstrations, it was determined that force was used by member(s) of the Traffic Division. An entry was made in the Use of Force Log, however, no incident report had been written. The officer(s) involved stated that they believed that a general incident report was being written which would cover all force used which didn't result in arrest, and that entry in the Use of Force Log covered their reporting responsibilities.

Commander (then Captain) Martel was interviewed as the commanding officer who signed off on the log. Commander Martel stated that the Use of Force Log came to him on May 15, 1992, fifteen days after the demonstrations. At this time he observed that force was being reported with no case numbers listed. Commander Martel spoke with the lieutenants who supervise the Traffic Division and went over the reporting responsibilities required by the Department when force is used. He did not require that reports be written after the fact for the past demonstration related incidents, but did take action to ensure that Department rules would be followed in the future. It was Commander Martel's belief that it was highly unusual that Traffic Division officers would be assigned to on-line duties during crowd control situations and because of this infrequent experience, they are not familiar with the specific reporting requirements. He felt that training in these areas would be beneficial to officers who may be called upon to perform crowd control functions on an infrequent basis.

Prepared by
Senior Investigator Barbara Attard

Date: 10/22/93

Approved by
Director Alfreda Davis Porter

Date: 10/29/93

THE POLICE COMMISSION

OFFICE OF CITIZEN COMPLAINTS

CITY AND COUNTY OF SAN FRANCISCO

ALFREDA DAVIS PORTER
DIRECTOR

555 SEVENTH STREET
ROOM 252
SAN FRANCISCO
CALIFORNIA
94103-4732
FAX. (415) 553-1192
(415) 553-1407

TO: CHIEF RIBERA

FROM: ALFREDA DAVIS PORTER

DATE:

RE: POLICY FAILURE RESOLUTIONS OF COMPLAINTS
VIOLATIONS OF GENERAL ORDER J-3

OCC CASE NUMBERS: 541-92, 742-92, 18-93

- -

SUMMARY OF ISSUES:

The above named cases each involved the issue of officers driving suspect's vehicles from the scene to department stations. At the time that the incidents occurred, officers driving suspect's vehicles was forbidden by General Order J-3, ". . .Members shall not move the vehicle of an arrested person." Departmental Bulletin 93-95 revised this policy. Officers are now allowed to moved suspects vehicles under specific circumstances and with the "express" permission of a supervisor.

FINDING:

The dispositions of this issue in the above named cases will be closed as "Policy Failure." Because the department has taken action to rectify this problem, OCC will not be making a policy recommendation.

c:\TOW

93-95
5/3/93

TOWING PROCEDURE UPDATES: MOVING THE VEHICLE OF AN ARRESTED PERSON AND ISSUANCE OF SFPD 387

Department General Order J-3, "Towing of Vehicles," prohibits officers from moving the motor vehicle of an arrested person prior to ordering a tow. Effective immediately, pending the forthcoming revised General Order J-3, officers may move the vehicle of an arrested person prior to ordering a tow *with the express permission of a supervisory officer,* and only when moving the vehicle is necessary for any of the following reasons:

- Officer or citizen safety;
- The protection of evidence; or
- When, in the supervisor's opinion, further investigation of the vehicle is necessary.

If you move a vehicle prior to a tow per the provisions described above, you must include the following information in your incident report:

- The reason for the tow;
- The reason for moving the vehicle;
- The name of the supervisor who gave you permission to move and tow the vehicle.

Officers are also reminded that, in order to comply with Section 22852 CVC, they must ensure that arrestees whose vehicles have been towed subsequent to an arrest must be given SFPD 387, the notice of towing. Officers must document the issuing of this form in the incident report, and include whether the person given the form is the owner of the towed vehicle.

POLICY RECOMMENDATION

OCC Case Number 0339-92

SUBJECT: Procuring Field Photographs of Citizens in Non-Arrest Situations

Recommendation:

That the Department establish written guidelines governing the taking of photographs of civilians in non-arrest situations including the manner and place of their storage, the purposes for which they may be used, and dates for their destruction.

Background:

In the referenced case, complainant claimed that she was forced, under threat of arrest, to be photographed on the street in front of the Motherlode Bar at the corner of Larkin and Post Streets by plainclothes officers.

Investigation of the case by the OCC revealed that the officers involved were assigned to the Vice Crimes Detail. Former Chief Richard Hongisto, reacting to complaints of prostitution in the area, after consulting with the District Attorney and various members of his command staff had decided to use §372 PC, public nuisance, to combat the problem. Officers were instructed to:

1. observe persons engaged in solicitation/prostitution activities,

2. detain them,

3. identify them,

4. admonish them as to the potentially criminal nature of continuing their actions,

5. photograph them and

6. release them.

Complainant was photographed with five other persons, and according to at least one officer, they were not free to leave until after the picture was taken. The complainant was not arrested or cited. She did not voluntarily consent to be photographed. The officers explained that photographs were taken for identification purposes as persons allegedly engaged in prostitution often change their appearance. In this case, most of the individuals photographed were of the transsexual, transgender, or transvestite communities. The photographs, once taken, were kept on file in the Vice Crimes Detail.

The Office of Citizen Complaints recommends that the Department establish written guidelines for detaining and photographing civilians in non-arrest situations. These guidelines should include instructions as to when photographs may be taken, how the photographs may be used and stored, and when the photographs may be destroyed.

Prepared by:

LARRY R. SHOCKEY — DATE 4-2-93
Investigator

Reviewed by:

BARBARA J. ATTARD — DATE 4/20/93
Sr. Investigator

Approved by:

ALFREDA DAVIS PORTER — DATE 5/10/93
Director

ls/22

POLICY RECOMMENDATION
OCC CASE NO. 582-92

SUBJECT: TRAINING / DOCUMENTATION OF EMBEZZLED OR STOLEN AUTOS

Recommendation
It is recommended that the Department undertake renewed training efforts in the area of embezzled (10855 V.C.) and stolen (10851 V.C.) autos. All officers responsible for completing incident reports should be trained to make accurate determinations as to when a motor vehicle is taken illegally from its legitimate owner, lease holder, or renter, and should be entered into the Stolen Vehicle System (SVS).

Officers should be able to differentiate between what constitutes a stolen vehicle and the elements for an embezzled vehicle; as well as what documents will be needed by the follow-up investigators in order to successfully prosecute for embezzlement (rental agreements, demand letters, etc.).

Officers should also know the difference between a suspicious circumstance stolen vehicle and an embezzled vehicle. This would be helpful so that every officer on the street would know when to refer complaints to the Auto Theft Section for a report and when they should be completing the reports themselves.

Finally, it is believed that a section of the hotsheet, or separate broadcasts should be made for motor vehicles stolen under suspicious circumstances, or embezzled (understanding that some embezzled vehicle cases may in fact be civil in nature). Officers should not be placed in a position of potential liability for deciding which vehicles should not immediately be brought to the attention of law enforcement as possible stolen or embezzled vehicles.

Background
In the case at hand, officers believed that a car taken by an acquaintance of the owner - who did not have any authority or permission to drive the vehicle - was an embezzled vehicle and referred the owner to the auto theft investigators, rather than taking a report and having the vehicle placed into the SVS. Fifteen hours later, when the owner went to the investigators, he was advised that the vehicle should have been reported as a stolen vehicle.

The confusion which arose over this incident stems from the practice of referring both suspicious circumstances stolen vehicle complainants and persons wishing to report embezzled vehicles to the investigators without completing reports. In both situations, the suspects are generally known by the vehicle owners. This should not be the sole determining factor in whether the vehicle is embezzled or a "suspicious circumstance" stolen vehicle. A change in the policy should result in less inconvenience to all victims of auto theft or embezzlement.

Submitted By: [signature] 7-16-93
John Parker, Sr. Investigator — Date

Approved By: Alfreda Davis Porter 7/16/93
Alfreda Davis Porter, Director — Date

POLICY RECOMMENDATION
OCC CASE NO. 132-93

SUBJECT: SPANISH MIRANDA ADMONISHMENT CARDS

Recommendation:

It is recommended that the Police Commission adopt a resolution to have the San Francisco Police Department print and distribute a Spanish Miranda Admonishment Card for its Spanish speaking officers. A Miranda Advisement Card which was printed by Concord Press for SFPD is attached and recommended by OCC as a possible card for this use.

Background:

During the course of an OCC investigation, it was determined that some patrol officers are using Miranda Admonishment cards in Spanish which the department published and distributed around 1979. According to the SFPD Planning Department, these cards were recalled sometime after 1979. Upon further inquiry to the SFPD Legal Division, the Department could not indicate whether or not the above mentioned cards were in fact recalled.

Although the cards are not in circulation, the investigation revealed that a number of Spanish speaking police officers have retained the old cards or acquired advisement cards from other sources. Spanish speaking officers have also translated the content of the Miranda Admonishment from English to Spanish since they were unable to find one in Spanish within the department.

It is apparent that Spanish speaking officers find Miranda Advisement cards useful and will find them from some source. It is important that the Department develop a card with an approved translation for Spanish speaking members to ensure consistency. Use of unclear or incorrect Miranda Advisements may present problems in subsequent criminal prosecutions.

Prepared by Investigator David Aulet	10/12/93 Date
Reviewed by Senior Investigator Barbara Attard	10/18/93 Date
Approved by Director Alfreda Davis Porter	11/8/93 Date

POLICY RECOMMENDATION
OCC Case No. 590-93

SUBJECT: TRAINING/OPERATIONAL RULES FOR HOJ SECURITY CHECK POINT

Recommendation

The OCC recommends that the Department develop a course of instruction in the operation of the security check point at the Hall of Justice. The course content should include fundamentals of the concept of building security, the correct operation of the security devices, and some basic rules for personnel staffing the check point.

Background

The OCC received a complaint from a jury panelist which alleged that a police officer staffing the security check point at the Bryant Street entrance to the Hall of Justice was inattentive to his duties at that location. Specifically, the officer allegedly waved people through the metal detector and failed to check them further, despite the fact that the machine had been set off.

During the course of the investigation, the OCC learned from Lt. D. Hallisy that there was no formal training for police officers (generally from Southern Station) who may be called upon to staff the security check point in the absence of the civilian personnel regularly assigned to handle such duties. The officer involved in the OCC complaint said that officers were expected to use "common sense" when assigned to this function.

The OCC also learned that both civilian and sworn personnel have been allowed to possess reading material while on-duty at the check point, and are regularly observed reading. This practice may result in inattention to duty. Rules should be established to prohibit any activity which may result in, or appear to indicate inattentiveness to duty.

Submitted by: [signature] 10-25-93
John Parker, Sr. Investigator — Date

Approved by: [signature] 11/1/93
Alfreda Davis Porter, Director — Date

TRAINING RECOMMENDATION
OCC Case No. 0671-93

SUBJECT: TRAINING IN THE NOTIFICATION OF OWNERS OF RECOVERED VEHICLES

Recommendation

The OCC recommends that the Department develop a course of instruction in the notification of owners of recovered stolen vehicles. An owner should be notified through a specific process by designated personnel, and a record of those responsible for any notification should be maintained. These personnel should be trained in the precise steps which need to be taken by the legal owner in order to secure the vehicle.

Background

The OCC received a complaint from the owner of a recovered stolen vehicle which alleged that despite three telephone calls, visits to Southern Station, and Rooms 150 and 154, after being notified of the vehicle's recovery, no one, either on the phone at Southern Station, Room 150, and Room 154, instructed the owner that he needed to obtain a waiver of charges and a release form prior to going to City Tow. It appeared that throughout the process, the places to report to with the required paperwork was not clearly defined from the initial call notifying the owner that the vehicle had been recovered.

Submitted by: Mary White 12-28-93
Mary White, Investigator Date

Approved by: Alfreda Davis Porter 12/22/93
Alfreda Davis Porter, Director Date

SUSTAINED CASE STATUS REPORT
CASES RECEIVED January 1, 1990 - December 31, 1993

ETN	SUSTND ALLEG.	DATE MCD	DATE RETURNED	REMARKS	COMPLAINT DATE
2	CRD	02/30/91	07/23/91	Not Sust. (OCCDB)	01/12/90
-\-	UA	02/22/91	07/23/91	Admonished	01/12/90
4	D	06/18/90	08/20/90	Admonished	01/16/90
1	ND	10/23/90	03/13/91	Admonished	01/16/90
1	UF.UA.CRD	01/07/92	11/06/92	20 days suspension: 15	01/20/90
-\-	-\-	-\-	-\-	not imposed(Commission)	01/20/90
1	UA	01/14/91	03/23/93	Not Sustained	01/23/90
-\-	UA	-\-	-\-	-\-	01/23/90
7	D	01/02/91	04/10/91	Ins.Evidence by chief	01/24/90
2	D	07/15/92	10/17/91	Proper Conduct by Chief	01/26/90
7	D,UA	10/31/90	01/31/91	Counselled & Admonished	01/29/90
2	UF	07/19/91	05/12/93	2days susp.held in abey	01/30/90
4	D,ND	11/08/90	07/23/91	Admonished	01/31/90
2	UA	01/10/91	09/10/91	Retraining	02/01/90
2	UA	05/31/91	11/29/91	Proper Conduct(OCCDB)	02/05/90
3	ND	10/01/90	12/28/90	Admonishement	02/07/90
2	UF	12/10/90	01/08/92	Not Sust. by Commission	02/07/90
1	CRD	10/23/90	03/22/91	Counselled	02/80/90
2	UA,ND	11/16/90	03/13/91	Admonishment/Retraining	02/09/90
1	CRD	01/18/91	01/25/91	Member retired,01/04/91	02/12/90
3	UF	08/09/91	10/26/92	Proper Conduct by Chief	02/20/92
2	CRD	11/29/90	03/13/91	Admonishment/Retraining	02/17/90
3	Policy	-\-	-\-	Policy Recommendation	02/22/90
1	UA	05/28/91	11/01/91	Insf.Evidence by Chief	02/28/90
?	UF,D	09/13/91	10/26/92	Not Sust. by Chief	02/26/90
4	ND	10/29/90	01/31/91	Not Sust. by Chief	03/05/90
-\-	ND,ND	-\-	-\-	Not Sust. by Chief	-\-
2	UF	07/30/91	11/05/92	Not Sust.Retrain. Chief	03/14/90
1	Policy	-\-	-\-	Policy Recommendation	03/15/90
3	ND	09/13/91	04/10/92	Admonished	03/21/90
1	D	01/10/92	02/03/92	Admonished	03/23/90
1	ND	07/27/90	11/21/90	Admonished	03/28/90
1	UF	06/21/91	06/27/91	No Charges MCD (OCCDB)	03/28/90
2	D,NDx2	12/20/91	06/26/92	Written Reprimand x 2	03/28/90
-\-	ND	-\-	-\-	NO MCD DISPO (OCCDB)	-\-
1	CRD	01/10/92	06/16/92	5 day suspension	04/02/90
1	ND	09/03/91	12/12/91	Reprimand	04/03/90
?	UA	10/11/91	12/12/91	Retraining	04/13/90
1	UA	07/17/90	05/31/91	Not Sustained	04/07/90
1	Policy	-\-	-\-	Policy Recommendation	04/06/90
2	ND	11/19/91		Pending - SFPD	04/12/90
1/1	ND	01/23/91	05/02/91	Not Sustained	04/16/90
1	ND,D	01/10/91	02/03/92	Written Reprimand	04/23/90
2	ND	07/21/92	05/03/93	Admonished	04/25/90
3	Policy	-\-	-\-	Policy Recommendation	04/25/90
1	D	03/23/92	03/31/92	Not Sustained	05/30/90
?	ND	11/21/90	04/23/91	Written Reprimand	04/30/90
?	ND/ND	12/19/91	12/31/91	Discipl. Hearing X 2	05/02/90
1	ND/ND	07/15/91	10/08/91	Not Sustained	05/30/90

SUSTAINED CASE STATUS - CONTINUED

ETN	SUSTND ALLEG.	DATE MCD	DATE RETURNED	REMARKS	COMPLAINT DATE
2	UF,UA,CRD	09/18/91	01/21/93	90 day susp. (per MCD)	05/05/90
-\-	X 3.ND X2	-\-	-\-	-\-	-\-
-\-	CRD.ND.ND	-\-	-\-	Retired (per MCD)	-\-
1	D	10/14/92	11/12/92	Not Sust. by Chief	05/12/90
1	UF	10/14/92	08/11/93	1 day suspension	05/23/90
2	D	05/16/91	06/25/91	Admonished	05/21/90
2	D,CRD,ND	12/17/91	07/20/92	Reprimand	05/24/90
-\-	RS	-\-	-\-	Reprimand	-\-
2	UF	01/10/92	11/12/92	P. Conduct by Chief	06/05/90
1	UA	07/27/90	11/21/90	Admonished	06/08/90
1	ND	11/08/91	01/22/92	Admonished	06/13/90
7	ND	08/09/91	09/12/91	Insuf.Evidence	06/14/90
1	UF,ND x 3	06/25/91	09/13/91	***Returned to OCC for	06/20/90
-\-	UFx2,NDx3	-\-	-\-	Prosecution*****	-\-
-\-	UF,ND/ND	-\-	-\-	***Resolution, c.12/93*	-\-
-\-	ND	-\-	-\-		-\-
-\-	ND	-\-	-\-		-\-
-\-	ND	-\-	-\-		-\-
-\-	ND	-\-	-\-		-\-
-\-	ND	-\-	-\-		-\-
-\-	ND	-\-	-\-		-\-
-\-	ND	-\-	-\-		-\-
-\-	ND	-\-	-\-		-\-
-\-	ND	-\-	-\-		-\-
-\-	ND	-\-	-\-		-\-
7	CRD	10/01/90	12/28/90	Admonished	06/25/90
2	ND	04/28/93			06/25/90
2	D	08/09/91	10/17/91	Reprimand	06/26/90
1	ND,CRD	01/18/91	07/23/91	Reprimand	07/12/90
2	ND	05/16/91	06/25/91	Admonished	07/12/90
1	CRD,ND,ND	01/12/91	02/03/92	Admonished	07/27/90
2	ND	03/13/92	05/07/92	1 day suspension	08/12/90
1	UA,UF,D	07/02/91	05/07/92	P. Conduct per Chief	08/06/90
-\-	UA,UF,D	-\-	-\-	P. Conduct per Chief	-\-
1	UA,ND,UA	04/03/91	11/06/92	Admonhisment/Retraining	08/07/90
-\-	ND,ND	-\-	-\-	Admonhised	-\-
4	ND	01/03/91	04/10/91	Not Sust. by Chief	08/14/90
1	Policy	-\-	-\-	Policy Recommendation	08/27/90
2	D	10/15/91	12/12/91	Admonished	08/28/90
5	ND	05/10/91	06/25/91	Admonished	08/31/90
1	Policy	-\-	-\-	Policy Recommendation	08/31/90
1	ND	01/10/92	04/05/93	Reprimand	09/04/90
2	UA/UA	05/11/92	06/16/92	P. Conduct per Chief	09/04/90
2	ND,ND	05/10/91	09/10/91	Retraining	09/10/90
1	UF	10/05/93	11/24/93	Written Reprimand	09/26/90
7	Policy	-\-	-\-	Policy Recommendation	10/02/90
5	UF,ND	05/19/92	11/19/92	Insuf. Evidence	10/05/90
5	ND/ND	05/19/92	11/19/92	Admonished/Admonished	10/05/90
2	UA	08/26/92	11/06/92	Admonished	10/09/90
2	UF	09/24/92	03/19/93	Not Sustained	10/11/90
2	UF	12/17/91	03/02/93	5 day suspension	10/15/90
2	ND	09/14/92	03/05/93	Admonished x 2(Per MCD)	10/18/90

SUSTAINED CASE STATUS - CONTINUED

ETN	SUSTND ALLEG.	DATE MCD	DATE RETURNED	REMARKS	COMPLAINT DATE
-\\-	ND/Policy	-\\-	-\\-	-\\-	-\\-
1	Policy	-\\-	-\\-	-\\-	10/26/90
2	UF.ND.ND	12/16/91	11/06/92	90 day Suspension	11/21/90
-\\-	ND	-\\-	-\\-	Reprimand	-\\-
2	ND.CRD	01/18/91	04/10/91	Reprimand	11/02/90
1	ND	01/18/91	04/17/91	Reprimand	11/07/90
1	ND/ND	07/23/92	08/12/92	Admonished/Admonished	11/13/90
1	UA	04/05/91	08/14/91	Reprimand	11/26/90
1/1	UF/UF	01/10/92	11/23/92	Insuf. Evidence	11/27/90
1	UA	12/23/92	05/24/93	Reprimand	12/04/90
1	ND	03/09/92	03/16/92	Policy Failure	12/07/90
1	UF.D	04/02/91	11/06/92	Not Sust./Admonish.	11/26/90
2	UA	07/15/91	07/23/91	Not Sustained	12/17/90
2	ND	01/23/93		Pending with MCD	12/18/90
?/1	CRD.ND	05/04/92	03/02/93	Reprimand	12/18/90
1	Policy	-\\-	-\\-	Policy Recommendation	12/19/90
?	UA x 3	09/19/91		??	12/26/90
1	ND/ND	07/10/92	11/16/92	Reprimand/Reprimand	01/04/91
1	UF2,CRD	04/23/91	07/19/91	Rturned/OCC prosecution	01/08/91
-\\-	ND2,D2	-\\-			-\\-
-\\-	ND/ND	-\\-			-\\-
?	UA	09/19/91		??	01/09/91
1	ND	04/21/92	???	Admonished	01/23/91
1	D	07/16/91	09/10/91	Admonished	01/11/91
1	CRD/ND	03/05/93	10/05/93	Reprimand	01/15/91
1	ND,ND	07/31/92	11/06/92	Retraining/Not Sust.	01/17/91
2	CRD/CRD	12/23/92		Pending with MCD	01/18/91
-\\-	CRD	12/23/92		Pending with MCD	-\\-
2	D	09/16/92	09/21/92	Reprimand	01/18/91
4	ND	08/13/91	04/10/92	Written Reprimand	01/23/91
1	Policy	-\\-	-\\-	Policy Recommendation	01/25/91
5	D	05/13/92	08/27/92	Admonished	01/25/91
1	ND	09/22/92	11/13/92	Admonished	01/30/91
1	ND	07/31/92	09/15/92	Written Reprimand	02/12/91
2	CRD	07/27/92	11/05/92	Reprimand	03/13/91
?	Policy	-\\-	-\\-	Policy Recommendation	03/12/91
2	UF,ND/ND	07/22/91	08/31/92	60 days susp.X 2	03/18/91
-\\-	UF,ND	-\\-	-\\-	60 days susp.(Per MCD)	-\\-
1	CRD	01/20/93	08/25/93	Reprimand	03/20/91
1	UA,D,CRD	09/03/91	11/06/92	Not Sus. by Commission	03/27/91
2	ND,UA	01/28/93	06/17/93	Admonishment x 2	04/02/91
2	ND,UA	-\\-	-\\-	Admonishment x 2	-\\-
4	Policy	-\\-	-\\-	Policy Recommendation	04/18/91
1	CRD	09/23/92	04/19/93	1 day Susp.held abey.	05/07/91
3	UF	06/25/91	08/31/92	60 day suspension (*)	05/05/91
-\\-	D	06/25/91	10/11/91	*Retrnd MCD Prosecution	-\\-
1/1	D	07/17/92	07/27/92	Not Sustained	05/08/91
1	UA	10/16/92	03/04/93	Retraining	05/10/91
1	CRD,ND,ND	10/28/93		Rtrnd MCD 02/21/93-	06/03/91
7	ND	-\\-		Hearing Request Denied	-\\-
1/1	UA	10/16/91	01/23/92	Written Reprimand	06/19/91
3	policy	-\\-	-\\-	Policy Recommendation	06/24/91

USTAINED CASE STATUS - CONTINUED

ETN	SUSTND ALLEG.	DATE MCD	DATE RETURNED	REMARKS	COMPLAINT DATE
1	D,ND	08/20/91	10/21/91	Member resigned	06/25/91
1	ND	08/09/91	11/08/91	Admonished & Retraining	06/15/91
?	ND	01/21/93	09/03/93	Reprimand	06/26/91
1	ND	09/10/92	11/06/92	Admonished	07/03/91
1	ND	12/17/91	12/31/91	1 day suspension	07/12/91
?	UA/UA	06/03/92	09/10/92	Admonished & Retraining	07/12/91
-\-	ND	04/14/93	09/10/93	Policy Failure(Per MCD)	07/25/91
-\-	ND	-\-	-\-	Policy Failure(Per MCD)	-\-
3	ND,D	08/26/92	11/06/92	5 days suspension	07/23/91
2	ND,ND	01/31/92	06/17/92	Written Reprimand	07/30/91
2	UF	01/21/93		Pending MCD	08/06/91
?	ND	12/20/91	03/17/92	1 day suspension	08/08/91
1	ND/CRD	05/01/92	03/04/93	Admonished/Admonished	08/10/91
?	ND	-\-	-\-	Chief's Discipl.Hearing	-\-
3	UA,CRD/ND	04/14/92		Pending MCD	
-\-	ND	-\-	-\-		
-\-	ND,UA,CRD	-\-	-\-		
-\-	ND&UAx2CRD	-\-	-\-		
1	CRD,RS,UF	04/21/92	10/04/92	Member resigned	08/18/91
-\-	ND	-\-	-\-	-\-	-\-
1/?	UF,SS,UA	01/17/92	05/19/92	Reprimandx2,Chief Hear.	08/19/91
1	UA	01/28/92	07/23/92	Admonished	No Date
2	ND	10/14/92	03/04/93	Written Reprimand	08/21/91
1	Policy	-\-	-\-	Policy Recommendation	08/27/91
1	ND,ND	01/17/92	07/22/92	Written Admonishment	09/04/91
?	UF,D	01/10/92		Pending MCD	09/08/91
3	ND	08/26/92	11/06/92	Admonished & Retraining	09/03/91
1	ND	01/20/93	03/31/93	Not Sustained	09/18/91
2	ND/ND	12/23/92	03/19/93	Not Sustained	09/18/91
1	CRD	05/13/92	05/26/93	Not Sustained	09/21/91
1	UA	08/12/92	09/15/92	Admonished & Retraining	10/17/91
1	ND/ND	01/28/93	06/03/93	Admonished/Admonished	10/24/91
-\-	ND	-\-	-\-	Admonished	-\-
1	CRD	03/16/92	07/20/92	Proper Conduct	10/24/91
2	ND,ND	06/17/92	09/15/92	Written Reprimand	10/31/91
1	Policy	-\-	-\-	Policy Recommendation	11/03/91
4	CRD,RS	03/09/92	07/20/92	40 Hour Suspension	11/05/91
1	ND	10/26/92	02/19/93	Retraining	11/13/91
1	CRD	08/26/92	11/05/92	Admonished	11/20/91
1	ND	07/15/92	09/09/92	1 day suspension	11/20/91
2	UF/Policy	10/26/92	11/20/92	5 days susp./4 in abey.	12/03/91
1	CRD	03/17/92	04/10/92	Admonished	12/09/91
2	UF	01/20/93		Pending MCD	12/16/91
1	CRD	05/04/92	07/20/92	Admonished	12/26/21
2	UA	06/03/92	06/10/92	Not Sustained	12/31/91
4	ND	01/28/93	08/11/93	1 day Suspension	01/27/92
2	D	06/01/92	07/22/92	Admonished	01/29/92
2	ND	09/10/92	09/14/92	Not Sustained	02/05/92
2	ND,ND,Pol	04/19/93		Pending MCD	03/06/92
2	ND	11/23/93		Pending MCD	02/16/92
2	ND	06/11/93		Pending MCD	02/21/92
2	UA	07/19/93		Pending MCD	02/25/92

SUSTAINED CASE STATUS - CONTINUED

ETN	SUSTND ALLEG.	DATE MCD	DATE RETURNED	REMARKS	COMPLAINT DATE
-\-		09/21/93		Rtrnd MCD	-\-
1	D	01/28/93	05/28/93	Admonished	02/26/92
2	Policy	-\-	-\-	Policy Recommendation	02/27/92
2	D,ND(L-1)	06/11/93		Pending MCD	03/12/92
2	ND	04/14/93		Pending MCD	03/16/92
3	UF,UF	07/13/93	01/27/94	Unfounded	03/19/92
2/6	D	07/15/92	11/06/92	Reprimanded	04/06/92
3	ND	09/21/92	11/06/92	Admonished	04/09/92
1	Policy	-\-	-\-	Policy Recommendation	04/17/92
2	UF,CRD,ND	06/11/93		Pending (Per MCD)	04/20/92
-\-	ND/ND	-\-	-\-	-\-	-\-
2	ND	03/05/93		Pending MCD	04/20/92
?	Policy	-\-	-\-	Policy Recommendation	04/29/92
1	Policy	-\-	-\-	Policy Recommendation	05/08/92
2	CRD	04/14/93		Pending MCD	04/29/92
1	ND/ND	04/14/93	06/15/93	Admonished/Admonished	05/06/92
1	UA/CRD	05/18/93	09/03/93	1 day susp.	05/11/92
3	ND	01/21/93	10/05/93	Reprimand	05/14/92
1	D	04/13/93	08/11/93	Reprimand	06/05/92
2	ND	01/28/93	08/11/93	Admonished	06/12/92
-\-	ND	01/28/93	08/11/93	Admonished	06/12/92
3/3	UA/CRDx2	01/21/93		Pending MCD	06/03/92
2	Policy	-\-	-\-	Policy Recommendation	
?	CRD	06/11/93	07/23/93	Not Sustained (per MCD)	06/30/92
1	CRD	07/28/93		Pending MCD	07/06/92
1	D	01/21/93		Pending MCD	07/02/92
1	-\-	-\-	-\-	Policy Recommendation	07/13/92
7	ND	04/14/93	01/11/94	Admonished	08/10/92
1	CRD	04/13/93	07/23/93	Admonished	08/14/92
1	UA	03/05/93	06/17/93	Admonished	08/19/92
2	D	09/28/93		Pending MCD	08/25/92
2	D/UA	-\-			-\-
	Policy	-\-	-\-	Policy Recommendation	08/30/92
1	ND	04/14/93		Pending MCD	09/09/92
1	D	03/05/93		Pending MCD	09/11/92
?	ND	08/03/93		Pending MCD	09/13/92
2	UA	10/20/93		Pending MCD	09/22/92
-\-	UA	-\-			-\-
?	ND	07/16/93		Pending MCD	09/23/92
4	ND	04/14/93	07/23/93	Admonished	10/01/92
?	UA/CRD/ND	10/20/93		Pending MCD	10/05/92
-\-	UA	-\-			-\-
	ND,D	11/29/93		Pending MCD	10/22/92
1	UA	10/20/93		Pending MCD	11/06/92
?	-\-	-\-	-\-	-\-	-\-
2	D	10/20/93		Pending MCD	10/24/92
?	UA	06/11/93		Pending MCD	11/18/92
1	RS	11/29/93		Pending MCD	11/25/92
1	CRD	08/03/93		Pndng MCD-Hearing Dend	11/30/92
1	ND	08/03/93	10/05/93	Not Sust. (MCD & OCCDB)	11/30/92
1	UA	09/10/93		Pending MCD	11/20/92
1	ND	08/11/93		Pending MCD	12/01/92

SUSTAINED CASE STATUS - CONTINUED

ETN	SUSTND ALLEG.	DATE MCD	DATE RETURNED	REMARKS	COMPLAINT DATE
?	ND	08/27/93		Fndng decision MCD/OCC	12/04/92
		11/29/93	12/23/93	Fndng OCC reevaluation	01/07/93
	Policy	-\-	-\-	Policy Recommendation	01/05/93
1	UA	10/28/93		Pending MCD	01/06/93
-\-	CRD	-\-			-\-
?	ND	04/28/93	07/01/93	Admonished	01/15/93
	Policy	-\-	-\-	Policy Recommendation	02/19/93
1	CRD	10/20/93		Pending MCD	03/16/93
?	CRD	10/20/93		Pending MCD	04/01/93
	ND	11/25/93		Pending MCD	04/08/93
?	CRD	10/20/93		Pending MCD	04/25/93
3	D	07/28/93	09/13/93	Admonished	05/14/93
3	UA	01/12/94		Pending MCD	05/26/93
?	CRD	10/28/93		Pending MCD	06/04/93
2	ND	11/23/93		Pending MCD	06/08/93
1	UA	11/23/93		Pending MCD	06/25/93
1	Policy	-\-	-\-	Policy Recommendation	07/21/93
	ND/ND			Pending OCC Resolution	07/28/93
1	ND	01/12/94		Pending MCD	
	Policy	-\-	-\-	Policy Recommendation	
	ND	11/23/93		Pending MCD	

Complainant Ethnicity Code:

1 White
2 Black
3 Hispanic
4 Asian
5 Filipino
6 Pac. Is./Amer. Ind.
7 Other

Summary of Action by S.F.P.D. on Sustained Cases Sent in 1993:

Pending...............41
Admonishment..........13
Reprimand.............6
Suspension............2
Not Sustained by MCD...5
Policy Failure by MCD..1

(Above numbers do not include OCC Policy Recommendations)

DEFINITIONS OF ALLEGATIONS

UF - UNNECESSARY FORCE: Any use of force which exceeds the level of force reasonably needed to perform a necessary police action.

UA - UNWARRANTED ACTION: An act or action not necessitated by circumstances or which does not effect a legitimate police function.

CRD - CONDUCT REFLECTING DISCREDIT ON THE DEPARTMENT: An act or action which, by its nature, reflects badly on the Department and undermines public confidence.

ND - NEGLECT OF DUTY: Failure to take action when some action is required under the applicable laws and regulations.

RS - RACIAL SLURS: Behavior or use of language meant to belittle or defame because of race or ethnicity.

SS - SEXUAL SLURS: Behavior or use of language meant to belittle or defame because of sex or sexual preference.

D - DISCOURTESY: Behavior or language commonly known to cause offense, including use of profanity.

DEFINITIONS OF OCC FINDINGS

1. **Sustained:** A preponderance of the evidence proved that the conduct complained of did occur, and that using as a standard the applicable regulations of the Department, the conduct was improper.

2. **Not Sustained:** The investigation failed to disclose sufficient evidence to either prove, or disprove the allegation made in the complaint.

3. **Proper Conduct:** The evidence proved that the acts which provided the basis for the allegations occurred; however, such acts were justified, lawful, and proper.

4. **Unfounded:** The evidence proved that the acts alleged in the complaint did not occur, or that the named member was not involved in the acts alleged.

5. **Policy Failure:** The evidence proved that the act by the member was justified by Departmental policy, procedure, or regulation; however, the OCC recommends a change in the particular policy, procedure, or regulation.

6. **Supervision Failure:** The evidence proved that the action complained of were the result of inadequate supervision when viewed in light of applicable law; training; and Departmental policy and procedure.

7. **Training Failure:** The evidence proved that the action complained of was the result of inadequate or inappropriate training; or a absence of training when viewed in light of Departmental policy and procedure.

8. **Information Only:** The evidence proved that the action complained of did not involve a sworn member of the Department; or that the action described was so obviously imaginary that their occurrence is not admissible by any competent authority. Information Only allegations are not counted as complaints against sworn members of the Department. Complaints against non-sworn employees of the Department are referred to Management Control Division. Complaints against employees of other agencies, are referred to the appropriate agency.

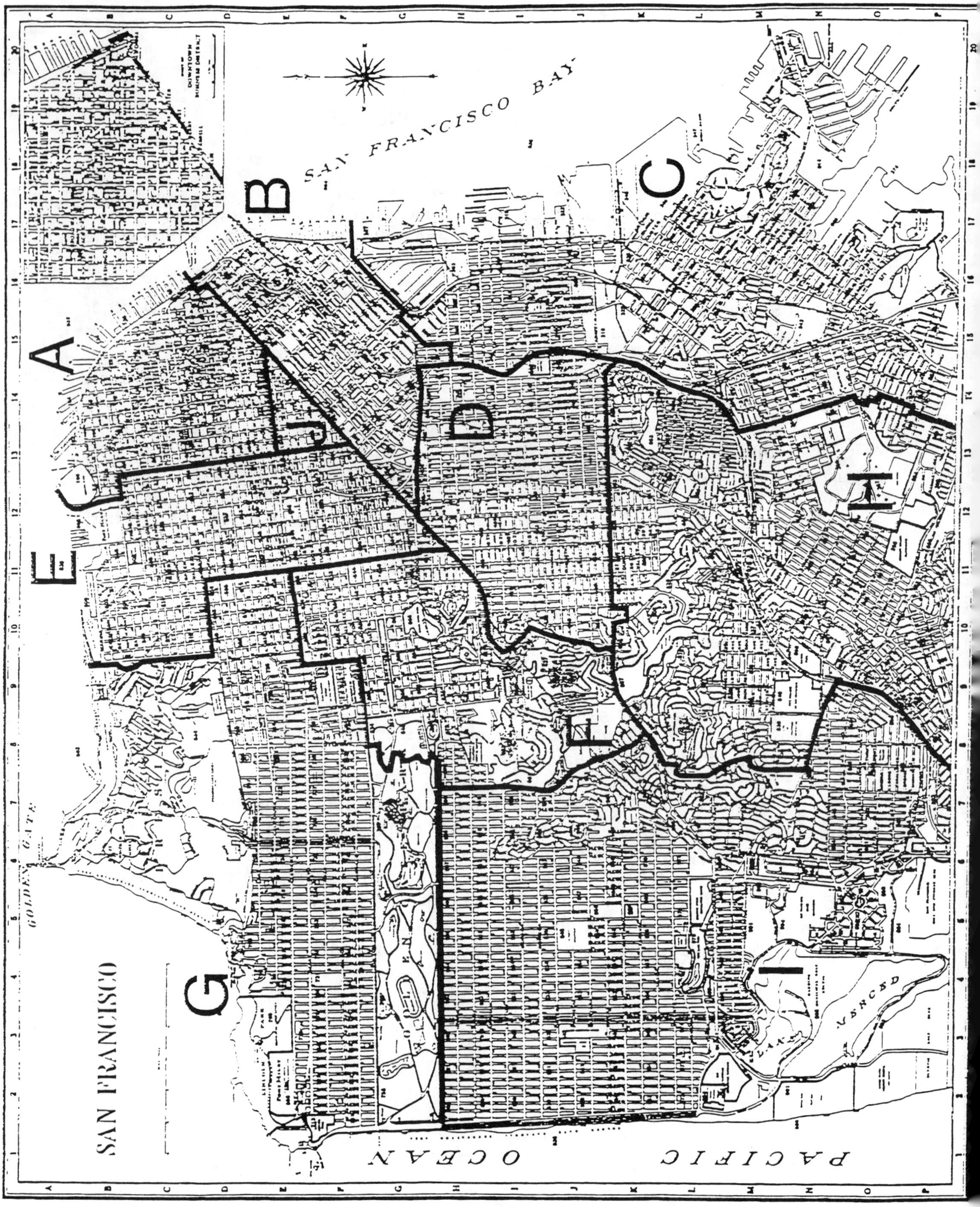
SAN FRANCISCO
SAN FRANCISCO BAY
PACIFIC OCEAN
GOLDEN GATE
LAKE MERCED
DOWNTOWN BUSINESS DISTRICT
A
B
C
D
E
F
G
H
I
J

Document No. 27

San Francisco

(citizen complaint form)

Police Commission for the City and County of San Francisco

OFFICE OF CITIZEN COMPLAINTS

~CITIZEN COMPLAINT FORM~

INSTRUCTIONS FOR COMPLETION OF THE CITIZEN COMPLAINT FORM:
Please answer questions in blocks 2, 3, 4, 5, 6, 8, 9, 10, 11, 15, 17, 20, 21, & 22. Leave all other blocks blank unless you know the information requested. Please **print** all information in **English**. If you do not have a telephone number, enter a message number or the number of a neighbor, friend or relative in block 4. If witnesses are available, write their names, addresses and telephone numbers on a separate sheet of paper and attach it to your complaint. Do not write them on the complaint form. If you do not know the officers name or badge number, include a complete physical description in the narrative (22). **Print** your narrative. Explain what happened from beginning to end. Be specific as to the nature of your complaint against each officer. Include who, what, where, when and why. If you need additional space, use separate sheets of paper and attach them to the complaint. **YOUR STATEMENT MUST BE A TRUE AND ACCURATE ACCOUNT OF THE INCIDENT** to the best of your knowledge and belief, and must be signed by you in block 25. If you have questions or need help, please call the OCC at 415-553-1407 between 8:00 a.m. and 5:00 p.m., or leave a message with our answering service after 5:00 p.m. You may also contact your local neighborhood center for help. Interpreters can be provided at no charge.

填寫公民投訴書說明：
請回答第2，3，4，5，6，8，9，10，11，15，17，20，21及22項問題。除非您知道我們所要求的資料，否則請將其他各項留空。所有資料，務請以正楷填寫清楚。如果您沒有電話號碼，請在第4項填上有可能聯絡您的電話號碼，或鄰居、親戚、朋友的號碼。如果有證人，請用另一張紙寫上他們的姓名，地址及電話，和投訴書夾在一起；切勿寫在投訴書上。如果你不知道涉及事件的警務人員姓名或編號，請將該員的身體特徵，以正楷詳盡寫在第22項上。請清楚說明事件的過程，及投訴的類別，包括涉及何人、何事、何處、何時及何由。如您認為投訴書不夠您填寫，可以另紙填寫資料，夾在投訴書上。您應根據您所知道及所相信的事實填寫資料，必須眞實及正確；填妥請在第26項簽名。如有疑問或需要幫助，請在上午八時至下午五時，致電415-553-1407「公民投訴組」，或在下午五時後，在該組的電話錄音機上留言。您亦可以與有免費翻譯員服務的「華埠建民中心」求助，電話415-391-5099。

INSTRUCCIONES PARA LLENAR EL FORMULARIO DE QUEJAS DE LOS CIUDADANOS: Por favor conteste las preguntas de las casillas 2, 3, 4, 5, 6, 8, 9, 10, 11, 15, 17, 20, 21, & 22. Deje sin contestar las demas preguntas a menos que sepa la información solicitada. El formulario debe ser contestado en **Ingles**. Si usted no tiene telefono escriba en la casilla 4 el número de un servicio de mensajes, o el de un vecino, amigo o pariente. Escriba en una hoja separada los nombres, direcciones y telefonos de los testigos (si los hay), y adjunte ésta información al formulario. En caso de que no conozca el nombre o número de insignia de los oficiales, incluya una descripción fisica completa (22). Describa los hechos en forma completa, sea especifico. Incluya quien, que, donde, cuando y porque. Su declaración debe ser un recuento exacto y verdadero del incidente y debe estar firmada por usted (25). Para pedir información o solicitar ayuda visite nuestras oficinas locales o llamenos al numero 415-553-1407, de 8:00 AM - 5:00 PM. El servicio de interpretacion es gratis. Formularios tambien pueden ser obtenidos en La Raza Information Center--415-826-5885.

PARAAN NE PAGSASGOT SA PORMANG ITO (CITIZEN COMPLAINT o REKLAMO NE MAMAMAYAN)
Mangyaring sagutin ang mga tanong sa blokeng 2, 3, 4, 5, 6, 8, 9, 10, 11, 15, 17, 20, 21, at 22. Kung wala kayo ng impormasyon hinihingi dito, paki-iwanan blanko ang blokeng hindi masagot. **Paki-limbag ang lahat na sagot ninyo.** Kung wala kayong telepono, paki-sulat lang ang inyong "message number", o ang numero ng inyong kapit-bahay, kaibigan, o kamaganak. Kung mayroon kayong mga saksi o testigo, isulat sa ibang papel ang kanilang mga pangalan, mga tirahan, at mga telepono at ikabit ito sa reklamo ninyo. Huwag gagamitin ang pormang ito. Kung hindi ninyo alam ang pangalan ng pulis o ang numero ng kanyang tsapa, isama sa inyong salaysay ang hitsura at pagmumukha ng pulis. Iimbag ang inyong salaysay. Liwanagin lahat ang nangyari magmula sa umpisa hanggang sa katapusan. Tiyakin o siguraduhin ang inyong sinusumbong o renireklamo. Sabihin o ilarawan kung sino, ano, saan, kailan at bakit sa pangyayari. Kung kulang ang pagsusulatan dito gumamit ng ibang papel at ikabit ito sa sumbong ninyo. Sa inyong kaalaman at paniniwala, ang inilahad ninyong nangyari ay dapat lubos na katotohanan at walang kamali-mali at kailangan ninyong pirmahan ang sumbong ito sa blokeng bilang 25. Itanong sa amin kung alinman dito ang hindi maliwanag sa inyo. Kung kailangan ninyo ng tulong, paki-tawagan kami, OCC, telepono 415-553-1407. Maaring tawagan din ninyo ang Dimasalang House sa telepono 415-495-5007 sa pagitan ng alas--otso ng umaga at alas--singko ng hapon o mag-iwan ng pahatid o "message" sa aming "answering service" paglampas dng alas--singko ng hapon.

OFFICE OF CITIZEN COMPLAINTS - USE BLACK INK ONLY!

(1) Day, Date & Time Complaint Received ______

Complaint Against: Personnel ☐ Policy ☐ Procedure ☐

How Received: Person ☐ Phone ☐ Letter ☐ SFPD ☐ Mail-In ☐ Other ☐: (specify)______

(2) **Primary Complainant:**

______
Last Name First Name Middle Initial

HOME ADDRESS:______
Street Apartment

______
City State Zip

WORK ADDRESS:______
Street Apartment

______
City State Zip

(3) **Personal Information**

Age:_____ Date of Birth:______

Sex:______

Ethnicity:______

Occupation:______

(4) **Telephone Numbers:**

Home: (_____)______

Work: (_____)______

(5) **Location of Occurrence:**

(6) **Type of Place**

(7) **District**

(8) **Day, Date, & Time Of Occurrence:** A.M. / P.M. (Circle one)

(9) **Incident Report or Citation No**

(10) **SECONDARY COMPLAINANT?** Yes☐ No☐ **Witnesses?** Yes ☐ No ☐ (If "Yes", attach separate sheet of paper.)
Taped Interview? Yes ☐ No ☐ **Criminal Case Pending in Relation to this matter?** Yes ☐ No☐

(11) **Injuries Claimed?** Yes ☐ No ☐ **Injuries Visible?** Yes ☐ No ☐ **Drug/Alcohol Related?** Yes ☐ No ☐

Photos Taken? Yes ☐ No ☐ By: Photo Lab ☐ O.C.C. ☐ Other:______

Type of Injury: **Medical Release Signed?** Yes ☐ No ☐

(12) Activity	(13) Type	(14) DISP.	(15) Uniform Yes	(15) Uniform No	(16) Rank	(17) Member's Name & Star Number	(18) Unit	(19) Svc	(20) Sex	(21) Eth

(22) **NARRATIVE OF INCIDENT:**

(23) **CASE DISPOSITION AND COMMENTS:**
(For O.C.C. use only!)

(24) **ASSIGNED TO:** **DATE:**

(25) I verify that the above statement is true and correct to the best of my knowledge and belief.

X

Complainant's Signature

Taken By:

Name Title/Star #

Station

After you have completed this form, return it to the Office of Citizen Complaints by folding it along the lines below so that the address shows on the outside. Drop in any mailbox. NO POSTAGE NECESSARY IF MAILED IN THE UNITED STATES.

在您填妥本投訴書後，請沿摺線摺妥（地址在外），投入郵箱，寄回「公民投訴組」。在美國境內寄出，不需郵費。

Despues de completar la forma,doblela sobre las lineas marcadas y depositela en el buzon. No necesita estampilla (sello postal).

Matapos buuin ang pormang ito, tiklupin sa mga linyang nakatatak sa baba upang makita sa labas ang aming "address". Ihulog sa anumang buson o "mailbox". Hindi kailangan ng selyo kung ipadadala lang sa loob ng America.

OFFICES LOCATED AT:
555-7th Street, Room 252
(Between Bryant and Brannan Streets)
San Francisco, California 94103

NO POSTAGE NECESSARY IF MAILED IN THE UNITED STATES

BUSINESS REPLY MAIL
FIRST CLASS MAIL PERMIT NO. 22978 SAN FRANCISCO, CA

POSTAGE WILL BE PAID BY ADDRESSEE

City and County of San Francisco
OFFICE OF CITIZEN COMPLAINTS
400 Van Ness Avenue, Room 67-A
San Francisco, California 94102-9946

Document No. 28

San Jose, Calif.

OFFICE OF THE INDEPENDENT POLICE AUDITOR

SECOND QUARTERLY REPORT
DECEMBER 14, 1993 TO MARCH 31, 1994

A REPORT TO THE
SAN JOSE CITY COUNCIL

TERESA GUERRERO-DALEY
INDEPENDENT POLICE AUDITOR

EXECUTIVE SUMMARY

The Second Quarterly Report encompasses the time from December 14, 1993, through March 31, 1994. The Office of the Independent Police Auditor tabulates its statistics by the number of allegations in each complaint. These allegations are taken directly from the reports submitted by the Internal Affairs Unit. During this quarter, 35 complaints were filed directly with the Auditor and the Internal Affairs Unit submitted 124 complaints for review. Our office reviewed a total of 159 complaints. These 159 complaints produced a total of 303 allegations. Eighty-eight of the 303 allegations were of Unnecessary Force.

The Auditor further narrowed down the 47 cases of Unnecessary Force in order to determine the types of force alleged. Of these cases, there are 48 instances involving the alleged use of hands and feet. These actions taken by the police officers indicate that they are complying with the Department's escalation of force policy.

The San Jose Police Department's response to the First Quarterly Report revealed the creation of a new system for classifying complaints. Misconduct Complaints are divided into two categories: Formal and Informal. The other two categories are Procedural and Policy Complaints. Besides creating a more concise system to classify complaints, all complaints are now typed and better documented which make auditing easier.

The Informal Misconduct Complaint is a new category and has been in place since January 1994. An audit of this new category resulted in a preliminary indication that this informal method of handling complaints is accomplishing its intended dual purpose: to assist first-line supervisors in the handling of minor transgressions involving their officers and to accommodate complainants who prefer not to file a Formal Complaint.

There were 218 Procedural Complaints audited during this quarter. Of these complaints, 61 were randomly selected for the purpose of establishing personal contact with the complainants in order to verify the nature of their complaints. This had been a problem area in the past because Misconduct Complaints were logged as Procedural Complaints. In those cases where contact was made, all but five Procedural cases were consistent with the complainants' statements.

The new classification system will be discussed in more detail in the Third Quarterly Report. The following issues have been raised by the complainants; however, there is not sufficient data to conduct a proper analysis. These issues are:

- Citizens allege that they are deterred from observing police practices.
- Police allegedly arrest or threaten to arrest citizens who use recording devices.
- Many Internal Affairs investigations take too long to complete and may affect the outcome through a loss of complainant interest or loss of witnesses.
- Unnecessary injuries are allegedly inflicted while handcuffed.
- Parents allege that youths are inappropriately stereotyped as gang members.

- Pre textual Arrests for drunk in public, resisting arrests or under the influence of a drug or narcotic charges are allegedly made.

- Unlawful home entries under the guise of "Welfare Checks" are allegedly made.

This office will monitor these issues and will report on any findings in the Third Quarterly Report.

TABLE OF CONTENTS

PAGE

I. INTRODUCTION....1

II. STATISTICAL DATA....2

A. METHODOLOGY....2

B. TOTAL NUMBER OF MISCONDUCT COMPLAINTS....3

1. Unnecessary Force....4

2. Other Types of Allegations....5

C TOTAL NUMBER OF PROCEDURAL COMPLAINTS....6

D. TOTAL NUMBER OF INFORMAL COMPLAINTS....6

III. POLICE RESPONSE TO THE FIRST QUARTERLY REPORT....7

A. DEFINING COMPLAINTS....7

B. AUDITING COMPLAINTS....9

C INTERVENTION COUNSELING AND PROCEDURAL COMPLAINTS....12

D. POTENTIAL BIAS WITHIN THE INTERNAL AFFAIRS UNIT....12

E OBJECTIVITY OF THE INTERNAL AFFAIRS PROCESS....13

IV. OBSERVATIONS....14

V. CONCLUSION....17

TABLE OF CONTENTS

APPENDIX A-1	Chart for Cases
APPENDIX A-2	Chart for Unnecessary Force Allegations
APPENDIX A-3	Chart for Alleged Uses of Unnecessary Force
APPENDIX A-4	Chart for Other Types of Allegations
APPENDIX A-5	Definitions of Findings

I. INTRODUCTION

This is the Second Quarterly Report produced by the Office of the Independent Police Auditor pursuant to the requirements of San Jose Municipal Code Section 2.06.020 c. The ordinance requires that the Auditor prepare a quarterly report including:

1. A statistical analysis documenting the number of complaints by category, the number of complaints sustained and the actions taken;
2. An analysis of trends and patterns; and
3. Specific recommendations for change.

This report will follow a similar format as the First Quarterly Report. It addresses quarterly and cumulative statistics, general and specific observations of the San Jose Police Department and the Internal Affairs Unit. The new classification system created by the Internal Affairs Unit as a response to the First Quarterly Report was reviewed. General impressions about the overall effectiveness of the Office of the Independent Police Auditor will also be discussed.

II. STATISTICAL DATA

A. METHODOLOGY

The statistical data compiled by the Office of the Independent Police Auditor encompasses the time from December 14, 1993, through March 31, 1994. The data presented reflects the research and calculations of the staff of the Office of the Independent Police Auditor.

The statistics collected by this office will differ from those collected and disseminated by the Internal Affairs Unit in some respects. The Office of the Independent Police Auditor uses the word *"complaint"* in generic terms to mean "an expression of dissatisfaction or discontent." When totaling the number of complaints filed with the office, the Auditor combines Procedural, Policy, and Misconduct Complaints[1], whereas Internal Affairs keeps separate statistics for each classification. Additionally, Internal Affairs uses the "Prevailing Case Classification" to account for the total number of complaints.[2]

The statistics presented in this report focus primarily on the number of allegations received and not the number of complaints.

---

[1]The distinctions among Procedural, Policy, Misconduct Complaints are addressed in detail in the section entitled "Police Response to the First Quarterly Report."

[2]The "Prevailing Case Classification" is a classification method where the allegations are a prevailing level number. This determines how the complaint shall be classified. For example, an allegation of Unnecessary Force is a level one, whereas an allegation of Improper Procedure is a level eight. If there is a complaint where there are two allegations, one for Unnecessary Force and the other for Improper Procedure, the complaint will be classified as an Unnecessary Force complaint because it is a level one.

For example, a single complaint filed by a citizen indicating that unnecessary force was used to effectuate his/her arrest may also state that the officer was rude, or that the officer improperly searched this person. This individual would have made a single complaint with three different allegations: Unnecessary Force, Rude Conduct and Unlawful Search.

The number of allegations reported are taken directly from the face sheets submitted by Internal Affairs. Internal Affairs classifies the type and the number of allegations.

B. TOTAL NUMBER OF MISCONDUCT COMPLAINTS

During the second quarter of operations, 35 complaints[3] were filed directly with the Auditor. In addition, the Internal Affairs Unit submitted 124 complaints[4] to the Independent Police Auditor for review. Of the 159 total complaints, the Independent Police Auditor officially closed[5] 47 complaints.[6]

---

[3]The San Jose Police Department defines a complaint as *an act of expressed dissatisfaction that related to Department operations, personnel conduct or unlawful acts. See* San Jose Police Department Duty Manual, Section C 1501.5. The 35 complaints filed directly with the Auditor were subsequently classified by Internal Affairs as 26 "Procedural", eight "Misconduct", and one "Informal" complaints.

[4]This number includes: (1) Complaints closed by Internal Affairs after the opening of the Office of the Independent Police Auditor; and (2) Complaints *opened* by Internal Affairs after the opening of the Office of the Independent Police Auditor, or which were *opened* at the time of the opening of the Office.

[5]The term "officially closed" used by the Office of the Independent Police Auditor is to describe cases where the Auditor concurs with the investigative process and finding, and no further investigation or action is required.

[6]*See* Appendix A-1

1. UNNECESSARY FORCE

The Independent Police Auditor reviews all complaints alleging excessive or unnecessary force. The Auditor monitors these cases by reviewing all the investigation conducted, and by periodically attending the interviews of civilian witnesses and police officers.

The review also includes reading all the investigative reports, listening to the taped statements of the witnesses and officers, and directly contacting the complainants and witnesses when necessary. The analysis may also result in requests for additional investigation.

In the second quarter, the Office of the Independent Police Auditor monitored 47 cases that contained 88 new allegations of Unnecessary Force. Of those allegations, two were sustained[7] and 28 resulted in a finding other than sustained.[8] There are 58 allegations that are still pending.[9]

The statistics below indicate that, if the force was necessary, the officers are following the escalation of force guidelines. Officers are trained to first use their hands to control, arrest or detain an individual. If that fails or is not proper, the next level of force is the OC spray. The baton and deadly force, respectively, are the last levels of force used.

---

[7]The allegations are sustained when the investigation disclosed sufficient evidence to clearly prove the allegations made in the complaint. *See* San Jose Police Department Duty Manual, Section C 1513.20.

[8]Internal Affairs employs several other findings to describe situations where an allegation is not proven. This report will not statistically address these other findings. These other findings include: Unfounded, Exonerated, Not Sustained, and No Finding. *See* San Jose Police Department Duty Manual, Section C 1513.20. *See* Appendix A-5 for definitions of other findings.

[9]*See* Appendix A-2.

The majority of the complaints alleging Unnecessary Force involved the use of hands. Of the 47 Unnecessary Force cases, there were 35 instances where the citizens complained that the officers unnecessarily shoved, pushed, tackled, pulled their hair or applied a wrist lock. Feet were allegedly used 13 times. These instances where feet were involved included kicking and stepping on the complainants to restrain them. The baton was allegedly used fourteen times. Of these fourteen baton uses, the majority were blows to the body other than the head. OC spray was allegedly used seven times. Seven complaints involved the alleged use of flashlights, body slams against the police car and the forcible taking of blood samples.[10]

The statistics also revealed there were more incidents of baton use than OC spray use. However, the use of OC spray, unlike the baton, requires that the person be facing the officer within a proper range in order to be effective.

2. OTHER TYPES OF ALLEGATIONS

The Independent Police Auditor is required to review at least 20% of complaints which relate to matters other than Unnecessary Force. These other types of allegations are Improper Procedure, Unlawful Arrest, Rude Conduct, Failure to Take Action, Excessive Police Service, Unlawful Search, Damaged and/or Missing Property, Discrimination and Unofficerlike Conduct.

The Auditor has reviewed a total of 215 other allegations. Of the 215 allegations, 25 were sustained and 56 resulted in a finding

[10]*See* Appendix A-3.

other than sustained. There are 134 allegations that are still pending as of the end of the second quarter.[11]

C. TOTAL NUMBER OF PROCEDURAL COMPLAINTS

During this quarter, there were 218 Procedural Complaints filed and audited. The total includes those Procedural Complaints initiated at the Auditor's office and at the Internal Affairs Unit. These are separate from the Misconduct Complaints.

D. TOTAL NUMBER OF INFORMAL COMPLAINTS

A total of 29 Informal Complaints were audited for this quarter. This is a new category that the Auditor will continue to monitor.

[11] *See* Appendix A-4.

III. POLICE RESPONSE TO THE FIRST QUARTERLY REPORT

There were five areas of concern that were addressed in the First Quarterly Report. These areas included:

A. Defining Complaints
B. Auditing Complaints
C. Intervention Counseling
D. Potential Bias within the Internal Affairs Unit
E. Objectivity of the Internal Affairs Process

A. DEFINING COMPLAINTS

Prior to the inception of this office, Internal Affairs used a two-prong system to classify complaints. The cases were classified as Misconduct or Procedural Complaints. This was an old system that incorporated but did not distinguish the Informal Misconduct Complaints from the truly Procedural Complaints.

Internal Affairs has created and implemented a system consisting of four types of complaints: Formal[12], Informal, Procedural and Policy.

Formal Complaints are those complaints which alleged a serious violation of Department policy or a violation of law by an officer. The complaints will continue to be investigated in the same manner and no change is noted.

Informal Complaints are those complaints involving allegations of minor transgressions on the part of a subject officer[13] which may

---

[12]Formal and Informal Complaints are complaints of misconduct.

[13]Subject officer refers to the officer of whom the complaint is about.

be handled informally by bringing the matter to the attention of the officer's chain of command at the complainant's request.[14] These are typically Rude Conduct complaints. However, if the complainant feels such conduct was in his/her opinion egregious that a formal complaint is warranted, Internal Affairs is then obligated to investigate this complaint as such. The complainant has ultimate control as to whether to treat the complaint as Formal or Informal.

Procedural Complaints are now defined in two separate portions. The first portion includes the following: "After the initial investigation by the Intake Officer, the Department determines the subject officer acted reasonably and within Department Policy and Procedure given the specific circumstances and facts of the incident and that despite the allegation of misconduct, there is no factual basis to support the allegation." At the end of the investigation, the assigned finding will be "Within Department Policy."[15]

A second portion of the definition includes: "The allegation is a dispute of fact case wherein there is no independent information evidence or witnesses available to support the complaint and there exists another judicial entity which is available to process the concerns of the complainant." A finding of "No Misconduct Determined" will be assigned to the dispute of fact cases.[16]

---

[14]San Jose Police Department, Response to Independent Police Auditor's First Quarterly Report, page 7, May 25, 1994.

[15]Ibid., page 6.

[16]Ibid., page 6.

For example, a person files a complaint alleging an Unlawful Search, where the complainant states that the police entered his/her home and conducted a search. After a preliminary investigation, the Internal Affairs Officer discovers that the complainant is on parole and has a search clause. The case will be closed with a finding of "No Misconduct."

Policy Complaints pertain to an established policy, properly employed by a Department member, which the complainant understands but believes is inappropriate or not valid. A complaint of this nature could be for the disapproval of a towing ordinance. These complaints do not focus on the conduct of the officer but on the policy or law with which the complainant disagrees.

There are many advantages to this new system if properly employed. The Formal, Informal and Procedural Complaints are all indexed by officers' names. The complaints will be retained for a period of six years. Not only will they be subject to Intervention Counseling, but they will also be subject to Motions for Discovery in criminal and civil proceedings. This tracking system will enable the Auditor and the police department to better identify trends or patterns as they develop.

B. AUDITING COMPLAINTS

Auditing procedural complaints was problematic because there were only two forms of documentation for these cases by Internal Affairs: the handwritten log and the individual investigator's handwritten notes. These writings were difficult to read and to understand, other than to the author.

All Internal Affairs investigators are now equipped with their own computers. All classifications of citizen complaints are typed and entered into the Internal Affairs' database. A cumulative log and an individual face sheet are prepared for these types of complaints. The complainants are now given an opportunity to review and sign their statements. They are also notified in writing regarding the disposition of their complaints and given information on how to access the Auditor's office.

Of the 218 Procedural Complaints, 61 complaints were randomly selected to survey and audit for this quarter. Personal contact with the complainant was achieved in 39 cases. Of the 39 citizens that were interviewed, 28 cases were found to be properly classified as Procedural. In five cases, according to the complainants, the allegations were not compatible with the Procedural Log. One case became a Formal Complaint.

In 22 of the 61 cases, the complainants were not contacted because they had either moved, had the phone disconnected or after repeated attempts did not return the phone calls.

Since January 15, 1994, Internal Affairs has been using the Informal Complaint system. This office has conducted an audit of this new classification method by personally contacting the citizens to verify if they were satisfied with the informal handling of their complaints.

In 22 cases, we successfully contacted the complainants. In six cases, we were unable to contact the complaining citizens. In one case, the complaint did not involve the San Jose Police Department.

Of the people contacted, the survey indicated that the allegations stated were compatible with the allegations in the Informal Log. Fifteen of the 22 complainants were satisfied with the informal handling of their cases. Of the four who were dissatisfied with the handling of their Informal Complaints, one person will seek to formalize the complaint and the three other citizens indicated that they did not wish to further pursue the matter. One person was unable to say if he/she was satisfied with the informal handling of his/her complaint. Another person contacted changed his/her Informal Complaint to a Formal Complaint. Finally, one other complaint involved a San Jose police dispatcher.

This audit revealed that the Informal Complaints as defined have been properly identified and handled. There were no complaints of undue pressure from Internal Affairs to have their complaints filed as Informal. Furthermore, the audit revealed that Internal Affairs investigators took time to explain to the complainants their options of filing a Formal or Informal Complaint.

The Auditor will continue to monitor these complaints to ensure that the complainants are not pressured into accepting this less formal method of investigating their cases. The Auditor will also review these cases closely to ensure that only minor transgressions are addressed in this manner. In addition, under this new system, the Unit Commander must approve the classification of a complaint as Informal. This will standardize the classification process so that there is uniformity in the Internal Affairs Unit.

C. INTERVENTION COUNSELING AND PROCEDURAL COMPLAINTS

Unlike Misconduct Complaints, Procedural Complaints were not subject to Intervention Counseling regardless of the fact that there were over four times as many Procedural Complaints as Misconduct Complaints. Misconduct Complaints, which include Formal and Informal Complaints, and Procedure Complaints are now tracked and indexed by the officers' names and will be subject to Intervention Counseling. Any officer receiving three or more Formal Complaints or five or more Procedural or Informal Complaints in a twelve-month period will receive Intervention Counseling.

D. POTENTIAL BIAS WITHIN THE INTERNAL AFFAIRS UNIT

In order to avoid potential bias, formalized written policy will be added to the Internal Affairs Procedure Manual requiring an Internal Affairs investigator to notify his/her Unit Commander of any potential conflict arising from prior contacts between the investigator and the subject officer or the complainant. The Auditor frequently communicates with the Internal Affairs investigators and has verified that they are aware of this policy and are in compliance.

E. OBJECTIVITY OF THE INTERNAL AFFAIRS PROCESS

During the first quarter, citizens frequently came to the Auditor's office to complain about the manner in which they were treated at Internal Affairs. They complained about leaving with the feeling that they were not believed or that Internal Affairs investigators were more interested in disproving rather than proving their case.

The second quarter has seen a decline in the number of citizens complaining about their interaction with Internal Affairs Investigators. All Internal Affairs investigators have been given specific direction by the Unit Commander on how to be more sensitive when interacting with the complainants. The Unit Commander receives feedback from the Auditor regarding any complaints involving the officers. The Auditor has met with the new investigators to acquaint them with the functions of this office and to inform them of particular areas of interest. Many hours are spent at the Internal Affairs Unit where the majority of the officer interviews take place. The investigators will also call the Auditor and alert her office of any particular problems with the cases and of upcoming witness interviews.

IV. OBSERVATIONS

The Office of the Independent Police Auditor continues to serve as an alternative forum in which citizens can file their complaints. This quarter appears to have a decline in the total number of new complaints filed, from 171 to 159. Because this office does not use the Prevailing Case Classification to account for the number of complaints, the number of cases are less even though the number of allegations rose by over 35%. The number of Unnecessary Force allegations rose from 63 to 88. The number of other types of allegations also rose significantly from 131 to 215.

The Auditor will continue to review all of the Unnecessary Force cases and the majority of all other cases. The Auditor will also monitor the new classification system. A more complete evaluation of this new method will be discussed in the Third Quarterly Report. Unannounced audits to compare the information sent to the Auditor and the information found in the files of Internal Affairs will also continue to be a function of this office.

The Auditor's office has continued to promote the office to the community. The following is a partial list of groups or organizations with whom the Auditor has met:

- PAT-7 meeting with Councilmember George Shirakawa,
- Kathy Meir, President and Chris Burdick, Executive Director of the Santa Clara County Bar Association,
- Bay Area Police Oversight Network,
- Kiwanis Pueblo de San Jose,
- John Crew, Staff Attorney Director from the ACLU,
- Story Road Business Association,
- Publisher and Editors of the San Jose Mercury News, and

- Citizen's Police Academy.

The Internal Affairs Unit and the Auditor's office are working closely towards developing and implementing effective ways for them to work together and to accomplish the mission of the Office of the Independent Police Auditor. There are open channels of communication between the Auditor, the Internal Affairs Unit and the Office of the Chief.

A sergeant has been assigned as the liaison for the Auditor's office. This sergeant is responsible for gathering and tracking all the information to and from Internal Affairs and the Auditor's office. The sergeant also facilitates the exchange of information and scheduling of witness interviews for those cases that are assigned to the Bureau of Field Operations for investigation.

An area that has been problematic for this office is the lack of resources to adequately research and authenticate issues that are raised by citizens' complaints. There are serious allegations that have been raised; however, this office lacks the means to do a historical analysis of the available data or statistics to adequately prove or disprove a hypothesis. In order to gather a sufficient quantity of data whenever an issue arises, the Auditor's office has to hand-search all the files. An issue may not become significant until the second or third quarter; therefore, there is a need to automate the data in the files in order to later retrieve the information.

The following allegations have been raised in several cases. However, there is not sufficient data in this quarter to do a proper analysis.

- Citizens allege that they are deterred from observing police practices.

- Police allegedly arrest or threaten to arrest citizens who use recording devices.

- Many Internal Affairs investigations take too long to complete and may impact the outcome through a loss of complainant interest or loss of witnesses.

- Unnecessary injuries are allegedly inflicted while handcuffed.

- Parents allege that youths are inappropriately stereotyped as gang members.

- Pre textual Arrests for drunk in public, resisting arrest or under the influence of a drug or narcotic charges are allegedly made.

- Unlawful home entries under the guise of "Welfare Checks" are allegedly made.

This office is sensitive to the City's budgetary constraints and has begun to address the needs for the proper collection and analysis of data. The Auditor's office is in the process of creating a database which would adequately contain the information in the files for later retrieval. The services of an analyst would be of great assistance. However, in the mean time the three person staff of this office will begin to input all the back data including all the incoming cases.

V. CONCLUSION

The Office of the Independent Police Auditor is performing the functions it was intended to accomplish. With the passage of time, the office is evolving into its role of serving as an alternative forum for citizens to file their complaints, for auditing the investigations of the aforementioned complaints and for reaching out into the community to help bring about greater confidence in the San Jose Police Department's Internal Affairs process.

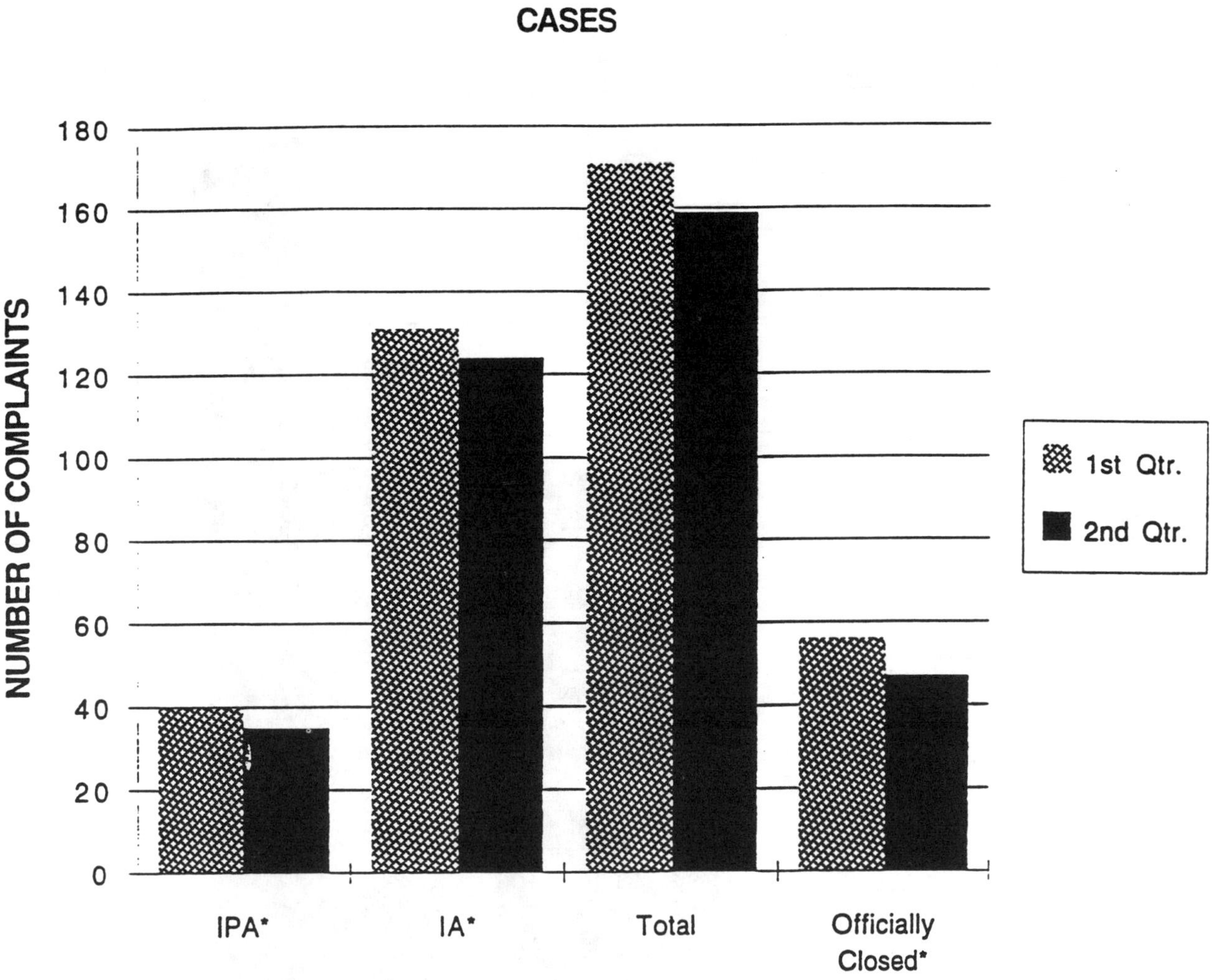

*IPA (Independent Police Auditor)- The number of complaints filed/updated at our office per complainant's request.

*IA (Internal Affairs Unit)- The number of complaints file directly at IA, including the department initiated cases.

*Officially Closed- This term is used by IPA is to describe cases where the Auditor concurs with the investigation process and finding, and no further investigation or action is required. The first quarter graphs contain cumulative allegations from the First Quarterly Report. These #s are not the same as the #s from the First Quarterly Report because they have been updated.

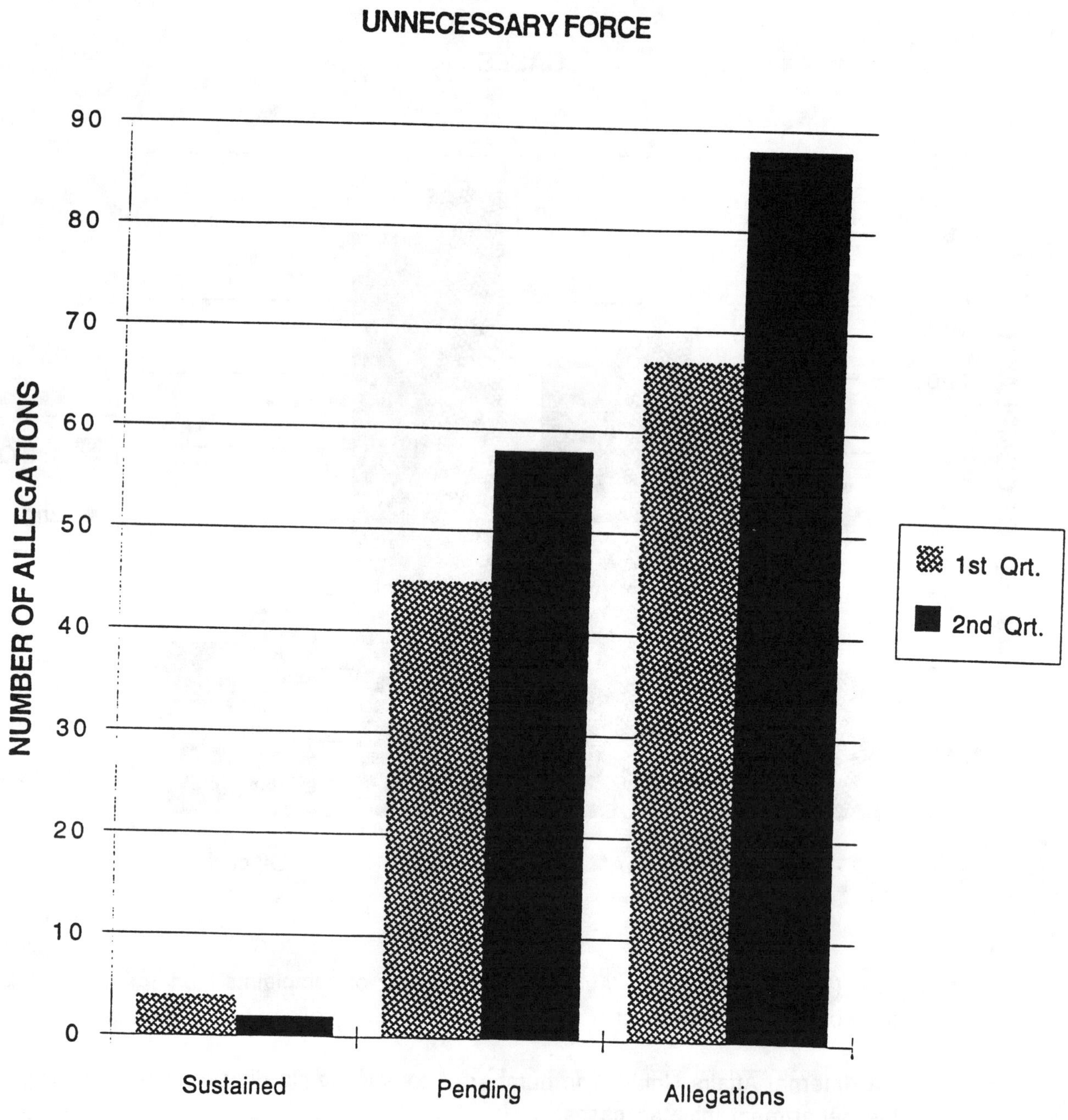

•The first quarter graphs contain cumulative allegations from the First Quarterly Report. These #s are not the same as the #s from the First Quarterly Report because they have been updated.

ALLEGED USES OF UNNECESSARY FORCE

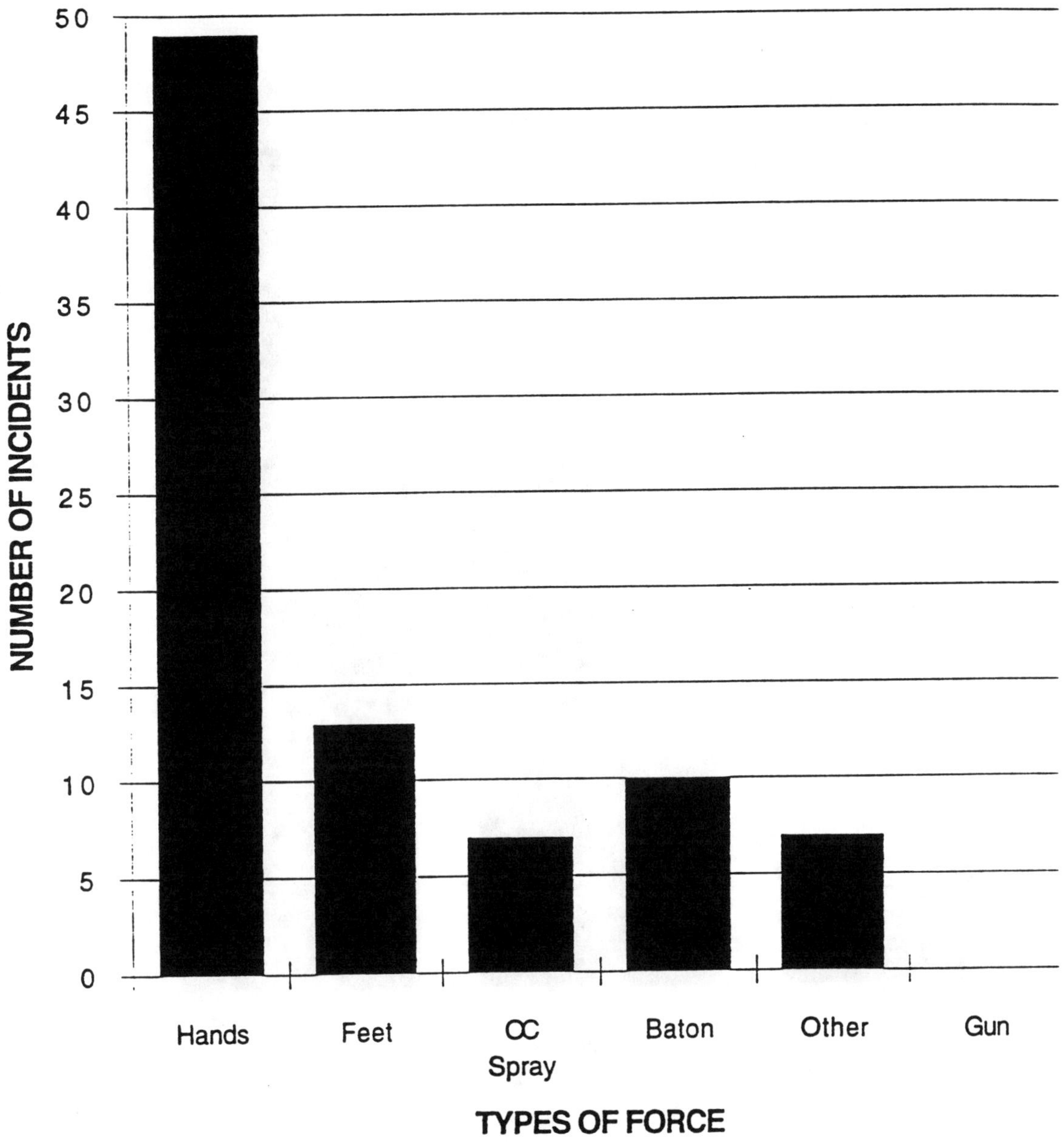

•This chart contains only second quarter statistics.

OTHER TYPES OF ALLEGATIONS

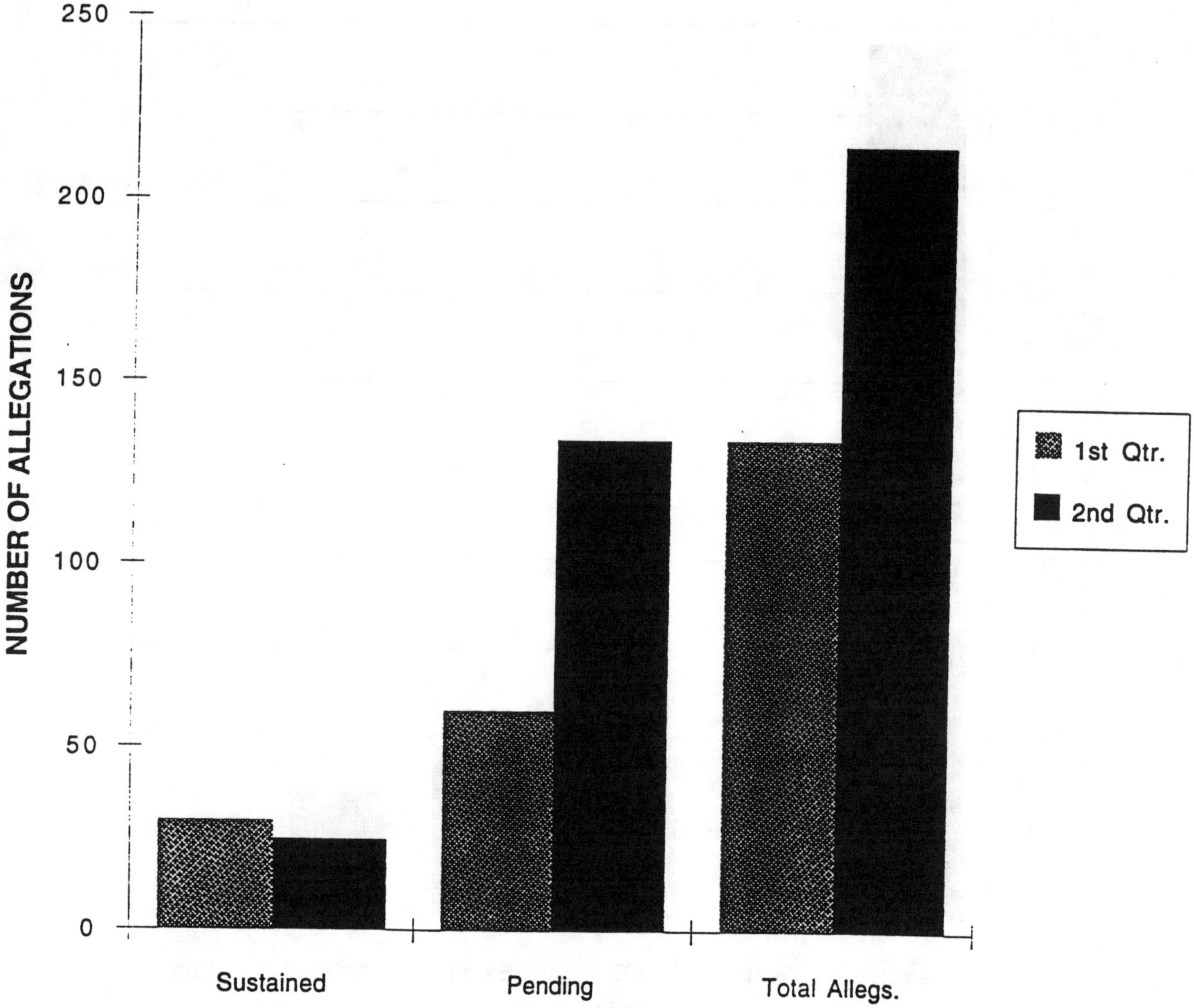

•The first quarter graphs contain cumulative allegations from the First Quarterly Report. These #s are not the same as the #s from the First Quarterly Report because they have been updated.

DEFINITIONS OF FINDINGS

1. **SUSTAINED**: The investigation disclosed sufficient evidence to clearly prove the allegation made in the complaint.

2. **NOT SUSTAINED**: The investigation failed to disclose sufficient evidence to clearly prove the allegation made in the complaint or to conclusively disprove the allegation.

3. **EXONERATED**: The acts which provided the basis for the complaint or allegation occurred; however, the investigation revealed that they were justified, lawful and proper.

4. **UNFOUNDED**: The investigation conclusively proved that the act or acts complained of did not occur. This finding also applies when the individual member(s) or employee(s) named were not involved in the act or acts which may have occurred.

5. **NO FINDING**: The complainant failed to disclose promised information to further the investigation; or the investigation revealed that another agency was involved and the complaint or complainant has been referred to that agency; or the complainant wishes to withdraw the complaint; or the complainant is no longer available for clarification.

Document No. 29

Seattle

SEATTLE POLICE DEPARTMENT

INTERNAL INVESTIGATIONS AUDITOR

OCTOBER, 1992 REPORT

I. INTRODUCTION:

Pursuant to ordinance No. 115975, I am submitting this report reviewing my first six (6) months as Internal Investigations Auditor. By way of background information, I decided to go beyond the literal requirements of the ordinance which details my responsibilities. My work since approximately April 1, 1992, has entailed a review of not only excessive force cases but every completed Internal Investigation Section (IIS) file (over 80), every contact log (over 200), and every line referral (several dozen). Also, I have met with interested community persons, Seattle Police Guild representatives, and city officials and staff. In addition, I have visited other cities (Cincinnati, Ohio and San Diego, California) and met with their respective internal investigation units. Finally, I have reviewed a significant amount of written materials which discuss police discipline - both within the Seattle Police Department and without.

With that background in mind, I have divided my report into three sections: General Impressions, Specific Recommendations, and Ordinance Reporting Requirements.

II. GENERAL IMPRESSIONS

A. Overall impression of Police Conduct

Based on information I have reviewed (both within and without the department) it is clear that the overwhelming majority of Seattle Police officers do their job in a professional manner on a daily basis under frequently difficult conditions. By and large this is an efficient, well-trained police department.

The traditional yardsticks of lawsuits, settlements, shots fired and complaints[1] show the overall positive impact of training, supervision and discipline. However, this should not be interpreted to suggest that there are not instances of serious misconduct by Seattle Police officers, including cases of excessive force. Such things do occur. Yet we need to recognize that, compared to other metropolitan police departments, this department has much to be commended.

B. Current Disciplinary System

Prior to the creation of the auditor position, Seattle utilized a traditional approach to police discipline, i.e. the entire intake, investigation, decision and discipline system was handled within the department. The auditor position permits civilian review of the paperwork in individual cases and the process , but with limited authority to act. Except for infrequent instances discussed below, the system functions much like it did prior to the establishment of the auditor. My biggest criticism of this system is that too much emphasis is placed on discipline and not enough on prevention. I recognize that the Chief makes a strong effort to use prevention within the discipline system, e.g., deferring findings and/or requiring assistance programs, but I don't believe enough is done. Minor instances of misconduct, which could lead to bigger problems later, are too often overlooked in a system that must, by necessity, focus on the more serious cases. In general, this has not promoted respect for IIS within the department. It is difficult to break the officers 'code of silence' or 'blue wall' where the chief emphasis is perceived to be on punishment[2] .

---

[1] There were 193 lawsuits for false arrest and/or excessive force from 3/85 through 1/92. Many of these lawsuits were closed without payment. Monies paid to claimants during those years averaged approximately $100,000/year. Also, amounts paid out in settlements from 1980-1992 averaged $1,740 plus $6,300 in costs and attorney fees per case. The number of complaints of excessive force was 129 in 1991 and 138 in 1990. The number of arrests in those years for serious crimes exceeded 60,000/year. Regarding shots fired, so far in 1992 there have been 9 (6 accidental, 3 justified); in 1991, 6 shots fired (1 accidental, 4 justified, 1 not justified); 1990, 12 shots fired (5 accidental, 7 justified). These numbers compare favorably to other cities or counties within Washington.

[2] This should not be construed as condoning a 'code of silence'. Instances where a complaint is sustained and an officer corroborated a fellow officer's story should be aggressively investigated. An officer's loyalty must first be to the public he/she serves - especially when faced with fellow officer misconduct. We know that officers can pay an enormous price for telling the truth about a fellow

Coincidentally, due primarily to state pension and federal law changes, fitness for duty examinations have been essentially eliminated. The issue of police officer 'burn out' concerns me and I think should be addressed outside the discipline system. Fitness for duty exams used to have a role. A question is raised as to whether legitimate issues of 'burn out' can or should be handled in a discipline system.

In my role as auditor I have had extraordinary cooperation from the police department. Both IIS and other sections have gone out of their way to answer my questions. In particular the Chief and officers within IIS have made themselves available on short notice. Also, I was able to review procedures outside my particular duties as auditor. For example, I attended a Complaint Advisory Board Hearing and have witnessed the Chief making decisions on completed IIS files following line review. My impression is that there is an honest effort by those involved in the discipline system to do a good job. The thoroughness of the IIS investigations appears, in general, to be of high degree and of professional quality. The leadership of the department appears committed to ensuring that sustained instances of misconduct, including excessive force cases, are not tolerated. But as noted above I am persuaded the present system can be made much more effective. A principal question remains whether the addition of civilian oversight improves the discipline system. I believe such oversight is essential.

C. <u>The Appropriateness of Civilian Oversight</u>

It is basic to keep in mind that the police, as an adjunct to maintaining public order, are citizens authorized to carry weapons and use force. With that authority carries a special responsibility to the public that should permit close scrutiny of discipline matters. The risk to the public is too great to suggest otherwise.

Civilian oversight of police discipline can be justified primarily to ensure the fairness of the system and to suggest improvements. In Seattle,

---

officer. But we can't permit a system that rewards a 'code of silence'. Fundamentally, it is a matter of confidence in the discipline system.

where the Chief is ultimately accountable to the Mayor and City Council, one can argue that there does already exist some civilian oversight. However, that position loses favor in the daily operations of the department which must look at discipline on a case-by-case basis. Without civilian oversight I would be concerned whether there may be a greater tendency to give an officer the benefit of the doubt.[3] My experience as auditor has shown me that civilians do look at some behavior differently than police officers. It seems entirely appropriate that Seattle continue some form of civilian oversight of police discipline. Although the present Chief obviously takes the matter of discipline seriously, the long term view suggests that civilian oversight would lessen the opportunities for abuse of the discipline system within the department. Also, my strong perception is that no public institution should conduct important public business without some form of accountability beyond its internal processes.

D. Form of Civilian Oversight

At this time I think it would be premature for me to suggest that a different form of civilian oversight than auditor is necessary. Six months is simply not enough time to gather anything other than initial impressions. I still believe that I have a lot to learn about a very complex issue and am requesting that such matters be more seriously probed in my next report.

Preliminarily, I do feel confident in expressing some frustration with a limited review of paperwork at the investigative stage. A far more preferable approach would permit input by the auditor at the discipline stage and perhaps authority to recommend investigation outside the police department in extraordinary situations of alleged criminal actions by police officers.

A collateral issue to the concept of civilian oversight is the level of confidentiality that IIS records receive. The convergence of court rulings and contract requirements present a legal quagmire when assessing the public's

[3] On the surface the rate at which complaints are sustained within the Seattle Police Department (less than 10%) is lower than many other cities. However, I am reluctant to make too much of this percentage at this time without learning more about whether other cities screen out minor complaints - which Seattle Police Department does not do. It is worthy of additional study.

right to know - which is in itself a form of civilian oversight. Although my initial impression is that more openness is beneficial to the department and the public, I am still researching this matter and would like to defer anything definitive until a future report. However, I do believe it is an issue of significance.

III. SPECIFIC RECOMMENDATIONS

A. Increase Authority of IIS[4]

It is my view that an unwavering commitment within the police department to discipline instances of misconduct and reasonable civilian oversight is the best protection for the public. But by limiting IIS to an investigatory role we remove the voice of those with the most knowledge and experience with misconduct from commenting on the facts. It also lessens the esteem of IIS within the department.

A more preferable system would permit direct input from IIS to the Chief as to whether an event happened. Likewise, the IIS commander should make recommendations, along with the chain of command, as to the appropriate discipline for sustained complaints. Although the present chief appears to welcome such input, the process needs to be institutionalized.

. Appointment of a Sergeant to IIS should be perceived as a more prestigious position and important to an officer's advancement within the department. By increasing the authority of IIS the discipline system would benefit.

B. Eliminate Line Review of Completed IIS Files

Under the present system, a complaint for which a complete IIS investigation occurs is sent through the investigated officer's chain of command for recommendation to the Chief as to whether an incident occurred. I question the utility and necessity for this procedure. (Please note

[4] Note that IIS is considering draft rules of administration which address the issue of the authority of IIS and some of the other matters discussed herein.

that I have no objection to input from the chain of command regarding appropriate discipline.)

Line commanders are no better than anyone else in determining whether misconduct occurred. In fact, previous perceptions of an officer could warp their view. Also, the Chief, who must ultimately make the decision, can face subtle obstacles when his view is different from that of the line. Likewise, this procedure causes more delay in a system that needs more prompt resolution of complaints. (See discussion below, III.D.) The input to the chief should be from a more neutral source, i.e. a strengthened IIS as discussed in III. A., Supra.

C. <u>Redirection of Rudeness or Demeanor Complaints</u>

Much of the work of IIS is spent deciding whether relatively minor accusations of misbehavior should be investigated as disciplinary matters. It is my belief these incidents are more appropriately viewed as management issues as opposed to discipline matters. Specifically, it would seem that minor complaints of misconduct should be handled at the precinct level by the officer's supervisor. A written record should be kept of the complaint and any remedial action. Nothing would be made a part of the officer's discipline history unless the infraction recurs within a negotiated period of time and is sustained.

This approach would place responsibility for such behavior where it belongs - on the officer and the officer's supervisor. Failure by the supervisor to respond to a complaint in timely fashion should itself subject the supervisor to disciplinary action. Also, this change could increase the promptness with which such complaints are handled and encourage more contact between citizens and the supervisors. In my experience so far, many citizens simply want a call from a supervisor acknowledging their complaint and that the matter was brought to the officer's attention. Such redirection of this category of complaint to the precinct level could improve the public perception of the police in their community by creating a closer relationship between them. Finally, behavior that might now be overlooked or viewed as minor would have to be dealt with - thereby improving the chances of preventing more serious misconduct later.

If contact logs are continued in their present form, I would urge that supervisors be required to meet with the officers regarding the allegation and a written record be made of the action taken in a log that can be accessed by IIS.

D. Promptness in Completing Investigations and Determining Discipline

This is a difficult issue. The increase in complaints during the past two years without any concurrent increase in staffing has placed an enormous burden on IIS. On the other hand, prompt investigation and imposition of discipline is essential to an effective disciplinary system. I would suggest a system that, absent a finding of good cause for delay stated in writing by the commander of IIS, all investigations will be completed within sixty days. Discipline, absent good cause, would be imposed in sustained cases within thirty days following decision.

I understand the difficulties inherent in this proposal. Many complainants or witnesses are unavailable or unresponsive. Also, civil litigation is an added complication. Yet in fairness to the officer and the public, promptness is a virtue - even if it means an investigation that is less than perfect. I have seen too many cases that linger in the investigatory stage for months. The passage of time makes meaningful investigations and discipline proceedings difficult to attain. I would be glad to work with IIS to help reduce the causes of delay.

E. Line Referrals Should Be Restructured or Eliminated

Presently IIS has the option of referring conduct that is beyond a contact log to the officer's chain of command for investigation (a line referral) rather than IIS. On the surface I am troubled by the appearance of objectivity of such a process. More practically, the quality of line referral investigations varies enormously.

My preference would be to eliminate such investigations completely. If financial or other considerations prohibit this, then limit those persons within a section or bureau who can conduct these investigations and train them accordingly. Frankly, permitting discipline investigations outside of IIS is asking for problems.

F. Results of Lawsuits Should Be Part of Discipline Files

Occasionally officers are sued for false arrest and/or excessive force. The outcome of this litigation should be part of the officer's disciplinary file. If exonerated, i.e. the case is dismissed or the jury finds for the officer, what better indication of the invalidity of the complaint? Conversely, an adverse finding by a neutral fact finder clearly should be a matter for possible discipline.

Right now the relationship between civil claims and discipline is murky. However, there is an obvious connection. Guidelines should be established to ensure a free flow of information between IIS and civil litigation against police officers.

G. Resisting Arrest/Obstructing Charges Should Be Compared to Complaints of Excessive Force

Many persons (including myself) believe an important clue to officers having trouble with the use of force may lie in the number of charges officers file against defendants for resisting arrest and/or obstructing. As IIS improves its computer programming, linkage could be established with the Seattle Municipal Court to compare complaints of excessive force and an officer's tendency to file resisting or obstructing charges against citizens.

The purpose is preventive. I am not suggesting such comparisons in themselves should give rise to discipline proceedings. However, an awareness of the incidence of such matters may enable supervisors to consider remedial action - outside of the discipline system.

H. Administrative Reviews Should Be Encouraged

Administrative reviews can be initiated by IIS where an officer has accumulated a certain number of complaints during a given period of time. I believe this procedure is crucial to identifying officers who may be developing escalating patterns of misconduct especially involving the use of force.

IIS is limited in their ability to initiate such reviews absent better computerization of records. Yet it should remain a priority and diligently pursued once IIS is capable of doing so. Administrative reviews permit a review of an officer's conduct on more than a case-by-case basis and are essential to a discipline system that not only punishes but also tries to help.

I. <u>IIS Brochure & Information About Complaint Process</u>

The disciplinary system within the Seattle Police Department needs to be understood and respected by the broad spectrum of our public. An important part of gaining public acceptance is a readable brochure. The current brochure is too complicated and cumbersome. A serious effort should be made to simplify and shorten the brochure which describes the complaint procedure along with appropriate translations from English. Also, the more publicity about the complaint process, the more effective will be the discipline system.

J. <u>Name Tags or Other ID Should Be Mandatory</u>

I was surprised by the number of complainants who could not identify the officer against whom they wish to make a complaint. Every officer should be required to have name and badge number visible to the public unless excused in writing from doing so by a supervisor. Rightly so, the inability of a citizen to readily identify an officer raises suspicions. Such a requirement should apply to off-duty, uniform employment as well. Failure to follow identification requirements should be strictly dealt with in the discipline system.

I recognize that plastic name tags are frequently broken or lost. I would suggest the department attempt other methods of permitting officer identification.

IV. SPECIFIC AUDITOR ORDINANCE REPORTING REQUIREMENTS

A. Number of Cases Reviewed

All completed IIS files (80), all contact logs (210), and all line referrals (65).

B. Number of Follow-up Investigations

Only a handful of follow-ups were suggested by me of completed IIS investigations. I would usually make a request for an additional interview or suggest another possible act of misconduct. None of my follow-up requests were denied.

C. Number of Full Investigations of Contact Logs Requested and Denied

There were perhaps 15 requests by me for further investigation of contact logs. IIS always looked into the matter further at my request. Whether a full investigation was done depended on what IIS reported back to me. Only on two or three occasions did a contact log go to a more thorough investigation. Usually IIS would supply additional information that persuaded me a complete investigation was not warranted. However, I would refer to III.C. for my concern with the system of contact logs.

D. Recommendations for Change

See discussion II, III, Supra.

V. CONCLUSION

"We know who the bad guys are. Reputations become well known, especially to the sergeants. ... We know the officers who are getting into trouble more than anyone else." (LAPD Assistant Chief, Jesse Brewer, retired, Christopher Report, 1991) This statement sharply focuses a principal challenge for any police discipline system. The ideal system will make reasonable efforts to ferret out the 'bad guys' and take appropriate steps.

However, perhaps an equally important challenge is to deal with problems early and promptly. Officers who wind up with serious complaints frequently showed signs that went unheeded. Remedial action such as training, counseling, or reassignment must be given serious attention.

The philosophy behind the details of this report is to: (1) remove many of the minor complaints from the disciplinary system and require supervisors to deal with the issues raised; and (2) permit a strengthened IIS to focus more on serious complaints and to expedite the process.

Finally, I believe civilian oversight is essential to assisting a police department in reaching the twin goals of prevention and fair discipline and to maintaining public confidence in the department. In my next report I plan to address issues involving the need for any changes in the auditor ordinance, the confidentiality of IIS records and the percentage of sustained complaints. We have a good police department. The recommendations in this report are submitted for the purpose of making it better.

Respectfully submitted this ___ day of November, 1992.

Terrence A. Carroll
Internal Investigations Auditor

Document No. 30

St. Petersburg, Fla.

STANDARD OPERATING PROCEDURES MANUAL

Citizen Review Committee

St. Petersburg, Florida

This manual is the property of the City of St. Petersburg.

Manual Number ____
May 1994

The committee member to whom this manual is issued is responsible for its maintenance and ensuring that directives issued subsequent to this date are properly inserted.

This manual is official committee property. It must be returned in good condition to the Citizen Review Committee Staff Coordinator upon expiration of your term.

This manual is issued to: ____
on (Date): ________________.

If found, please return to the Office of the Mayor, City of St. Petersburg, City Hall, 175 Fifth Street North, St. Petersburg, Florida 33701.

Approved:

____
David J. Fischer
Mayor

INTRODUCTION

External review of police practices has been spreading rapidly throughout the United States, as well as in England, Canada, Ireland, and Australia. The idea is not a new one and has been the topic of debate for over the last three decades.

In some municipalities around the country, the impetus behind external review has been public displays of police brutality and insensitivity towards the very citizens they are duly authorized to protect. As complaints are made against officers, a mechanism within the police department called Internal Affairs, is responsible for investigating the alleged acts and also serves as the internal system of checks and balances. Although this process is expedient, other serious questions have been posed as to its effectiveness and integrity.

In St. Petersburg, the impetus behind external review stemmed from the public's perception that some brutality existed and the police department's complaint process was a closed system. In a closed system in which those who are complained against investigate whether there exists legitimate grounds for a complaint, simply opposes the rules of natural justice and are therefore imperfect. Even if there does not exist an inherent bias in the internal system, distrust of it could persist, and could erode citizen confidence in the police in general. Citizen involvement can ensure the development of systems which are not merely structured around internal departmental policies, but which are reflective of community needs.

In mid-1990 in the City of St. Petersburg, research began on external review mechanisms of law enforcement agencies. By late 1991, members of the City Council concluded that there was a need to create a review process wherein citizens were given an opportunity to review internal police investigations. Thus, on November 21, 1991, City Council appropriated funds and directed the creation of the City of St. Petersburg Citizen Review Committee.

The purpose of the Citizen Review Committee is to review citizen complaint cases and cases which have received a high level of community interest, which have been investigated and adjudicated by the Police Department. Through its review, the Committee determines through consensus, the adequacy and appropriateness of the investigations and findings.

In its final form, the Citizen Review Committee is a three subcommittee panel group consisting of twenty-three members which reports directly to the Mayor. Committee member selection is made by the Mayor. Committee members are required to meet the following qualifiers and disqualifiers:

QUALIFIERS

- Must be a resident of St. Petersburg
- Willingness to make a commitment of up to three (3) years
- Willingness to attend a minimum of twenty (20) hours of training
- Willingness to spend the necessary time required to review cases and attend meetings

DISQUALIFIERS

- Have any prior felony convictions or any violation of a City ordinance involving moral turpitude
- Hold any political office
- Be a City of St. Petersburg employee
- Work for any law enforcement agency
- Be related to members of St. Petersburg Police Department

I-1 MISSION, DISTRIBUTION AND REVIEW, INDEXING

ISSUE DATE: May 1994 EFF. DATE: Immediately

I. MISSION

A. The mission of the Citizen Review Committee is to provide a forum for discussing issues that are important to the community and Police Department and to serve as a means of informing the Mayor, City Council, Chief of Police, and the citizens of St. Petersburg with its views as to the quality of the police service delivery system.

The Mayor is committed to ensure that all persons are treated with dignity and respect. All complaints against the Police Department will be fairly and impartially investigated. All police officer's rights shall be protected during the investigation of complaints.

The Citizen Review Committee shall review cases that have been internally investigated by the Police Department as a result of a citizen complaint or otherwise has received a high level of community interest.

B. All committee members should become familiar with all the procedures described herein; all members will be held responsible for strict compliance with these procedures.

C. These rules provide for the impartial, independent, prompt review and evaluation of complaints in a manner which protects both the public and the City. All members of the public are encouraged to bring forward legitimate complaints of alleged abuses or improper conduct to either the Internal Affairs Section of the police department or the Staff Coordinator for the Committee located in the Mayor's Office.

II. DISTRIBUTION AND REVIEW

A. Copies of this manual will be distributed to the Mayor, City Council, the Chief of Police, the Internal Affairs Section Commander, and all members of the Citizen Review Committee.

B. This manual will be reviewed yearly or as indicated by committee members. Any changes to this manual:

1. Shall be presented by committee forum to the Staff Coordinator.

2. The Staff Coordinator shall, in conjunction with other appropriate staff, determine the reasonableness based upon policy inherent in the City Charter, City of St. Petersburg Rules and Regulations of the Personnel Management System, Florida State Statutes, Police Officer's Bill of Rights; and, the Police Benevolent Association (PBA) contract.

III. INDEXING

The key processes shall be numbered consecutively with the prefix of a Roman Numeral for the chapters as follows:

I. Mission, Distribution and Review, Indexing, Organization and Meetings

II. Case Management

III. Complaint Review Procedures

IV. Reporting Requirements

V. Public Information

VI. Preservation of Rights

IV. DEFINITIONS

As used in these Standard Operating Procedures and Council Resolution No. 91-961:

A. **Alternate Member** is an appointed member of the Committee who shall review cases in the event a quorum is not present in any one of the subcommittees. Alternate member status does not, however, preclude that member from any voting rights afforded primary members.

B. **Chief of Police** is the top administrator of the St. Petersburg Police Department.

C. **Chief of Staff** is the administrative official who is responsible for the Citizen Review Committee, as well as several other departments.

D. **City** means City of St. Petersburg.

E. **Co-chair** is one of two individuals elected to chair the Citizen Review Committee.

F. **Committee** refers to the City of St. Petersburg Citizen Review Committee.

G. **Complainant** refers to the individual making a complaint/allegation against a sworn police officer.

H. **Complaint** is an allegation made by a citizen regarding the conduct of a sworn police officer.

I. **Exonerated** means the act or acts which provided the basis for the complaint or allegation occurred; however, investigation revealed that they were justified, lawful, and proper.

J. **Finding(s)** refers to the outcome of an investigation and specifically is concerned with whether or not a complaint is sustained.

K. **Formal Case** is an allegation of misconduct on the part of an employee (sworn officer), where the misconduct is of a serious nature and does require a detailed investigation, e.g., unnecessary force, conduct unbecoming an employee (sworn officer). (Ref: General Order II-10, II. B.)

L. **Internal Affairs** is a police department unit which is an extension of the Chief of Police, whose function is to vigorously investigate all complaints in order to bring to light any employee (sworn officer) misconduct or inappropriate activity while protecting the employee (sworn officer) from unfounded and unwarranted accusations.

M. **Mayor** means the Chief Administrative Official who is the head of government in the City.

N. **Not Sustained** means the investigation failed to disclose sufficient evidence to prove the allegations made in the complaint.

O. **Primary Member** is an appointed member of the committee who shall review cases in a subcommittee forum.

P. **SPPD** shall refer to the St. Petersburg Police Department.

Q. **Staff Coordinator** is the individual appointed by the Mayor to provide staff support to the Committee.

R. **Subcommittee Chairperson** is the head of a review subcommittee.

S. **Subcommittee Co-chair** is a subcommittee member selected by his/her subcommittee to preside in the subcommittee chairperson's absence, as well as assist the chair when requested.

T. **Sustained** means the investigation disclosed sufficient evidence to prove clearly the allegation made in the complaint.

U. **Unfounded** means the investigation conclusively proved that the act or acts complained of did not occur.

I-2 ORGANIZATION AND MEETINGS

ISSUE DATE: May 1994 EFF. DATE: Immediately

I. COMPOSITION OF COMMITTEE

A. The committee shall consist of twenty-three (23) members appointed by the Mayor. It shall be racially diverse in nature in order to reflect the representative composition of the City of St. Petersburg's population.

B. The twenty-three members shall include two (2) co-chairs, three (3) subcommittees comprised of six (6) members each, and three (3) alternate members. Each subcommittee shall have a chairperson elected from among its six members. The chairperson shall designate a subcommittee member as a subcommittee co-chair to act as chairperson in his absence.

C. Each subcommittee shall be racially diverse and composed of one 1-year member, three 2-year members, and two 3-year members.

D. Members of the subcommittees shall be rotated annually in order to ensure that all members are given the opportunity to interact with each other on cases.

II. RECRUITMENT, SELECTION AND APPOINTMENT

A. The recruitment process shall be open and appropriate efforts shall be made to achieve the highest level of representative participation.

B. Initially, committee composition shall include concerned citizens and individuals from the following organizations:

- Ambassador Club
- Chamber of Commerce
- Clergy
- Community Alliance
- Council of Neighborhood Associations (CONA)
- Federation of Inner City Organizations (FICO)
- NAACP
- School Administration
- Southern Christian Leadership Conference (SCLC)
- Urban League

C. For subsequent years of committee membership, the composition shall include individuals from other organizations and interested citizens from the community. The vehicle for acquiring nominations shall be a public notice of vacancy. Those interested citizens will be directed to submit a letter outlining reasons why they seek membership along with a resume addressed to the Mayor at the committee's official address. The initial screening of letters and resumes will be performed by the Mayor's Office.

D. The official (physical) address of the committee is:

Citizen Review Committee
Office of the Mayor
175 Fifth Street North
St. Petersburg, FL 33701

The mailing address of the committee is:

Citizen Review Committee
Office of the Mayor
Post Office Box 2842
St. Petersburg, FL 33731

E. During the interview process, the following shall be stressed to each candidate:

1. The mission of the committee,

2. The experience and impartiality of the applicant,

3. The approximate time and personal commitment expected of the members,

4. The extensive training program necessary for accomplishment of the committee's mission, and

5. The necessity of at least a minimum of twenty-four (24) hours (one shift per district) of ride-along experience with an officer.

F. A personal interview shall be conducted with committee candidates by the Mayor or his designate and the Staff Coordinator of the committee after which a complete background screening will be conducted.

G. Appointment

1. Appointments to the City of St. Petersburg Citizen Review Committee shall be made by the Mayor annually or as needed.

2. Each appointee shall be notified by letter of his appointment.

3. All unsuccessful candidates shall be notified by letter of their status.

4. The final list of appointees shall be made public as soon as the interview and screening processes are completed.

III. TRAINING

A. Training is a mandatory requirement for membership on the committee.

B. A comprehensive training course will be provided to each committee member prior to reviewing any cases. Such training shall include, but not be limited to familiarization with:

1. Police Department General Orders, Instructional Orders, Special Orders and Legal Notices;

2. The Standard Operating Procedures for the Uniform Services Bureau, Investigative Services Bureau, Community Policing Division and the Internal Affairs Section;

3. Investigative techniques utilized by Internal Affairs;

4. City Rules and Regulations;

5. City Charter, State Statutes, and the Police Officer's Bill of Rights;

6. Police Recruitment and Selections Standards and Police Training programs;

7. Policy on Use of Force;

8. Policy on Discipline;

9. Appeal and Grievance Procedures for police;

10. Complaint Processing;

11. Confidentiality;

12. History of police review in the United States and St. Petersburg,

13. Exposure to other cities' experience with external review mechanisms; and,

14. Mandatory review of hypothetical complaint cases.

C. After the initial training period, additional training sessions for update on policies, etc. shall be conducted on an as needed basis.

IV. ELECTION OF OFFICERS AND THEIR RESPONSIBILITIES

A. Co-chairs

1. The two co-chairs, each from a different race, shall be elected from within the membership yearly.

2. The co-chairs are responsible for presiding over full committee meetings and the quarterly community meetings on an alternate basis.

B. Subcommittee Chairpersons

1. A subcommittee chairperson shall be elected by each of the three individual subcommittee memberships.

2. The subcommittee chairperson shall be responsible for presiding over Internal Affairs case reviews, reporting the results of those reviews with comments to the full committee; and maintaining attendance records during the case reviews.

C. Subcommittee Co-chair

Each subcommittee shall select a co-chair/designee from the remaining members of the subcommittee to preside in the chairperson's absence and assist the chairperson, whenever needed.

V. SELECTION OF PRIMARY AND ALTERNATE MEMBERS AND THEIR RESPONSIBILITIES

A. **Initially**, primary and alternate assignments are determined through drawing of lots. All members of the committee draw for primary or alternate positions.

B. Members who have chosen primary assignments shall be assigned to one of the three subcommittees. No more than six primary members shall serve on any one subcommittee.

C. If a member initially draws a primary slot and subsequently learns that such a choice presents a problem, it should be brought to the immediate attention of the Staff Coordinator for alternative resolution. The determination of alternative measures rests solely with the Staff Coordinator and is binding upon the member.

D. Primary members are responsible for the diligent review of completed Internal Affairs cases and are required to attend all scheduled meetings.

E. Alternate members may be utilized when a quorum is not available for case reviews. The Staff Coordinator shall request an alternate's participation in the review process at this time and insure that the member has adequate time to review case files prior to their scheduled review date. They are also responsible for the diligent review of assigned case files and are required to attend all other scheduled meetings.

F. Alternate members may also be utilized to fill an uncompleted term vacated by primary committee members.

G. For **subsequent years**, appointed members shall serve in the same term capacity vacated by both expiring primary and alternate members.

VI. TERMS

A. Committee co-chairs shall serve for a period of one year. A co-chair may decide to submit his/her name to serve a second one-year term. A majority vote decides if he/she will be retained.

B. All subcommittee primary members shall serve on a staggered term basis of one to three years.

C. Subcommittee chairs and co-chairs shall serve for six months irrespective of the staggered term chosen or assumed.

D. Alternate members shall serve for a period of one year. At the end of the one-year term, they may assume expired one-year member vacancies.

E. As terms expire, the Mayor shall appoint new members utilizing those procedures discussed at Operating Procedures I-2, Section II.

VII. COMPENSATION

Members of the Committee shall serve without compensation.

VIII. COMMITTEES

The Committee shall, as a whole, determine the need for creation of committees to staff special projects and review and develop internal procedures for the Committee.

Any committee so selected shall report its findings and recommendations to the Committee as a whole, in writing, within the established timelines.

IX. ATTENDANCE AND REMOVAL

A. All members are required to attend their appropriate subcommittee case reviews, all full committee and quarterly community meetings, unless **excused**. Satisfactory excuses must be provided to the Mayor's Office.

Notification of non-attendance at any meeting should be made 3 days in advance of the scheduled meeting with the Staff Coordinator.

B. Each member shall be advised of the number of his/her **unexcused** absences on a quarterly basis. As members approach the limits for unexcused absences, they will be notified by mail, telephone contact, or both of an impending violation. Absent such notices, the members shall be considered **Members in Good Standing**.

C. Guidelines for unexcused absences are as follows:

1. Case Reviews - only **3 unexcused absences** will be allowed during any quarter.

2. Full Committee Meetings - only **1 unexcused absence** will be allowed during any quarter.

3. Quarterly Community Meetings - only **1 unexcused absence** will be allowed during any quarter.

D. Surpassing the limit in either meeting category alone, will necessitate removal from the Citizen Review Committee.

E. Removal Process

1. The member's record of attendance shall be forwarded to the co-chairs as a **Notice of Removal** for their review. The violating member shall be notified concurrently.

2. A meeting of the full committee shall be called to officially remove the member through a majority vote. The member shall be notified of this meeting date.

3. If the member represents an organization, that group shall be notified at the time the Notice of Removal is forwarded to the co-chairs and be requested to provide a successor for the unexpired balance of the predecessor's term.

X. STAFF SUPPORT

A. Staff Coordinator

1. The Mayor's Office shall appoint this position. The staff coordinator shall report directly to the Mayor's Office.

2. The Staff Coordinator, with the approval of the Mayor, shall supervise personnel necessary to discharge the functions of the Citizen Review Committee.

3. It shall be the coordinator's responsibility to serve as liaison between the Mayor's Office and the St. Petersburg Police Department.

B. Administrative Secretary

1. The Staff Coordinator shall select for this position through a job vacancy announcement coordinated through the Employee Relations Department.

2. The secretary shall carry out all the duties and responsibilities ascribed to that position in the Citizen Review Committee's office.

XI. TRANSACTION OF BUSINESS

A. Subcommittee Meetings

1. Subcommittee meetings are held when a case review has been scheduled. Case reviews meetings shall be conducted on an as needed basis.

2. All case reviews shall occur at 5 p.m., in Room 101 in City Hall, located at 175 Fifth Street North and are open to the public. Reasonable notice shall be given to the members, the complainant(s) and the public prior to convening a subcommittee meeting.

3. The dates of case review meetings shall be aired over the Government Access Channel (cable channel 15) and shall be listed

in the Weekly Meeting Schedule. This schedule is available at the Mayor's Action Center in City Hall; at City Hall in the Mall (Tyrone Square Mall); the public library (3745 Ninth Avenue North) and at the Enoch Davis Center (1111 18th Avenue South).

4. A quorum (4) must be present for the transaction of business.

5. A quorum being present, the order of business at the meeting of the subcommittee shall follow the prescribed review agenda (CRC Form 001.A and B):

   a. Call to Order

   b. Attendance

   c. Introduction/Old Business

   d. Conflict of Interest

   e. Investigation and Materials Review

      1. Comments on investigation and materials

      2. Recommendation(s) to the mayor

   f. Findings of Chain of Command Review Board

      1. Comments on findings

      2. Vote

         (a) Agree, no comment

         (b) Agree with comment

         (c) Disagree, no comment

         (d) Disagree with comment

         (e) Request additional/clarifying information

(f) Refer to the full committee

3. Recommendation(s) to the Mayor

g. Discipline Review

1. Comments of Discipline

2. Vote

(a) Agree, no comment

(b) Agree with comment

(c) Disagree, no comment

(d) Disagree with comment

(e) Request additional/clarifying information

(f) Refer to the full committee

3. Recommendation(s) to the Mayor

h. Additional Comments

i. Adjournment

6. Minutes of each meeting shall be prepared by the support staff.

B. Full Committee Meetings

1. Full committee meetings shall be held to address the following:

a. Affirmation of subcommittee case review results

b. Committee business

c. Training issues

d. Presentations by guest speakers

e. Community outreach

2. All full committee meetings shall be held at City Hall located at 175 Fifth Street North unless otherwise indicated. These meetings are open to the public. Reasonable notice shall be given to the members and the public prior to convening a full committee meeting.

3. The dates of full committee meetings shall be aired over the Government Access Channel (cable channel 15) and shall be listed in the Weekly Meeting Schedule available at those sites indicated in A.3. above in this section.

4. A majority of all the members of the committee shall constitute a quorum (12) for the transaction of business.

5. A quorum being present, the order of business at the meeting of the full committee shall be as follows:

   a. Call to Order

   b. Attendance

   c. Approval of Minutes

   d. Staff Coordinator's Report

   e. Communications

   f. Old Business

   g. New Business

   h. Public Comment

   i. Committee Reports

   j. Adjourn

6. Minutes of each meeting shall be prepared by the support staff.

7. Prospective committee members shall attend at least one meeting where time permits. They have no vote and cannot be counted towards making a quorum.

C. Quarterly Community Meetings

1. The full committee shall conduct quarterly meetings. These meetings allow for presentation to the public the results of case reviews that have been completed by the committee. These meetings also provide a forum for extensive public participation.

2. Quarterly community meetings shall be held in various community locations. Notice of these meetings shall be made utilizing various public announcement vehicles (e.g., newspapers, radio, television).

3. Dates of quarterly community meetings shall be aired over the Government Access Channel (cable channel 15) and shall be listed in the Weekly Meeting Schedule at those sites indicated in A.3 above in this section.

4. Agendas for the community meetings shall be made available within a reasonable timeframe at the sites mentioned at A.3. and at the specific meeting location.

5. The order of business at the community meetings shall be as follows:

   a. Call to Order

   b. Introduction of Panelists and Opening Remarks

   c. Staff Coordinator's Report

   d. Report on Case Review Results

   e. New Business

   f. Public Comment

   g. Adjournment

6. Minutes shall be prepared by the support staff.

II-1 CASE MANAGEMENT

ISSUE DATE: May 1994 EFF. DATE: Immediately

I. CASE RELEASE

No case shall be released for review by the Committee until such time that it has been completely investigated by the Police Department and, is a public record.

II. PUBLIC RECORDS POLICY

A. For the purpose of public record, completed Internal Affairs cases must be absent of <u>all</u> the following conditions **before** it can be reviewed by the Committee:

1. The subject matter of the complaint is under investigation by the State Attorney's Office or is the subject of criminal judicial proceedings.

2. The accused officer in a sustained case is in the grievance and appeal process.

3. If the accused officer is terminated as a result of the Internal Affairs investigation, and invokes the appeal process.

B. All the above conditions serve to defer action on complaint cases. The review of these cases shall remain pending until such conditions have reached a final disposition.

III. PUBLIC INTEREST CASES

Cases which have received a high level of community interest shall be reviewed by the Committee. Cases which obtain this status are those that appear in local area newspapers (i.e., St. Petersburg Times, Tampa Tribune, The Weekly Challenger).

IV. PROCESSING COMPLAINTS

A. The Staff Coordinator shall request notification from the Internal Affairs

Section commander when an investigation or proceedings regarding a citizen-initiated complaint has reached a final disposition.

B. In addition, the Staff Coordinator shall periodically peruse the Internal Affairs' intake log for complaints filed by citizens and maintain a record as a source of future case reviews. Each month the staff coordinator shall contact the Internal Affairs commander and ascertain final disposition in these cases.

C. All cases received shall be entered into a Master Control File in numerical order preceded by the year. This file shall be maintained by the staff coordinator and contain the following information:

1. Control number (includes I.A.'s # as a cross-reference)
2. Date and time of the incident
3. Date of complaint taken
4. Allegation(s)
5. Internal Affairs investigator's name
6. Date investigation initiated
7. Complainant's name
8. Complainant's race/sex/age
9. Complainant's address (if listed)
10. Complainant's phone number (if available)
11. Accused's name
12. Accused's race/sex/age
13. Accused's payroll number
14. Accused's assignment

15. Accused's duty status at time of incident (on/off duty)

16. Length of service at time of incident

17. SPPD's disposition of the case

18. Disciplinary action taken

19. Date CRC received the case

20. Subcommittee assigned the case for review

21. Scheduled date for review by CRC

22. Results of CRC review

23. Date of notice of review to complainant

24. Complainant's comments

25. Staff coordinator's comments

D. The Staff Coordinator shall also maintain the following on a monthly basis:

1. Total number of cases reviewed

2. Total number of cases pending

III-1 COMPLAINT REVIEW PROCEDURES

ISSUE DATE: May 1994 EFF. DATE: Immediately

I. POLICY

A. It is the policy of the Committee to encourage citizens who have complaints concerning the conduct of sworn police officers of the St. Petersburg Police Department to file the complaint with the Police Department. If citizens do not wish file the complaint with the Police Department, they have the option of registering their complaints with the Office of the Staff Coordinator at City Hall. The Staff Coordinator would then coordinate with Internal Affairs for the citizens to file their complaints.

B. The Committee shall make every effort to ensure that complaints against any sworn police officer of the City are evaluated and reviewed in an impartial manner.

C. Priority shall be given, when appropriate, within the Internal Affairs Section to those cases that are to be reviewed by the Committee.

II. PROCEDURES

A. Administrative Guidelines

1. The staff coordinator shall review all case files received from Internal Affairs to insure that a complete file has been received (i.e., no missing pages, all investigative forms have been signed by the appropriate individuals, accused officer(s) 18-month Internal Affairs history is included, etc.).

2. The complaint cases shall be assigned in a timely manner to the appropriate subcommittee. A notice of the review date, time and place shall accompany the case file. The complainant(s) in the case shall be notified via letter that the complaint has been submitted to the Committee for review. A copy of the complainant's notification letter can be found at Exhibit A, following this section.

3. The Internal Affairs commander shall be requested to attend all case reviews. The purpose of the commander's presence shall be

to answer questions from the subcommittee and clarify details. At the discretion of the commander, the specific Internal Affairs investigator may be present.

3. In order to allow a reasonable turnaround period, all cases shall be reviewed within ten days of receipt.

4. After receipt of the file, each subcommittee member has three days to declare a substantial conflict of interest and excuse himself/herself from the review. The case shall be returned immediately to the staff coordinator for reassignment to an alternate member, should a quorum not exist. Substantial conflict shall mean such a conflict of interest where there is reasonable probability that it might tend to affect the judgment or actions of the subcommittee member. (See Conflict of Interest Statements at Exhibit B.) Conflict of interest statements shall become part of the case file.

5. In accordance with "Government in the Sunshine", case review meetings shall occur in a public place, usually City Hall.

6. The staff coordinator shall attend all subcommittee case reviews.

B. Procedural Guidelines - Content of Allegation

1. The case review shall be conducted in accordance with procedures outlined in Operating Procedures I-2, Section XI. A. Transaction of Business: Subcommittee Meetings.

2. The subcommittee shall conduct its review by comparing standards of investigation as set forth in the Internal Affairs Section Standard Operating Procedures manual and the policies set forth in the Police department's General Orders, Instructional Orders, Special Orders and Legal Notices with the case contents, noting any discrepancies.

3. At the end of the review, the subcommittee shall consider the findings of the department's investigation and determine whether the investigation was adequate and appropriately conducted. The Police department findings are classified as:

a. Sustained,

b. Not sustained,

c. Exonerated, and

d. Unfounded.

(NOTE: See definitions at Operating Procedures I-1, Section IV.)

6. The subcommittee shall make its decision and complete the appropriate form indicating whether its members:

   a. Agree with the findings, no comment,

   b. Agree with the findings with comment,

   c. Disagree with the findings, no comment,

   d. Disagree with the findings with comment,

   e. Request additional/clarifying information, or

   f. Refer case to the full committee.

   (See case review forms at the end of this section.)

7. At least four subcommittee members must agree on the same review conclusion. If not, the case will be placed on an agenda and considered by the full committee for vote.

8. If the subcommittee decides on options 6.a. through 6.d., the matter shall be reported at a full Committee during affirmation of case review results.

9. If the subcommittee decides on option 6.e., the staff coordinator shall return a completed Request for Additional/Clarifying Information form to the Chief of Police and the Internal Affairs Commander. A subsequent meeting shall be conducted to discuss the nature of the case and the content of the request. This meeting shall be attended by the originai subcommittee members, the Mayor or his designee, the Internal Affairs commander and the staff coordinator.

10. Option 6.f. is chosen only when the subcommittee completely disagrees with the findings in a case due to a perceived lack of adequate rationale. Cases decided in this manner shall be presented to the full committee for its determination on the case findings.

11. Any recommendations made by the subcommittee should be noted on the case review forms.

12. The minority/dissenting members shall be given the opportunity to document their position. This opinion shall become part of the permanent case file. (See Dissenting Opinion Form at end of this section.)

C. Procedural Guidelines - Content of Discipline

1. The Committee shall also review the discipline imposed on officers found guilty of misconduct in the cases received from Internal Affairs.

2. The review shall be conducted with respect to Police Department General Orders, City Rules and Regulations, and the appropriate policies found in the Police Benevolent Association's contract with the City. The review shall also take into consideration, the officer's 18-month Internal Affairs history. This history provides a listing of allegations made and their outcomes based on the date of the incident and then 18 months backwards in time.

3. When the review has been completed, the subcommittee shall consider the discipline imposed and determine whether it was adequate and appropriately determined.

4. Once a decision has been made, the subcommittee shall indicate its findings on the same form referred to at Section II. B. 6.a. through 6.d.

5. At least four subcommittee members must agree on the same review conclusion. If not, the case will be placed on an agenda and considered by the full committee for vote.

6. If the subcommittee decides on Section II. B., options 6.a. through

6.d., the matter shall be reported to the full Committee during affirmation of case review results.

7. The options described at Section II. B. 6.e. and 6.f. shall not be considered as choices since discipline is imposed on a progressive basis by the City as well as the Police department.

8. Any recommendations made by the subcommittee should be noted on the case review forms.

9. The minority/dissenting members shall be given the opportunity to document their positions. This opinion document shall become part of the permanent case file. (See Dissenting Opinion Form at end of this section.)

D. Completed Reviews

1. All case reviews completed by subcommittees each month shall be summarized and distributed to all committee members, the Internal Affairs commander, the Chief of Police, the Chief of Staff, and the Mayor.

2. A full committee meeting shall be scheduled to affirm the findings in all the cases. Enough notice shall be given so as to allow the Chief of Police and his staff time to respond to unresolved questions and intended actions on recommendations made by the Committee. Those responses shall be presented at the meeting.

3. A **summary** of the cases, including questions, answers and intended actions on recommendations shall be forwarded to City Council, the Mayor, and Chief of Staff.

EXHIBIT A

April , 1994

(Complainant's name)
(Complainant's address)

Dear :

The Internal Affairs Section of the St. Petersburg Police Department has forwarded your complaint case # , against Patrol Officer , to our committee for review.

The Citizen Review Committee was established in November 1991 by City Council. The purpose of the Committee is to formally review cases that have been internally investigated by the Police Department as a result of citizen complaint or have otherwise attained a high level of community interest. Through its review, the Committee determines through consensus, the adequacy and appropriateness of the investigations and findings. As a result of these findings, the Committee provides recommendations for policies within the department which conveys a sense of fairness, competency of investigations and concerns for the interests of both the civilian complainants and the officers.

The Committee will review your case on **(day, date), at 5 p.m., in Room 101 of City Hall**. City Hall is located at 175 Fifth Street North, St. Petersburg.

You are invited to attend the case review. Subcommittee # will conduct the review. Any comments or questions you may have for the subcommittee members should be withheld until the case review has been completed. You may not introduce any new evidence.

Enclosed is a brochure which outlines what the Committee is about. If you have any questions, please contact me 893-7229 between the hours of 8 a.m. and 5 p.m.

Sincerely,

Debra Bynum, Staff Coordinator
Citizen Review Committee

/db
Enc.

EXHIBIT B

CONFLICT OF INTEREST STATEMENT

I, ______________________________ (print name), am personally associated with/a relative of the complainant(s) or personally associated with/a relative of the accused officer(s) in Internal Affairs # ______, being reviewed today.

I, therefore, excuse myself from this review.

____________________________ Signature of Subcommittee Chairperson	____________________________ Signature of Subcommittee Member
	____________________________ Date

CRC FORM 002

CITIZEN REVIEW COMMITTEE
Case Review Form

Master Control No. ___ ___ X-Ref. I.A. No. ______

Employee(s) Name(s)/Number(s): ____

____

____

Allegation(s): ____

____

Complainant: ____

Subcommittee No. __

Recommendations: ____

____

____

____

____

____

____

____

____

____

Chairperson: ________________ Date: ________________

Members: ________________

________________ ________________

________________ ________________

CRC FORM 003.A Page __ of __

CITIZEN REVIEW COMMITTEE
Case Review Form Supplement

Master Control No. ______ X-Ref. I.A. No. ______

Recommendations continued: ____

Chairperson: ______________ Date: ______________

Members: ______________

______________ ______________

______________ ______________

CRC FORM 003.B Page __ of __

CITIZEN REVIEW COMMITTEE
Dissenting Opinion Form

Master Control No. ______ X-Ref. I.A. No. ______

Employee(s) Name(s)/Number(s): ____

____

____

Allegation(s): ____

____

Complainant: ____

Subcommittee No. __

Dissenting Opinion: ____

____

____

____

____

____

____

____

____

____

____

____

____

____

Chairperson/Member Date

CRC FORM 004.A Page __ of __

CITIZEN REVIEW COMMITTEE
Dissenting Opinion Form Supplement

Master Control No. ______ X-Ref. I.A. No. ______

Dissenting Opinion continued: ____________________

____

____

____

____

____

____

____

____

____

____

____

____

____

____

____

____

____

____

____

____

Chairperson/Member Date

CRC FORM 004.B Page __ of __

CITIZEN REVIEW COMMITTEE
Request for Additional/Clarifying Information

Master Control No. ______ X-Ref. I.A. No. ______

Employee(s) Name(s)/Number(s): ______________________________

____

Allegation(s): ______________________________

____

Complainant: ______________________________

Subcommittee No. ___

Requested Information and Reason(s) for Request: ______________________________

____

____

____

____

____

____

____

____

____

____

Chairperson: ______________ Date: ______________

Members: ______________

______________ ______________

______________ ______________

CRC FORM 005.A Page __ of __

CITIZEN REVIEW COMMITTEE
Request for Additional/Clarifying Information Supplement

Master Control No. ______ X-Ref. I.A. No. __ __

Request and Reason(s) continued: ______________________________

Chairperson: ________________ Date: ________________

Members: ________________

________________ ________________

________________ ________________

CRC FORM 005.B Page __ of __

CITIZEN REVIEW COMMITTEE
SUBCOMMITTEE # __

CHAIRPERSON NOTES

Master Control No. ______ X-Ref. I.A. No. _____

Employee(s) Name(s)/Number(s): ______________________________

____

____

____

____

Allegation(s): ______________________________

____

Complainant: ______________________________

____

____

____

____

____

____

____

____

____

____

____

____

____

____

____

CRC FORM 006.A Page __ of __

CITIZEN REVIEW COMMITTEE
SUBCOMMITTEE # __

CHAIRPERSON NOTES SUPPLEMENT

Master Control No. ______ X-Ref. I.A. No. _____

CRC FORM 006.B Page __ of __

III-2 COMMUNITY OUTREACH

ISSUE DATE: MAY 1994 EFF. DATE: Immediately

I. INITIATING OUTREACH

A. During the course of its reviews, the subcommittees may identify trends and patterns in citizen complaints. If it is determined that the source of these trends and patterns appears to be attributable to a lack of or misunderstanding on the citizen's part, then the issue(s) may be presented to the full Committee for action. A meeting shall be scheduled in which the full Committee shall:

1. Hear presentation from the proposing subcommittee,

2. Determine its merit through a majority vote,

2. Address the issue(s),

3. Recommend a course of action, and

4. Present the action to the Mayor for approval.

B. The action presented to the Mayor shall contain the basis for the proposal and how it shall be presented to the public.

C. A speakers bureau shall be established within the Citizen Review Committee. Members of the bureau shall make every effort to speak to citizens groups, by invitation, to describe the operations of the Committee and to seek input on improving community relations between the Police and the citizenry.

D. Community outreach shall be consistent with Operating Procedures XI. B. 2. and 3. Transaction of Business: Full Committee Meetings as to notification of meeting.

II. SCOPE OF OUTREACH

The Citizen Review Committee shall make every effort to reach as much of St. Petersburg as is possible in order to educate the public about the complaint process and recommendations it makes regarding improving police services in St. Petersburg.

IV-1 REPORTING REQUIREMENTS

ISSUE DATE: May 1994 EFF. DATE: Immediately

I. COMMUNITY MEETINGS

A. The Citizen Review Committee shall conduct quarterly community meetings to report on the results of Internal Affairs cases to-date and receive public input related to community feelings regarding the delivery of police services and to make recommendations on improving police services in St. Petersburg.

B. Notice of the meeting time and place shall be consistent with Operating Procedures XI. C. 2. and 3. Transaction of Business: Quarterly Community Meetings.

C. The Chief of Police, Internal Affairs Commander, PBA president and the general police department populations shall be extended an invitation to attend the meetings.

II. BI-ANNUAL REPORTS

A. Bi-annual reports shall be made and distributed to the Chief of Police, Mayor, Council and the public.

B. These reports shall contain, at a minimum, the results of case reviews and information concerning the delivery of police services to the citizens of St. Petersburg.

III. REVIEWS AND EVALUATIONS

A. At the discretion of the Mayor's Office, general reviews shall be conducted to evaluate the effectiveness of the complaint and review process. This will include an analysis of trends and patterns in citizen complaints, investigations and discipline.

B. The scope of the review shall include:

1. Evaluation of the complaint procedures of the Police Department;

2. Interviews with personnel designated to process complaints;

3. Survey and interviews of the complainants previously involved in the complaint process;

4. Survey and interviews of the witnesses involved in the complaint process;

5. Review of statistical reports related to the complaint process; and,

6. Review of discipline imposed to identify trends.

V-1 PUBLIC INFORMATION

ISSUE DATE: May 1994 EFF. DATE: Immediately

I. PRINTED MATERIAL

A. A pamphlet describing the purposes and procedures of the Citizen Review Committee shall be prepared and distributed by the Mayor's Office.

B. For purposes of the Review Committee, all files are a matter of public record.

C. All files shall be retained by the Support Staff.

II. PRESS RELATIONS

A. The Committee Co-chairs shall be the spokespersons for the Committee. In the event both are absent or unavailable, another member shall be temporarily designated as such.

B. In all cases, public comment on matters relating to the Citizen Review Committee, shall be deferred to and given by the Committee Co-chair or designate only.

C. Citizen Review Committee members are prohibited from giving "personal opinions". Opinions shall only be given as a body by the Co-chairs.

D. Citizen Review Committee members and Co-chairs are permitted to report that a case is being reviewed or has been reviewed. For a report on the results, members shall defer to the Co-chairs.

E. When questioned about the results of a vote, the Co-chairs shall answer in the following manner:

"There was a split vote ..." OR "There was a unanimous vote ..."

F. In cases of a split vote, a unanimous disagreement, or dissenting opinions, the report given by the Co-chair should take the form of:

"The nature of the dissent centered around ..."

III. POLITICAL ACTIVITY OR RELATIONSHIPS

All Citizen Review Committee members are prohibited from discussing or speaking about case deliberations with members of Council.

When the review is completed, the Co-chairs may discuss the case with members of Council.

VI-1 PRESERVATION OF RIGHTS

ISSUE DATE: May 1994 EFF. DATE: Immediately

These procedures shal: be in addition to and not in derogation of:

A. The procedures existing for the preservation of rights of police officers pursuant to the Police Officer's Bill of Rights.

B. The contract between the City (Police Department) and the Police Benevolent Association.

C. The applicable laws, ordinances, statutes and Constitution of the State of Florida and the St. Petersburg City Charter.

Document No. 31

Tucson, Ariz.

ADOPTED BY THE
MAYOR AND COUNCIL

MAR 24 1980

ORDINANCE NO. 5123

RELATING TO COMMUNITY AFFAIRS; CREATING AND RESERVING NEW SECTIONS 10A-81 THROUGH 10A-85 OF THE TUCSON CODE; ADDING A NEW ARTICLE VIII TO CHAPTER 10A OF THE TUCSON CODE CONSISTING OF NEW SECTIONS 10A-86 THROUGH 10A-93, CREATING A CITIZENS-POLICE ADVISORY COMMITTEE.

BE IT ORDAINED BY THE MAYOR AND COUNCIL OF THE CITY OF TUCSON, ARIZONA, AS FOLLOWS:

SECTION 1. That Chapter 10A of the Tucson Code be amended by creating and reserving new Sections 10A-81 through 10A-85 to read as follows:

Secs. 10A-81 -- 10A-85. Reserved.

SECTION 2. That Chapter 10A of the Tucson Code be amended by adding a new Article VIII to Chapter 10A of the Tucson Code, consisting of new sections 10A-86 through 10A-93 to read as follows:

ARTICLE VIII. CITIZENS-POLICE ADVISORY COMMITTEE.

Sec. 10A-86. Declaration of policy.

It is the policy of the city to [foster and encourage a citizen-police partnership in the prevention of crime and the undertaking of constructive action to develop and improve positive communication and mutual understanding between the police and the community.]

Sec. 10A-87. Creation.

In order to promote the goals and objectives of the above-stated policy, there is hereby established an entity to be called the Citizens-Police Advisory Committee.

Sec. 10A-88. Functions, powers, duties, goals and purposes.

The committee shall:

CITY CLERK'S NOTE:
City Ordinance 5123, as adopted, will be included as Article VIII, Sections 10A-86 through 10A-93 with appropriate sections reserved. (Approved by F. S. Dean, DLM/mb/rwb)

(a) Consult with the governing body from time to time as may be required by the mayor and council.

(b) Assist the police in achieving a greater understanding of the nature and causes of complex community problems in the area of human relations, with special emphasis on the advancement and improvement of relations between police and community minority groups.

(c) Study, examine, and recommend methods, approaches and techniques to encourage and develop an active citizen-police partnership in the prevention of crime.

(d) Promote cooperative citizen-police programs and approaches to the solutions of community crime problems, emphasizing the principle that the administration of justice is a responsibility which requires total community involvement.

(e) Recommend procedures, programs and/or legislation to enhance cooperation among citizens of the community and police.

(f) Strive to strengthen and ensure throughout the community the application of the principle of equal protection under the law for all persons.

(g) Consult and cooperate with federal, state, city and other public agencies, commissions and committees on matters within the committee's charge.

(h) The Committee may ask for and shall receive from the Police Department, a review of action taken by the Department in incidents which create community concern or controversy.

(i) The Committee shall have the authority should it so desire to use a specific incident as a vehicle for the examination of police policies, procedures and priorities.

(j) At the discretion and express direction of the mayor and council, assume and undertake such other tasks or duties as will facilitate the accomplishment of these goals and objectives, except as hereinafter provided.

Sec. 10A-89. Composition, appointment and terms.

(a) Composition. The Tucson Citizens-Police Advisory Committee shall be composed of thirteen (13) members. All appointed members shall be residents of the City of Tucson and shall not have ever been convicted of a felony.

(b) Appointment. The mayor and each councilmember shall appoint one (1) member of the committee. The Fraternal Order of Police, Lodge No. 1, shall nominate, for appointment by the mayor and council, two (2) members from the Police Department who hold a rank no greater than sergeant. The Tucson Crime Commission shall nominate, for appointment by the mayor and council, one (1) member. The Tucson Human Relations Commission shall nominate, for appointment by the mayor and council, one (1) member. The city manager and the chief of police, or their designated representatives, shall be continuing ex-officio, non-voting members.

(c) All appointments shall be for two (2) year terms, except that members directly appointed by the mayor and each councilmember shall not serve beyond the term of the mayor or councilmember making such appointment.

Sec. 10A-90. Committee organization.

The committee chairperson and vice-chairperson shall be selected by a majority of the committee from those members directly appointed by the mayor and council. The committee shall adopt rules and regulations relating to its powers and duties; may appoint from its members such standing or special committees as determined necessary; and shall meet at such times and places throughout the city as determined by the committee.

Sec. 10A-91. Reports and Minutes.

The committee shall present to the mayor and council an annual report on or before March 1, and shall submit such additional reports as it deems necessary or as requested by the mayor and council. Minutes of the committee shall be filed with the city clerk.

Sec. 10A-92. Limitation of powers.

Neither the committee nor any member thereof, except as otherwise authorized by law, shall:

(a) Incur city expenses or obligate the City of Tucson in any way without prior authorization of the mayor and council.

(b) Make any written or oral report of any committee activity to any individual or body other than to the mayor and council without prior authorization by the governing body.

(c) Investigate or review the conduct of individual police officers or disciplinary decisions of the police department.

(d) Conduct any activity which might constitute or be construed as a quasi-judicial review of police actions.

(e) Conduct any activity which might constitute or be construed as establishment of city policy.

(f) Violate the confidentiality of any information related to matters involving pending or forthcoming civil or criminal litigation.

The activities of the committee at all times shall be conducted in accordance with all applicable federal, state, and local laws. Information available to the committee shall be governed by the provisions of A.R.S. §41-1750 and Subpart B of the Federal Regulations, 28 CFR 20, as amended. Action in excess of the authority of the committee, or in violation of the limitations set forth herein, shall result in automatic forfeiture of membership on the committee.

Sec. 10A-93. Cooperation.

The various city officers and employees are hereby authorized and directed to perform all acts necessary or desirable to give effect to this article. The city manager is hereby authorized and directed to provide or make provisions for such clerical services as are reasonably needed to support the committee's activities.

SECTION 5. WHEREAS, it is necessary for the preservation of the peace, health and safety of the City of Tucson that this Ordinance become immediately effective, an emergency is hereby declared to exist, and this Ordinance shall be effective immediately upon its passage and adoption.

PASSED, ADOPTED AND APPROVED by the Mayor and Council of the City of Tucson, Arizona, MAR 24 1980.

MAYOR

ATTEST:

CITY CLERK

APPROVED AS TO FORM:

CITY ATTORNEY

REVIEWED BY:

CITY MANAGER

Document No. 32

Winston-Salem, N.C.

O-Ch. 6
O. No. 4092

AN ORDINANCE AMENDING CHAPTER 2 OF THE CITY CODE ENTITLED "ADMINISTRATION"

BE IT ORDAINED, by the Board of Aldermen of the City of ~~Winston-Salem~~, as follows:

Section 1. A new Article XVII to be entitled "City of Winston-Salem Citizen Police Review Board" is hereby created as follows:

"ARTICLE XVII WINSTON-SALEM CITIZEN POLICE REVIEW BOARD

Section 2-242. Creation and duties.

There is hereby created a board to be known as the City of Winston-Salem Citizen Police Review Board. The board shall serve as an advisory board to the City Manager and the Public Safety Committee thereby removing the Public Safety Committee from the current citizen complaint hearing process involving police matters. The board shall review appeals of police complaints, conduct appeal hearings which includes receiving and evaluating testimony and issuing findings of fact to the City Manager and perform such other duties as may be assigned to it from time to time by the Public Safety Committee or the Board of Aldermen.

Section 2-243. Membership and appointment.

The board shall be composed of eleven (11) members who shall be appointed by the Board of Aldermen upon recommendation of the Mayor. Prior to the appointment by the Board of Aldermen, the Public Safety Committee and members of the Board of Aldermen shall be provided with the names and background information on all applicants and nominees. All members of the board shall be residents of the City of Winston-Salem.

Section 2-244. Term of office, vacancies and compensation.

Initially six (6) members shall be appointed for three (3) years and five (5) members for two (2) years. All subsequent appointments shall be for a three (3) year term. Members shall hold office until their successors are appointed. Any vacancy resulting from a cause other than expiration of term shall be filled only for the unexpired portion of the term. Vacancies shall be filled in accordance with the provisions of Section 2-243. Members shall serve no more than two (2) consecutive terms. Members shall serve without compensation.

Section 2-245. Officers.

The Board of Aldermen, upon recommendation of the Mayor, shall appoint the initial chairman who shall serve for the duration of his initial appointment to the board. Thereafter, the board shall elect its own chairman to serve for a three (3) year term. The board shall elect from its membership a vice-chairman to serve for the duration of the initial appointment to the board, and thereafter the vice-chairman shall serve for a three (3) year term.

Section 2-246. Removal.

Members of the board shall serve at the pleasure of the Board of Aldermen and may be removed by the Board of Aldermen.

Section 2-247. Meetings and quorum.

The Board shall hold regular meetings not less than once a quarter. Special meetings may be called by the chairman upon notification of an appeal of a complaint to the board or for any other reason by giving notice in writing and personally to each member or left at his residence not less than forty-eight (48) hours prior to the time fixed for the meeting. Six (6) members of the board shall be considered a quorum for conducting regular business, and the affirmative vote of a majority, a quorum being present, shall be required before any recommendation is made on any matter considered. Seven (7) members of the board shall be considered a quorum and a majority vote shall be required for determining the necessity of a hearing, conducting hearings and making finding of facts.

Section 2-248. Rules of procedure.

The board shall adopt rules and regulations as may be necessary for the proper discharge of its duties and shall file said rules and regulations with the city secretary.

Section 2-249. Complaint procedure.

(a) A person claiming to be aggrieved by the actions of the police department or an officer or employee thereof may file a written complaint with either the Police Internal Affairs Division, the City Secretary's Office or the Human Relations Office. When a complaint is filed with any one of these offices, a copy of the complaint will be forwarded to the chairman of the board, the complainant and the Internal Affairs Division of the Police Department.

(b) All complaints will be investigated by the Internal Affairs Division of the Police Department. Upon completion of an investigation by the Internal Affairs Division, the Police Chief will notify the complainant by letter of the investigative results and consistent with state law indicate disciplinary or other actions taken. The complainant shall also be informed of his right to appeal the decision to the review board.

Section 2-250. Appeal Procedure.

(a) All appeals must be filed in writing with the City Secretary's Office. The appeal must state the reason for the appeal.

(b) Staff will prepare a summary of the case and notify the board that a meeting is necessary to discuss the appeal request. The chairman of the board may call a special meeting pursuant to Section 2-247.

Section 2-251. Review by the board.

(a) Unless there are extenuating circumstances, within thirty (30) days of receipt of the request for appeal, the board, in executive session, shall consider the appeal by reviewing the request, the case summary and other pertinent information and, by majority vote, shall determine the necessity of a hearing.

(b) In public session, the chairman shall indicate whether or not a hearing has been scheduled, the date, time and place of hearing. The chairman shall notify the complainant and other involved parties in writing of the decision, hearing date, time and place, if any.

Section 2-252. Hearings before the board.

(a) If the board decides to conduct a hearing, the hearing shall be scheduled within thirty (30) days of said decision unless there are extenuating circumstances. The hearing shall be conducted in executive session and at least seven (7) members of the board must all be present for all of the hearing.

(b) Members, who in a particular case have a conflict of interest, shall not attend nor participate in the hearing and decision making process.

(c) All witnesses shall testify under oath or affirmation.

(d) All of the proceedings before the review board shall be recorded.

(e) All parties involved shall have the right to be represented by counsel or any other person of his choice. The city attorney's office shall provide legal counsel to the board on procedural matters.

(f) The complainant may offer evidence first in support of his complaint. The department or employee(s) shall have the right to cross-examine the complainant and his witnesses. Thereafter, the department or employee(s) shall have the right to offer evidence and the complainant shall have the right to cross-examine the witnesses. At the conclusion of all the evidence, the complainant or his representative followed by the department or employee may make a closing statement. Members of the board may question any witness, request additional information or further investigation at any point in the process.

(g) Unless there are extenuating circumstances, within twenty (20) days after the conclusion of the hearing, the board shall issue its findings of fact to the City Manager for review and the Public Safety Committee for informational purposes. The findings of fact must be approved by a majority, a quorum being present.

Section 2-253. Action by the City Manager.

(a) The City Manager shall review the findings of fact of the board and any other information at his disposal and take such action as he deems appropriate, consistent with state law and city policy.

(b) The City Manager shall notify all parties including the hearing board of his resolution of the complaint consistent with state law."

Section 2. Section 2-49. Notice of meetings is hereby amended by adding the "City of Winston-Salem Citizen Police Review Board" to the list of public bodies.

Section 3. This ordinance shall be effective upon adoption.

Document No. 33

Yonkers, N.Y.

POLICY & PROCEDURE

YONKERS POLICE DEPARTMENT

No. 1.06.03

SUBJECT:		EFFECTIVE DATE:
Police Professional Standards Review Committee		11/4/93
DISTRIBUTION: All Members	AMENDS/SUPERSEDES: New	Page 1 of 6 Pages

I. **PURPOSE**

To establish criteria for selection of committee members and to identify protocol for referral of designated internal investigations to the Police Professional Standards Review Committee.

II. **POLICY**

It is the policy of the Yonkers Police Department to investigate completely all allegations of misconduct involving members of the force in order to preserve the integrity and reputation of the department as well as to protect personnel against unjust accusations. As the department recognizes that the general public has a vested interest in it's police department, it supports the institution of the Police Professional Standards Review Committee, comprised of civilians and sworn personnel. Representation on the committee will afford the community an opportunity to review internal investigations that significantly impact on their interests. The Police Professional Standards Committee shall consist of the following:

III. **MEMBERSHIP**

The Police Professional Standards Committee shall consist of the following:

A. Three (3) Yonkers Police Department members of the rank of sergeant or above, selected by the Commissioner of Police, who are <u>not supervising</u> officers of the personnel who are the subject of the complaint and who are not otherwise subject to disqualification because of a personal bias or prejudice.

B. One (1) Yonkers Police Officer, recommended to the Police Commissioner by the President of the Police Benevolent Association. Provided however, that such nominee is not subject to disqualification due to a personal bias or prejudice. In the event that the

APPROVED:

COMMISSIONER OF POLICE

Police Commissioner believes that such a personal bias or prejudice exists, the Police Commissioner and the PBA president or his designee will meet to determine whether a prospective committee member nominated by the Police Benevolent Association has a personal bias or prejudice and if so to disqualify such nominee from serving on the committee and select an alternative candidate nominated by the Police Benevolent Association.

C. Four citizen panelists from the Yonkers community, selected by the Police Commissioner, in consultation with the Task Force on Police - Community relations; civil rights, civil liberties and religious organizations; and other community and civic organizations in the City of Yonkers. Provided, however, that such panelists shall:

1. Reflect the diversity of the City's population;

2. not be subject to disqualification due to a personal bias or prejudice;

3. shall not be a present holder of any public office; and

4. not have experience as a law enforcement professional or be a former member of the Yonkers Police Department.

For purposes of the foregoing, experience as a law enforcement professional shall include experience as a police officer, criminal investigator, special agent, or managerial or supervisor employee who has exercised substantial policy discretion on law enforcement matters in a federal, state, or local law enforcement agency, other than as an attorney in a prosecutorial agency.

D. Four alternate panelists, selected by the Police Commissioner, in a consultation with the Task Force on Police - Community Relations who will be utilized in the event that a panelist is disqualified, excused, sick or otherwise unable to serve when needed.

E. A committee member shall be disqualified from any consideration of a complaint if s(he) has a demonstrated personal bias or prejudice, or the appearance thereof, in the outcome of a complaint. This does not include holding or manifesting any political or social attitude or belief that does not preclude objective consideration of a case on its merits.

Examples of personal bias or prejudice include, but are not limited to:

1. Having a familiar relationship, close friendship or close working relationship with parties material to the complaint;

2. witnessing events material to the inquiry;

3. being a party to the complaint;

4. holding a bias for or against a particular party that is sufficient to impair the committee member's impartiality;

5. having a financial interest in the outcome of the review of a complaint.

A member of the committee may withdraw from the committee or from consideration of a complaint whenever that member deems himself or herself to be disqualified.

A motion to disqualify a member from consideration of a complaint on grounds of personal bias or prejudice may be introduced by any member of the committee. A majority vote will determine the disqualification.

IV. QUALIFICATIONS OF CIVILIAN PANELISTS

A. Yonkers resident for a continuous period of one year.

B. No felony or misdemeanor criminal convictions.

C. Consistent with the intent of the New York State Civil Rights Law, section 50 - a, panelists must be willing to sign a confidentiality agreement and maintain the confidentiality of all records reviewed.

D. Within one year of being selected, panelists must attend and successfully complete the Yonkers Civilian Police Academy. Within one year of being selected all committee members must also attend and successfully complete a series of workshops on the civil rights and civil liberties of civilians during encounters with law enforcement representatives.

E. All committee members including alternate committee members shall serve two year terms. A member may be removed from the committee by the Police Commissioner only for a good cause.

Any one of the following shall constitute good cause for removal actions by the Police Commissioner:

1. Failure to attend at least sixty-six (66%) percent of committee meetings in any six (6) month period unless such absences have been excused by a vote of the committee;

2. persistent failure to perform the duties of committee members.

A motion for removal may be made by any member of the committee. Written notice of the motion shall be sent to the business and home address of the member concerned. The motion shall be considered at the next regularly scheduled meeting of the committee.

Upon the concurrence of a majority of the members of the committee, as a result of a vote following such a consideration, a recommendation to remove a member from the committee shall be forwarded to the Police Commissioner, and to the organization(s), if any, that recommended that the member concerned serve on the committee.

F. As previously defined, civilian panelists may not have any prior professional law enforcement experience.

G. May not be a present holder of any public office.

V. FUNCTIONS AND RESPONSIBILITIES

The Police Professional Standards Committee will be convened by the Police Commissioner in order to review investigations into allegations of police misconduct. The functions and responsibilities of the Professional Standards Committee will include, but not be limited to, the following:

A. Receive from the commanding officer of the Office of Professional Standards completed investigation(s) into complaints of police misconduct that allege:

1. use of excessive force;

2. abuse of authority:

3. discourtesy: and/or

4. use of offensive language, including, but not limited to, slurs relating to race, ethnicity, religion, gender, sexual orientation and disability.

B. Review other selected cases as requested by the Commissioner of Police.

C. Review the fairness, thoroughness, completeness, and timeliness of completed investigations and identify other potential areas for further investigation.

D. Return to the commanding officer of the Office of Professional Standards any investigation which the committee feels is deficient, giving reasons therefore.

E. Vote as a group on conclusions reached by the Office of Professional Standards and prepare a report of findings for the Commissioner of Police with dissenting opinions if a unanimous conclusion is not reached. Findings shall include (1) the deposition of each allegation included in all complaints investigated by the Office of Professional Standards; and (2) any policy and practice recommendations as described in Section V (F).

F. Recommend changes or review of policy, procedures, or training for forwarding to the Commissioner of Police.

G. Maintain strict confidentiality of all information contained within the reports submitted by the Office of Professional Standards as well as all matters discussed by the committee.

VI. PUBLIC EDUCATION

The committee, through the Office of the Police Commissioner, shall institute public education campaign to (1) inform the public of the existence and purpose of the City of Yonkers Police Professional Standards Committee; (2) educated people as to their rights in encounters with police officers and procedures for filing a complaint of police misconduct; and (3) update the public regularly through published reports as to the activities of the committee.

The committee's public education campaign shall utilize print and electronic media and shall include a telephone information service available twenty-four (24) hours a day.

The committee's public education campaign shall include the participation of committee members in educational forums in communities throughout the City of Yonkers.

The Yonkers Police Commissioner will issue bi-annual reports on the committee's activities. Bi-annual reports shall include:

(1) The total number of complaints filed and disposition of complaints;

(2) The number of cases recommended for discipline or other action, including dismissal of allegations by the committee;

(3) The actions taken by the Police Commissioner in each of those cases recommended for discipline or other action, including dismissal of allegations.

VII. COMMANDING OFFICER OF THE PROFESSIONAL STANDARDS

The commanding officer of the Professional Standards will be the liaison to the P.P.S.C. and provide administrative support to the P.P.S.C. as necessary.

